AN INTRODUCTION TO
THE LAW OF

HEALTH & SAFETY

AT WORK IN SCOTLAND

AUSTRALIA
LBC Information Services—Sydney

CANADA and USA
Carswell—Toronto

NEW ZEALAND
Brooker's—Auckland

SINGAPORE and MALAYSIA
Thomson Information (S.E. Asia)
Singapore

AN INTRODUCTION TO THE LAW OF

HEALTH & SAFETY

AT WORK IN SCOTLAND

by
Victor Craig
Professor of Employment Law,
Heriot-Watt University

and
Kenneth Miller
Professor of Employment Law,
University of Strathclyde

W. GREEN/Sweet & Maxwell Ltd
EDINBURGH
2000

First published 1995
reprinted 1998
Second Edition 2000

Published in 2000 by W. Green & Son Ltd
21 Alva Street
Edinburgh EH2 4PS

Typeset by LBJ Typesetting Ltd
of Kingsclere
Printed and bound in Great Britain by
MPG Books Ltd, Bodmin, Cornwall

No natural forests were destroyed to make this product;
only farmed timber was used and replanted

A CIP catalogue record for this book is available from
the British Library

ISBN 0 414 01375 1

PREFACE TO SECOND EDITION

When the text of the first edition of this short work was completed, following as it did on a period of almost frenetic activity, both at European and domestic level, it might have been expected that the area of health and safety at work would lie fallow for some considerable time. However, that has proved to be anything but the case.

While the development of the common law in fields like liability for mental and physical stress related to or caused by work has continued, the major developments, as one would expect, have been the product of statutory intervention.

Many of the regulations covered in the first edition have been revised, most notably the Management of Health and Safety at Work Regulations 1992. Significant changes have resulted from the revocation of the 1992 Regulations and their replacement by the Management of Health and Safety at Work Regulations 1999. Unfortunately, at the time of writing, the Health and Safety Executive have not yet produced the code of practice that will accompany the 1999 Regulations. Most significantly, however, the 1999 Regulations incorporate the principles upon which preventative measures have to be adopted. Previously, the Approved Code of Practice made reference to some of these matters, but their incorporation into the regulations themselves is likely to be significant.

Wholly new sets of regulations include the Working Time Regulations 1998, the Fire Precautions (Workplace) Regulations 1997, the Consultation with Employees Regulations 1996, the Control of Lead at Work Regulations 1998, and the Construction (Health, Safety and Welfare) Regulations 1996, complementing the Construction (Design and Management) Regulations 1994. Also the Manual Handling Operations Regulations of 1992 must now be seen in the light of the Lifting Operations and Lifting Equipment Regulations 1998.

Undoubtedly, the Public Interest Disclosure Act 1998, whose germ can be traced to recommendations of the Cullen Report, will fortify employees and other workers who are required to work in less than reasonably safe circumstances in making public their working conditions which may create risks not merely for themselves but members of the public, like patients and customers.

Interestingly, in common with the Working Time Regulations, the Public Interest Disclosure Act extends its protection well beyond the narrow confines of the employment contract, while the collective aspect of health and safety at work continues to be emphasised by the Working Time Regulations 1998, which permit flexibility but only through certain collective, or workforce, agreements. All of this, however, must be seen in the context of the Employment Relations Act 1999 which, whether a trade union is recognised or not, entitles employees to be accompanied during health and safety grievance hearings by a trade union official or fellow employee.

It would be foolhardy to suggest that a plateau has now been reached, when a code of practice on stress at work will be published later this year, and the possible impact of the Human Rights Act 1998 in the field of health and safety has not yet been experienced. When there is added to those areas the prospect of legislation being introduced to deal with corporate killing, it is clear that whilst this second edition incorporates considerable new material, health and safety at work has a somewhat elusive horizon.

Even an introductory text, however, requires considerable encouragement and support from colleagues, editors and publishers and in that respect, we have to extend our thanks to the staff of Greens for encouraging us to undertake this second edition and prompting us for the delivery of manuscript when necessary, while recognising that that exercise had to be located within the teaching, research and ever-increasing administrative activities of two authors.

While it is hoped that this text covers the main principles and elements of health and safety at work law, at a level that is suitable for legal and occupational health and safety practitioners and students, any errors or omissions are of course the responsibility of the authors who have sought to state the law as at January 1, 2000.

Vic Craig and Kenny Miller
Edinburgh and Strathclyde
January 31, 2000.

PREFACE TO FIRST EDITION

It is the purpose of this book to provide a concise and up-to-date introduction to the law of health and safety at work as it applies in Scotland. This approach necessitates us considering the common law, the older regulatory statutes, the Health and Safety at Work, etc. Act 1974 and the regulations made under it, and, of increasing importance, European law. It is true that much of the law is common to all of the United Kingdom. Yet sufficient differences do exist to merit the treatment of the subject in a Scottish context. There can be no doubt that decisions in Scottish cases have made a unique and positive contribution to the development of the common law of health and safety in both Scotland and throughout the English speaking world. Equally, many of the landmark cases as regards the older regulatory statutes are also Scottish.

This in itself cannot be the sole justification for writing a book from a Scottish perspective. We also wished to produce a book which emphasised the continuing importance of Scots law in this area. Decisions of the Scottish courts continue to play a central role in the development of health and safety law at a United Kingdom level and wherever possible we have sought to rely on Scottish authority where it exists. In other areas where English law is more developed we have speculated on the likely response of the Scottish courts. We also thought it important to write a book which located the law within the legal system of Scotland. For example, there are special features about the award of damages in Scotland ⋅ and this is reflected in our treatment of the subject in Chapter 7 where we use recent Scottish case law in order to illustrate how damages are calculated here. Nevertheless given the commonality of the current statutory material on health and safety we hope that the book will be useful not only to readers whose interest is primarily Scottish but also to others who may be interested in a text which attempts to treat the general principles of the law of health and safety at work in a contemporary and straightforward way.

The book has been written at a time of great change in health and safety law. As already indicated, European law has started to play a major role in this area and this has necessitated significant alterations to domestic law. Equally, the Government's preference for deregulation is beginning to have an impact on health and safety issues. Thus the recent review of health and safety law conducted by the Health and Safety Commission is likely to lead to the repeal of all the remaining older statutory provisions. Wherever possible we have sought to reflect these developments in the book. Thus a significant portion of the book is devoted to a consideration of European directives and the way in which they have been implemented in domestic law. However, given the pace of development, we do not claim that this book is an exhaustive statement of the law. For one thing, we have had to be selective as regards the health and safety regulations which we discuss. Nonetheless we believe that we have discussed the most important ones.

We would like to thank all our colleagues at Heriot-Watt and Strathclyde Universities for their support and encouragement. In particular, thanks are due to Jenifer Ross for her constructive comments, to Michael Allan and Amanda Cooke for assisting us with the research and to Barbara Syme for her patient transcription of the manuscript. We would also like to thank Greens for agreeing to publish the book and for their sterling editorial support.

Any errors or omissions remain those of the authors and we have sought to state the law as at March 1, 1995.

Vic Craig and Kenny Miller
Edinburgh and Glasgow
March 31, 1995.

Contents

TABLE OF CASES

TABLE OF STATUTES

TABLE OF STATUTORY INSTRUMENTS

TABLE OF EUROPEAN TREATIES

TABLE OF EUROPEAN DIRECTIVES

CHAPTER 1

INTRODUCTION

1.1 Few areas of the law can have been transformed, in a relatively short period of time, to the same extent as that area conveniently described as the law of health and safety at work. While there had been a gradual development of the responsibilities of those at work via the common law duty of care as well as occasional but important bench-mark setting legislation in the form of various enactments to regulate factories, mines, offices and certain other premises, radical shifts in the approach of the law to health and safety at work were stimulated first by the Report of the Robens Committee[1] and then by the Council of Ministers approving[2] the First Action Programme on Health and Safety at Work, drawn up by the Commission of the European Communities. The former resulted in the passage of the Health and Safety at Work Act 1974, which embraced an entirely new philosophy of enacting general duties supported by Codes of Practice and enforced through the criminal law, while the latter saw the adoption of various Directives, most notably the Framework Directive[3] which made express the employer s duty to be proactive by assessing the risks to health and safety and take the necessary implementing measures, thereby equating the area of health and safety with other areas of management. Other important developments would include the Cullen Report on the Piper Alpha disaster,[4] which recognised the need to ensure that employees who were safety representatives be protected against dismissal and action short of dismissal for carrying out safety functions. The necessary legislation was originally contained in the Offshore Safety (Protection against Victimisation) Act 1992, whose extended provisions are now to be found in the Employment Rights Act 1996[5] and the Public Interest Disclosure Act 1998,[6] in respect not just of "employees" who are

---

[1] Safety and Health at Work, Cmnd 5034 (1972).
[2] Council Resolution 78/C165/1.
[3] Directive on the Introduction of Measures to improve the Health and Safety of Workers at Work (89/392).
[4] Report of the Public Inquiry into the Piper Alpha Disaster, Cm. 1310 (1990).
[5] s. 100.
[6] ss. 2–5.

employed offshore, but all "workers" who make disclosures that a person has failed to comply with a legal obligation (which clearly would include a legal obligation regarding health and safety of workers) or that the health and safety of any individual has been or is likely to be endangered. Another important development was the adoption of the Treaty for the Single European Act, which added *inter alia* Article 118a to the E.C. Treaty to permit the adoption, by qualified majority voting, of directives to improve the working environment as regards health and safety of workers, and the effect of this has already been felt through the adoption of the Directive on the Organisation of Working Time[7] and the introduction, with effect from October 1, 1998, of the United Kingdom implementing measure the Working Time Regulations 1998. The Treaty of Amsterdam[8] makes further provision for European initiatives in the area of health and safety at work.[9]

The common law

1.2　While the early common law recognised that the "master" was, as a general rule, liable for the injuries to the "servant"[10] this was subject to the servant not continuing in the face of a known danger; indeed the impression might be gained from some of the early decisions that if workmen were properly compensated for injuries sustained in the course of their employment they might be encouraged to omit normal caution and diligence in the exercise of their work.[11] Similarly, from a moral standpoint, the conduct of the employer could be regarded as "highly reprehensible as I think they were in the present instance. The workman who depends on his employment for the bread of himself and his family is thus tempted to incur risks to which, as a matter of humanity he ought not to be exposed. But looking at it from a legal point of view if a man for the sake of his employment takes it or continues in it with the knowledge of all the risks he must trust to himself to keep clear of injury."[12] Although this notion of implied consent seems to have

---

[7] Directive 93/104.

[8] The Treaty came into force on May 1, 1999 after ratification by all 15 Member States, and has the effect of renumbering Articles in the E.C. Treaty; however, throughout this text, unless dealt with expressly, where reference is made to the E.C. Treaty it is to that Treaty prior to its amendment by the Treaty of Amsterdam, on the grounds that it was in reliance on the provisions of the E.C. Treaty before the Treaty of Amsterdam became effective that the Directives discussed here were adopted.

[9] For a more detailed discussion of the effect of European Union law, see Chap. 2.

[10] Fraser, *Master and Servant* (3rd ed.), pp. 177 *et seq.*; and see Chap. 3.

[11] *Priestley v. Fowler* (1837) 3 M. & W. 1. And see *Seymour v. Maddox* (1851) 20 L.J. Q.B. 327, in which a singer's action failed because she had as good an opportunity of seeing the danger (a hole in the floor) as the employer.

[12] *Woodley v. Metropolitan District Railway Co. Ltd* (1877) 2 Ex. D. 384, *per* Cockburn C.J.

had its origins in England, sadly it seems to have been readily accepted in Scots law.[13] Nor was Scots law able to resist the introduction of the cognate doctrine of common employment[14]—a doctrine which required a workman to be regarded as agreeing to accept the risks of working alongside others in whose selection he had not been involved! Of course there were from time to time judicial attempts to temper some common law rules. Thus the personalisation of the duty of care was, to an extent, intended to obviate the effects of common employment[15] and the limitations imposed on the circumstances in which the employer could plead *volenti non fit injuria*[16] were judicial recognition of the reality of the insecure status of employment, in the absence of any protection against arbitrary dismissal and of any system of welfare benefits. Even the most modest of reforms were the result of legislation. Thus the eradication of the doctrine of common employment and the effects of an employee's contribution to his injuries both required legislative intervention[17] and, arguably, in at least one case legislation is still awaited.[18] Further, because the common law operates *ex post facto* to compensate an injured employee, it is obvious that any generally normative measures which would operate to prevent or reduce injuries at work by setting standards of performance would require legislation. This is not to say that the common law, through the flexible concept of the duty of care, is unable to respond to new risks and dangers. Thus the problems encountered in attempting to recover damages for long-term exposure to noise over periods of employment with different employers were tackled in *Thompson v. Smith Shiprepairers (North Shields) Ltd*,[19] while the contemporary dangers of repetitive strain

---

[13] See for example *McNeill v. Wallace* (1853) 15 D. 818, *Robertson v. Adamson* (1862) 24 D. 1231.

[14] See Chap. 3, para. 3.3.

[15] *ibid.*

[16] See Chap. 3, para. 3.53.

[17] See Chap. 3, paras 3.3 and 3.53.

[18] There still exists the possibility of an insurer requiring, on the basis of a subrogation clause, that an insured employer sue an employee for damages for breach of the implied contractual duty to perform with reasonable care which has resulted in a claim being brought against the employer by a third party. See Chap. 3, para. 3.48.

[19] [1984] I.C.R. 237 (QBD). And see *McGhee v. National Coal Board* [1973] 1 W.L.R. 1 (HL) where the House of Lords treated proof that a breach of duty had increased the risk of dermatitis as proof that the breach had actually caused the disease, which as Lord Wilberforce pointed out (p.7) was a fiction adopted in the interests of justice to prevent the plaintiff from losing his claim through a failure to prove what in the current state of medical knowledge he had no means of proving.

injuries or work-related upper limb disorders[20] and stress[21] have shown the ability of the common law to respond. Nevertheless the nature of the risks and dangers of modern employment conditions requires not merely that remedies are available for those who suffer occupational injury or disease; the public interest is also involved, in that those who are rendered incapable of economic activity, or whose economic activity is reduced by such injury or disease, impose charges on the public health and welfare systems of the state. Thus there is a need for legislation to (1) complement the common law and create a framework of provisions which are preventative, applicable to specific dangers where necessary, educative and mandatory, (2) create the necessary reforming and enforcement agencies and (3) translate into domestic law requirements of European Union Directives and such instruments as are necessary to ensure compatibility with the European Convention on Human Rights, introduced into Scots law by a combination of the Human Rights Act 1998 and the Scotland Act 1998.

Statutory intervention

1.3 Principally because until about the end of the eighteenth century there were in Scotland only "labouring individuals" in agriculture[22] Acts of the Scots Parliament, although they gave magistrates of Royal Burghs the power to fix prices and wages, were not required to deal with the occupational dangers which accompanied the post-Union industrial revolution. Many of the early examples of statutory intervention were addressed to the protection of children (apprentices) and women.[23] As a result of the extension of the Poor Law of 1601, destitute children were located in Industrial Schools and Workhouses. Their exploitation was highlighted by the outbreak of fever in 1784 in the Ratcliffe Cotton Works in Lancashire and, by 1794, magistrates and Justices of the Peace together had powers to prohibit indentures and fine masters who ill treated apprentices. In 1802 the Health and Morals of Apprentices Act was passed and, in 1819, in spite of opposition on the grounds that regulation by the state would inhibit trade and reduce living standards, the Factory Act prohibited employment in a cotton mill of those under the age of nine, and limited the

---

[20] *Bettany v. Royal Doulton (U.K.) Ltd* (1993, unreported); *cf. Mughal v. Reuters Ltd* [1993] I.R.L.R. 571 (H. Ct); *Pickford v. Imperial Chemical Industries plc* [1998] I.R.L.R. 435 (HL).

[21] See *Johnstone v. Bloomsbury Health Authority* [1991] I.C.R. 269, CA; and *Petch v. Commissioners of Customs and Excise* [1993] I.C.R. 789, CA. See also *Ward v. Scotrail Railways Ltd*, 1999 S.C. 255, discussed in Chap. 3.

[22] Johnson, *History of the Working Class in Scotland.*

[23] For coverage of early statutory intervention see Hutchins and Harrison, *History of Factory Legislation* (1926).

Introduction 5

working day of those under 16 to 12 hours. The Factory Act 1833
set up His Majesty s Inspectorate of Factories and introduced rules
regarding provision of fences and guards for dangerous machines,
and by 1901 a rudimentary system of notification of accidents and
disease was set up by the Factory and Workshop Act of that year.
In 1959 the Factories Act 1937 was amended to include provisions
dealing with dangerous fumes and substances, hoists, lifts, floors
and stairs. In 1961 the Factories Act was passed to consolidate
many of the earlier provisions and that legislation, although now
largely repealed and replaced by regulations[24] designed to give
effect to European Union Directives,[25] still serves as the basis of
health and safety of the many workers engaged in factories.
However, as the different industries developed, similar and frequently duplicating legislation was enacted to regulate health and
safety in mines and quarries, shops, offices and railway premises,[26]
but was still typified by legislative reaction to particular disasters or
hazards in certain types of work, and by the late 1960s there were
over five hundred pieces of legislation and regulations in force.

Thus until the enactment of the Health and Safety at Work Act
1974, statutory intervention typically took the form of a response to
specific dangers and was restricted to particular types of workplace.
Many people were excluded from the protection of legislation
because, for example, the injury was sustained in a type of
workplace which was not to be covered—like a school or a
hospital[27]—or the legislation protected only those who were
employed under contracts of employment,[28] or the particular
activity was outside the scope of the legislation.[29] Also, prior to
1974, legislation was frequently expressed in the form of a prescrip-
tive absolute duty which encouraged the belief that responsibility
for safety and health at work was a matter for inspectors and
ultimately the criminal courts, with the effect that both employers
and employees felt little ownership of health and safety issues and

---

[24] See for example the Workplace (Health, Safety and Welfare) Regulations
1992.
[25] See Chap. 6.
[26] See Chaps 4 and 5.
[27] See for example *Bromwich v. Ear Nose and Throat Hospital* [1980] 2 All E.R.
663 in which, had it not been held that a workshop, which formed part of a hospital,
was in law a "factory", the injured plumber would not have been able to rely on the
provision of the Abrasive Wheels Regulations 1970.
[28] *Herbert v. Harold Shaw Ltd* [1989] 2 Q.B. 138.
[29] Consider the issue in *Morganite Crucible Ltd v. Nurse* [1989] I.C.R. 15 (HL);
namely whether the demolition of structures made partly of asbestos was, for the
purpose of the Factories Act 1961 and the Asbestos Regulations 1969, a "process".
Had it not been a "process", compliance with the Regulations, which ensured
provision of respiratory protective equipment and the escape of asbestos dust,
would not have been supported by a criminal sanction. And see *Watt v. Fairfield
Shipbuilding and Engineering Co. Ltd*, 1998 G.W.D. 39-2051.

there was no guarantee that the different inspectorates applied consistent standards. Finally, but perhaps most important of all, enforcement relied on the criminal law which was concerned only very indirectly with the avoidance of dangers and the minimising of risks. One of the main aims of the Health and Safety at Work Act 1974 was to sweep away many of these illogical and outdated distinctions on which the entire structure of health and safety law had been erected, and to replace legislation which targeted specifics and contained narrow, technical definitions with legislation which enacted universally applicable general duties supplemented where appropriate with guidance and Codes of Practice, while retaining the criminal sanction. However, the 1974 Act's general duties reflect the common-law duty of reasonable care in that they are qualified by the test of reasonable practicability,[30] and in that respect the Act acknowledges that in many cases there is a balance between health and safety on the one hand, and cost, administrative convenience and feasibility on the other, and it is open to question the extent to which such a balance is consistent with the relevant Directives.[31]

The effects of European Union

1.4 This is dealt with in more detail in Chapters Two and Four, but in the meantime it is sufficient to note that much recent and expected health and safety legislation originates in the form of European Union Directives which, in accordance with the Single European Act and Article 118a[32] of the Treaty establishing the European Economic Community, may be adopted by qualified majority. The distinction between legislation which is to encourage improvements as regards health and safety of workers which may be achieved through the adoption by qualified majority of Directives, and working conditions generally for which Directives would until recently have required unanimity was the subject of much debate in *United Kingdom v. Council of the European Community*,[33] in which the United Kingdom challenged the legal validity of the Directive on the Organisation of Working Time.[34] As the Advocate General (Leger) pointed out, Article 118a refers particularly to the "working environment", which has to be given

---

[30] And see the Workplace (Health, Safety and Welfare) Regulations 1992, reg. 12(3).
[31] See Chap. 2, para. 2.18 and Chaps 5 and 6.
[32] Art. 118a was added by the Single European Act and provides for the Commission to propose Directives on health and safety for adoption by the Council of Minister by qualified majority.
[33] [1997] I.R.L.R. 30 (ECJ).
[34] Directive 93/104. The Working Time Regulations 1998 introduced to implement the Directive are discussed in detail in Chap. 4.

the wide meaning ascribed to that phrase in Denmark which introduced the concept of the working environment into Article 118a at the stage of its drafting. The opinion of the Advocate General was endorsed by the Court, which upheld the validity of the Directive on the grounds that there was nothing in Article 118a which justified a restrictive interpretation of "working environment", "health" or "safety". The Court's broad approach to working environment was required to include limitations on working time; this approach is supported by the World Health Organisation whose constitution defines health as a state of complete physical, mental and social well-being that does not consist only in the absence of illness or infirmity.

Following the Treaty of Amsterdam concluded on October 2, 1997, the United Kingdom agreed to end its opt-out of the Social Chapter which had been in place since the Member States had agreed the Maastricht Treaty. The effect of ending the opt-out was to incorporate the Social Chapter into the E.C. Treaty so that the Council of Ministers may, with effect from 1999, take decisions by qualified majority voting with regard to improving the working environment to protect workers' health and safety, and working conditions.[35] Interpretation of domestic legislation has to take place against the background of its European origins, and that requires that wherever possible the implementing domestic law has to be given a meaning which comports with its European parent.[36] Furthermore, even where the domestic provision is contradictory or absent the provisions of a Directive, if sufficiently precise and unconditional,[37] can be relied on against the state or an "emanation of the state" like a public health authority.[38] While an employee in the private sector who suffers loss as a result of his own Member State failing to implement a Directive may have a right of action against his own government,[39] a Directive does not give rise to rights or restrictions between private individuals.[40]

---

[35] See Chap. 4.
[36] *Litster v. Forth Dry Dock and Engineering Company Ltd*, 1989 S.L.T. 540 (HL); *Webb v. EMO Air Cargo (U.K.) Ltd* [1995] I.R.L.R. 645 (HL). Indeed it is probably the case that a U.K. court has to give effect to a Directive unless the domestic statute is directly contradictory (*Marleasing S.A. v. La Commercial Internacional de Alimentacion S.A.* [1992] C.M.L.R. 305 (ECJ); *Faccini Dori v. Recreb Srl* [1994] E.C.R. I–3325 (ECJ).
[37] See *Faccini*, above.
[38] *Marshall v. Southampton, etc. Health Authority* [1986] I.C.R. 335. As to what is an emanation of the state, see *Foster v. British Gas* [1991] I.C.R. 84 (ECJ). And see *Gibson v. East Riding of Yorkshire District Council* [1999] I.R.L.R. 358 regarding the enforceability of the Directive on the Organisation of Working Time (Art. 7).
[39] *Francovich v. Italy* [1991] I.R.L.R. 84 (ECJ).
[40] *R v. Secretary of State for Employment, ex p. Seymour-Smith* [1997] I.R.L.R. 315 (HL).

What the future holds

1.5 After an exhaustive review of health and safety legislation the Health and Safety Commission has issued a report,[41] and the government has accepted all of its proposals and recommendations. While the report acknowledges that there is room for improvement in certain areas, it proposes no change to the "architecture" of the present system as established by the Health and Safety at Work Act 1974. Nevertheless, in addition to the need to generally rationalise and simplify the many provisions, the Commission recognises the need to (1) clarify the respective roles of legislation, Codes of Practice and guidance, (2) update or remove at least 100 sets of regulations and primary legislation and simplify the existing provisions regarding completion of forms and records, and (3) reduce inconsistencies in enforcement. Accordingly, and in keeping with the philosophy of the Deregulation and Contracting-Out Act,[42] a comprehensive system of review was undertaken which resulted in almost all the pre-1974 legislation being removed.[43] Undoubtedly in this respect the Commission will be influenced and prompted by European Directives but, standing the decision in *R v. Secretary of State for Employment, ex p. NACODS*,[44] there is no requirement to amend or repeal section 1(2)[45] of the 1974 Act because where the Secretary of State believes that the new regulations satisfy the statutory criteria, the court must not review the respective merits of the new proposed legislation.

1.6 The Working Time Directive itself exemplifies the much broader understanding of health and safety at work in other legal systems of the European Community[46]—an understanding which more closely correlates with our concept of "welfare" and this is likely to have a continuing effect on the content of health and

---

[41] *Review of Health and Safety Legislation* (1994).

[42] The Task Force of the Department of Trade and Industry made several proposals for the amendment of health and safety legislation, and highlighted the need to assess whether the administrative and compliance costs are justified by the costs of the risks present. For an assessment of the effect of this see M. Beatson, "Balancing Costs and Benefits of Risk Reduction", *Health and Safety Bulletin*, January 1998, p. 16.

[43] And see K. Williams, "De-regulating Occupational Health and Safety" (1994) 24 I.L.J. 133.

[44] 1994 H.S.I.B. 222.

[45] s. 1(2) permits the Secretary of State to amend existing provisions by regulations "designed to maintain or improve standards of health safety and welfare" established by or under those provisions.

[46] And see D.R. Walters, "Occupational Health and Safety Strategies in Europe", Vol. 1, *The National Situations* (1996, Office for Official Publications of the European Communities).

safety law. Arguably the conditions which prevailed at the time that Lord Robens Committee reported have now changed, and new conditions require to be considered.[47] Undoubtedly the challenge ahead will require re-appraisal of the role of trade unions in health and safety at work in light of the fall in union membership[48] and the extent to which non-union representation is effective.[49] One study has concluded that where there are joint committees in which all of the employee representatives are union appointees, workplace injuries are considerably reduced when compared with workplaces in which management alone determines health and safety arrangements,[50] and the Health and Safety (Consultation with Employees) Regulations 1996, which requires consultation either with employees directly or their representatives but not necessarily trade union representatives, have to be seen in this light. The fact that under the Employment Relations Act 1999 all except small businesses may be required to recognise trade unions may have an impact, not just on terms of employment, but if only indirectly health and safety records.[51]

1.7 The structure of the workforce at the time Robens reported has changed considerably. Workers are more mobile (spatially and temporally) and less concentrated, with the result that organisation and representation is more difficult, and the test will be whether the law can respond to these changes while at the same time recognising that health and safety at work embraces protection of workers against work-related stress disorders and hours of work, and even the style of human resource management[52] which includes bullying and humiliation of subordinates—also, the first case in Scotland to seek damages for bullying and humiliation by a superior has been lodged.[53]

The European Convention on Human Rights

1.8 The Human Rights Act 1998 which becomes fully effective in the United Kingdom on October 1, 2000, will incorporate the

---

[47] See the interesting Interim Import from the Institute of Employment Rights by D. Walters and P. James, *Robens Revisited* (1998) (ISBN 1873271 9).

[48] 1999 saw the first and modest increase in union membership in the U.K. for 19 years.

[49] See Chap. 5 on the Health and Safety (Consultation with Employees) Regulations 1996.

[50] B. Reilly *et al.*, "Unions, safety committees and workplace injuries", B.J.I.R., Vol. 33, p. 273.

[51] Note the restricted definition of collective bargaining in Sched. A1 to the Trade Union and Labour Relations (Consolidation) Act 1992, inserted by the Employment Relations Act 1999, Sched. 1.

[52] According to a TUC study conducted in 1998, 11% of employees had been bullied at work by middle managers who themselves had been treated in the same way when younger.

[53] See "Nurse in landmark workplace bullying lawsuit", *The Herald*, May 7, 1999. See also *Rorrison v. West Lothian College*, 1999 Rep. L.R. 102.

Convention into United Kingdom law by requiring that legislation be interpreted and given effect to in a way that is compatible with Convention rights, and by making it unlawful for public authorities (defined to include any person whose functions are of a public nature) to act in a manner which is incompatible with Convention rights. It is beyond dispute that bodies like the Health and Safety Executive, the Scottish Environmental Protection Agency and local authorities are public authorities, and although the Convention does not deal expressly with health and safety, it is likely that Article 6 (right to a fair trial and impartial tribunal), Article 8 (right to respect for private and family life), as well as Article 1 of the First Protocol (right to peaceful enjoyment of possession) will impact on the broader health and safety issues. It is unlikely that health and safety at work law will be totally insulated from the sea-change the Convention will bring about.

CHAPTER 2

SOURCES AND INSTITUTIONS

INTRODUCTION

2.1 The legal provisions which operate in the area of health and safety at work have such a variety of sources and qualities that they may fairly be described as kaleidoscopic. The area sees a confluence of common law principles and statutory codes, criminal and civil jurisdictions, contractual and delictual obligations (and civil remedies for breach of statutory duty), private and public law regimes, the intervention of the ordinary courts and specialist employment tribunals as well as domestic and European Community legislation, both primary and secondary. A proper understanding of health and safety at work law therefore requires an appreciation of these distinctions and how they interact, and while a comprehensive treatment of these matters is beyond the scope of this work it is necessary to give at least an indication of the operation of the different provisions in the context of health and safety.

The criminal law

2.2 Many particular risks or dangers have been the subject of express statutory provisions commonly enacted to protect the interests and welfare of women, young persons and children employed in factories or mines. Thus the Factories Act 1833[1] established a 12-hour maximum working day for young persons while for women and children the figure was 10 hours, although the effect of this was considerably lessened by the decision in *Ryder v. Mills*[2] by construing the statute to permit relay working. These modest early statutes, however, set the pattern for future and contemporary measures by introducing criminal sanctions on employers for infringements.[3] However, it was not until the

---

[1] And see the Ten Hours Act 1857.
[2] (1850) 3 Exch. 853.
[3] Interestingly the Factories Act 1844 and the Coal Mines Inspection Act 1850 allowed the Home Secretary a power to award part of any fine imposed on an employer to a worker injured as a result of the employer's breach of the statutory provision—a power little used until its eventual abolition in 1959.

appointment of a Royal Commission in 1875 that there occurred the first attempt at comprehensive factory legislation[4]; a trend continued in later years and typified by the Mines and Quarries Act 1954, the Factories Act 1961 and the Offices, Shops and Railway Premises Act 1963, but eventually departed from with the enactment of the Health and Safety at Work Act 1974 which, following the recommendation of the Robens Committee on Health and Safety,[5] signalled the commencement of a move away from legislating against specific dangers in particular places of employment to legislating for all places of employment in terms of general duties.[6] While undoubtedly the coherent development of the law of health and safety at work has been the province of statutory regulation enforced through the criminal law[7]—a pattern of development which has recently been continued by the passage of delegated legislation to implement the many Directives on health and safety at work made by the European Community's Council of Ministers—it is also important to note that while that development remains almost exclusively statutory it has, since the enactment of the Health and Safety at Work Act 1974, taken the form of subordinate legislation and Approved Codes of Practice (ACOPs) under the enabling powers contained in the 1974 Act itself[8] or the European Communities Act 1972.[9]

2.3 Regulations made in reliance on the powers contained in section 15 of the Health and Safety at Work Act 1974 are known as "health and safety regulations",[10] and while a government Minister is required to consult the Health and Safety Commission before exercising such enabling powers,[11] they may be exercised for any of the purposes contained in Schedule 3 to the 1974 Act.[12] However, whether the legislation be primary or secondary, the sanction is

---

[4] Factory and Workshop Act 1878.

[5] Robens Committee on Health and Safety at Work (Cmnd. 5034).

[6] Contrast for example Factories Act 1961, Pt II dealing with such specific matters as cleaning of prime movers by women and young persons (s. 20) and cranes, ropes and lifting tackles (s. 26) with the general duties in Health and Safety at Work Act 1974 (HASAWA), ss. 1–7.

[7] Factories Act 1961 ss. 155, 158, 164, and see Chap. 4.

[8] Health and Safety at Work Act 1974, ss. 15, 16.

[9] Thus the Working Time Regulations 1998 & 1999 (S.I. 1998 No. 1833 and S.I. 1999 No. 3372) were made under the 1972 Act.

[10] HASAWA, s. 15.

[11] HASAWA, s. 50.

[12] Where the subordinate legislation is to implement a European Union Directive which extends beyond the area of health and safety at work, a Minister may have to rely on the enabling powers contained in the European Communities Act 1972, s. 2; see, for example the Supply of Machinery (Safety) Regulations 1992 (S.I. 1992 No. 3073).

eventually[13] invariably criminal.[14] Thus it is provided[15] that it is an offence for any person to fail to discharge a duty imposed by the 1974 Act itself or to contravene any of the health and safety regulations or any requirement or prohibition imposed under any such regulations. It is therefore unnecessary for health and safety regulations[16] expressly to provide that their breach is an offence.[17]

2.4 Where an offence is due to the wrongful[18] act or default of some other person that other person may be charged[19] and where the offence is committed by a body corporate with the consent or connivance of, or to have been attributable to,[20] any neglect on the part of any director, manager,[21] secretary or similar officer he too shall to be guilty of the offence.[22]

The civil law

2.5 Where a person suffers injury at work, compensating such a person for the losses he sustains as a result of that injury is of course the province of the civil law, which may for present purposes be subdivided into (a) delictual and contractual, and (b) breach of statutory duty. It may be said therefore that the principle objective of the current statutory regime is "the suppression of dangers before they arise . . . rather than guarding against risks which have been allowed to occur",[23] whereas the civil law proceeds on the basis that breaches of duty will occur and provides compensation to the victims of such breaches. The relevant principles of the laws of delict and contract are treated in detail later,[24] but it requires to be emphasised here that legislation which imposes a criminal penalty in respect of a failure to comply with the statutory provision may also give rise to a civil law action for

---

[13] Initially breach of a statutory provision may result in the issuing of an Improvement Notice, but a failure to observe the terms of such a notice is itself an offence (HASAWA, s. 33(1)(g)).

[14] And see the value attributed to administrative sanctions by the report of the Robens Committee on Health and Safety at Work (Cmnd. 5034), Chap. 9.

[15] *ibid*, s. 33(1)(a)–(c).

[16] Namely those regulations made under HASAWA, s. 15.

[17] And see the similar provisions in the Factories Act 1961, s. 155 and the Offices, Shops and Railway Premises Act 1963, s. 63. *Cf.* the Supply of Machinery (Safety) Regulations 1992 (S.I. 1992 No. 3073), Pt IV.

[18] *Noss Farm Products Ltd v. Lilico* [1946] 2 All E.R. 609.

[19] HASAWA, s. 36.

[20] *Wotherspoon v. H.M. Advocate*, 1928 J.C. 74.

[21] Those who are responsible for deciding corporate policy or strategy are "managers" (*R. v. Boal (Francis)* [1992] Q.B. 591).

[22] *ibid*, s. 37.

[23] Redgrave, Fife and Machin, *Health and Safety* (2nd ed.), p. v.

[24] See Chap. 3.

breach of statutory duty.[25] Whether a criminal provision also gives
rise to an action for breach of statutory duty at the instance of an
injured party is a matter of interpretation in order to determine
what was the intention of Parliament in enacting the duty concerned,[26] although civil liability will be inferred where the predominant purpose of the statute or the subordinate legislation is the
protection of a particular class of workmen by imposing a duty on
their employers, the duty of taking special measures to protect
their safety.[27] However, the pursuer must prove on the balance of
probabilities that it was the breach of statutory duty which caused
the injury.[28] In this context it is important to note therefore that
while nothing in Part I of the Health and Safety at Work Act 1974
shall be construed as conferring a right of action in any civil
proceedings for a failure to comply with any duty imposed by
sections 2 to 8, or as affecting the extent (if any) to which breach of
a duty under an existing statutory provision[29] is actionable, breach
of a duty imposed by health and safety regulations[30] shall, in so far
as it causes damage,[31] be actionable, except in so far as the
regulations provide otherwise.[32]

Approved Codes of Practice (ACOPs)

2.6 In recognition of the difficulty of framing effective statutory
regulations and the need to provide "intelligibility and flexibility",[33]
the Robens Committee[34] recommended the enactment of the
general principles of the responsibilities for health and safety at

---

[25] See also Chap. 4.

[26] *Atkinson v. Newcastle Waterworks Co.* (1877) 2 Ex. D. 441; *Pullar v. Window Clean Ltd*, 1956 S.C. 13; and see *McArthur v. Strathclyde Regional Council, The Times*, May 20, 1994.

[27] *Black v. Fife Coal Co.*, 1912 S.C. (H.L.) 33; *Bett v. Dalmeny Oil Co.* (1905) 7 F. 787.

[28] *Wardlaw v. Bonnington Castings Ltd*, 1956 S.C. (H.L.) 26. *Cf. Kelly v. Glebe Sugar Refining Co.* (1893) 20 R. 833, where Lord Adam opines that neglect of the criminal duty creates a prima facie case of fault against the employers.

[29] See HASAWA, s. 53(1), Sched. 3.

[30] Namely regulations made under HASAWA, s. 15.

[31] If this phraseology would exclude interdict from the scope of s. 47(2), where the regulation was passed to implement a European Directive it would offend against the rule that domestic law ensures an effective remedy for breach of provisions contained in a Directive (*Rewe Handelsgesellschaft-Nord GmbH v. Hauptzollamt Kiel* [1981] E.C.R. 1805).

[32] HASAWA, s. 47(1) and (2). See for example the Management of Health and Safety at Work Regulations 1999, reg. 22(1); however, reg. 22(2) disapplies the exclusion of civil liability for regs 16 and 19, which implement E.C. Directive 92/85 regarding protection of new and expectant mothers and young persons. And see Chap. 7.

[33] Report of Robens Committee (Cmnd. 5034), Chap. 5.

[34] Cmnd. 5034.

work supported by regulations and codes of practice, the latter to be used extensively to provide "detailed specifications and guidance on the implementation" of these principles but not to impose legal obligations, although to be taken into account where necessary in enforcement proceedings.[35] Effect to that recommendation has been given by sections 16 and 17 of the Health and Safety at Work Act 1974. Thus the Health and Safety Commission may approve and/or issue codes of practice which it regards as suitable for the purpose of providing practical guidance to the requirements of (a) sections 2–7 of the 1974 Act, and (b) health and safety regulations.[36] The consent of the Secretary of State for Employment is required before the Health and Safety Commission can approve a code,[37] but many codes of practice have been issued and several British Standards have been approved as codes of practice, thereby acquiring the legal characteristics attached to codes of practice by section 17 of the 1974 Act, namely that a failure on the part of any person to observe the code shall not of itself render him liable to any civil or criminal proceedings.

However, where in any criminal proceedings a party is alleged to have committed an offence under any provision mentioned in section 16(1) of the 1974 Act[38] in respect of which provision there existed an approved code, any part of such a code as appears relevant to the alleged offence shall be admissible in evidence. Further, a failure to comply with an approved code results in the accused being required to show that the relevant statutory provision or regulation was complied with otherwise than by observing the provision(s) of the code.[39] Although section 17 makes no provision for the effect of a failure to comply with an approved code of practice, in civil proceedings there would seem to be nothing to prevent it being adduced as evidence of the standard of care to be expected of an employer in an action based on breach of the common law duty of care.[40] Indeed it is well established that guidance and advice in official documents or leaflets may be referred to for showing the proper precautions to be taken or standard of care to be achieved even although, strictly, the guidance does not apply to the circumstances in which the injury occurred.[41] Similarly it has been held that reference may be made

---

[35] *ibid.*, Chapter 5.
[36] Namely regulations made under HASAWA, s. 15 (HASAWA, s. 53(1)).
[37] *ibid.*, s. 16(2).
[38] Namely HASAWA, ss. 2–8; health and safety regulations and existing statutory provisions.
[39] HASAWA, s. 17(1) and (2); see *West Cumberland By Products Ltd v. DPP* [1988] R.T.R. 391; *Lockhart v. Kevin Oliphant*, 1993 S.L.T. 179.
[40] See Chap. 3.
[41] *Dickson v. Flack* [1953] 2 Q.B. 464; and see *Butt v. Inner London Education Authority* (1968) 66 L.G.R. 379, CA.

to a statutory provision for the purpose of setting the standard of care required for performance of the common law duty of care.[42] However, while compliance with an official document or a code of practice is of evidential value there is no presumption that it demonstrates the defender has performed to the required common law standard of reasonable care[43] and the common law duty of care is not necessarily superseded by a detailed statutory provision.[44]

The role of the European Community[45]

2.7 As noted earlier in this chapter, one of the recommendations of the Robens Committee was to replace the piecemeal approach of legislating for particular industries and places of employment which had produced a "mass of ill-assorted and intricate detail" with a system of comprehensive provisions founded on basic principles which would extend to all employers, employees and the self-employed and would be self-regulating. While the Health and Safety at Work Act 1974 enacted basic principles of responsibility for health and safety at work, it is doubtful whether the system which resulted therefrom was generally self-regulating. Interestingly, however, the principle of self-regulation under the guise of risk assessment is at the heart of the present approach to health and safety embodied in the European Commission's Third Programme on Health and Safety at Work of 1987 and the Social Charter and Action Programme of 1989.

2.8 It is beyond the scope of this work to deal in detail with the European dimension of health and safety at work, but it is necessary here to deal with the major developments which were outlined in Chapter 1.[46] The main reasons for the European Community's intervention into the field of health and safety at work are (a) different safety standards result in price differentials which would inhibit the free flow of products; (b) a reduction in the social and economic costs of accidents result in the enhancement of the quality of life for the whole Community; (c) safe and therefore efficient work practices produce increase in productivity

---

[42] *Hewett v. Alf Brown's Transport Ltd* [1991] I.C.R. 471 (Control of Lead at Work Regulations 1980 (S.I. 1980 No. 1248)).

[43] *Bux v. Slough Metals Ltd* [1974] 1 All E.R. 262 (strictly by providing goggles the employer had complied with the relevant statutory regulations, but the common law standard required that he encourage their use). And see Chap. 3.

[44] *Matuszczyk v. NCB*, 1953 S.C. 8; and see Chap. 3.

[45] Technically with effect from November 1, 1993 as a result of the Treaty of Maastricht the European Community has been embraced by the European Union of which it is a "pillar".

[46] For a detailed coverage see (eds) Neal and Wright, *European Community Health and Safety Legislation* (1992).

and improved industrial relations; and (d) major industrial incidents can have cross-border effects and their treatment requires to be harmonised. Also the social policy provisions of the Treaty of Rome[47] themselves demonstrate that the European Community is not concerned only with economic expansion, and notably Article 118, when combined with the high number of workplace accidents, prompted the Commission to embark on an initiative to develop, in stages, a preventative policy. Until 1974 the Commission's approach focussed on occupational illnesses and diseases. However, in each year there were 100,000 deaths and 12,000,000 injuries resulting from accidents at work, and these figures resulted in the Commission, encouraged by the adoption by the Council of Ministers of a resolution,[48] drawing up a series of Action Programmes and the setting up of the Advisory Committee for Safety, Hygiene and Health Protection at Work,[49] comprising 72 representatives of governments, trade unions and employers, and the Dublin Foundation,[50] an autonomous Community body to conduct research into working environment and the impact of new technologies.

Until 1978 there were two significant legislative initiatives.[51] However, in that year the First Action Programme on health and safety at work was drawn up[52] for the period to 1982, to take action leading to improving the aetiology of accidents and diseases, providing protection against dangerous substances, preventing dangers and harmful effects of machines, and bringing about an improvement in attitudes in the workplace. 1980 saw the adoption of the First Framework Directive[53] dealing with harmonisation of measures for protection against chemical, physical and biological agents at work and its four "daughter" Directives, which are early examples of self-assessment operating as a mechanism to trigger more specific provisions. Thus, for example, a daughter Directive[54] provides that where any activity is likely to involve a risk of exposure to dust from asbestos the risk must be assessed to determine the nature and degree of exposure. Where the assessment shows the presence of asbestos fibre below the maximum but above other specified levels, a range of special and detailed provisions are activated. In 1984 the Second Action Programme

---

[47] Arts 117–128. The Treaty of Amsterdam revised and renumbered many of the Articles. Arts 117–128 have been renumbered 136–151.
[48] January 21, 1974.
[49] Council Decision 74/325.
[50] Set up by Council Regulation of May 26, 1976.
[51] Directive 77/576 (safety signs at workplace); Directive 76/610 (exposure to uynie chloride monomers).
[52] Council Resolution 78/C165/1.
[53] Directive 80/1107.
[54] 83/477.

was set in motion by a Council Directive[55] which, when later combined with the amendments to the treaty of Rome introduced by the Single European Act, encouraged the Commission to make policy initiatives in reliance of the new Articles 118a and 118b by which the Council was permitted to act by qualified majority.[56] This in turn was followed by the Community Charter of Fundamental Social Rights of Workers,[57] the eventual text of which was agreed at Strasbourg in December 1989 by all Member States except the United Kingdom, and provided *inter alia* for social aspects to be given the same importance as economic ones.[58]

2.9 Perhaps the most significant step of all was taken by the adoption of the Framework Directive 89/391—the first Directive to be introduced under the new Article 118a. Unlike Directive 87/1107 the Framework Directive went beyond self-assessment and imposed certain basic duties on employers and workers. Of particular significance is Article 16 of the Framework Directive, which provides that the Council, acting on a proposal of the Commission based on Article 118a of the Treaty of Rome, shall adopt individual Directives in the areas listed in the Annex to the Framework Directive; namely (a) workplaces, (b) work equipment, (c) personal protective equipment, (d) work and visual display units, (e) handling of heavy loads, (f) temporary or mobile worksites and (g) fisheries and agriculture. Individual Directives have been adopted in respect of all areas except (g).[59] However, while Articles 100a and 118a of the amended Treaty of Rome allowed the Council to act by qualified majority, at the insistence of the United Kingdom, Article 100(2) provides that the power to act by qualified majority shall not apply to any provisions regarding the rights of employed persons.

2.10 When the Treaty on European Union (TEU) was negotiated at Maastricht in 1992 the United Kingdom refused to accept the changes proposed by the other 11 member states to the Social Chapter of the European Economic Community Treaty, and to secure the other changes to the decision-making processes it was agreed in a Protocol on Social Policy that the other 11 member states would be able to make use of the institutional and decision-making processes of the Community to further develop social

---

[55] Directive 84/C67/02.

[56] Until 1987 only six health and safety Directives had been issued in reliance on Art. 100 which requires unanimity.

[57] Com. (89) 568.

[58] See below para. 2.11.

[59] Other directives adopted under the Framework Directive include the Protection of Workers from Risks Related to Carcinogens at Work Directive (90/394) and the Protection of Pregnant Workers Directive (92/87).

policy. The United Kingdom was not to be bound by any measures adopted nor participate in the deliberations.

Charter or Chapter?

2.11 Although frequently used interchangeably these terms require to be distinguished. The Social Charter describes the document entitled the "Community Charter of Fundamental Social Rights of Workers",[60] which sets out a list of social and employment rights or principles including freedom of movement, fair remuneration, paid leave, right to associate in trade unions, the right to strike, the right to information and consultation prior to the introduction of workplace change, and rights for the young, elderly and disabled to which the Community was to be committed. The Charter itself did not create any legal rights and perhaps of more significance was the Action Programme prepared by the Commission for the purpose of "operationalising" the general principles in the Charter itself.[61]

2.12 The Social Chapter on the other hand are the Social Provisions (Arts. 117 to 122) contained in what was originally Chapter 1 of Title III of the E.C. Treaty. As indicated above, in 1987 two new Articles (118a and 118b) were added by the Treaty for the Single European Act, by far the more significant being Article 118a, which permitted the Council of Ministers to adopt directives by Qualified Majority Voting (QMV) to improve the working environment as regards health and safety of workers. In 1992 the Treaty on European Union changed the name of (and renumbered) Title III of the E.C. Treaty to reflect the aims of the Social Charter so that it became Title VIII Social Policy, Education, Vocational Training and Youth, with Chapter 1 (the Social Chapter) continuing to deal with social provisions.[62] The effect of the Social Protocol Agreement (the Agreement) for the Member States except the United Kingdom was to extend Community competence to introduce—by QMV—Directives in the area of

---

[60] It was adopted (the U.K. dissented) by the Council of Ministers in October 1989.

[61] The Action Programme reflected the Charter by proposing measures on a variety of matters including living and working conditions, vocational training and health and safety at work.

[62] It had been intended that the principles set out in the Social Charter be enshrined in the E.C. Treaty itself but because of the opposition of U.K. the substance of the Chapter had remained unchanged. Instead, all Member States agreed to the Social Protocol, which noted that 11 Member States wished to continue along the path laid down by the 1989 Charter of Fundamental Social Rights of Workers, and to that end they adopted the Social Protocol Agreement (the Agreement). Any Acts adopted by the Council on the basis of the Agreement did not bind the U.K.

improvement in the working environment, and working conditions. Article 4 of the Agreement allowed for an agreement—a framework agreement—between the social partners (essentially trade unions and employers) to act as the basis for a Commission proposal and eventual Council decision.

The Labour Government and the Social Chapter

2.13 Soon after the General Election in 1997 the United Kingdom indicated a willingness to endorse the Agreement, with the result that there was incorporated into the E.C. Treaty itself the provisions of the Agreement from which the United Kingdom had previously withheld its consent. This required amending the Maastricht Treaty and the E.C. Treaty. The necessary amendments were achieved at an Inter-governmental Conference in Amsterdam in June 1997, which resulted in the Treaty of Amsterdam. Health and safety and employment lawyers should note that this Treaty repeals the original E.C. Treaty provisions comprising the Social Chapter and replaces them with a series of new articles now numbered Articles 136–145. The result is that the Council of Ministers is now authorised to achieve the objectives of the Agreement by virtue of the legislative process of the E.C. Treaty itself with regard to the whole Community and not merely the subscribing Member States.

The new Social Chapter

2.14 Article 136 (117)[63] now makes express reference to the European Social Charter signed at Turin on October 18, 1961, and Community Charter of the Fundamental Social Rights of Workers and, to those ends, provides that the Community and the Member States shall promote employment and improve living and working conditions, while highlighting the possibility of progress through dialogue between management and labour—the social partners. Article 137 (118) empowers the Council, acting by QMV, to adopt directives in a variety of areas, including (a) the working environment to protect workers' health and safety and (b) working conditions.

2.15 The revised Social Chapter gives more prominence to dialogue and consultation between employers and trade unions or worker representatives. Thus under Article 138 (118a) the Commission has the task of promoting the consultation of management and labour at Community level and shall take any relevant measure

---

[63] The numbers in brackets are the numbers of the nearest equivalent articles of the E.C. Treaty before amendment by the Treaty of Amsterdam.

to facilitate dialogue by ensuring balanced support for the parties, while Article 139 (118b) allows management and labour to conclude contractual relations, including framework agreements which may form the basis of a Commission proposal and Council decision.[64]

2.16 Assuming a Directive is validly made what is its legal effect in Scots law? Although Directives are addressed to Member States and can lead to infraction proceedings at the instance of the Commission or another Member State in the European Court of Justice, in constrast to self-executing Treaty provisions,[65] in order to have legal effect require to be translated into domestic law by Member States[66] Directives can, however, affect legal rights within the domestic legal regimes in certain circumstances. Thus where a Member State has failed to properly translate a Directive into domestic law it cannot rely on its own failure to do so in an issue with an individual such as an employee of an emanation of the state,[67] on the grounds that it would be incompatible with the binding nature which Article 189 of the EEC Treaty confers on directives to hold that the obligations imposed thereby cannot be relied upon. The European Court of Justice has therefore deduced that a member state which has not adopted the necessary implementing measures may not plead, as against individuals, its own failure to perform the obligations the Directive entails.[68] The result is that individuals are entitled, in an issue with an emanation of the state, to rely on a Directive which is unconditional and sufficiently precise. This can be seen in *Gibson v. East Riding of Yorkshire District Council*[69]; the EAT has held that a swimming instructor employed by a local authority—an emanation of the state—who was paid an hourly rate and was not paid during school holidays, was entitled to four weeks' paid annual leave under Article 7 of the Working Time Directive.[70] The EAT noted that the Directive was

---

[64] It was on this basis that the Parental Leave Directive and the Directive on Part-time Work were adopted.

[65] *e.g.* EEC Treaty, Art. 119 (equal pay).

[66] EEC Treaty, Arts 169 and 170. For a full account of European Community law see D. Lasok & J.W. Bridge, *Law and Institutions of the European Communities* (5th ed., Butterworths).

[67] An emanation of the state has been held to include an area health authority (*Marshall v. Southampton and South West Hampshire Area Health Authority (Teaching)* [1986] I.C.R. 335 (ECJ)), a police authority (*Johnston v. Chief Constable of the Royal Ulster Constabulary* [1987] I.C.R. 83 (ECJ)) and a nationalised industry (*Foster v. British Gas plc* [1991] I.C.R. 84 (ECJ)), *cf. Doughty v. Rolls-Royce* [1992] I.R.L.R. 126, CA.

[68] *Marshall v. Southampton and S.W. Hampshire Area Health Authority (Teaching)* [1986] I.C.R. 334 (ECJ); *Becker v. Finanzamt Münster Innenstadt* [1982] E.C.R. 53 (ECJ).

[69] [1999] I.R.L.R. 358.

[70] Directive 93/104.

concerned with the further harmonisation of health and safety conditions within the community and, *inter alia*, granting minimum annual periods of rest in order to ensure safety of workers, the structure of the Directive was consistent with it having direct effect, and Article 7 was clear and precise and admitted of no ambiguity or conditionality.

2.17 Secondly, where the Parliament of the United Kingdom has enacted legislation to implement a Directive, the House of Lords has encouraged domestic courts and tribunals to be prepared to take a progressive attitude to statutory interpretation if necessary to achieve compatibility with Community law.[71] Thus, in *Litster v. Forth Dry Dock and Engineering Co.*,[72] in order to give effect to Directive 77/187/EEC their lordships were prepared to write into the implementing domestic regulations[73] words which had not been in the regulations approved by Parliament, and which incidentally have not since been added although the same regulations have in other respects been amended to comply with other provisions of the Directive. Following the decision of the European Court of Justice in *Marleasing v. La Commercial Internacional d'Alimentacion SA*[74] (in which it was held that in applying national law, whether it is passed to implement a Directive or whether it pre-dates a Directive, the domestic court is obliged to do everything possible to achieve the result laid down by the Directive) it has been argued that the distinction between domestic legislation which pre-dates and post-dates a Directive is inconsistent with Community law,[75] and the House of Lords has now accepted[76] that it is the duty of a United Kingdom court to construe domestic legislation to accord with a Directive as interpreted by the European Court of Justice, whether the domestic leglislation came before or after the Directive, subject to two important reservations—(a) that the construction did not distort the meaning of the legislation and (b) only if it is possible for the domestic court to do so in the context of health and safety. Finally in *R v. Secretary of State for Transport, ex p. Factortame*[77] the European Court of Justice has held that, if a rule of domestic law prevented the enforcement of a Community law, domestic law had to be set aside, and in *Francovich v. Italian Republic*[78] it was held that a

---

[71] *Pickstonne v. Freeman's plc* [1988] I.C.R. 697 (HL).

[72] [1989] I.C.R. 341 (HL).

[73] Transfer of Undertakings (Protection of Employment) Regulations 1981 (S.I. 1981 No. 1794).

[74] [1990] E.C.R. I–4135 (ECJ).

[75] See, for example, *Porter v. Cannon Hygiene Ltd* [1993] I.R.L.R. 329 (NICA).

[76] *Webb v. EMO Air Cargo UK Ltd* [1993] I.R.L.R. 27 (HL).

[77] [1990] E.C.R. I–2433 (ECJ).

[78] [1992] I.R.L.R. 84 (ECJ). And see "Beyond Francovich", Ross [1993] M.L.R. 55.

member state which fails to properly implement a Directive could be liable in damages.

2.18 From these principles it follows that where domestic regulations have been introduced to give effect to a Directive they have to be construed so far as possible to conform with the Directive, and it is arguable that in some respects the regulations introduced to give effect to the Framework Directive 89/391/EEC and its daughter Directives[79] fall short of doing so. Thus unlike the Directives, the domestic regulations and their accompanying codes of practice are frequently limited by the insertion of the phrase "as far as reasonably practicable" a limitation of responsibility not usually found in the Directives. The Framework and its daughter Directives only permit a reduction of employers' responsibility where occurrences are due to unusual and unforeseeable circumstances, beyond the employer's control, or to exceptional events whose consequences could not have been avoided despite all due care,[80] and this seems a more stringent requirement than "not reasonably practicable". However, in accordance with the decision of the House of Lords in *Webb v. EMO Air Cargo Ltd*[81] a domestic court may be able to construe the test of reasonable practicability to give effect to the Directives. Similarly, breach of a provision in a code of practice of itself, although probably of evidential value in a civil action, certainly does not activate a criminal sanction, and it is arguable that, where a Directive is implemented by a code of practice and not a regulation the requirement of Community law that for breach of the provisions of a Directive there is an effective remedy, may not be met. However, in *Officier van Justitie v. Kolpinghuis Nijmegen BV*[82] it has been held that because the national court's obligation to interpret domestic law to comply with a Directive is limited by the general principles of law—in particular the principles of legal certainty and non-retroactivity—there was not, in the context of criminal proceedings, a duty to comply with a Directive which a Member State government itself had not implemented. Finally, because the Management of Health and Safety at Work Regulations 1999[83] which purport to complete the implementation of the Framework Directive exclude civil liability—except in respect of regulation 16 (risk assessment and pregnancy) and regulation 19 (young persons)—it is arguable that such an exclusion of civil liability offends against the requirement of

---

[79] Directive 89/654; Directive 89/655; Directive 89/650; Directive 89/686; Directive 90/269 and Directive 90/270.
[80] Directive 89/391, Art. 5(4).
[81] [1993] I.R.L.R. 27 (HL).
[82] [1987] E.C.R. 3969 (ECJ).
[83] S.I. 1999 No. 3242.

Community law that legal actions available in the courts of Member States for enforcement of rights which are the product of domestic law should also be available for ensuring observance of Community law.[84] Thus, although an employer who fails to carry out a risk assessment as required by the Management of Health and Safety at Work Regulations 1999[85] would not be liable for breach of statutory duty, it is arguable that the failure to carry out such "a suitable and sufficient assessment"[86] may also lead to a breach of the common law requirement to provide a safe system of work.

The Institutions of the law of Health and Safety at Work

2.19 As mentioned earlier in this Chapter health and safety law depends on the concentration of different types of legal provisions from different sources and so it is with regard to what may conveniently be called the institutions or agencies of health and safety law. Clearly many of those legal provisions are subject to the jurisdictions of the ordinary civil and criminal courts, or the employment tribunals.[87] However, the effective prosecution of the recommendations of the Robens Committee[88] required the creation of new, or the reorganisation of existing, structures. Thus there has been created the Health and Safety Commission and Executive (HSC and HSE) under whose aegis various inspectorates[89] and directorates operate. Following the White Paper on the civil service (*Continuity and Change*) the HSE has undergone substantial internal reorganisation and the diagram in the appendix hereto shows the main operating divisions of the HSE.

2.20 The HSC has published its Plan of Work for 1998–1999 which sets out the priorities for the HSC and the HSE. The five priorities are:

To build on the success of "Good health is good for Business" campaign;

To work with others including employee representatives and local authorities to improve health and safety;

---

[84] *Rewe Handelsgesellschaft-Nord GmbH v. Hauptzollamt Kiel* [1981] E.C.R. 1805.
[85] S.I. 1999 No. 3242, reg. 3.
[86] *ibid.*, reg. 3(1).
[87] See, for example, the jurisdiction given to the employment tribunals to hear appeals against Improvement and Prohibition Notices (HASAWA 1974, s. 24); and see Chap. 4.
[88] Cmnd. 5034.
[89] In *Harris v. Evans and the HSE*, April 24, 1998, CA, it was held that neither the HSE nor its inspectors are liable in respect of negligent advice which results in economic loss.

To cut injury rates particularly in agriculture and construction;
To help small firms comply with the law;
To implement the Control of Major Hazards Directive.

The composition and powers of the Health and Safety Commission and Executive are dealt with in Chapter Four but it is necessary here to place these and other agencies in perspective. The Health and Safety at Work Act 1974 created a two tier structure consisting of the Health and Safety Commission (HSC) and its operational arm the Health and Safety Executive (HSE) to which it may give directions.[90] Amongst the HSC's powers is the power to make agreements whereby (1) other agencies can perform functions on behalf of the HSC or HSE,[91] or (2) the HSE can perform appropriate functions on behalf of a Minister, government department or public authority.[92] The HSE is empowered to appoint inspectors,[93] and the former inspectorates of factories, mines and quarries, nuclear installations, industrial pollution and explosives have been transferred to the HSE. Also, with effect from April 1, 1991 the HSE exercises functions previously conferred on the Secretary of State for Trade and Industry by the Mineral Workings (Offshore Installations) Act 1971.[94] Since 1898 there had been a medical branch of the Factories Inspectorate, and in 1972 the functions of that branch were extended and placed on a statutory footing by the Employment Medical Advisory Service Act 1972 which provided for the establishment, organisation and function of the Employment Medical Advisory Service (EMAS) and the abolition of the position and functions of appointed factory doctors. The purpose of setting up the EMAS was to ensure that those concerned with the health of employed persons and those in training for employment would be kept informed of matters concerning the safeguarding and improvement of such persons.[95] Part II of the Health and Safety at Work Act 1974 repeals, in part, and re-enacts with some amendments the 1972 Act. The work of EMAS, with its headquarters in London, is carried out on a

---

[90] HASAWA 1974, s. 11(4).

[91] See for example the agreements entered into under HASAWA, s. 13 with (a) the National Radiological Protection Board whereby that Board performs the HSC's function regarding radiation dangers and (b) the Gas and Oil Measurement Branch of the Department of Trade and Industry, whereby that branch performs functions for the HSE with respect to the Gas Quality Regulations 1992.

[92] See for example HSE's acceptance of responsibility for enforcement of the Employers Liability (Compulsory Insurance) Act 1969 under S.I. 1975 No. 194.

[93] HASAWA 1974, s. 19.

[94] And see Chap. 6 regarding the change of responsibilities following the Cullen Report on *Piper Alpha* and Offshore Safety Act 1992, and Chap. 5 regarding the inspection of shops, offices, leisure facilities, hotels, restaurants and places of worship, carried out by the local authority environmental health officers.

[95] Employment Medical Advisory Service Act 1972, s. 1(1).

regional basis, a Senior Employment Medical Advisor being appointed for each region.[96]

European institutions

2.21 It is the responsibility of the European commission to take enforcement proceedings against any Member State which fails to implement directives. The Commission also has the responsibility for drawing up proposals for directives but, before doing so and before entering into consultations with the European Parliament, it will take advice from the Advisory Committee on Safety Hygiene and Health Protection at Work,[97] which consists of representatives of employees, employers and Member States. In 1994 the Council of Ministers established a European Agency for Safety and Health at Work[98] to encourage improvements in the working environment and to provide technical and scientific data for use in health and safety at work.[99] To achieve its objectives the Agency, after consulting the Commission and the Advisory Committee, adopts annual programmes of work which generally form part of a four-year rolling programme. The Agency is based in Bilbao, to which the HSE has sent personnel on secondment.

2.22 In 1995 the Commission set up a Committee of Senior Labour Inspectors[1] and a Scientific Committee for Occupational Exposure Limits to Chemical Agents.[2] In 1996 the Commission set up a Major Accident Hazards Bureau to assist the Commission on the implementation of policy to control major hazards.

---

[96] The Scottish Headquarters is Belford House, 59 Belford Road, Edinburgh EH4 3UE; tel. 0131 247 2000.
[97] Established by Council Decision 74/325.
[98] Council Regulation 2062/94.
[99] In 1995 (Council Regulation 1643/95) the composition of the Agency's Administrative Board was changed giving more influence to Member States.
[1] Decision 95/319.
[2] Decision 95/320.

CHAPTER 3

THE COMMON LAW

INTRODUCTION

3.1 While the systematic development of health and safety at work is today overwhelmingly the province of statutory regulation (domestic and European) it is important to note that common law, because of the generality of its principles and their flexibility of application, is still an important source of legal rights and duties. Until very recently, Scots health and safety at work law, like its English counterpart, at least in terms of civil liability, consisted of the general principles of delict (or tort in England) supplemented by specific statutory provisions which related to particular workplaces, for example factories,[1] mines and quarries,[2] shops and offices,[3] or to particular operations, for example, the use of particular machines or equipment[4] and substances.[5] While the Health and Safety at Work Act 1974 enacted general duties which would apply, irrespective of the nature of the workplace or the operation being undertaken,[6] that statute operates only in the field of the criminal law, section 47(1) providing "[n]othing in . . . Part [I] shall be construed (a) as conferring a right of civil action in any civil proceedings in respect of any failure to comply with any duty imposed by sections 2 to 7; or (b) as affecting the extent (if any) to which breach of a duty imposed by any existing statutory provisions is actionable".

3.2 It is noticeable, however, that since 1974 the statutory regulation of health and safety at work has adopted the "generalist" approach of the 1974 Act. Thus the regulations made under the

---

[1] Factories Act 1961.
[2] Mines and Quarries Act 1954.
[3] Offices, Shops and Railway Premises Act 1963.
[4] See the Woodworking Machine Regulations 1974.
[5] See, for example, Highly Flammable Liquids and Liquified Petroleum Gases Regulations 1972; Ionising Radiation (Unsealed Substances) Regulations 1968.
[6] See, for example, Health and Safety at Work Act 1974, ss. 2–7.

Health and Safety at Work Act 1974 which, in accordance with section 47(2),[7] create civil liability unless they provide otherwise, apply to risk-creating work operations and are couched in the flexible terminology of "reasonable practicability". Examples of this current approach can be seen in (a) the Manual Handling Operations Regulations 1992,[8] which may apply in circumstances as different as a nurse lifting a patient in a hospital, a dancer lifting a fellow performer in a theatrical production,[9] or a factory worker carrying a box from one part of the factory to another, and (b) the Workplace Health and Safety Regulations 1992, which may apply equally to the provision of sanitary facilities for agricultural fieldworkers[10] and the arrangement of workstations in a college or university.[11]

One result of this approach to statutory regulation of health and safety at work has been, at least in some respects,[12] the convergence of the approach of common law and statute, in that in each case the concepts of "reasonableness" and "practicability" form the basis of legal rules which apply generally to risks and dangers at work. A by-product of this convergence has been a cross-fertilisation of the statutory and common law systems which has come about in two ways. First the decision of a court dealing with an employee's common law claim, based as it is on an employer's duty to take "reasonable care", is capable of influencing a court entertaining an employee's claim based on breach of statutory duty which will frequently turn on whether an employer took such steps as were "reasonably practicable"; secondly, there can be no doubt that a court, when faced with a question as to whether an employer has acted reasonably, whether dealing with an action based on common law or for breach of statutory duty, will be much influenced by formal, normative documents like

---

[7] s. 47(2) provides that "breach of a duty imposed by health and safety regulations . . . shall so far as it causes damage be actionable except in so far as the regulations provide otherwise".

[8] reg. 2(1) defines "load" to include any person or animal. But note the accompanying Guidance provides that an implement, tool or machine is not considered a load while in use for its intended purpose. See *King v. Carron Phoenix Ltd*, 1999 G.W.D. 9-437: that applying force to a spanner was not supporting or moving a "load".

[9] Thus Mr Kevin Woods, principal dancer in *Aspects of Love*, raised an action under the Manual Handling Operations Regulations 1992 against the theatre company claiming that his role required him to execute a series of complicated and strenuous lifts.

[10] Workplace (Health, Safety and Welfare) Regulations 1992, regs. 3, 22.

[11] *ibid.*, reg. 11.

[12] Clearly in many areas statutory regulations prescribe absolute standards where necessary because of special risks which a particular operation may involve: see, for example the Miners and Quarries Act 1954 and the Agriculture (Threshers and Balers) Regulations 1960.

approved codes of practice[13] as well as informal guidance given by the Health and Safety Executive[14]; similarly the failure to perform a statutory obligation, such as carry out a risk assessment, may be taken into account in considering a common law claim.[15]

However, this cross-fertilisation will not always be the case and care must be taken to distinguish the standard required for a common law claim from that brought for breach of statutory duty. Thus in *Hall v. City of Edinburgh Council*,[16] where a blacksmith sued his employer for a back injury both at common law and for breach of the Manual Handling Operations Regulations 1992 founding on guidance produced by the Health and Safety Executive (HSE), his case at common law failed because the HSE guidance was prepared in relation to the Regulations which involved a lower threshold of risk, whereas for the common law case, while the employer would be required to have regard to the guidance he would also be entitled to take account of other relevant experience; namely that the operation had been carried out by a blacksmith experienced in relatively heavy work virtually daily for many years without complaint or injury.[17] Similarly in *Cullen v. North Lanarkshire Council*,[18] while under regulation 4(1)(a) of the Manual Handling Operations Regulations 1992 the standard required of the employer was that of reasonable practicability the risk to be guarded against was the foreseeable *possibility* of injury and not the foreseeable *probability* of injury, and it was wrong to say that the Regulations added little to the

---

[13] Under the Health and Safety at Work Act 1974, s.16(1), the Health and Safety Commission may, with the consent of the Secretary of State for Employment, approve codes of practice which contain practical guidance with respect to the requirements of various statutory provisions.

[14] The interrelationships between the common law, statutory regulation and a code of practice is well illustrated by *Hewett v. Alf Brown's Transport Ltd* [1992] I.C.R. 530, CA. And see *King v. Carron Phoenix Ltd*, 1999 G.W.D. 9-437, that a reasonable employer would have been alerted by the HSE document "Work related Upper Limb Disorders" to carry out an assessment of the pursuer contracting upper limb disorders.

[15] *Logan v. Strathclyde Fire Board* (O.H., unreported, January 12, 1999); although the decision concerns mainly the duties required under the Manual Handling Operations Regulations 1992 the common law case was upheld partly on the basis that there has been no risk assessment carried out.

[16] 1999 S.L.T. 744, O.H. And see *Mearns v. Lothian Regional Council*, 1991 S.L.T. 338 (O.H.), distinguishing the common law duty from the statutory one in reg. 4 of the Merchant Shipping (Safe Movement on board Ships) Regulations 1988.

[17] And see *Devizes Reclamation Co. Ltd v. Chalk*, *The Times*, April 2, 1999, CA, that no liability arose where an experienced labourer acting on his own initiative injured his back in performing a one-off task requiring the use of common sense and for which no instruction could have been given. *Cf. Oliver v. Brown and Root MacDermott Fabricators Ltd* (O.H., unreported, March 12, 1999) (employer liable for setting to work an untrained and inexperienced employee) and *Fraser v. Winchester Health Authority*, *The Times*, July 12, 1999, CA.

[18] 1998 S.L.T. 847 (I.H.).

common law case.[19] Somewhat analogously it has been held that legislation whose primary purpose was to protect employees may also extend to members of the public.[20]

DEVELOPMENT OF THE EMPLOYER'S OBLIGATION
BEFORE *BARTONSHILL*

3.2 Until the infamous *Bartonshill Coal Company* cases[21] the essential principle of an employer's duty to his employee was not in doubt and is comprehensively stated by Lord Justice Clerk Hope in *Dixon v. Rankin*[22]:

"The master's primary obligation in every contract of service in which his workmen are employed in a hazardous and dangerous occupation for his interest and profit, is to provide for, and attend to the safety of the men. That is . . . paramount even to that of paying for their labour. This obligation includes the duty of furnishing good and sufficient machinery and apparatus to enable them, with safety to their lives, to perform the work they are employed to his profit, and to keep the same in a reasonable and good condition. . . . In this obligation is equally included—as he cannot do everything himself—the duty to have all acts, by others whom he employs, done properly and carefully, in order to avoid risk. The obligation to provide for the safety of the lives of his servants by fit machinery, is not greater, or more inherent in the contract, than the obligation to provide for their safety from the acts done by others whom he also employs."

This approach therefore prevented an employer escaping liability by showing that the injury was caused by the negligence of another employee and in the same year in *Nisbett v. Dixon & Co.*[23] the First Division thwarted an early attempt to avoid liability by interposing an independent contractor. Dixon & Co., having entered into a

---

[19] *ibid.*, at p. 850. And see *Anderson v. Lothian Health Board*, 1996 Rep.L.R. 89.

[20] Thus in *Banna v. Delicato*, 1998 G.W.D. 34-1758, a customer who caught her foot in a basket on the shop floor was able to rely on the Workplace (Health, Safety and Welfare) Regulations 1992 which in respect of traffic routes are more specific than the Occupiers Liability (Scotland) Act 1960. *Cf. Thomson v. Barbour*, 1996 S.L.T. 920, emphasising that for the purpose of a criminal charge under Health and Safety at Work Act 1974 (s. 7(a)) the employee must be "at work".

[21] *Reid v. Bartonshill Coal Co.* (1858) 17 D. 1017; *Bartonshill Coal Co. v. McGuire* (1858) 3 Macq. 300.

[22] (1852) 14 D. 420 at p. 424; and see *Sword v. Cameron* (1839) 1 D. 493.

[23] (1852) 14 D. 971.

lease of ironstone workings, engaged Nimmo and Watson to extract the ironstone. Due to the negligence of Watson an adjacent coal mine was damaged by fire (and the necessary steps taken to extinguish it) and the issue arose of whether Dixon & Co. could, by employing contractors, get rid of their responsibility to the landlord. Although the case did not involve an employer's duty of safety the reluctance of the court to allow the avoidance of responsibility by engaging third parties—unless they are truly contractors exercising an independent calling—is clearly illustrated by the judgments and, as Fraser points out,[24] the cases support the principle that where a person is legally bound to do a thing he cannot delegate his responsibility to a contractor. The non-delegability of the employer's duty is beyond doubt by 1854 when the First Division upheld the decision in *Baird v. Addie*[25] in which the Lord Ordinary had opined:

"Assuming that the law imposes upon a coalmaster the duty of looking to the safety of the workmen employed in his service, it would be subversive of the whole benefit of the principle, to hold that he could exonerate himself by merely changing the mode of his operations, and by engaging one person to undertake the whole service, instead of himself employing the men. The primary obligation being imposed on the coal master, it is clear that if he employs another to fulfil it, he is liable for any failure or neglect in its fulfilment; he must be answerable for anything left undone, if it were his duty to see it done by himself or others in his employment. The contractor is, with reference to parties in the position of the pursuer . . . to be regarded in the light of a servant, for whose neglect or fault he is responsible."

Similarly in *Macdonald v. Wyllie & Son*[26] a new trial was granted when Macdonald's employer escaped liability for his (Macdonald's) injury following a direction by the trial judge:

"That if the jury are satisfied that the defender, not having the knowledge and skill to erect the scaffolding in question, selected a tradesman having skill and experience of such work, and contracted with him to provide such a scaffold, he would not be liable as for fault if the scaffolding fell in consequence

---

[24] *Master and Servant* (3rd ed.), pp. 291 *et seq.*
[25] (1854) 14 D. 420. Contrast the approach adopted in *Baird* with the English decision in *Wigmore v. Jay* [1850] 19 L.R. Ex. 300 in which a builder was held not liable for the death of a bricklayer killed as a result of a defect in a scaffold erected under supervision of builder's foreman.
[26] (1898) 1 F. 339; and see *Wilson v. Merry & Co. Ltd* (1867) 5 M. 807.

of it not having been erected in a skilful manner through the
fault of the skilled person who contracted to erect it."

COMMON EMPLOYMENT

3.3 However, a major development occurred in 1858 when in
Reid v. Bartonshill Coal Co.[27] the House of Lords imposed on
Scotland law "the fatuous rule"[28] that there was implied into the
contract of employment a term that the employee took the risk of
injury by the negligence of a fellow employee or one in "common
employment" with himself. Having been applied in America in
Farwell v. Boston and Worcester Railroad Corporation[29] the rule was
adopted in England in *Hutchison v. York, Newcastle and Berwick
Railway Co.*,[30] where it was stated that "[t]he principle is that a
servant, when he engages to serve a master, undertakes as between
himself and his master, to run all the ordinary risks of the service;
and this includes the risk of negligence upon the part of a fellow
servant, when he is acting in the discharge of his duty as servant of
him who is the common master of both." Whether any other
implied term could have such far reaching consequences is difficult
to imagine and, of course, it resulted in those who needed the
protection most being deprived of it. Thus Alderson B. in
Hutchison noted that "[i]t may . . . be proper . . . to add that we do
not think that a master is exempt from responsibility to his servant
for an injury occasioned to him by the act of another servant where
the servant was not at the time of the injury acting in the service of
his master. In such a case the servant injured is substantially a
stranger and entitled to all the privileges he could have had if he
had not been a servant." In spite of attempts by the Scottish courts
to limit the scope of the doctrine of common employment,[31] it was
not until the passage of the Employers Liability Act 1880 that the
erosion of the doctrine began. By this Act an employee had a
remedy against his employer where he was injured by reason of any
defect in the ways, works, machinery or plant or from the
negligence of some person placed in the position of supervisor or
superintendent whose orders the employee had to obey. Only in
1948 was the doctrine of common employment abolished by the

---

[27] (1858) 17 D. 1017.
[28] Gow, *Mercantile and Industrial Law of Scotland*, p. 724.
[29] [1842] 4 Metc. 49; the judgment of Shaw C.J. is reproduced at (1858) 3 Macq.
316.
[30] [1850] 19 L.J. Ex. 296.
[31] See the interesting discussion in Miller, *Industrial Law in Scotland*, pp. 158–
163.

enactment of the Law Reform (Personal Injuries) Act. That Act, while repealing the Employers Liability Act 1880 provided (i) that it shall not be a defence to an employer who is sued in respect of personal injuries caused by the negligence of a person employed by him, that that person was at the time the injuries were caused in common employment with the person injured, and (ii) that any provision in a contract of employment or apprenticeship or any collateral agreement is void in so far as it would have the effect of excluding or limiting any liability of the employer in respect of personal injuries caused to the person employed by the negligence of persons in common employment with him. *Lindsay v. Connell & Co. Ltd*,[32] adopting a firm purposive approach to the interpretation of the statute, rejected the argument that it did not make an employer liable for what were "merely casual acts which emerged in the course of the day's work, . . . which the master could not guard against". The effect of the 1948 Act was to "replace the doctrine of common employment by the old maxims and by what before 1858 was the law of Scotland".[33] However, as has been remarked elsewhere,[34] the development of the law after 1858 took place in order to avoid the defence of common employment.

THE NATURE OF AND BASIS FOR THE EMPLOYER'S DUTY

3.4 Before addressing this issue it is necessary to spend some time considering the nature of the contract of employment. A more detailed discussion of judicial identification of the contract of employment may be found elsewhere.[35] For present purposes it is important to note that the test currently applied[36] is nothing if not flexible and may be fairly described as the "multiple and variable test", in that it requires the tribunal of fact to consider and evaluate a wide range of factors. It is therefore capable of application where the underlying issue involves whether the "worker" benefits from a statutory protection limited to those employed under a contract of employment[37] or whether the "employer" owes a duty of care for the "worker's" safety[38]; its

---

[32] 1951 S.C. 281.

[33] *per* Lord Blades, 1951 S.C. 281 at p. 285.

[34] Gow, *Mercantile and Industrial Law of Scotland*, p. 724.

[35] For a more detailed account of the concept of the employment contract and the judicial attempts to promulgate definitive tests reference may be made to V. Craig & K. Miller, *Employment Law in Scotland* (2nd ed.), Chap. 2.

[36] See for example *Short v. J & W Henderson*, 1946 S.C. (H.L.) 24; *Market Investigations Ltd v. Minister of Social Security* [1969] 2 Q.B. 173.

[37] See for example *Massey v. Crown Life Insurance Co.* [1978] I.R.L.R. 31.

[38] See for example *Ferguson v. Dawson and Partners Ltd* [1976] I.R.L.R. 346.

flexibility also allows particular significance or weight to be attached to one or more factor. Thus in a case dealing with casual staff including agency workers[39] or homeworkers, greater weight will be attached to the factor of "mutuality of obligation".[40] Many of the recent cases which have required a consideration of the nature of the relationship between employer and worker have concerned the application of statutory rights in which the multiple and variable test has permitted emphasis to be given to a particular factor or factors.

When considering whether the employer owes a duty of care and whether he is vicariously liable, the recent approach by Scottish courts has been to emphasise the factor of control. Thus in *Rennie v. Dorans*[41] where Rennie was approached by Dorans who had secured some painting work with which he required assistance, it was held that he owed Rennie a duty of care on the grounds that Dorans agreed to pay Rennie a daily rate and was "entitled in some reasonable sense to control the work of the pursuer and in particular the method adopted by him in carrying out the work for the defender" and the "agreement was such as to contain that factor of superintendence and control as has frequently been treated as critical of the legal quality of the relationship between [employer and employee]".[42] On the other hand the English courts seem to have been more concerned with the policy of the law and have doubted the ability of a worker to have the benefit of being self employed for purposes of taxation while claiming the status of being employed for claiming compensation for injuries.[43] Thus in *Lane v. Shire Roofing Co. (Oxford) Ltd*[44] the Court of Appeal expressly recognised, in the field of health and safety at work, for policy reasons[45] the law had to properly distinguish employees from independent contractors and while the element of control was important in the case of skilled employees the question was broadened to whose business was it. "Was it the workman carrying on his own business, or was he carrying on his employer's?"[46]

3.5 How to classify the relationship is of course important not merely in order to determine whether the employer owes a duty of

---

[39] See *McMeechan v. Secretary of State for Employment* [1997] I.R.L.R. 353, CA.

[40] See for example *Nethermere (St Neots) Ltd v. Taverna and Gardiner* [1984] I.R.L.R. 240; *O'Kelly v. Trust House Forte plc* [1983] I.R.L.R. 369.

[41] 1991 S.L.T. 443 (O.H.).

[42] *per* Lord Cameron of Lochbroom, 1991 S.L.T. 443 at 444 L. And in relation to vicarious liability see *Marshall v. William Sharp & Sons Ltd*, 1991 S.L.T. 114 (I.H.) and *United Wholesale Grocers Ltd v. Sher*, 1993 S.L.T. 284 (O.H.).

[43] See *Ferguson v. Dawson and Partners Ltd* [1976] 1 W.L.R. 1213; *Lee Ting Sang v. Chung Chi-Keung* [1990] 1 W.L.R. 1173 (PC).

[44] [1995] I.R.L.R. 493, CA.

[45] These were that there are far more self-employed people and fewer in employment, and that there are advantages for both workmen and employers in not creating an employment relationship.

[46] [1995] I.R.L.R. 493, *per* Lord Justice Henry.

care to the workman. If the relationship is one of employment it also makes the employer vicariously liable for the negligence of the employee[47] and may bring into play the operation of the Employers' Liability (Compulsory Insurance) Act 1969[48] and the Employers' Liability (Defective Equipment) Act 1969.[49] The significance of the technical concept of the contract of employment is to an extent being eroded due in part at least to the influence of European Community law,[50] which in the field of health and safety is generally concerned with a relationship wider than that encompassed by the contract of employment. Thus the Directive on the Introduction of Measures to encourage Improvements in the Safety and Health of Workers at Work[51] (the Framework Directive) applies to a worker who is defined to mean "any person employed by an employer including trainees and apprentices (but excluding domestic servants)" and to an employer who is defined to mean "any natural or legal person who has an employment relationship with a worker and who has responsibility for the undertaking or establishment". While the domestic Regulations introduced to give effect to the Framework Directive[52] are in some respects restricted to "employees",[53] the Regulations[54] giving effect to the Directive on the Organisation of Working Time[55] apply to "workers", who include those who work under contracts of employment and those who work under other contracts whereby an individual undertakes to perform personally work for another party to the contract who is not a client or customer of any business carried on by the individual.[56] The Working Time Regulations also apply to agency workers[57] (who would not be embraced by the definition of worker by virtue of the fact that while they undertake to perform personally work, they do not necessarily undertake to work for the other party to the contract) and non-employed trainees.[58] Whether

---

[47] See Chap. 3, paras 3.48 *et seq.*
[48] See Chap. 7, para. 7.46.
[49] See Chap. 3, para. 3.40.
[50] See Chap. 1.
[51] Directive 89/391 (O.J. 1989, No. L 183/1).
[52] Management of Health and Safety at Work Regulations 1999 (S.I. 1999 No. 3242).
[53] And see similarly the Workplace (Health, Safety and Welfare) Regulations 1992, Provision and Use of Work Equipment Regulations 1998, Personal Protective Equipment at Work Regulations 1992, Manual Handling Operations Regulations 1992 and Health and Safety (Display Screen Equipment) Regulations 1992, which were introduced to give effect to the five "daughter" directives adopted to deal with specific risk areas.
[54] Working Time Regulations 1998 (S.I. 1998 No. 1833).
[55] Directive 93/104 (O.J. 1993 L 307/18).
[56] Working Time Regulations 1998, reg. 2(1).
[57] *ibid.*, reg. 36.
[58] *ibid.*, reg. 42.

this extension of statutory health and safety rights to "workers" is due to the determination of the current Government to extend employment law rights generally[59] or the realisation that the Framework Directive requires the application of its principles and those of its "daughter" Directives to a wider class is important; if it is due to the former then it would be a matter for the Government to decide how far it wishes such an extension to go, but if it is due to the latter it may require that other statutory health and safety provisions will require to be applied to "workers" and not just to "employees" (that is, those with contracts of employment).

Contract or delict?[60]

3.6 In England it is been accepted for some time that the employer's duty to take reasonable care for the safety of his employees may be based on tort or by a term to that effect being implied into the contract of employment,[61] and the employee may elect whether to sue in contract or in tort.[62] While in some fields of law there has been a declared unwillingness to develop liability in tort where the parties are in a contractual relationship,[63] it has been stated[64] that such an approach is not in point when considering the employer's duty of safety. Nevertheless although the substance of the employer's duty has been developed in the context of litigation based on tort, English law now clearly recognises that a failure to take care for the safety of the employee will give rise to contract law remedies,[65] and in *White v. The Chief Constable of South Yorkshire Police*[66] the House of Lords, whilst confirming that

---

[59] See the White Paper Fairness at Work and the Employment Relations Act 1999.

[60] And see Chap. 7, para. 7.3.

[61] *Matthews v. Kuwait Bechtel Corporation* [1959] 2 Q.B. 57.

[62] And see *Coupland v. Arabian Gulf Oil Co. Ltd*, *The Times*, June 23, 1983, CA.

[63] See, for example, the dictum of Lord Scarman in *Tai Hing Cotton Mill Ltd v. Liu Chong Hing Bank Ltd* [1986] A.C. 80 at p. 107, *National Bank of Greece SA v. Pinios Shipping Co. No 1* [1990] 1 A.C. 637 at p. 650 and *Banque Keyser Ullman SA v. Skandia (U.K.) Insurance Co. Ltd* [1990] 1 Q.B. 665 at p. 799.

[64] *Johnstone v. Bloomsbury Health Authority* [1991] I.C.R. 269 per Stuart-Smith L.J. at p. 276. And see the decision of the House of Lords in *Arbuthnott and Others v. Fagan & Feltrim Underwriting Agencies Ltd* [1994] 3 W.L.R. 761 to the effect that a plaintiff who had available to him concurrent remedies in contract and tort could choose the most advantageous remedy.

[65] *Johnstone v. Bloomsbury Health Authority* [1991] I.C.R. 269, CA (injunction and damages for breach of contract); *Dutton & Clark Ltd v. Daly* [1985] I.C.R. 780 (EAT) (rescission—constructive dismissal); *Jagdeo v. Smiths Industries Ltd* [1982] I.C.R. 47 (EAT) (lawfulness of transfer to work involving unsafe conditions); *British Aircraft Corporation v. Austin* [1978] I.R.L.R. 332 (EAT) (constructive dismissal—employer failing to investigate complaint about provision of safety equipment); *Graham Oxley Tool Steels Ltd v. Firth* [1980] I.R.L.R. 135 (exposure to intolerable cold for several months). And see Chap. 7, para. 7.14.

[66] [1999] I.R.L.R. 110 (HL).

the duty may be formulated in contract, expressed the view that the contractual duty could not be wider than that imposed by the law of tort.

Scots law also recognises the employer's duty of safety may be expressed as a matter of contractual or delictual liability and there would appear to be no reason for Scots law to accept the approach advocated by Lord Scarman, in that there is nothing to the advantage of the law's development "in searching for a liability in tort where the parties are in a contractual relationship".[67] Although all of the early Scots decisions are the result of delictual actions of reparation for the death or personal injury of a workman, these same decisions recognise that the duty is based on the existence of a contract of service. Thus in *Dixon v. Rankin*[68] the Lord Justice-Clerk opined that "[t]he master's primary obligation in every contract of service in which his workmen are employed in a[n] . . . occupation for his interest and profit, is to provide for and attend to the safety of the men. Similarly in *Macdonald v. Wyllie & Son*[69] Lord Young observed that "[a]ccording to the law of Scotland in the contract of master and servant . . . it is implied that the employer is responsible to his workmen for the condition of the scaffolding which he has provided for them to work upon". While more recently still Lord Murray has stated[70]—in the context of a discussion of the standard of the employer's duty of safety—that "contractual obligations which are implied at common law are not absolute". The position in Scots law would appear to be that not just is the contractual relationship of employer and employee one which is sufficiently close to bring the duty of care into play,[71] but also there is a parallel implied contractual term which, in the event of its breach will allow the employee to rescind. Indeed in *Knight v. Barra Shipping Co. Ltd*[72] the EAT has indicated it is an important term of the contract that the employer will not require an employee to work in conditions which are "intolerable", Lord Coulsfield adding that conditions which present a danger to life can "properly be regarded as intolerable"; although this terminology suggests a development of the existing duty, the term could also be expressed as a failure to take reasonable care or to provide a safe system of work. In the result there would appear to be no reason why in Scots law the employee whose employer fails in his duty to take reasonable care for his safety may not raise his legal proceedings on the basis that there has been a breach of an implied term of

---

[67] *Tai Hing Cotton Mill Ltd v. Lin Chung Hing Bank Ltd* [1986] A.C. 80 at 1078.
[68] (1852) 14 D. 420 at p. 424.
[69] (1898) 1 F. 339 at 344.
[70] *Bain v. Fife Coal Co. Ltd*, 1935 S.C. 681 at 701.
[71] cf. *Keatings v. Secretary for Scotland*, 1961 S.L.T. (Sh.Ct.) 63; *K. R. Page v. J. Read* (C.A.), 85/441 (unreported); and see *Rennie v. Doran*, 1991 S.L.T. 443.
[72] Case No. 187/92 (unreported); and see *Graham Oxley Tool Steels Ltd v. Firth* [1980] I.R.L.R. 135 (EAT).

his contract or that his employer has failed to perform his delictual duty of care depending on where the advantage might lie. Generally the rules regarding the assessment of damages will dictate that the employee injured as a result of the breach or failure (fault) of his employer will sue in delict and not in contract and, although it might be arguable that an award of damages for breach of contract would not suffer a reduction in respect of the pursuer's contributory negligence,[73] Lord Davidson has opined[74] that damages for breach of contract may be reduced for contributory negligence, but only if the breach can also be described as a "fault" within the meaning of section 5 of the Law Reform (Contributory Negligence) Act 1945; namely a "wrongful act, breach of statutory duty or negligent and (or omission) which gives rise to the defence of contributory negligence". In *Lancashire Textiles*[75] carpet layers had sued the carpet suppliers for breach of contract on the basis that the carpeting was not of merchantable quality and not reasonably fit for the purpose. While the pursuers relied on section 14 of the Sale of Goods Act 1979 Lord Davidson was of the view that that did not mean that they (the pursuers) sued in respect of a breach of statutory duty in the sense in which that expression is used in section 5.[76] It has to be observed that the history, terminology and circumstances of the 1945 Act would seem to suggest that Parliament did not envisage the Act would have any bearing on breach of contract claims.[77]

THE PERSONAL ELEMENT

3.7 While the employer's duty may be simply stated as "has the employer taken reasonable care for the safety of the workman?"[78] or "the basic duty of the employer is to take reasonable care that the employee is not exposed to unnecessary risk",[79] frequently the

---

[73] See the interesting discussion in A.S. Burrows, *Remedies for Torts and Breach of Contract* (1987), pp. 73–79.

[74] *Lancashire Textiles (Jersey) Ltd v. Thompson, Shepherd and Co. Ltd*, 1986 S.L.T. 41.

[75] 1986 S.L.T. 41.

[76] Interestingly in England the definition of fault in which "negligence" is substituted for "wrongful act" seems less ambiguous and for this reason the approach of English decisions require to be treated with caution and it has been held there that the provisions of the 1945 Act did not entitle a defendant to raise contributory negligence as a defence (*Barclay's Bank PLC v. Fairclough Building Ltd*, *The Times*, May 11, 1993, CA).

[77] See H.C. Debs, Hansard 1945.

[78] *per* Viscount Simonds, *Davie v. New Merton Board Mills Ltd* [1959] A.C. 604 at 618.

[79] *Longworth v. Coppas International (U.K.) Ltd*, 1985 S.L.T. 111.

duty is said to be tripartite in that it requires the employer to (a) provide and maintain suitable materials (plant, machinery and equipment), (b) keep premises safe and devise and operate a safe system of working, and (c) exercise care in the selection of competent fellow-employees. A fundamental issue which arises is whether and to what extent the employer can perform his duty by delegation to others, be they his employees or agents, suppliers of materials, or independent contractors. Put another way, to what extent is the duty personal to the employer so that, where the employee is injured because of the negligence of the delegate, the employer cannot escape liability. The issue of delegation has been examined particularly with regard to those aspects of the duty requiring the devising and operating a safe system of working and the provision of suitable materials.

A safe system of work

3.8 As Gow has remarked,[80] much of the law relating to the safe system of work was developed in order to forestall the defence of common employment, in that there became established a critical distinction between defects of a "permanent and continuous" nature and defects of a "transitory kind which may emerge in the course of a day's working". Responsibility for the former resided with the employer and could not be affected by the doctrine of common employment which of course applied only where an employee had been injured by the negligence of a fellow employee. The English attempt in *Fanton v. Denville*[81] to relieve the employer of virtually all responsibility for his employee's safety (by allowing the employer to perform his duty towards the employee by selecting competent persons to whom he would delegate the provision of materials and adequate plant) was emphatically rejected in *Bain v. Fife Coal Company Ltd.*[82] According to Lord Justice-Clerk Aitchison the decision in *Fanton v. Denville*:

> "ignores . . . a fundamental doctrine of the law of master and servant namely that there are certain duties owed by a master to his servant so imperative and vital to safety that the master cannot divest himself of responsibility by entrusting their performance to others so as to avoid liability in the event of injury arising to the servant through neglect of any of these duties . . . [I]n the eye of the law they are duties that cannot be delegated. If in fact they are entrusted by the master to

---

[80] Mercantile and Industrial Law of Scotland, p. 724; and see the judgment of Lord Reid in *Davie v. New Merton Board Mills Ltd* [1959] A.C. 604 at 637.
[81] [1932] 2 K.B. 309.
[82] 1935 S.C. 681.

others, the maxim *qui facit per alium facit per se* applies if the master entrusts the duty to someone else instead of performing it himself, he is liable for injury caused through want of care of that someone else, as being, in the eye of the law, his own negligence."[83]

Interestingly the importance of the issue of delegation is itself recognised by the Framework Directive which provides that the "employer shall have a duty to ensure the health and safety of workers in every aspect related to the work" and "where . . . an employer enlists competent external services or persons this shall not discharge him from his responsibilities".[84] That the employer's duty to provide a safe system of working was personal to the employer and non-delegable was confirmed by the House of Lords in *English v. Wilsons and Clyde Coal Company Ltd*.[85] English was injured when he was struck by a train of hutches while he was walking along the main haulage road from his workplace to the pit bottom. He sued the owners of the mine, contending that it was a necessary part of a safe system of working that the haulage of coal by hutches should be stopped while the men were making their way to the pit bottom at the end of their shift. The employers owned several collieries and had appointed an agent to look after the mining side of their business and the agent had in turn selected a manager for each colliery whose appointment had to be approved by the employers. The employers argued (i) that if an employer delegates his duty to take care of the safety to competent subordinates, his responsibility in respect of his primary common law duty ceases, unless there is proof of knowledge by him not acted upon and (ii) by the Coal Mines Act 1911[86] neither an owner nor his agent could take part in the technical management of a mine unless properly qualified, so that in effect by law the employers had no alternative but to delegate. The first argument was rejected because "the negligence lay in a failure to provide a safe system, not in the working of the system provided"[87] and as such was "non-delegable"; the second was rejected because "there is no reason in principle that a compulsory delegation should displace the . . . responsibility of the employer, if a *de facto* delegation, which is often unavoidable, has not this effect. . . . [H]e is answerable either directly for his own negligence or vicariously for his servant's

[83] *ibid.*, at 693.

[84] Directive 89/391, Art. 5(1), (2). And see reg. 7(8) of the Management of Health and Safety at Work Regulations 1999, that where there is a competent person in the employer's employment that person shall be appointed in preference to one not in his employment.

[85] 1937 S.C. (H.L.) 46.

[86] s. 2(4).

[87] *ibid.*, *per* Lord McMillan at 58.

negligence, if the negligence affects the provision of a safe system of working."[88] A more modern application of the principle of non-delegation is seen in *McDermid v. Nash Dredging and Reclamation Co. Ltd*[89] in which McDermid, an employee of Nash Dredging, worked as a deckhand on a tug owned by Steven, a wholly owned subsidiary of Nash Dredging and which employed Sas as the tugboat captain. McDermid's duties included the unhitching of mooring lines between the tug and a dredger working in tandem and, so that Sas would know when the mooring ropes had been unhitched, Sas instructed McDermid to bang twice with his hand on the wheelhouse to indicate that the mooring lines were aboard the tug and that it was safe to move the tug. McDermid was injured when Sas—without receiving the signal from McDermid—put the tug astern with the result that McDermid's leg was trapped by a mooring line. On the personal nature of the duty the Lord Chancellor, Lord Hailsham of Marylebone, stated[90]:

"the defendants did not and could not dispute the existence of ... a duty of care, nor that it was 'non-delegable' in the special sense in which that phrase is used in this connection. This special sense does not involve the proposition that the duty cannot be delegated in the sense that it is incapable of being the subject of delegation, but only that the employer cannot escape liability if the duty has been delegated and then not properly performed. ... There was no double knock because ... Sas did not attempt to operate the correct sequence and did operate the engines with the ... rope still on ... the dredger. The 'system' was therefore not being operated and was therefore not being 'provided' at all. It matters not whether one says that there was no 'system' in operation at all or whether one says that the system provided was unsafe, or whether one says that the system in fact provided was not in use at the crucial stage. In any event the defendants had delegated their duty to the plaintiff to ... Sas, the duty had not been performed and the defendants must pay for the breach of their 'non-delegable' obligation."

Lord Brandon of Oakbrook divided:

"the relevant legal principle into three parts. First an employer owes to his employee a duty to exercise reasonable care to

---

[88] *English v. Wilsons and Clyde Coal Company Ltd*, 1936 S.C. 883, *per* Lord President Normand at 902, quoted with approval by Lord Thankerton in the House of Lords, 1937 S.C. 46 at 57.
[89] [1987] I.C.R. 917 (HL).
[90] *ibid.*, p. 922.

ensure the system of work provided for him is a safe one. Secondly the provision of a safe system has two aspects: (a) the devising of such a system and (b) the operation of it. Thirdly the duty . . . (is) personal or non-delegable . . . the essential characteristic of the duty is that if the duty is not performed it is no defence for the employer to show that he delegated its performance to a person, whether his servant or not his servant, whom he reasonably believed to be competent to perform it. Despite such delegation the employer is liable for non performance. . . . In the present case . . . the defendants delegated both the devising and the operating of [the] system to . . . Sas, who was not their servant. However . . . Sas did not operate that system . . . and for this failure by . . . Sas to operate the system which he had devised, the defendants, as the plaintiff's employers, are personally, not vicariously liable to him."[91]

Thus where an employee is dispatched to work on a site not under the control of his own employer the latter is liable for any injury the employee may sustain as a result of an unsafe system of work,[92] although the standard of performance to be required of an employer may be affected by the fact that the employer is not in possession or control of the premises.[93] Thus in *Fox v. British Railways Board*[94] it was held that where an employee was injured while taking part in a management training programme organised by a third party, the employer's responsibilities were limited by the fact that the employee was at the time working on premises under the control of a third party. However, emphasising that the employer cannot escape liability merely by asserting that the employee was working on premises which were under the control of a third party, the Lord Ordinary accepted that employers were under an obligation to safeguard against danger where it was anticipated, and that this would require very precise pleading, including an averment that the activity was inherently dangerous. A less demanding, and—it is suggested—correct, approach may be seen in *Crombie v. McDermott Scotland Ltd,*[95] where Lord Hamilton, adopting a similar approach to that in *Cook v. Square D*

[91] *ibid.*, pp. 930–931.
[92] *Morris v. Beaverglen Ltd* [1993] I.R.L.R. 350, CA; *Brown v. Josiah Wedgwood & Sons (Aust) Pty Ltd* (1989) 51 S.A.S.R. 81.
[93] See *McQuilter v. Goulandris Bros Ltd*, 1951 S.L.T. (Notes) 75 and *Cook v. Square D. Ltd* [1992] I.C.R. 262, CA which, with respect may be regarded as unsatisfactory in failing to emphasise the distinction between an employer's non-delegable duty and an isolated act of negligence which could not have been avoided by any system.
[94] 1995 G.W.D. 38-2245 (O.H.), applying *M'Quilter v. Goulandris Bros Ltd.*
[95] 1996, S.L.T. 1238 (O.H.).

Ltd,[96] expressed the view that older authorities which suggest that an employer has no duty to safeguard his employees against dangers arising from the state of premises of third parties are not consistent with the modern law. Accordingly whether such a duty arises is to be determined by having regard to a variety of factors including the number of employees being sent and the periods for which they are sent. Lord Hamilton also held that "potentially relevant" are the nature of the premises including the character of the working conditions which the employers could have anticipated their employees would experience at the premises of the third party and "what grounds if any the employers had for supposing that others would put in hand and properly maintain safety arrangements at the site". Does this suggest that the employer's duty in such circumstances is delegable, or does it merely relate to the standard of care required of the employer?[97] In light of the composition of the contemporary workforce, and that many workers are mobile or work in premises which are not under the control of their own employer the extent to which the common law requires their employers to operate safe systems of work raises important issues. Interestingly the Management of Health and Safety at Work Regulations 1999 requires a risk assessment to be carried out by every employer in respect of his employees while they are "at work."[98] While that phrase is unqualified it might be argued that it would apply to employees at work anywhere. However by implication it appears that "at work" means at work in premises in Great Britain since it is provided[99] that the Regulations apply to premises and activities outside Great Britain only in certain circumstances.[1]

Plant and Materials

3.9 The rule in *English v. Wilsons and Clyde Coal Co. Ltd*[2] was subsequently analysed and explained in *Davie v. New Merton Board Mills Ltd*[3] a case in which it was sought to apply the "non-

---

[96] [1992] I.C.R. 262, CA. Similarly see *Johnson v. Coventry Churchill International Ltd* [1992] 3 All E.R. 12 where it was held that an English company which recruited in the U.K. employees to work in Germany may have a duty of care regarding the safety arrangements at the German construction site.

[97] Probably Lord Hamilton is dealing only with standard of care because at the same part of his opinion he refers to the issue of practicability.

[98] reg. 3(1).

[99] reg. 16.

[1] See the Health and Safety at Work etc. Act 1974 (Application outside Great Britain) Order 1995 (S.I. 1995 No. 263). The effect of the Order was to apply the Management of Health and Safety at Work Regulations 1992 to offshore installations, wells and pipelines. See now the Management of Health and Safety at Work Regulations 1999, reg. 23.

[2] 1937 S.C. (H.L.) 46.

[3] [1959] A.C. 604 (HL).

delegability" principle so that an employer would be liable to his employee for injury sustained by using a defective tool which the employer had provided but which had been negligently made by a reputable manufacturer.

3.10 Davie, an employee of *New Merton Board Mills Ltd*, was injured when a piece of metal flew off a metal drift, provided by his employer for his use. The drift, although apparently in good condition, had been negligently manufactured by reputable makers, who had sold it to the firm of suppliers who then sold it to Davie's employers; it was excessively hard and was in the circumstances a dangerous tool. Although the employer's system of maintenance and inspection was not at fault Davie sued them on the ground that they had negligently supplied him with a defective tool. Viscount Simonds described Davie's case thus:

> "The employer, it was said, was under a duty to take reasonable care to supply his workman with proper plant and machinery including such tools as drifts. . . . It was then said that the employer could not escape responsibility by employing a third party, however expert, to do his duty for him. So far so good. . . I agree. But then comes the next step—but I would rather call it a jump, and a jump that would unhorse any rider. Therefore, it was said, the employer is responsible for the defect in goods that he buys in the market, if it can be shown that the defect was due to the want of skill or care on the part of anyone who was concerned with its manufacture."

However all of their Lordships rejected this argument because although *English v. Wilsons and Clyde Coal Co. Ltd*[4] had decided that the employer was liable for the acts of himself, his servants and agents and, possibly, independent contractors a manufacturer could not "by any legitimate use of language be considered the servant or agent of, or an independent contractor with, the employer who buys his manufactures in the market."[5] Lord Reid viewed *English* as a case in which there was no question of the employer being liable for the negligence of some person who was not their servant noting that "agent" as used in that case was merely the technical name of the chief servant of the coal mine owner. His Lordship was justified in his opinion that *English* did not decide that the employer's duty was such that he was responsible for the negligence of a manufacturer or supplier by examining the law of Scotland before it was interrupted by the introduction of the rule of common employment.[6] He concluded:

[4] 1937 S.C. (H.L.) 46.
[5] *Davie v. New Merton Board Mills Ltd* [1959] A.C. 604, *per* Viscount Simonds at 624–625.
[6] *ibid.*, 636–645.

"an employer besides being liable to his servant for injury caused by the negligence of his own servants, is in some cases liable in respect of the negligence of others. Where, then is the line to be drawn? On the one hand it appears that an employer is liable for the negligence of an independent contractor whom he has engaged to carry out one of . . . his personal duties on his own premises and whose work might normally be done by the employer's own servant—at least if the negligent workmanship is discovered by reasonable inspection. On the other hand . . . I am of opinion that he is not liable for the negligence of the manufacturer of an article which he has bought, provided he has been careful to deal with a seller of repute and has made any inspection which a reasonable employer would make."[7]

Clearly delegation, in the sense of being able to escape liability for the negligence of the supplier or manufacturer, is effective where the employer's duty involves the provision of safe plant and equipment. However, the effect of the decision in *Davie* has been reversed by the Employer's Liability (Defective Equipment) Act 1969.[8]

Competent Staff

3.11 As earlier indicated another aspect of the employer's duty is to take reasonable care to select competent staff[9] and the question must arise whether this aspect may be performed by delegation to someone other than an employee. If one takes the view that an employment agency can be equiparated with a "supplier" the principles enunciated in *English v. Wilsons and Clyde Coal Co. Ltd*[10] as applied in *Davie* could permit an employer to escape liability for injury to an employee caused by the incompetence of another employee who had been selected through the negligence of an independent employment agency. However such a result would run counter to the older Scottish decisions which have held that the duty to select competent employees is personal to the employer and that if an employee is injured as a result of the actions of an incompetent employee the employer is responsible,[11] and it has been held in England[12] that the aspect of the employer's duty

---

[7] *ibid.*, 645–646.
[8] See para. 3.40.
[9] *McCarten v. McRobbie*, 1909 S.C. 1022. And see para. 3.43 below.
[10] 1937 S.C. (H.L.) 46.
[11] *Donald v. Brand* (1862) 24 D. 295 (inebriate employee); *Wilson v. Merry & Cunningham* (1868) 6 M. (H.L.) 64; *McCarten v. McRobbie* 1909 S.C. 1020 (incompetent driver).
[12] *Hudson v. Ridge Manufacturing Co. Ltd* [1957] 2 Q.B. 348; *Smith v. Crossley Brothers Ltd* (1951) 95 S.J. 655.

relating to the provision of competent staff is non-delegable and this may be valuable where an employee is injured as a result of the actions of an incompetent employee acting outwith the course of their employment.

To whom is the duty owed?

3.12 It is clear that the duty to take reasonable care is owed to those with whom the employer has entered into contracts of employment or apprenticeship. However, that duty must be circumscribed by the notion of the scope of, or course of the employee's or apprentice's employment.[13] It is long established that the employee who is injured in engaging in activity outwith the scope of his employment cannot recover damages from his employer for his injury[14] unless he took the action to save life or limb,[15] commonly referred as a rescue-type case.[16] However, some observations require to be made. First many of the older cases[17] take a strict and perhaps unrealistic view of what might be regarded as in the course of employment. Contrast *Hosie v. Fred M. Walker Ltd*,[18] in which an employee employed to use a machine to plane planks of wood was held not to be acting in the course of his employment when he used the machine to cut a piece of wood which he would use to keep his stand clear of cuttings, with *National Coal Board v. England*[19] in which a miner, who was injured while, against instructions and against the Coal Mines Order 1954, he assisted a shotsman to set up for shot-blasting, was held by the House of Lords to be acting in the course of his employment.[20] Arguably employees who are injured while engaging in activities which they are not contractually bound to do, have benefited from a willingness of the courts to extend the notion of "scope or course of employment" in cases where one employee is injured as a result of the negligence of another in order to fix vicarious liability on the employer.[21] Secondly, as the doctrine of common employment vividly illustrated, the older law was more prepared to imply an acceptance of risk by the employee entering into the contract whereas the modern approach emphasises the delictual principle that the greater the danger the higher is the

---

[13] And see para. 3.48 below.
[14] *Morris v. Boase Spinning Co. Ltd* (1895) 22 R. 336.
[15] *Wilkinson v. Kinneil Coal Co. Ltd* (1897) 24 R. 1001.
[16] See paras 3.44 *et seq.*
[17] See the cases referred to in Glegg on *Reparation*, p. 403.
[18] 1907 S.C. 134.
[19] [1954] 1 All E.R. 546 (HL).
[20] And see *Davidson v. Handey Page Ltd* [1945] 1 All E.R. 235; *Nancollas v. Insurance Officer* [1985] 1 All E.R. 833.
[21] See para. 3.48.

degree of care required. Contrast *Clark v. Caledonian Railway Co. Ltd*,[22] in which the widow of an engine driver (who was killed when, his engine having been stopped at a signal, he fell over an unfenced bridge while walking ahead to the signal box without a torch to ascertain the reason for the stoppage) was unable to recover damages because "if a servant takes an unusual course and an unusual risk he cannot transfer the risk . . . to his employers"[23] with *Paris v. Stepney Borough Council*,[24] in which it would have been unthinkable to plead that the partially sighted employee had only himself to blame. Thirdly, the fact that the employee has had to assume responsibility for matters which may, strictly, fall outside his duties itself may indicate that the employer has failed to give sufficient attention to the devising of a safe system of work.[25] Accordingly today only if the evidence clearly demonstrates the employee has taken himself outside the scope of his employment will the employer's personal duty be inapplicable.

Self-employed workers

3.13 While it cannot be doubted that the employer's duty to devise and operate a reasonably safe system of work extends to those with contracts of employment and apprenticeship—on the grounds that those relationships permit the employer to dictate not merely the work objective but the work method as well—whether the employer owes any duty to other classes of workers also arises. In this respect the source of the obligation becomes of significance in that, if the obligation originates purely as an implied term in the contracts of employment and apprenticeship it would follow that those who work under other contractual arrangements or those who might, technically, have exceeded the scope of their own employment would not benefit. If, however, the obligation to employees and apprentices is merely one example of the employer's general duty of care, there is no reason why in principle it may not also extend to other classes of worker who, in the eyes of the principles of delict, the employer should regard as his "neighbour in law", adopting the words of Lord Atkin's dictum in *Donoghue v. Stevenson*.[26] Thus in *Calder v. H. Kitson Vickers & Sons (Engineers) Ltd*[27] the Court of Appeal held that, although when

---

[22] (1877) 5 R. 273.
[23] *ibid., per* Lord Shand, 276.
[24] [1951] A.C. 367.
[25] Thus in *Hosie v. Fred M. Walker Ltd*, 1907 S.C. 134, the only reason Hosie attempted to use his machine to make a scraper was because the system of work devised by the employer to keep Hosie's stance level and safe was patently ineffective.
[26] 1932 S.C. (H.L.) 31 at 44.
[27] [1988] I.C.R. 232, CA.

Calder was injured as a result of the negligence of one of the defendant's employees he was operating as a self-employed contractor, nevertheless his status and the financial arrangements between himself and the defendants could not affect the duty of care owed to him which required that they would not operate the crane in such a way as to expose Calder to danger. The trial judge, who was of the view that (even if Calder was not an employee of Kitson) the nature of the relations and the degree of control exercised by Kitson were such that Kitson owed Calder a duty of care to see that the operation was reasonably safe and was reasonably safely carried out opined that "Kitson . . . supplied a sling or hook which had no safety chain [and] failed to ensure the 'snatch' would operate smoothly (and) to see Calder had a suitable safety chain and that it was used."

However, Ralph Gibson L.J. opined that while the duty of care owed by Kitson was not as extensive as that formulated by the trial judge, there was at least a duty on Kitson not to operate the equipment provided by them in a way which to their knowledge exposed Calder to a danger which his team appeared to be disregarding, but to give clear warning to the team of that danger. "If the risk was severe I think there was a duty to refuse to operate the gear unless it was clear that all those affected by the risk were fully aware of it".[28] However, as the existence of the duty of care is dependent upon the issue of reasonable foreseeability, different circumstances and facts can have a major impact on whether a duty was owed, and a more typical result is seen in *K. R. Page v. J. Read*[29] in which Page, a self-employed painter, was engaged by the main contractor on a building site. Page was required to paint the fascia boards of a house and, in the absence of any scaffolding, while sitting on the roof and leaning over to paint the boards he fell and was injured. While the Court of Appeal recognised that everyone must refrain from doing things which they ought reasonably to know will harm their neighbour, and this duty would require a contractor who provides equipment to a sub-contractor to ensure the equipment is safe for the purpose for which it is provided, there is no positive duty of supervision or to offer safety equipment; in that sense the duty to the independent contractor is lower than that owed by an employer to his employee.

Seconded employees, *pro hac vice* and contractors

3.14 It is a common phenomenon for an employer to dispatch one of his own employees to work on the site or premises of another enterprise. Such an occurrence presents two problems.

---

[28] [1988] I.C.R. 254–255.
[29] (1985) unreported case no. 85/441, CA.

First, which of the two employers is liable to a third party[30] injured by the employee's negligence, and secondly to what extent, if any, are the responsibilities for the safety of the employee transferred to the secondary or temporary "employer"? Both problems require consideration of whether the employee of the original, or general, employer has at the relevant time—that is the time a third party sustains injury as a result of the employee's negligence or the time the employee himself is injured as a result of a failure to take reasonable care for his safety—become the employee of the secondary or temporary employer *pro hac vice*. Whether such a transfer has taken place depends principally on whether the secondary employer is authorised to control not merely what the employee does but how he does it[31]; although each case very much depends on its own circumstances which, for there to be a transfer *pro hac vice*, must show that the employee either expressly or impliedly consented to accept the secondary employer.[32] It is clear that where such a transfer has taken place the secondary employer becomes vicariously responsible for the negligent acts and omissions of the employee while acting in the course of his employment.[33] However, it would seem that the primary employer remains responsible for ensuring there is provided and operated a reasonably safe system of work for the *pro hac vice* employee on the view that that test (of authority to exercise detailed control) is relevant only to the question of vicarious liability.[34] It is now doubtful whether there is any difference between the case of an employee hired out as the operator of a piece of complicated machinery and the provision of an unskilled labourer to another person who himself occupied the factory, provided all the tools and equipment and advised on the system of working,[35] and where the contract of hire provides that the hirer is to be responsible for the negligence of an employee of the owner of the equipment "as if" he (the hirer) were the employer of that employee that will tend to indicate that no transfer has taken place.[36]

---

[30] "Third party" would of course include an employee of the employer for whom an employee works *pro hac vice*: *Moir v. Wide Arc Services Ltd*, 1988 H.S.I.B. 146.

[31] *Mersey Docks and Harbour Board v. Coggins and Griffiths* [1947] A.C. 1; and see *McGregor v. J. S. Duthie Ltd*, 1966 S.L.T. 133; *McAllister v. Oban Transport and Trading Co. Ltd*, 1971 S.L.T. (Notes) 71.

[32] *Malley v. LMS Ry Co.*, 1944 S.C. 129.

[33] *McGregor v. J. S. Duthie Ltd*, 1966 S.L.T. 133.

[34] *Morris v. Breaveglen Ltd t/a Anzac Construction Co.*, 1993 I.R.L.R. 350, CA, in which the English authorities are extensively reviewed. *Cf. Denham v. Midland Employers Mutual Assurance Ltd* [1955] 2 Q.B. 437, CA; *Gibb v. United Steel Companies Ltd* [1957] 1 W.L.R. 668.

[35] See the suggestion to this effect in *Garrard v. A. E. Southney & Co.* [1952] 2 Q.B. 174, *per* Parker J. at 179.

[36] *Kerr v. Hailes (Plant) Ltd*, 1974 S.L.T. (Notes) 31. Complicated indemnity provisions in the contract of hire will not influence the question whether there has been a transfer *pro hac vice*: *ibid.*; and see *McConkey v. Amec plc*, *The Times*, February 16, 1990, CA.

3.15 Also it is axiomatic that the employer's duty for the safety of his employees is non-delegable and it would be inconsistent with that if an employer could escape all liability for injury to his employee while working for a secondary employer *pro hac vice*. The issue was considered in *Morris v. Breaveglen Ltd*,[37] in which Morris was employed as a building site worker by Breaveglen, who entered into a contract with Sleeman for the supply of labour at a building site where Sleeman was carrying out work. While working under the direction of Sleeman, Morris was permitted to operate a dumper truck although he had never been given any proper instruction in its use by Breaveglen Ltd. While operating the truck under the instructions of Sleeman the truck went over the edge of the tipping site and Morris sustained injuries. Lord Justice Beldam held that Breaveglen were liable to Morris for their "failure to lay down and operate a safe system of work. They had delegated their task to the foreman of Sleeman on site. He had clearly fallen down by failing to provide precautions to prevent the dumper going over the edge of the dumping ground and clearly they were responsible". In *Crombie v. McDermott Scotland Ltd*[38] Lord Hamilton reviewed the Scots position and concluded that some of the older authorities which tended to show that employers were not obliged to safeguard workers against risks arising from the state of premises of third parties were no longer to be relied on as being inconsistent with the principles of modern law.[39] Crombie was employed by Orion Ltd, who contracted out his services under a labour-only arrangement to Bailey & Co. Ltd, who themselves had sub-contracted electrical work from McDermott, the main contractors, in overall control of the site, and was injured when crossing a walkway which gave the only means of access to his work. Although the decision proceeded on the assumption that Orion were Crombie's employers and that they alone owed him the duties of care arising from the employment relationship, on the primary issue of whether Orion had a duty to acquaint themselves with the access arrangements it was held that the test was whether in all the circumstances the performance of the employer's duty of reasonable care required them to acquaint themselves with the physical circumstances in which employees were required to work; Orion's duty to Crombie was not negatived by their supplying his skilled labour unsupervised, and that the fact that Orion did not control

---

[37] [1993] I.C.R. 766, CA. And see *Nelhams v. Sandells Maintenance and Another, The Times*, June 15, 1995, CA.

[38] 1996 S.L.T. 1283 (O.H.).

[39] Lord Hamilton distinguished *Durie v. Main (Andrew) & Son*, 1958 S.C. 48 on the ground that it proceeded on the consideration that inspection of a ship is a highly technical matter and doubted the width of the statements in Glegg on *Reparation* (4th ed.) at p. 385, and Walker on *Delict* (2nd ed.) at p. 575.

his work was an important but not decisive factor. Crombie's averment that Orion ought to have acquainted themselves with his working conditions and to have taken reasonable steps to secure a safe walkway by providing it themselves or by requesting McDermott to do so were relevant and should be admitted to probation.

3.16 There is no general rule that an employer is not liable for breach of his duty to take reasonable care for his employee who is injured as a result of the negligence of an independent contractor engaged by the employer; whether the employer has performed his duty to take care for the employee by selecting a competent contractor of good reputation depends on the facts and circumstances.[40] However, in keeping with the maxim *qui facit per alium facit per se*, where an employer engages a contractor and retains sufficient control of the work so as to direct the contractor and his employees as to how the work is to be done, the contractor and his employees become *pro hac vice* the employees of the employer.[41] Similarly where a main contractor engages sub-contractors to perform part of the contract, by virtue of his exercising control over the whole site, the main contractor may have responsibility for supervising the work of the sub-contractors so that work is conducted in a reasonably safe manner to make the main contractor liable for injuries sustained by an employee of one sub-contractor who fell through a hole in a roof left by the employees of another sub-contractor.[42] However, such a case must be distinguished from that of an occupier of premises such as a building site who has contracted for work to be done on the site. While such an occupier may have a duty of care to protect the visitor,[43] a pre-condition of liability for the condition of the premises and operations carried out there is that the occupier is in control of the premises in the sense of being able to license or forbid entry thereto,[44] and in an English case the House of Lords has held that the occupier is not usually liable to an employee of a contractor carrying out work on his (the occupier's) premises because his own employer failed to operate a safe system of work, because it would not be reasonable to expect the occupier to supervise the contractor.[45]

---

[40] See *Davie v. New Merton Board Mills*, 1959 A.C. 604 (HL).
[41] *Gregory v. Hill* (1869) 8 M. 282; *Stephen v. Thurso Police Commissions* (1876) 3 R. 535.
[42] *McArdle v. Andmac Roofing* [1967] 1 All E.R. 583.
[43] See para. 3.35 regarding liability under the Occupiers Liability (Scotland) Act 1960.
[44] *Murdoch v. A & R Scott*, 1956 S.C. 309.
[45] *Ferguson v. Welsh* [1987] 3 All E.R. 777 (HL).

GENERAL DELICTUAL ISSUES

3.17 As the existence of the employer's duty to take reasonable care for the health and safety of his employees is merely one facet of general delictual principles, a proper understanding of the duty and liability for breach thereof requires here at least a general treatment of foreseeability, causation and standard of duty. For more detailed coverage of these matters the reader is referred to specialist texts.[46]

Foreseeability

3.18 As pointed out earlier, the relationship between employer and employee, apprentice and independent contractor, is such as to make it reasonably foreseeable that the employer's action or inaction would cause harm to the employee, apprentice or contractor. However, forseeability also relates to the kind of harm which may be occasioned; unless the kind of harm was reasonably foreseeable the employer will have no liability even although the injury sustained by his employee was undoubtedly the result of the employer's act or omission,[47] so that an employer will not be liable for an employee's psychiatric illness where an ordinary bystander as opposed to a psychiatrist would have foreseen something more than the employee being dissatisfied, embarrassed or frustrated.[47a] Thus the employers of a deceased employee owed no duty of care to his widow, who died of mesothelioma after hand-washing her husband's asbestos impregnated working clothes from 1948 to 1965, because before 1965 no employer could reasonably have foreseen the risk of physical injury from domestic exposure to asbestos—there was no medical literature on the subject neither warnings nor guidance in industrial or official publications and, even if the defendants had engaged specialist medical personnel, it was unlikely they would have become aware of the risk from domestic exposure to asbestos dust before 1965.[48] Similarly, the

---

[46] See for example "The Analysis of Negligence" in *Introductory Essays on Scots Law* (2nd ed.) by W. A. Wilson. "Introduction to the Scots Law of Delict" by W. J. Stewart is an excellent but concise statement of the relevant principles; for a different and in some respects more detailed text see D. M. Walker, *Delict*.

[47] *Hughes v. Lord Advocate*, 1963 S.C. (H.L.) 31.

[47a] *Rorrison v. West Lothian College*, 1999 Rep. L.R. 102, O.H.

[48] *Gunn v. Wallsend Slipway & Engineering Co. Ltd, The Times*, January 23, 1989, QBD; and see *Hewett v. Alf Brown's Transport Ltd* [1992] I.C.R. 530, CA, to effect that generally an employer does not owe a duty of care to an employee's family (wife) for lead oxide powder taken home on work clothes and as in the instant case the husband's exposure to lead was below the lowest end of the scale set out in the relevant Code of Practice it was so insignificant no duty was owed in the particular circumstances. *Cf.* the settlement arrived in 1998 at the widow of a worker who contracted mesthelioma after washing asbestos dust from her late husband's clothing; *M. v. Alcan International* (Coroner's Health and Safety Case Law Report, Issue No. 17).

employers of a crane operator were not liable for his contracting vibration white finger (VWF) because there had never been a previous case of a crane driver recovering compensation for VWF and there was no evidence that the employers ought reasonably to have known that the operative, whose work did not involve using hand held tools, was at risk of contracting the disease.[49] On the other hand the employers of a ship's painter were under a duty not to expose him to asbestos dust because the risks of asbestosis had been known since 1947[50]; similarly the employers of a ballistics expert were liable for injury to his hearing when they advised him to combat ringing in his ears by putting cotton wool into them when it was widely known that such a procedure was useless,[51] and whether an employer ought to have known that employees may contract illnesses through being exposed to the cigarette smoke of fellow employees has been allowed to go to proof[52]; the test of reasonable forseeability requires an employer to anticipate an employee using equipment incorrectly although this may raise the issue of contributory negligence.[53]

3.19 Particularly where statutory regulations have been enacted to eliminate a risk of harm—but for a technicality do not apply— the harm will be something the employer should reasonably have foreseen. Therefore, while the lighting provisions of the Construction (Working Places) Regulations 1966 did not apply to power stations, the employer owed a duty of care to an employee who was injured when he put himself in a dangerous position which he would not have been required to do had adequate lighting been provided.[54]

3.20 However, the nature of the work being undertaken clearly affects what harm an employer should reasonably foresee. Thus where "an ordinary piece of furniture (filing cabinet) was being moved by two ordinary men through an ordinary department of an

---

[49] *Heyes v. Pilkington* [1998] P.L.Q.R. 303, CA.

[50] *Bryce v. Swan Hunter Group* [1987] 2 Lloyd's Rep. 426; and see *Balfour and Others v. William Beardmore*, 1956 S.L.T. 205 (O.H.) (following the interim report of Committee on Dust in Steel Foundries, employers could not plead they could not reasonably have foreseen the danger of pneumoconiosis being contracted by employees) and *Douglas Reilly v. Robert Kellie & Son Ltd*, 1990 S.L.T. 205 (O.H.), regarding liability for exposure to isocyanate fumes.

[51] *McCafferty v. Metropolitan Police Receiver* [1977] 2 All E.R. 756; and see *Burgess v. Thorn Consumer Electronics (Newhaven)*, *The Times*, May 16, 1983 (employer previously advised of risk of tenosynovitis by Health and Safety Executive).

[52] *Rae v. Glasgow City Council and Strathclyde Joint Police Board* [1999] S.C.L.R. 959.

[53] *Sampson v. Hunslet Holdings Ltd* (1984) unreported case 84/357, CA.

[54] *Lyons v. Babcock Energy plc and Another* (1992) H.S.I.B. 202 (O.H.).

ordinary factory and then through an ordinary door at the end of the department", the employer could not reasonably foresee that the operation would result in one employee injuring his hand when the other employee pushed the cabinet in a particular way,[55] but an employer of an employee who was injured while attempting to lift a large sheet of glass weighing almost 30kg should have foreseen that lifting of the glass would be likely to cause injury to the average employee who had not received any special training.[56]

The requirement that the kind of harm be reasonably foreseeable is demonstrated by contrasting *Doughty v. Turner Manufacturing Co. Ltd*[57] with *Rowark v. National Coal Board.*[58] Doughty was injured when, along with other employees, he stood near a crucible containing molten sodium cyanide which was kept at 800°C whose lid, made of a special asbestos compound, was accidentally knocked into the sodium cyanide. There was a great explosion and Doughty was injured, not by splashes of molten cyanide, but by exposure to the great heat given off and the ensuing fire. Only later was it discovered that sodium cyanide at over 500°C reacted violently with water, and that water was given off by the asbestos compound at high temperature. Doughty's employer escaped liability because, although injury by splashing was a foreseeable danger, the heat produced by the chemical reaction was of a completely different type. In contrast Rowark developed tenosynovitis (inflammation of wrist tendons) after his work over a period of three months required him to haul wagons of waste weighing half a ton along a 400 yard track. His employer's defence that this particular condition could not have been reasonably foreseen as a result of the type of work involved was rejected because some kind of strain to the wrist was foreseeable.[59] The classification of the harm as one type or another can become very important; too strict an approach by the courts would result in obvious unfairness, and a less strict approach may be seen in *Morrison v. Safeway Stores plc,*[60] in which the employers of a shelf-stacker in a supermarket ought to have foreseen that the pursuer would suffer "some symptons in his knees, including pain" so that the fact "that the pain did not . . . come from bursitis but from another cause (osteo-arthritis) did not . . . matter." Similarly, if gloves provided by an employer would protect against a glancing

---

[55] *McGown v. George McLellan & Co. Ltd*, 1962 S.L.T. (Notes) 30.
[56] *Fotheringham v. Dunfermline District Council*, 1991 S.L.T. 610 (O.H.).
[57] [1964] 1 All E.R. 98.
[58] 1986, unreported case no. 86/45, CA.
[59] And see *Bradford v. Robinson Rentals Ltd* [1967] 1 All E.R. 267 (frostbite not reasonably foreseeable but some injury due to extreme cold was); *Ping v. Esselte-Letraset* 1992 C.L.Y.B. 231 (generally upper-limb disorders were reasonably foreseeable).
[60] O.H., unreported, January 15, 1999.

blow but not a piercing injury, the fact that the evidence did not disclose which type of injury was sustained was immaterial because these two types of blow are not entirely different types of injury but are merely manifestations of the same type of injury; namely a cutting injury.[61]

3.21 However, even where the type of harm is forseeable it has been held that for policy reasons senior police officers who are responsible for deploying officers to control serious public disorder are generally not liable to individual officers under their command if those officers are injured by attacks from rioters because to hold otherwise would be detrimental to the control of public order because critical decisions should not be affected by fear of a potential negligence claim,[62] and in *White v. Chief Constable of South Yorkshire*[63] the House of Lords refused to compensate police officers who were actively involved in the aftermath of the Hillsborough football stadium disaster and who suffered psychiatric injury in the form of post traumatic stress disorder; in the words of Lord Steyn "the common law regarded reasonable foreseeability as an inadequate tool for the disposal of claims in respect of emotional injury". There was no doubt that the Chief Constable as employer was negligent, but the case failed on the policy grounds that an award of damages to police officers would not be consistent with the denial of compensation to bereaved relatives and, if the moral argument was that police officers were entitled to compensation, many other categories of workers like doctors and nurses would also have to be compensated and, unlike the police, would not always retire with a statutory pension. Public policy is an unpredictable creature, however, so that where a female police officer was attacked by a prisoner, although there was no general legal duty of a fellow officer to intervene to protect her from injury, public policy required that the law should accord with common sense and public perception and the court had been right to say that the public would be greatly disturbed if the law held there was no duty of care owed to the officer under attack.[64]

Causation

3.22 The general principle may be stated that the breach of duty must have been the predominant or effective cause of the event or

[61] *Muir v. Cumbernauld and Kilsyth District Council*, 1993 S.L.T. 287.
[62] *Hughes v. National Union of Mineworkers and Others* [1991] 4 All E.R. 278 (QBD).
[63] [1999] I.R.L.R. 110 (HL).
[64] *Costello v. Chief Constable of Northumbria Police, The Times*, December 15, 1998, CA.

occurrence which resulted in the injury to the employee; alternatively the breach of duty must be the *causa causans* and not merely a *causa sine qua non* of the accident.[65] The distinction is illustrated by the decision of the Lord Ordinary in *McLean v. Caledonian Macbrayne Ltd*[66] in which the pursuer who was employed as a ships carpenter injured himself while climbing over a railing on board a ship. Because there was no gateway through the railing the pursuer was required to climb over the railing to remove a sign. The Lord Ordinary accepted that the pursuer sustained his injury while stepping down from the railing to the walkway but not while actually climbing over the railing. It was submitted for the defenders that the absence of a gate in the railing was a *causa sine qua non* but not the *causa causans* and, echoing the words of Lord Hoffmann in *Banque Bruxelles SA v. Eagle Star*[67] that "normally the law limits liability to those consequences which are attributable to that which made the act wrongful", Lord MacFadyen stated:

> "Applying that to the circumstances of the present case, the pursuer can . . . succeed only if his accident was the consequence of the danger which made it the defender's duty to provide a gate in the . . . railing. In my view it was not. If he had lost his balance or footing while carrying out the precarious manoeuvre at the top of the railing the accident would have been caused by the defender's negligence. But . . . he fell and slipped after the perilous stage of the manoeuvre. . . . He fell while stepping from the lower rail to the walkway . . . I am therefore of opinion that although the defenders ought to have provided a gate, the pursuer's accident was not . . . caused by their failure to do so.

However, while it is not necessary to show that the employer's breach of duty was the whole cause of the harm it must, in order to become the legal cause, materially increase the risk of the harm. Thus a workman, whose normal duties were carried out in a pipe kiln, was required to work in a brick kiln, contracted dermatitis and sued his employers who, he alleged, failed to perform their duty of care to him by not providing showering facilities at his place of work. It was held by the House of Lords that as the employer's

---

[65] For a discussion of the policy issues involved in causation see Atiyah, *Accidents Compensation and the Law*, chap. 4.

[66] Unreported, Lord MacFadyen, January 8, 1999, upheld on appeal to Inner House, October 28, 1999. And see *King v. Carron Pheonix Ltd* (O.H., unreported, January 26, 1999) that it is not enough to show that the employer has failed to carry out a risk assessment without also proving what the employers should have done thereafter to prevent the pursuer's injuries.

[67] [1997] A.C. 191 (HL).

breach of duty had materially increased the risk of the harm, that breach could be regarded as the legal cause, the *causa causans*.[68] However, the application of this rule may only occur where two (or more) causes could have resulted in the harm in which case the law should presume, in favour of the plaintiff, that the breach of duty was responsible for the damage. Thus in *Kay's Tutor v. Ayrshire and Arran Health Board*[69] the pursuer's son was admitted to hospital suffering from meningitis and was negligently given an overdose of penicillin which caused convulsions and hemiparesis. As a result of prompt remedial measures he promptly recovered from the latter and eventually from the meningitis but was deaf. The evidence that the penicillin would damage the hearing was rejected and there was no known case of penicillin overdose causing deafness, but many where deafness had been caused by meningitis. Although the health board had breached its duty by administering the overdose the House of Lords held that it was no cause at all of the deafness. Applying the principle of *McGhee*[70] was therefore to no avail because the evidence did not disclose two (or more) competing causes of the deafness.

Proof

3.23 As a general rule the onus is on the employee to prove, on the balance of probabilities,[71] that his injuries have been caused by the employer's breach of duty[72] and, particularly where an employee is working alone, the absence of corroboration[73] as to how the injuries occurred have prevented the employee overcoming that onus. An important exception is found in the legal presumption *res ipsa loquitur* (the thing speaks for itself) which applies where the thing is shown to be under the exclusive

---

[68] *McGhee v. NCB*, 1973 S.C. (H.L.) 37.

[69] 1987 S.L.T. 577.

[70] *McGhee v. NCB*, 1973 S.C. (H.L.) 37.

[71] A pursuer does not have to prove every fact on which his case is based however, as it is permissible for a court to draw from the evidence certain inferences; thus in *Cousins v. Lambeth, Southwark and Lewisham Health Authority* (1986, unreported case 86/225) the Court of Appeal has held that though there was no direct evidence of a slippery floor or a failure to mop it the first instance judge was entitled to infer from the evidence that more probably than not the pursuer, a nurse, slipped on a wet floor, the water must have come from a washbasin, it was likely that another nurse caused the spillage and the continued presence of water on the floor was due to the failure of other staff to mop it up.

[72] *Hendry v. Clan Line Steamers*, 1949 S.C. 320.

[73] Strictly, in accordance with the Law Reform (Miscellaneous Provisions) (Scotland) Act 1968, s. 9, in an action for damages for personal injuries corroboration is not necessary nevertheless an employee's uncorroborated evidence is unlikely to counter other indicators as to how an accident occurred. See for example *Hill v. Brian W. Coleman Fumigation Services*, 1993 G.W.D. 9-647 and *Hetherington v. Robertson*, 1993 G.W.D. 2-138.

management and control of the defender and the accident is such that, in the ordinary course of things if those who have the management use proper care, it affords reasonable evidence in the absence of an explanation of the defendants that the accident arose from want of care.[74] Thus where an employee was injured when an explosion in a hose caused him to leap, in fright, from the platform on which he was working, the employers were liable because (i) the most probable cause was the failure of a filter to prevent rust getting into the hose, (ii) at the material time they were in control of the hose and (iii) hose pipes do not usually explode.[75] However, the maxim does not apply if there is direct evidence of the cause of the accident, and if the pursuer can reasonably be expected to know the cause of the accident he must prove negligence,[76] although in order to do so the House of Lords has held that the pursuer will be entitled to see an employer's internal report into the cause of an accident notwithstanding that one of the purposes of preparing the report was to obtain legal advice in anticipation of litigation.[77]

3.24 The Second Division has pointed out in *Porter v. Strathclyde Regional Council*[78] that *McGhee*[78a] is most appropriate to apply "to the case of an industrial disease to which there may have been a number of contributory factors" but was "wholly inappropriate to apply to a fall caused by food on the floor which . . . should not have been there at the time."[79] Thus when Mrs Porter fell after slipping on food which had dropped on to the floor she had to establish whether the system of supervision and removal or covering of the dropped food (which a careful employer would have adopted) would probably have prevented the accident, and the Lord Ordinary had been wrong to require merely that such a system would have materially diminished the risk of the accident. Although certain parts of the judgment in *Porter* might suggest that, where a pursuer shows there occurred a failure to take a precaution designed to reduce a danger, it inevitably follows that had the precaution been taken the accident would probably have been prevented, the First Division in *Muir v. Cumbernauld and*

---

[74] *Murray v. Edinburgh District Council*, 1981 S.L.T. 253 (O.H.); distinguished in *Buchanan v. Drummond Miller, WS* (O.H., unreported, March 5, 1999): when a ceiling suddenly and without warning collapses onto an innocent employee an explanation is called for from her employers who had exclusive control and management of it.

[75] *Devine v. Colvilles*, 1969 S.C. (H.L.) 67.

[76] *Gavin v. Rogers* (1889) 17 R. 206.

[77] *Waugh v. British Railways Board* [1979] I.R.L.R. 364.

[78] 1991 S.L.T. 446.

[78a] *McGhee v. NCB*, 1973 S.C. (H.L.) 37.

[79] 1991 S.L.T. 446 at 448.

Kilsyth District Council[80] has emphasised that *Porter* "in no way derogates from the accepted test which is that a pursuer must prove on a balance of probabilities that breach of duty caused or materially contributed to his injury." However, it is not sufficient for the pursuer to prove that there would have been "a materially better chance" of avoiding the injury if the defender had not been negligent because such an approach does not take account of the requirement of proof on the balance of probabilities.[81] Even if it is established that the employer has breached his duty of care by not providing safety equipment, the pursuer is still required to prove on a balance of probabilities that he would have used the equipment,[82] and in the absence of medical evidence about the pursuer's mental condition the court is entitled to take account of his evidence that he would not have worn safety goggles even if they had been provided.[83] Of particular significance for repetitive strain injuries (RSI), the Court of Appeal has stated that where there is a clear choice between physical and psychogenic explanations and the psychogenic case is wholly unconvincing "it is simple logic to conclude that physical case is more probable."[83a]

Novus actus and contributory negligence

3.25 The chain of causation may begin with the employer's breach of duty, but a subsequent event may relieve him of liability for the employee's eventual injury because the chain of causation may be broken by the subsequent event; a sequence of events described by the maxim *novus actus interveniens*. The *novus actus* may be the act of a third party or indeed the pursuer himself. Thus where as a result of his employer's negligence an employee sustained minor injuries from which he would have recovered in about two weeks sustained a more serious injury to his right leg when, on experiencing a sudden weakness in his left (injured) leg he jumped down a number of steps to the next landing, his employers were held not liable for the injuries to his right leg because the injury was caused by the pursuer's unreasonable conduct—in putting himself in a position whereby he had to jump downstairs—which was a *novus actus interveniens*.[84] Alternatively the intervention of the pursuer or a third party may mean that the

---

[80] 1993 S.L.T. 287.

[81] *Farrer v. Lothian Health Board* (O.H., unreported, March 14, 1999).

[82] *McWilliams v. Sir William Arrol & Co.*, 1962 S.L.T. 121 (HL); *Bux v. Slough Metals Ltd* [1973] 1 W.L.R. 1358.

[83] *McKinlay v. British Steel Corporation*, 1988 S.L.T. 810.

[83a] *Alexander v. Midland Bank plc* [1999] I.R.L.R. 723.

[84] *McKew v. Holland & Hannen & Cubitts (Scotland) Ltd*, 1970 S.L.T. 68 (HL).

type of harm could not reasonably have been foreseen by the defender.[85]

3.26 More commonly the action of the injured employee will be a co-operating or contributing cause of his injuries rather than a *novus actus*. Until the enactment of the Law Reform (Contributory Negligence) Act 1945 where the negligence of the employee contributed to his injury, his employer was relieved of all liability.[86] Since 1945 a finding of contributory negligence merely permits the court to fix liability between the pursuer and the defender(s) in such proportions as reflects their shares of the responsibility[87] and this is so whether the action lies at common law or for breach of statutory duty.[88] The standard of care required of the pursuer for his own safety is such as is reasonable in the circumstances,[89] and an employee will be contributorily negligent if he ought reasonably to have foreseen that if he did not act prudently he might hurt himself, taking account of the possibility of others being careless[90]; it does not depend on the existence of a legal duty of care for his own safety—"[t]he real question being not whether the [pursuer] was neglecting some legal duty but whether he was acting as a responsible man and with reasonable care".[91] Thus although the employers of a nurse who sustained a back injury while lifting a patient were negligent in not ensuring that her assistant had been properly trained, the pursuer was conributorily negligent because she had previously suffered a back injury and had been given medical advice not to undertake heavy lifting work and had not arranged the patient's bed so as to maximise the best way of lifting[92]; although particularly where the pursuer is an employee, courts have accepted that familiarity with dangers breeds contempt and that workmen become careless and take risks.[93] Unless the trial

---

[85] See *Jolley v. Sutton London Borough Council, The Times*, June 23, 1998, CA; it was foreseeable that children would play on an abandoned boat left beside council houses and might injure themselves because of its rotten condition, but not that older children would jack the boat up in an attempt to repair it. The same result could be achieved by saying that it was the older boys' act which created the situation which resulted in the accident.

[86] *Caswell v. Powell and Duffryn Assd Collieries* [1940] A.C. 152; and see the report of the Law Revision Committee (Cmd. 6032, 1939) that the question is "whose act caused the wrong?"

[87] Law Reform (Contributory Negligence) Act 1945, s. 1(1); note that s. 1(1) does not operate to defeat any defence which arises under a contract and the Act applies to claims brought by dependants of a deceased (s. 1(4)).

[88] *Grant v. Sun Shipping Company*, 1948 S.C. (H.L.) 73; and see chap. 4, para. 4.13.

[89] *Porter v. Strathclyde Regional Council*, 1991 S.L.T. 446.

[90] *Jones v. Livox Quarries* [1952] 2 Q.B. 608, *per* Denning L.J. at 615.

[91] *Davies v. Swan Motor Co.* [1949] 2 K.B. 291.

[92] *McCaffery v. Datta*, 1997 P.I.Q.R. 164, CA.

[93] See for example *Flower v. Ebbw Vale Steel Company* [1934] 2 K.B. 132; *Caswell v. Powell Duffryn* [1940] A.C. 152; *Hutchinson v. LNER* [1942] 1 K.B. 481.

judge has manifestly gone wrong to a substantial degree the appeal court will not interfere with his apportionment of responsibility.[94] Each case very much depends on its own circumstances but sometimes it is difficult to comprehend the trial judge's apportionment of responsibility. Thus a 50 per cent allocation of responsibility was made and upheld where a nursery assistant had injured herself when she slipped on a small amount of mince and potato which had fallen on to the floor in a room where young children were being fed. She was so intent on carrying a fractious baby at the time that she forgot to look for food on the floor but she ought to have done so because food on the floor was a common occurrence.[95] On the other hand a 30 per cent allocation of responsibility was made and upheld where an experienced factory worker attempted to complete single-handed a task, involving the use of a hydraulic ram, normally performed by two people; his hand was injured when a punch, which he held between thumb and forefinger on the rivet head, slipped while he allowed the ram to come down with some force.[96] It is for the defender(s) to prove contributory negligence.[97]

The standard of the employer's duty

3.27 The duty owed to the employee can be stated in general terms as a duty to take reasonable care for the employee's safety[98] which involves a question of fact,[99] with the result that previous decisions are invariably merely examples of applications of the principles rather than statements of the law. Although it has been authoritatively stated that the standard of foresight of the reasonable man is an impersonal one which is independent of the idiosyncrasies of the particular person in question, there is to an

---

[94] *McCusker v. Saveheat Cavity Wall Insulation Ltd*, 1987 S.L.T. 24; *McIntosh v. NCB*, 1988 S.L.T. 348. But see *Calder v. H. Kitson Vickers Ltd* [1988] I.C.R. 3232, CA, where Ralph Gibson L.J. felt able to adjust the trial judge's apportionment on the ground that the latter concluded the contract was one of service, whereas Ralph Gibson L.J. considered the contract between Calder and the defendants to be for services.

[95] *Porter v. Strathclyde Regional Council*, 1991 S.L.T. 446; a similar allocation was made where an employee who knew goggles were available and the risk of working without them was injured when not availing himself of the goggles; *Crouch v. BREL*, 1988 I.R.L.R. 404, CA.

[96] *Jenkinson v. Brook Motors Ltd* (1985) unreported case no. 85/280, CA; and see *McMillan v. Lord Advocate*, 1991 S.L.T. 150 (30% allocation of responsibility to employee who tripped on a door seal which projected not more than one-half inch above the floor because "it was not clearly visible and it would be easy to forget about it").

[97] *Porter v. Strathclyde Regional Council*, 1991 S.L.T. 446.

[98] *Davie v. New Merton Board Mills* [1958] 1 All E.R. 67; *Muir v. Glasgow Corporation*, 1943 S.C. (H.L.) 3.

[99] *Qualcast (Wolverhampton) Ltd v. Haynes* [1959] A.C. 743.

extent a subjective element, in that it is left to the judge to decide
what in the circumstances of the particular case the reasonable
man would have had in contemplation and what the party sought
to be made liable ought to have foreseen.[1] Thus where a man is in
a position which requires special skill or knowledge, a failure to
exercise such skill or knowledge will breach the duty of care—and
this applies just as much to doctors and other professions as it does
to managers of industrial undertakings—and it has been fairly
commented that this is one reason why, in general, a higher
standard of care will be expected of employers than their
employees.[2] The fact that the employer is following trade practice
is not conclusive proof that he has taken reasonable care[3]; in every
case it is a question of whether the circumstances entitle the court
to conclude that there has or has not been a failure to exercise
reasonable care.[4]

3.28 In *Morton v. Dixon*[5] Lord Dunedin opined that where the
negligence consists of a fault of omission, proof should be one of
two kinds—either that the thing which he did not do was a thing
which was commonly done by persons in like circumstances, or that
it was a thing which was so obviously wanted that it would be folly
in anyone to neglect it and, although Lord Normand had coun-
selled that Lord Dunedin's opinion did not permit a "facile finding
that a precaution is necessary when there is no proof that it is one
taken by other persons in like circumstances but it does not detract
from the test of conduct and judgment of the reasonable and
prudent man".[6] Lord President Cooper in a later case[7] adhered to
the view that it was only in the extreme case where it was obvious
that some precaution was needed and inexcusable or folly to omit
it, that it was permissible to ignore current practice and rely on the
judgment of the reasonable man. More recent decisions[8] of the

---

[1] *Muir v. Glasgow Corporation*, 1943 S.C. (H.L.) 3, *per* Lord Macmillan at 10.

[2] Munkman, *Employers' Liability* (11th ed.), p. 36.

[3] "[N]o one can claim to be excused for want of care because others are as
careless as himself"; *Blenkiron v. Great Central Gas Consumer Co.* (1860) 2 F. & F.
437, *per* Cockburn C.J.

[4] *Cavanagh v. Ulster Weaving Co. Ltd* [1960] A.C. 145 (HL), (NI), explaining
Morton v. Wm. Dixon Ltd, 1909 S.C. 807. And see *Potec v. Edinburgh Corporation*,
1964 S.C. (H.L.) 1 (guard rail not provided at any refuse depot and they would have
impeded the operative's activities); *Martin v. Greater Glasgow Health Board*, 1977
S.L.T. (Notes) 66 (bannisters in nurse home same height as at other similar
institutions). And see *Marshall v. Wiliam Sharp & Sons Ltd*, 1991 S.L.T. 114 (I.H.)
regarding reference to manufacturers instructions.

[5] 1909 S.C. 807.

[6] *Paris v. Stepney Borough Council* [1951] A.C. 367.

[7] *Gallagher v. Balfour Beatty & Co. Ltd*, 1951 S.C. 712 at 718.

[8] See for example *General Cleaning Contractors Ltd v. Christmas* [1953] A.C. 180,
Cavanagh v. Ulster Weaving Co. Ltd [1960] A.C. 145.

House of Lords, however, have re-affirmed that the correct approach is that long-established practice in a trade, although not necessarily conclusive is generally regarded as strong evidence of reasonableness, and Lord Reid, stressing the need to have regard to what in *Paris v. Stepney Borough Council*[9] amounted to a "folly", namely something unreasonable or imprudent, has opined that Lord Dunedin's statement in *Morton v. Dixon*[10] must be read with Lord Normand's gloss,[11] and it is now accepted that where a precaution is shown to be reasonably practicable it is not necessary to prove a practice elsewhere.[12]

3.29 It is clear that where knowledge is developing, employers must keep abreast of it and not be slow to apply it[13]; they must be familiar with codes of practice,[14] pamphlets[15] and other guidance[16] issued by the Health and Safety Executive and other organisations concerned with occupational safety,[17] and a large undertaking will be expected to attain a higher standard of care in this respect than the corner shop.[18] Where the evidence discloses that the employers took all reasonable steps to inform themselves of the up-to-date position (regarding safe vibration limits for chain saws) and applied them, the fact that the technical aspects of the information were not examined in depth will not prevent the court finding for the employer,[19] and attempts by employers to promulgate their own limits and standards after collating information about health risks are frequently accepted as indicators of reasonableness.[20] Also, while it has been stated that "the law does not expect the employer

---

[9] [1951] A.C. 367.

[10] 1909 S.C. 807.

[11] *Morris v. West Hartlepool Steam Navigation Co. Ltd* [1956] A.C. 552 (HL); and note the criticism of Lord Dunedin's statement in *Donohue v. Union S.S. Co. of New Zealand* [1951] N.Z.L.R. 862 at 879.

[12] *Macdonald v. Scottish Stamping and Engineering Co. Ltd*, 1972 S.L.T. (Notes) 73 (no evidence of practice of safety clamps at other establishments).

[13] *Stokes v. Guest, Keen & Nettlefold* [1968] 1 W.L.R. 1776. And see *Lodge & McSherry v. British Telecom* (unreported, 1992).

[14] Codes of practice may be approved by the Health and Safety Commission under s. 16 of the Health and Safety at Work Act 1974, and are declared to be admissible in criminal proceedings, but there would seem to be no reason why they could not be relied on in civil proceedings without the statutory presumption against the employer which is applied by s. 17(2) in criminal proceedings; see chap. 5, paras 5.82 *et seq.*

[15] *Clifford v. Charles H. Challen & Son* [1951] 1 K.B. 495.

[16] *Burgess v. Thorn Consumer Electronics (Newhaven)*, *The Times*, May 16, 1983.

[17] *Balfour & Others v. William Beardmore & Co. Ltd*, 1956 S.L.T. 205 (O.H.) (Report of Committee on Dust in Steel Industries).

[18] *Wright v. Dunlop Rubber Co. Ltd and ICI Ltd* (1972) 13 K.I.R. 255, CA; *Cartwright v. G.K.N. Sankey Ltd* (1973) 14 K.I.R. 349.

[19] *Murphy v. Lord Advocate*, 1981 S.L.T. 213 (O.H.).

[20] *ibid.*; *Sloan v. British Railways Board*, 1981 S.L.T. 239 (O.H.).

of bricklayers' labourers to study and become conversant with the complexities of dermatology",[21] the decision seems to have turned on the fact that there was no evidence of a contrary practice in the building industry or any official or trade publication on conditions on building sites indicating that labourers are liable to contract dermatitis; and the rejection of the pursuer's submission that a careful employer should take steps to find out if a risk exists and, if it does, take steps to protect against it, is consistent with neither (a) the approach in *Sloan v. British Railways Board*[22] in which the identification and monitoring of train drivers at risk of neurosensory loss was rejected because it would not have detected the pursuer's sensitivity before his injury had become manifest, nor (b) the current statutory philosophy of risk assessment[23]; indeed it is respectfully suggested that the employer's statutory duty to carry out a risk assessment will become a prominent feature of common law claims. Of course the degree of awareness of the risk will change,[24] in which case the issue is from what date would a reasonable employer with proper but not extraordinary solicitude for the welfare of his workers have identified the problem (of excessive noise), recognise that it was capable of solution, weighed up the potential advantages and disadvantages of that solution, decided to adopt it, acquired a supply of protectors, set in train a programme of education, experimented with the system and put it into effect.[25]

3.30 Similarly, while an action at common law is distinct from an action for breach of statutory duty,[26] the former cannot be considered in complete dissociation from the latter. Thus on the one hand it would be difficult to maintain that an employer who had complied with a cognate statutory provision had failed in his common law duty to take care[27] and compliance with the statutory provision may be of evidential value,[28] while on the other hand the

---

[21] *Riddick v. Weir Housing Corporation Ltd*, 1971 S.L.T. 24, *per* Lord Thomson at 25. Lord Migdale suggested the employer's duty varied depending on whether the materials were new or had been in use for a long time.

[22] 1981 S.L.T. 239 (O.H.).

[23] See the Management of Health and Safety at Work Regulations 1999 (S.I. 1999 No. 3242).

[24] See for example *Graham v. C.W.S. Ltd* [1957] 1 All E.R. 654 (not known that mahogany dust could cause cancer); *Tremain v. Pike* [1969] 3 All E.R. 1303 (not at one time known in farming community that Weil's disease could be contracted through contact with rats' urine).

[25] *Thompson v. Smiths Shiprepairers (North Shields) Ltd* [1984] Q.B. 4058.

[26] *Caswell v. Powell Duffryn Associated Collieries* [1940] A.C. 152 (HL).

[27] *Franklin v. Gramophone Company Ltd* [1948] 1 KB 542, CA.

[28] *Qualcast (Wolverhampton) Ltd v. Haynes* [1959] A.C. 743 (HL), *per* Lord Keith of Avonholm at 756. Also while the Management of Health and Safety at Work Regulations 1999 do not impose civil liability it could be argued that failure to observe the regulations about risk assessment would be evidence of negligence.

very fact that there has been enacted a statutory provision may be relied on by a pursuer to show that a reasonable employer would have foreseen the risk which the statutory provision was designed to avert and would have taken appropriate action in the performance of his common law duty of care[29]; although clearly that does not apply where the facts and circumstances of the case take it outside the statutory provisions, in which case the common law issue has to be resolved without reference to the statute or regulations.[30] However, an examination of judicial decisions discloses that this concept of reasonable care involves consideration of the following issues—(a) the risk or probability that damage or harm will be done by the conduct or activity; (b) the magnitude of resultant damage or harm; (c) the value or utility of the object to be achieved by the conduct in question; (d) the practicability, cost, time and trouble of taking precautions against the risk of injury.[31]

Probability

3.31 Thus where an employee was bitten by one of her employer's two West Highland terriers while cleaning the windows of the veterinary surgery where she worked as a receptionist, the main issue was whether the injury was reasonably foreseeable and approving of the test set out in *Bolton v. Stone*.[32] Lord Weir stated the question was whether the risk of damage to the pursuer was sufficiently probable as to lead the defenders to anticipate it, and:

"there is no doubt in my mind that a stranger entering the back garden was at risk of being attacked and at risk of injury, and from the description of the dogs' behaviour I do not consider that the risk was remote or fanciful but a real one. . . . The evidence . . . gives the clear impression that these particular terriers were capable of turning nasty while in the garden and. . . . I cannot believe that the defenders could have been unaware prior to the incident of the vicious

---

[29] *Franklin v. Gramophone Company Ltd* [1948] 1 K.B. 542, *per* Somervell L.J. at 558; *National Coal Board v. England* [1954] A.C. 403 (HL). And see *Butt v. Inner London Education Authority* (1968) 66 L.G.R. 379; *Hewett v. Alf Brown's Transport Ltd* [1992] I.C.R. 530, CA, in which the standard of the common law duty was determined by reference to the Control of Lead at Work Regulations 1980 on the grounds that they made clear what risks were foreseeable.

[30] *Matuszczyk v. National Coal Board*, 1953 S.C. 8; *Chipchase v. British Titan Products Company Ltd* [1956] 1 Q.B. 545; and see *Bux v. Slough Metals Ltd* [1974] 1 All E.R. 262, CA.

[31] *Morris v. West Hartlepool Steam Navigation Co. Ltd* [1956] A.C. 552; applied with approval in *Brisco v. Secretary of State for Scotland*, 1997 S.C. 14 (I.H.); and see Atiyah, *Accidents, Compensation and the Law* (3rd ed., 1980), p. 44.

[32] [1951] A.C. 850; *cf. Whitefield v. Barton*, 1987 S.C.L.R. 259, *Lamond v. Glasgow Corporation*, 1968 S.L.T. 291.

tendencies of Shona and Dornie. I am satisfied that there was a foreseeable and not remote risk that . . . one or other of [the dogs] would show aggression towards a stranger who for any reason appeared in the garden and that this aggression might take the form of a physical attack".[33]

Similarly where an employee who was carrying a bottle tripped over a metal strip which protruded half an inch above floor level, the argument that the hazard was more apparent than real was rejected because "to catch a foot on the rim of this threshold was something which was liable to happen from time to time unless someone was looking where he was going and . . . it was only a matter of time before this would lead to a fall and to injury"[34]; or where an employee slipped on the spillages (from coffee or tea-cups) on a pseudo marble floor the probability test was met because:

> "the records had shown that spillages had been common, so that it had been almost inevitable that sooner or later an accident would occur; indeed staff had, several times each year by means of bulletins, been besought to take better care and to put a saucer or tray beneath any cup or mug which they carried from the kitchen."[35]

Although there was a foreseeable risk that a police constable who, to observe the spectators at a football match stood with her back to the play, would be injured if a player was impelled from the pitch the risk was so small that a reasonable man would not guard against it, with the result that the Chief Constable of Strathclyde Police was not liable for the injuries sustained by a police officer who was injured while supervising the crowd during a match between Airdrieonians and Celtic, when a Celtic player, in endeavouring to control the ball, left the pitch at such speed that he collided with her and propelled her into a barrier; the only similar incident appeared to have occurred 17 years ago at Sunderland.[36] By contrast a reasonable professional football player who committed a forceful and high challenge would know that it carried with it a significant risk of serious injury to the other player.[37]

[33] *Hill v. Lovett*, 1992 S.L.T. 994 (O.H.).

[34] *McMillan v. Lord Advocate*, 1991 S.L.T. 150 (O.H.); cf. *McClafferty v. British Telecommunications plc*, 1987 S.L.T. 327.

[35] *Bell v. Department of Social Security, The Times*, June 13, 1989, CA; cf. *Latimer v. AEC Ltd* [1953] 2 All E.R. 449, *Hanlon v. British Railways Board*, 1991 S.L.T. 228 (O.H.).

[36] *Gillon v. Chief Constable of Strathclyde Police*, 1997 S.L.T. 1218 (O.H.); cf. *Alexander v. Midland Bank plc* [1999] I.R.L.R. 723, CA, that where a psychogenic case is wholly unconvincing in a case of RSI it is "simple logic" to conclude that physical case is more probable.

[37] *Watson v. Gray and Another, The Times*, October 29, 1998, H.C.

The magnitude of the risk

3.32 As a general proposition it may be stated that the law exacts a degree of care commensurate with the risk created[38] so that the greater the risk of serious injury the more rigorous is the standard of care. Thus in the *locus classicus, Paris v. Stepney Borough Council,*[39] an employee who was known[40] by the employers to be already blind in one eye was using a hammer to loosen a bolt when a piece of metal flew off into his good eye, rendering him blind; his employers were liable for failing to provide protective goggles even although no goggles were provided to other men engaged in the same type of activity. Similarly, although an employer by making protective gloves available to his employee, a cleaner, could have avoided or at least reduced the risk of contact dermatitis, he failed in his duty of reasonable care by not warning his employee of the risk of contracting this "disease . . . [which] could become quite serious in that it could take a long time to heal and could become a long term problem."[41] On the other hand where the risks of injury are not great and an experienced employee knows the risks, it may be sufficient for the employer to make the safety equipment available[42]; and while an employer must warn an employee of the health risks a job involves where knowledge of the risks would be likely to affect the decision of a sensible, level-headed person about accepting the offer of employment, the duty was not activated by the prospect of the employee suffering from Reynaud's syndrome (a numbing of the fingers) which merely caused minor discomfort and trivial inconvenience with no effect on capacity for work.[43] Although in *Halliday v. Tayside Health Board*[44] the employer was not liable after a nurse who had already injured her back while lifting a patient was transferred to a ward where the lifting duties were more strenuous and frequent damaged her back again, the decision seems to have turned on the evidence which did not show that she was subject to a high risk of injury and that the employee's doctor had not indicated that she be given lighter work. In *Brisco v.*

---

[38] *Henderson v. Carron Co.* (1889) 16 R. 633.

[39] [1951] 1 All E.R. 42 (HL); *cf. Sloan v. British Railways Board*, 1981 S.L.T. 239 (O.H.).

[40] See *James v. Hepworth & Grandage* [1968] 1 Q.B. 94.

[41] *Campbell v. Lothian Health Board*, 1987 S.L.T. 665 (O.H.). And see *Stokes v. Guest Keen and Nettlefold Ltd* [1968] 1 W.L.R. 1776 (possible risk of developing scrotal cancer not publicised to workforce because resultant "turmoil's" possible effect on production).

[42] *Qualcast (Wolverhampton) Ltd v. Haynes* [1959] 2 All E.R. 38 (HL) (molten metal splashed on to foot of experienced employee to whom spats and boots were available.

[43] *White v. Holbrook Precision Castings Ltd* [1985] I.R.L.R. 215, CA; and see *Condo v. South Australia* [1987] S.A.S.R. 584.

[44] 1996 S.C. 434 (I.H.).

Secretary of State for Scotland[45] the claim of a prison officer who was injured while engaged in a simulated riot for training purposes was rejected on the ground that the risk of him being seriously injured was very small and the risk had to be balanced against the need to provide realistic training. Where the employee is inexperienced, however, a greater degree of training is required so that, where a resident support worker at a home for disabled people was sent on a camping holiday with a resident was injured while changing a cylinder on the gas cooker near the tent, the employer was liable even although the employee admitted she should have been aware of the risk from a lighted candle because she had been provided with the bare minimum of equipment (a torch but no battery) and no given instruction.[46] Also, training in the use of equipment when operated with a suitable guard will be of no effect where the machine used does not have a guard.[47]

Value of activity

3.33 There are few reported cases of courts concluding that the value to attach to the activity or conduct in question outweighs the duty to reduce or eliminate the risk, but it has been held that in wartime the need to make use of all available vehicles could justify the risks involved in using a vehicle with a defective signalling system,[48] and where a prison officer taking part in a training exercise was injured by a heavy fence post being dropped on to his foot the court noted that the officer had been provided with protective clothing and a helmet to protect the more vulnerable parts of the body and that "the whole purpose of the exercise was to give the trainees realistic experience of the conditions with which they might be faced in a genuine riot and that . . . the use of heavy missiles was required for that purpose."[49] However, economic expedience or the inconvenience of carrying out repairs during a busy period will probably not justify the risks of postponing repairs.[50]

---

[45] 1997 S.C. 14 (I.H.). And see *McErlean v. J & B Scotland Ltd*, 1997 S.L.T. 1326 (O.H.) (risk of minor bruising foreseeable but not disabling injury).

[46] *Fraser v. Winchester Health Authority, The Times*, July 12, 1999, CA.

[47] *English v. North Lanarkshire Council*, 1999 S.C.L.R. 310 (O.H.).

[48] *Daborn v. Bath Tramways Motor Co.* [1946] 2 All E.R. 333.

[49] *Brisco v. Secretary of State for Scotland*, 1997 S.C. 14 (I.H.).

[50] *Macdonald v. British Transport Commission* [1955] 3 All E.R. 789; and see *Stokes v. Guest, Keen and Nettlefold (Bolts and Nuts) Ltd* [1969] 1 W.L.R. 1776 (failure to issue warnings and introduce checks for scrotal cancer for fear that resultant turmoil would interfere with production); *Macdonald v. Scottish Stamping and Engineering Co. Ltd*, 1972 S.L.T. 73 (fitting safety device would slow down production and reduce employees' piece-rate earnings). *Cf. Wood v. Redpath*, 1993 G.W.D. 3-193 (uneconomic to employ winch operator).

Practicability, cost, time and trouble

3.34 The extent to which an employer is required to reduce or eliminate a risk is influenced by the difficulty and expense involved in taking such risk-reducing procedures and the effectiveness of protective measures. Thus it has been held that it is not reasonably practicable to prop every part of a mine,[51] to provide a barrier cream as protection against dermatitis where there were doubts about the effectiveness of the protection,[52] or to provide ear defenders to engine drivers where they would reduce the noise but also the driver's ability to hear audio-warning signals.[53] Similarly in *General Cleaning Contractors Ltd v. Christmas*[54] the risk of injury to a window cleaner by the top sash slipping down to cause a "guillotine" effect on his fingers as they held on to the lower sash thereby causing him to lose his grip and fall could have been eliminated by provision of simple wedges; other methods would have been to do all the cleaning from ladders or inserting bolts into the walls at either side of each window, but neither of these was practicable.[55] While the transfer of cash between £1,500–£2,000 did not require the employment of security specialists provided the employee had received adequate training in ways of reducing injury to himself,[56] the employers of an employee injured while manually moving a 45-gallon drum weighing 450lb were liable for the employee's injuries when they already had at their disposal a vehicle and a hoist; there was no extra cost and only minor inconvenience involved.[57]

THE SUBSTANCE OF THE EMPLOYER'S DUTY

3.35 Although the employer's duty is a general one, alternatively expressed as a duty to "provide in every way for the safety of

---

[51] *Marshall v. Gotham & Co. Ltd* [1954] A.C. 360.
[52] *Brown v. Rolls Royce Ltd*, 1960 S.C. (H.L.) 22; [1960] 1 All E.R. 577.
[53] *Sloan v. British Railways Board*, 1981 S.L.T. 239 (O.H.).
[54] [1952] 2 All E.R. 1110 (HL).
[55] And see *Cook v. Square D Ltd* [1992] I.C.R. 262 (CA), in which it was stated unrealistic to require employer of one employee sent abroad to inspect site, but the standard may change where a number of employees are involved or an employee is being sent for considerable period. However, in the earlier Scottish case of *M'Quilter v. Goulandris Bros Ltd*, 1951 S.L.T. (Notes) 75 it was made clear that where the employee was working on premises within the possession and control of a third party that does not absolve the employer from exercising reasonable care for the safety of the workmen, although the scope of the duty is circumscribed by the fact that the work is being done on premises not within the possession and control of the employer. See also *Crombie v. McDermott Scotland Ltd*, 1996 S.L.T. 1238 applying *M'Quilter*.
[56] *Charlton v. The Forrest Printing Ink Co. Ltd* [1980] I.R.L.R. 331 (CA).
[57] *Crawford v. Post Office* (1984) unreported case no. 84/85 (CA). *Cf. Wood v. Redpath* 1993 G.W.D. 3-193.

workmen against the risks which their employment involves", to make "such provision for the safety of the workman as is reasonable and necessary", or "to take reasonable care that the employee is not exposed to unnecessary risks",[58] which will include the dangers created by the actions of third parties where such a danger would have been very likely to occur,[59] it is frequently considered in relation to particular components or elements of the duty.

However, although for convenience it is possible to arrange decisions under particular headings it must be noted that each decision is very much related to its own facts and frequently will involve consideration of other relevant issues like foreseeability, causation and standard of care. Decisions relating to the substance of the employer's duty involve the use of words like "adequate", "maintain", "provide" and "inspect" which are also used in the context of statutory provisions,[60] and decisions dealing with their meanings in such a context may occasionally provide assistance where the words arise in litigation based on common law. However, care has to be taken to ensure that the word in its statutory context has not been given a special meaning either by judicial interpretation of the word in its statutory context[61] or by virtue of an interpretation clause in the statute itself.[62]

3.36 As indicated earlier[63] the planning of the work method or the promulgation of a system of work is the personal responsibility of the employer. Just what is a system of work and what is required by way of a system depends on the circumstances and the nature of the work being undertaken, but "system" generally denotes that which is permanent as opposed to transitory or casual,[64] and may range from the giving of instructions for the safe accomplishment of a work objective[65] to the provision of no, or inadequate,

---

[58] *McNeill v. Wallace* (1853) 15 D. 818; *Bett v. Dalmeny Oil Company* (1905) 7F. 787.

[59] *Longworth v. Coppas International (UK) Ltd*, 1985 S.L.T. 111.

[60] Thus the duty to provide a safe place of work is regulated by at least three statutory provisions: Occupiers Liability (Scotland) Act 1960, Health and Safety at Work Act 1974, s. 2(2)(d), and Workplace (Health, Safety and Welfare) Regulations 1992.

[61] See, for example the meanings ascribed to (a) "maintained" in *Millar v. Galashiels Gas Co. Ltd*, 1949 S.C. (H.L.) 31 and (b) "effective provision" in *Davies v. Massey Ferguson* [1986] I.C.R. 580.

[62] See, for example, the Personal Protective Equipment at Work Regulations 1992, reg. 7, regarding the meanings of "maintain".

[63] See paras 3.37 *et seq.*

[64] *Marshall v. William Sharp & Sons Ltd*, 1992 S.L.T. 114 (I.H.).

[65] *Wood v. Redpath*, 1993 G.W.D. 3-193 (failure to instruct marine apprentice to stop winch before attempting to free snagged rope); *Eltringham v. G. B. Papers plc*, 1993 G.W.D. 9-635 (failure to instruct employee to close stopcock to when high pressure hosepipe not in use to prevent formation of airlocks). *Cf. Couper v. Remploy Ltd*, 1993 G.W.D. 27-1715.

equipment,[66] although it may not include the provision of transport at the end of work.[67] In *Gandy, Herrick and Gerrard v. Matteson's Walls Ltd*[68] employees working on a sausage production line were required to do work which was highly repetitive and was performed at speed, and developed repetitive strain syndrome for which their employer was held liable as it had operated a system of work in which production rates were too high and job rotation and rest periods were inadequate.[69]

Place of work

3.37 Ensuring the employee's place of work is safe extends not just to tangible physical things like floors, doors, windows and means of access and egress, but also to environmental conditions like temperature and noise. By far the most common means by which a workplace can become unsafe is by spillages on, or obstruction of, floors or walkways. Generally,[70] where spillages are likely to occur an employer is required to institute and operate a reasonably adequate system of detecting and dealing with them, and what might be an adequate system inspection in one place (office block) may not be adequate in another (supermarket).[71] Thus the employers and the rig operator were jointly liable for the injuries sustained by an oil platform rigger who slipped while descending a ladder because his boots were made slippery by an accumulation of oil and mud on the deck and walkways; the danger of slipping had been known for several days before the accident.[72] However, a duty of care does not arise if the pursuer is unable to establish that the employers knew or ought to have known of the presence of the slippery substances,[73] and much will depend on the circumstances of each case so that the employers of a fireman who slipped in the fire station on a wet floor made of embossed quarry tiles, which were generally satisfactory for station activities, were held to have taken reasonable care,[74] while the employers of a

---

[66] *Weir v. Edinburgh Woolen Mill Ltd*, 1993 G.W.D. 1-54 (standing on top of ladder to remove shelving which habitually stuck).

[67] *Ramsay v. Wimpey Ltd*, 1951 S.C. 692 (I.H.).

[68] (1997) 9 C.L. 330, county court.

[69] See now the Working Time Regulations 1998, particularly reg. 8, that employers must ensure adequate rest breaks where work is monotonous or the work rate is predetermined. *Cf. Pickford v. Imperial Chemical Industries plc* [1998] I.R.L.R. 435 (HL) that a person of the plaintiff's intelligence (secretary) could reasonably be expected to take breaks from typing without being told.

[70] *cf. Cook v. Square D Ltd* [1992] I.C.R. 262, CA.

[71] Contrast *Bell v. Department of Health and Society Security, The Times*, June 13, 1989, with *Ware v. Tesco Stores Ltd* [1976] 1 W.L.R. 810.

[72] *Breslin v. Britoil plc*, 1992 S.L.T. 414 (O.H.); and see *Bell v. Department of Health and Social Security, The Times*, June 13, 1989.

[73] *Hanlon v. British Railways Board*, 1991 S.L.T. 228 (O.H.).

[74] *Dixon v. London Fire and Civil Defence Authority, The Times*, February 22, 1993, CA.

nurse who slipped on a small patch of oil on a terrazzo floor which resulted from the lubrication of the wheels of moveable machinery should have introduced a system of ensuring oil did not get on to the floor in this way.[75] Similarly an employer may be required to advise or enjoin the evacuation of an employee where the location of his work might expose him to unnecessary risks which could be caused by the intervention of a third party[76] and in the context of an unfair dismissal case it has been held that an employee could refuse to obey an order to go to Belfast (but not Wexford, Eire) on the grounds that it involved a serious risk not contemplated at the time of the contract.[77] Some decisions are difficult to reconcile and eventually will turn on the court's view of the remoteness of the risk.[78]

3.38 With regard to environmental conditions, these can extend to the provision of washing facilities,[79] lighting,[80] noise,[81] temperature,[82] work and shift patterns,[83] and presence of dangerous animals.[84] Exposing employees to the risks of passive smoking may also give rise to breach of duty[85] and while it has been held that an

---

[75] *Buchanan v. Lanarkshire Health Board*, 1983 S.L.T. 456 (O.H.); and see *Bloxham v. Swan Hunter Shipbuilders Ltd* (1985) unreported case 85/208, CA; and *Markwell v. Suffolk Coastal District Council* (1985) unreported case 85/815, CA (icy patches on private road and yard).

[76] *Longworth v. Coppas International (U.K.) Ltd*, 1985 S.L.T. 111.

[77] *Walmsley v. UDEC* [1972] I.R.L.R. 80 (I.T.).

[78] Contrast *Brown v. Redpath Brown & Co. Ltd*, 1963 S.L.T. 219 (I.H.) with *McMillan v. Lord Advocate*, 1991 S.L.T. 150.

[79] *McGhee v. National Coal Board* [1972] 3 All E.R. 1003 (HL).

[80] *Garcia v. Harland & Wolff Ltd* [1943] 2 All E.R. 477; *Russell v. Criterion Film Productions Ltd* [1936] 3 All E.R. 627 (injury to eyes by use of abnormally bright lights); *M'Quilter v. Goulandris Brothers Ltd*, 1951 S.L.T. (Notes) 75 (falling into open hatch through inadequate lighting); *Lyons v. Babcock Energy plc* (1992) H.S.I.B. 202 (injury by crushing when employee unable to see that heavy pipe might slip because of inadequate lighting).

[81] *Thompson v. Smiths Repairers (North Shields) Ltd* [1984] 1 All E.R. 881; *Baxter v. Harland and Wolff Ltd* [1990] I.R.L.R. 516, CA.

[82] *Bradford v. Robinsons Rentals Ltd* [1967] 1 W.L.R. 337; in *Graham Oxley Tool Steels Ltd v. Firth* [1980] I.R.L.R. 135 (EAT) the duty was expressed as a contractual one to provide a proper working environment.

[83] *Johnstone v. Bloomsbury Health Authority* [1991] I.R.L.R. 118, CA.

[84] *Hill v. Lovett*, 1992 S.L.T. 994 (O.H.) (employer allowing pugnacious dogs into area where employee worked).

[85] *Rae v. Glasgow City Council and Strathclyde Joint Police Board* [1999] S.C.L.R. 959. The action brought by Veronica Bland against her employers, Stockport Metropolitan Council, was settled by a payment of £15,000 compensation but without admission of liability after Miss Bland was required to share an office with three others who smoked up to 20 cigarettes a day even after the employer's occupational health doctor recommended she be moved to a non-smoking room (*The Times*, January 28, 1993); the same employer settled another case (Mrs Roe) without admission of liability for £25,000 when she retired on grounds of ill-health (*The Scotsman*, July 12, 1995).

employee had no contractual right to smoke at work[86] it would seem eminently arguable that the dismissal of an employee for non-compliance with an employer's non-smoking policy would be fair at least on substantive grounds.[87]

Equipment, plant and materials

3.39 With regard to these the employer's duty is to ensure the employee is provided with such equipment, plant and materials as are adequate for the safe performance of the job and to introduce a system of inspection and maintenance. Thus the employer was liable for the injuries sustained by an employee who was injured while raising piping from the ground to 70 feet up a steel structure; neither a crane nor a chain block and tackle was provided and the employee extemporised by using a rope block and tackle.[88] However, an experienced workman may be expected to select the correct equipment for the task where such equipment is available.[89] "Provision" may merely require making available the equipment for the employee's use when required[90] but there may be circumstances which require the employer to ensure that each employee receives a personal issue.[91] However, equipment will not be adequate if improper use by the employee which could lead to injury should have been foreseen by the employer.[92] Maintenance of equipment requires not merely repair and renewal as necessary, but also the introduction of a system of appropriate inspection. Thus the operators of a bus were liable when the bursting of a tyre caused the bus to crash; the operators should have known of the possibility of undetectable defects in tyres due to unduly harsh treatment, and should have introduced a system of reporting heavy blows to the tyres of their vehicles[93] and, where equipment has failed, a failure to produce evidence of any system of inspection being operated may result in the employer being liable.[94] The

---

[86] *Dryden v. Greater Glasgow Health Board* [1992] I.R.L.R. 469 (EAT).

[87] Contrast *Unkles v. Milanda Bread Ltd.* [1973] I.R.L.R. 76.

[88] *Machray v. Stewarts and Lloyds Ltd* [1964] 3 All E.R. 716; and see *Lovell v. Blundells and T. Albert Crompton & Co. Ltd* [1944] 1 K.B. 502; *General Cleaning Contractors v. Christmas* [1953] A.C. 80.

[89] *Qualcast (Wolverhampton) Ltd v. Haynes* [1959] 2 All E.R. 38 (HL); *Johnson v. Croggan Co. Ltd* [1954] 1 All E.R. 121; *Richardson v. S. Clarke Ltd* [1969] 3 All E.R. 705.

[90] *Qualcast (Wolverhampton) Ltd v. Haynes* [1959] 2 All E.R. 38 (HL).

[91] Contrast *Crouch v. British Rail Engineering Ltd* [1988] I.R.L.R. 404, CA; with *McKinlay v. British Steel Corporation*, 1987 S.L.T. 522; 1988 S.L.T. 810.

[92] *Sampson v. Hunslet Holdings Ltd* (1984) unreported.

[93] *Barkway v. South Wales Transport* [1950] 1 All E.R. 392; *cf. McDonald v. British Transport Commission* [1955] 3 All E.R. 789.

[94] *Henderson v. Henry E. Jenkins & Sons* [1969] 3 All E.R. 756.

extent to which an employer is required to enforce the use of safety equipment depends on all the circumstances, including the level of experience of the employee and the type of risk involved.[95] Thus while an employer was required to take very strict measures to enforce the wearing of goggles where employees were sharpening metal tools on a carborundum grinding stone,[96] the employer was not liable for the injuries sustained by an experienced fitter who attempted to perform a two-man task in the absence of his mate because in the circumstances the employer, having constituted a safe two-man work method, was not also required to expressly instruct the experienced employees not to devise a short cut or proceed single-handed.[97]

Employers' Liability (Defective Equipment) Act 1969

3.40 Where the plant or equipment is manufactured by a third party the common law rule is subject to a statutory proviso[98] which counteracts the effect of the decision of the House of Lords in *Davie v. New Merton Board Mills Ltd*.[99] The law prior to *Davie* was to the effect that the employers who provided the equipment were as one with the negligent manufacturers, and therefore liable for any injuries caused by a latent defect resulting from negligent manufacture.[1] In *Davie* the employer was not liable for the injury sustained by an employee when the drift he was using splintered because, although the drift had been negligently manufactured, it was apparently in good condition and the employer had obtained it from a reputable source.[2] The effect of the decision in *Davie* was that an injured employee would be unable to recover damages for his injuries where the negligent manufacturer had gone out of business, was situated abroad in another jurisdiction, or could not

---

[95] *Qualcast (Wolverhampton) Ltd v. Haynes* [1959] 2 All E.R. 38 (HL); *Cummings v. Sir William Arrol & Co.* [1962] 1 All E.R. 623 (HL).

[96] *Nolan v. Dental Manufacturing Co. Ltd* [1958] 2 All E.R. 449; and see *Bux v. Slough Metals Ltd* [1974] 1 All E.R. 262, CA.

[97] *Rundell v. English Clays Loverin Pochin & Co. Ltd*, unreported case no. 85/649, CA.

[98] Employers Liability (Defective Equipment) Act 1969. But see the special provisions in the Employment Act 1989, s. 11, regarding the wearing of safety helmets by Sikhs on construction sites: s. 11 provides (i) that any requirement to wear a safety helmet shall not apply to a Sikh wearing a turban and (2) where a person (*e.g.* employer) does not comply with such a requirement no action in reparation shall be brought against him in respect of injury, loss or damage.

[99] [1959] A.C. 604.

[1] See *Donnelly v. Glasgow Corporation*, 1953 S.C. 107.

[2] After *Davie* to succeed the employee injured as a result of a latent defect had to prove either that his employer was not entitled to rely on the skill and care of the manufacturers or that he (the employer) should have discovered the defect by reasonable diligence (*McMillan v. BP Refinery (Grangemouth) Ltd*, 1961 S.L.T. (Notes) 79 (I.H.)).

be located. The Employer's Liability (Defective Equipment) Act 1969 has reinstated the principle of law enunciated in *Donnelly*[3] by providing that, where an employee suffers personal injury in the course of his employment as a result of a defect in equipment provided by his employer for the purpose of his employer's business and the defect is attributable to the fault of a third party, whether identified or not, the injury shall be deemed to be also attributable to negligence on the part of his employer, whether or not he is liable for the injury apart from the Act. The significance of admitting that the fault was due to a third party is vividly illustrated in *Edwards v. Butlins Ltd*[4] where an employee sustained injuries when a calorifier exploded because, he averred, a release valve had been screwed down too tightly by the supplier's employee. The Lord Ordinary assoilzied the employer on the grounds that the employee had not shown who had screwed the valve down too tightly and had therefore not shown the defect was "the fault of a third party". On appeal, however, it was held that, as the employer of the injured employee had admitted that there was a defect in equipment caused by the fault of a third party, this itself rendered them liable.

"Equipment" is widely defined to include "any plant, machinery, vehicle, aircraft and clothing",[5] and has been held to include a bulk carrier,[6] industrial soap issued for cleaning mop heads,[7] and a flagstone to be laid by a road maintenance worker, on the grounds that there is no reason to suppose that Parliament had deliberately omitted the word "materials" in juxtaposition to the word "equipment".[8] On the other hand the concept which the Act involves is the "tools for the job" so that actuators which formed part of the braking system of axles which the pursuer was building were not "equipment"[9]; but this has to be distinguished from a case in which a heavy goods vehicle driver was injured when a load which had been packed in Japan shifted causing the lorry to overturn—the packaging was "equipment" for the purposes of the Act as it had been supplied to the driver for the purpose of his work, namely, the transportation of the load from one place to another.[10]

However, the Act contains some difficulties for the employee,[11] the most serious of which is the need to demonstrate that the

---

[3] *Donnelly v. Glasgow Corporation*, 1953 S.C. 107.
[4] 1998 S.L.T. 500 (I.H.).
[5] Employers Liability (Defective Equipment) Act 1969, s. 1(3).
[6] *Coltman v. Bibby Tankers Ltd (The "Derbyshire")* [1988] A.C. 276.
[7] *Ralston v. Greater Glasgow Health Board*, 1987 S.L.T. 386 (O.H.); and see *Yuille v. Daks Simpson Ltd*, 1984 S.L.T. 115.
[8] *Knowles v. Liverpool City Council* [1993] I.R.L.R. 6, CA.
[9] *Loch v. British Leyland Ltd U.K. Ltd*, 1975 S.L.T. (Notes) 67.
[10] *Davison v. A. R. Allen (t/a Allen's Transport)*, 1998 C.L. 333, county court.
[11] See, for example, Lang (1984) 47 M.L.R. 48.

defect is attributable wholly or partly to the fault of a third party, whether identifiable or not, and as Lang[12] has argued an employee will invariably fail where there is more than one cause of the accident if he cannot explain the precise nature of the alleged defect. It has been suggested that an employee injured by a defective product may be better served by an action of damages based on the Consumer Protection Act 1987, on the grounds that in the latter (a) proof of negligence is not required, (b) the definition of product is wider, (c) there is no requirement that the product be provided by the employer or that the employee be injured in the course of his employment, and (d) damages are not limited to personal injury although, in respect of damage to property, they are subject to a limit of £275.00; on balance the employee will have better prospects of success by raising an action against the employer under the 1969 Act.[13]

Information, instructions and warnings to employees

3.41 Of course the provision of inherently safe plant, materials and safety equipment itself may be insufficient. Although much depends on the circumstances,[14] it will frequently be necessary for the employer to take further steps, for example by instituting regular medical checks,[15] a programme of training,[16] or by providing information[17] about the risks and dangers involved in work activity and how these can, by using appropriate equipment, be reduced or eliminated. Where dangers are obvious it will normally be sufficient to issue simple instructions[18] which the employee can easily follow. Thus an employer was not liable for the injuries sustained by a window cleaner who fell when the handle on a sash gave way in his hand where the evidence demonstrated the

---

[12] *Op. cit.*

[13] Blaikie, 1993 S.L.T. 153.

[14] *McKinlay v. British Steel Corporation*, 1988 S.L.T. 810 (I.H.).

[15] In *Stokes v. Guest, Keen and Nettlefold* [1968] 1 W.L.R. 1776 it was held the employer had been negligent in not instituting a system of periodic medical examinations where it was known that employees who came into regular and prolonged exposure to mineral oil might develop scrotal warts which may become malignant. *Cf. Sorman v. Royal Scottish National Institution Board of Management*, 1961 S.L.T. 217, in which the court seems to have become unnecessarily concerned with compulsory examination and the individual's right to privacy of medical records.

[16] Of course the training must be such as would have prevented the accident or minimised the risk (*McCormick v. City of Aberdeen Council*, 1993 G.W.D. 1-54).

[17] This has been held to include an information system to advise the driver of a fire engine on the likely state of roads (*Spinks v. Strathclyde Regional Council* 1992 (unreported)).

[18] Thus the employers were liable for not instructing an employee to switch off a winch before attempting to free a snagged rope (*Wood v. Redpath*, 1993 G.W.D. 3-193).

employer had given clear instructions not to clean any window that looked difficult or dangerous and the employee could clearly see that the window was rotting,[19] and it has been held that a foundry labourer who was transferred to grinding work must have known of Raynaud's phenomenon (vibration white finger) so that his employer was not required to warn him of its dangers, which were not regarded as serious as it did not cause occupational disability and had not been made a prescribed industrial disease[20]; nor is an employer required to tell a person of a secretary's intelligence to take breaks from typing to avoid developing repetitive strain injury.[21] Where dangers are latent, however, clear, regular and more detailed information and advice will be required. Thus the employers were liable where hospital cleaners who contracted dermatitis were given no regular instructions or advice about the effectiveness of wearing rubber gloves which were available for their use[22]; the employers "had a duty to inform their servants . . . that they were exposed to a risk of irritant contact dermatitis and that the risk could be countered by wearing rubber gloves".[23] Similarly where employees engaged on general tasks in the printing industry developed upper limb disorders such as tenosynovitis, tennis-elbow and trigger-thumb, their employers were liable because they failed to give adequate warnings (including an explanation of the reason for, and the importance of reporting any wrist or arm pain immediately) before the work was begun.[24] Thus although it will be sufficient for the employer to warn of the risk of a general type of injury (for example hand injury caused by repetitive work) without specifying a particular condition which might be contracted (tenosynovitis),[25] recent decisions indicate that

---

[19] *Wilson v. Tyneside Window Cleaning Ltd* [1958] 2 All E.R. 265; and see *Vinnyey v. Star Paper Mills Ltd* [1965] 1 All E.R. 175. In *Woolger v. West Surrey and North East Hampshire Health Autrhority, The Times,* November 8, 1993, it was held that the method which a trained nurse would use to lift a patient was a matter for the nurse's individual judgment and a warning against lifting generally may suffice for an experienced employee (*Couper v. Remploy Ltd,* 1993 G.W.D. 27-1715).

[20] *White v. Holbrook Castings Ltd* [1985] I.R.L.R. 215, CA.; in fact Raynaud's phenomenon was made a prescribed (PDA11(a)–(c)) in 1985. And it has been held that it was not negligent for an employer to fail to warn an employee of the risks of developing "white finger" because a warning could cause unnecessary alarm to all the employees for the sake of the exceptional vulnerable one: *Joseph v. Ministry of Defence (The Times,* March 4, 1980); *sed quaere?*

[21] *Pickford v. Imperial Chemical Industries plc* [1998] I.R.L.R. 535 (HL).

[22] *Campbell v. Lothian Health Board,* 1987 S.L.T. 665, noted with approval in *Pape v. Cumbria County Council* [1991] I.R.L.R. 463.

[23] *ibid., per* Lord McCluskey at 667.

[24] *Ping v. Esselte-Letraset* [1992] C.L.Y 3211.

[25] *Wyeth v. Thames Case Ltd,* unreported case no. 86/533, CA; note the employers had frequently warned the employees of the need to rotate their individual tasks but they had refused to do so as this affected their work rate. *Cf. Kossinski v. Chrysler U.K. Ltd,* 1974 K.I.R. 225, CA.

Lord Radcliffe's advice in *Qualcast (Wolverhampton) Ltd v.*
Haynes[26] that courts be circumspect in filling out the duty to
provide adequate equipment with the much vaguer obligation of
encouraging, extorting or instructing workmen to make regular use
of what is provided, may now be regarded as unnecessarily
cautious.

Repetitive strain injury

3.42 In *Mughal v. Reuters Ltd*[27] Deputy High Court Judge Prosser
held that repetitive strain injury (RSI) was not a condition known
to medical science because it has no pathology and no clinical
symptoms that can be pointed to as confirming that a patient is
suffering from it and did not represent a condition promoted by
repetitive work; he therefore rejected the damages claim of the
plaintiff (a newspaper sub-editor who operated a VDU); although
"reflex sympathetic dystrophy" (RSD) had clinically observable
signs he did not know what the term meant.[28] However, *Mughal*
contrasts with *Lodge & McSherry v. British Telecom*[29] in which two
data processors were awarded damages for RSI as a result of poor
posture and prolonged and repetitive keyboard work, the repetitive
stereotype movement of unsupported arms and hands, the strain
being substantially added to by the strains which arose from the
poor working systems in place and the poor posture due to poor
ergonomics of the work station, unsuitable chairs and the uncor-
rected bad habits of the operators, and *Bettany v. Royal Doulton
(United Kingdom) Ltd*[30] in which, although none of the doctors
could detect any physical or demonstrable symptoms and the
medical evidence was divided as to the cause of the pain, it was
held on the balance of probabilities that Bettany, a crockery
painter, had suffered a work-related injury.[31] In light of the
approach adopted in *Mughal*, it is recommended where possible to
avoid general terms like "repetitive strain injury" and "work
related upper limb disorders" in favour of more specific medically
better recognised conditions like tenosynovitis, carpal tunnel syndrome, bursitis epicondylitis, etc. Where that is not possible there

---

[26] [1959] 2 All E.R. 28 (HL).
[27] [1993] I.R.L.R. 571.
[28] Note also that Judge Prosser observed that where employees work with
computer keyboards and visual display units each operator has to find by trial and
error the position which is comfortable for him/her and that there is little more the
employer can do except provide British Standard equipment, but this approach
seems to shift the responsibility from the employer to the employee.
[29] Unreported (1992).
[30] Unreported (1993).
[31] The employer's defence that the only cause of pain was psychological possibly
induced by the publicity about upper-limb disorders circulating in the industry was
rejected.

is no reason why a claim for non-specific musculo-skeletal should not succeed, provided there is evidence of the cause being work-related, even although the precise aetiology of the condition was not known.[31a]

Interestingly in *Bettany*, while the court accepted that the injury was work-related it did not agree that the employers had been negligent because (a) they had drawn the employee's attention to (i) the risk of upper limb disorder developing and (ii) the need to report promptly any pain or other symptoms, (b) there was in place a system which ensured that Bettany would be seen first by a nurse and then by the work's doctor, (c) the system also involved her being advised to consult her own general practitioner, (d) the system resulted in her being transferred to other work where rapid and repetitive movement was not required, and (e) all of these procedures had operated promptly and effectively after Bettany had reported pain. In *Mountenay (Hazard) v. Bernard Matthews plc*[32] the employer was liable for injuries (ganglion, tenosynovitis and trigger thumb) sustained by poultry processors (including new recruits) who had not received adequate warnings about the risks of contracting upper limb disorders and had not been subject to a proper system of job rotation.

Competent Staff

3.43 This facet of the employer's general duty requires reasonable care to be taken to ensure that employees are not exposed to risks by the appointment of fellow employees, and there would appear to be no reason in principle that this would extend to selection of others, for example independent contractors, with whom an employee may be required to work. Appointment of an inexperienced under manager and fireman,[33] a drunken wagon-driver,[34] an incompetent driver,[35] an unqualified fireman[36] and a negligent foreman[37] have all been held to give rise to claims by employees injured as a result of the incompetence of the staff.

ECONOMIC LOSS, NERVOUS SHOCK AND STRESS

3.44 It is clear that if an employee is injured as a result of his employer not introducing a safe system of work he is entitled to

---

[31a] See *Morrison v. Safeway Stores plc* (O.H., January 15, 1999, unreported) and *Alexander v. Midland Bank plc* [1999] I.R.L.R. 723.

[32] 1994 H.S.I.B. 219.

[33] *Black v. Fife Coal Company*, 1912 S.C. (H.L.) 33.

[34] *Donald v. Brand* (1862) 24 D. 295.

[35] *McCarten v. McRobbie*, 1909 S.C. 1020.

[36] *Ferguson v. N.B. Ry*, 1915 S.C. 566.

[37] *Flynn v. McGaw* (1891) 18 R. 554.

damages for all his loss which flows from the employer's delict. Thus an employee who injures his back will be entitled to damages to cover his pain and suffering, and any reduction in his earning power and, in that respect, his economic loss is recoverable. In such a case damages may be recovered for the physical injuries, the mental or psychological injuries—whether or not the employee was more susceptible than others to such injury[38]—and the economic damage resulting from the injuries. Such economic loss has been described as "derivative"[39] in that it arises as a consequence of physical injury to the person or property. In most cases injury sustained as result of breach of duty by an employer will be in the form of physical injury to the person. However, in *Reid v. Rush & Tompkins Group plc*[40] Reid, while acting in the course of his employment in Ethiopia, was injured due to the negligence of a third party/driver who could not be traced, and contended that his employers were liable for his economic losses in that (a) they had failed to arrange suitable insurance in the event of him sustaining injury as a result of the negligence of a third party or (b) they failed to advise him to obtain suitable insurance for himself. The first contention was rejected because it would be inappropriate for the common law to devise such a duty which Parliament could have, but had not, imposed,[41] and the second because the employer's duty was, in the absence of a contractual term, limited to protecting the employee against physical harm or disease, and such judicial conservatism has been endorsed by the English Court of Appeal which refused the extension of the duty of care to require a school to advise parents of the dangers of rugby football or by taking out insurance.[42] However, in a slightly different context a Scottish court has held that a receiver owed a duty of care to employees of the company not to terminate a pension scheme without first indicating his intention to do so,[43] and it may be that an obligation to advise of the need to take out special insurance or other protection would be more readily introduced through an implied contractual term, although this too was rejected in *Reid*.[44]

---

[38] *Graham v. David A. Hall Ltd*, 1996 S.L.T. 596.

[39] See A. Wilkinson and A. Forte, "Economic Loss", 1985 J.R. 1.

[40] [1990] 1 W.L.R. 212, CA.

[41] Ralph Gibson L.J. noted that "[t]he legislation has not in general extended the duty of compulsory employer's liability insurance in respect of employment out of this country [and] it has not been suggested that the master is required to provide personal accident insurance where in this country his servant is exposed to the risk of suffering injury . . . through the fault of a third party who cannot pay".

[42] *Van Oppen v. Clerk to the Bedford Charity Trustees* [1990] 1 W.L.R. 235, CA.

[43] *Larsen's Executrix v. Henderson*, 1990 S.L.T. 498.

[44] But note the willingness of the House of Lords in *Scally v. Southern Health and Social Services Board* [1991] I.R.L.R. 522 to imply a contractual term requiring employer to advise employees of the need to apply for a benefit within a certain time.

3.45 It is well established that where a person suffers nervous shock (without also suffering a physical injury) as a result of another's breach of duty he will have a claim against that other person.[45] However, nervous shock is a medical condition and is not to be confused with simply getting a fright,[46] and probably the correct analysis is that in certain cases damages are recoverable for psychiatric illness following nervous shock[47]; similarly the distinction has been made between extreme grief and a recognisable psychiatric illness, with the latter being actionable but the former not.[48] However, even that distinction is subject to qualification in that grief constituting pathological grief disorder is a recognisable psychiatric illness.[49] Accordingly where an employee suffers a psychiatric illness following nervous shock, without also having sustained a physical injury, he may be able to recover damages for his mental or psychological injury.[50] Typically this type of injury occurs as a result of a person being placed in a position in which he fears for his own safety[51] or where he witnesses a physical injury to another. Thus a seaman, although not on board the vessel, who suffered a psychiatric illness as a result of assisting bereaved relatives and identifying colleagues after he volunteered to assist in the *Herald of Free Enterprise* tragedy recovered damages for his injuries.[52] However, a person who was aboard a firefighting ship and witnessed the *Piper-Alpha* disaster was unsuccessful in his claim because the court was of the view that the platform operators could not reasonably have foreseen that someone in the plaintiff's position would suffer psychological injuries.[53] Although not connected with health and safety at work, *Alcock v. Chief Constable of*

---

[45] *Bourhill v. Young*, 1943 S.L.T. 105.

[46] *Simpson v. ICI*, 1983 S.L.T. 601; and see *Nicholls v. Rushton* (CA, unreported, April 19, 1992).

[47] *Alcock v. Chief Constable for South Yorkshire Police* [1991] 3 W.L.R. 1057.

[48] See *White v. Chief Constable of South Yorkshire Constabulary* [1999] I.R.L.R. 110 (HL) *per* Lord Steyn at para. 99. In *Reilly v. Merseyside Regional Health Authority, The Independent*, April 29, 1994, the Court of Appeal held that where employees were stuck in a lift and experienced extreme fear and claustrophobia there had been no recognisable psychiatric injury but merely "normal human emotion".

[49] *Vernon v. Bosley* [1997] 1 All E.R. 577, *per* Thorpe L.J.

[50] Although not within the scope of this chapter, a statutory duty to take practicable precautions to prevent danger (from an electrically charged cable) has been held not to be restricted to physical electrocution but to include the shock of seeing a workmate electrocuted: *Young v. Charles Church (Southern) Ltd, The Times*, May 1, 1997, CA. And see *Allison v. Isleburn Ltd*, 1999 S.C.L.R. 791 (O.H.).

[51] *Ross v. Glasgow Corporation*, 1919 S.C. 174; *Brown v. Glasgow Corporation*, 1922 S.C. 527; *Walker v. Pitlochry Motor Company*, 1930 S.C. 565; *Simpson v. ICI Ltd*, 1983 S.L.T. 601 (I.H.).

[52] *Dundee Courier*, October 3, 1991, regarding the settlement of Mr Rapley's claim.

[53] *McFarlane v. E. E. Caledonia Ltd, The Times*, September 30, 1993, CA; *The Scotsman*, August 30, 1993.

South Yorkshire[54] must now be regarded as the leading case. The House of Lords held that the victim of a psychiatric illness caused by the shock of witnessing injury to another had to show not only that such injury was reasonably foreseeable but that the relationship between the pursuer and the defender was sufficiently proximate and that the relationship between the victim and the persons injured was based on ties of love and affection, the closeness of which would have to be proved in each case; also there had to be propinquity of the pursuer in time and space to the accident or its immediate aftermath. The effect of applying these principles was that two plaintiffs who had been at the Hillsborough football ground at which a section of the crowd was crushed by an inrush of spectators, admitted at the discretion of a police officer, lost their claims because although they had, respectively, brothers and a brother-in-law in the section of the crowd affected there was no evidence that their relationships with them were "particularly close ties of love and affection".[55] There would seem to be no reason in principle why an employee who witnessed the injury or death of a close work colleague due to the negligence (personal or vicarious) of his employer could not recover damages for a psychiatric illness suffered as a result of hearing or seeing the accident, provided the conditions set out in *Alcock* were met. However, the issues have been re-examined recently in the context of employment in *White v. Chief Constable of South Yorkshire Constabulary*[56] in which the plaintiffs were police officers who were on duty at the same football stadium when the supporters were crushed to death by the inrush of fans. As a result of carrying out their duties the police officers suffered post-trauma stress disorder and they sued the Chief Constable, who admitted negligence but denied he owed the plaintiffs any duty of care. It was argued on behalf of the police officers that the case could be decided by reference to the duty of an employer to take reasonable care for the safety of his employees and to safeguard them from harm. However, Lord Steyn was of the view that it was a *non sequitur* to say that, because an employer was under a duty not to cause an employee physical injury the employer should, as a necessary consequence of that duty, be under a duty not to cause the employee psychiatric injury or harm because the rules of employers' liability are the rules of tort which contain restrictions on the recovery of damages for psychiatric injury. In so far as the police officers based their claims on being "rescuers", they failed, for in order for such claims to succeed Lord Steyn held

---

[54] [1991] 3 W.L.R. 1057 (HL).
[55] *ibid.*, per Lord Keith of Kinkel at p. 1101. On the other hand in the case of a filial relationship or the relationship between fiancés "the closest ties of love and affection fall to be presumed" (*ibid.*).
[56] [1999] I.R.L.R. 110 (HL).

that, in order to be able to recover, a rescuer must either expose himself to danger or at least believe that he was so doing.

3.46 Aside from the nervous shock cases, where the employee's injuries are entirely psychological there is no reason in principle why he cannot recover damages from an employer whose breach of duty resulted in the employee developing a psychiatric disorder or a depressive illness.[57] This situation falls to be distinguished from that considered in *White v. Chief Constable of South Yorkshire Constabulary* because it involves primary as opposed to secondary victims,[58] in that the police officers (secondary victims) suffered their psychiatric injury as a result of witnessing injury to others.[59] Although in *Petch v. Commissioners of Customs and Excise*[60] the case failed on the facts, it would seem to establish that (a) an employee's duty extends to taking reasonable care for the mental and psychological health of the employee caused by the strain of doing his work; (b) the employer will be in breach of that duty if, through their senior managers, they were aware or ought to have been aware that an employee's workload carried the real risk that he would have a breakdown or suffer some other psychological illness but took no steps to prevent it occurring; and (c) where an employee has already suffered a psychological illness, then on his return to work the employer may be in breach of his duty of care if he fails to take appropriate steps to ensure that the workload is adjusted or to arrange a transfer to less demanding work where possible. Indeed an employer has been held to be in beach of his duty of care where an employee suffered a mental breakdown as a result of the stress and anxiety created by his job.[61]

However, in Scotland it is necessary to show that the pursuer suffered a recognised psychiatric illness; it is not sufficient that the employer's conduct resulted in a nervous breakdown in the form of depression and anxiety.[61a] However, Lord Reed[61b] recognises liability for psychiatric illness has expanded, provided that such an illness is reasonably foreseeable by an ordinary bystander rather than a psychiatrist. Accordingly Rorrison's claim that her fellow employees should have foreseen that their conduct (unjustified criticism, pressure on time, lack of understanding of her role)

---

[57] *Johnstone v. Bloomsbury Health Authority* [1991] I.C.R. 269; *Petch v. Commissioners of Customs and Excise* [1993] I.C.R. 789, CA.

[58] [1999] I.R.L.R. 110 (HL), *per* Lord Hoffmann at 144.

[59] In the Court of Appeal, Rose L.J. thought that the police officers were primary victims partly because of the duty owed to them as employees.

[60] [1993] I.C.R. 789, CA; and see *Wilton v. Cornwall & Isles of Scilly Health Authority*, 1993 H.S.I.B. 482, CA.

[61] *Walker v. Northumberland C.C.* [1995] I.R.L.R. 35.

[61a] *Rorrison v. West Lothian College*, 1999 Rep. L.R. 102, O.H.

[61b] Strictly this part of Lord Reed's judgment is *obiter*.

would result in her feeling unsatisfied, frustrated and embarrassed, that was a "far cry from . . . a psychiatric disorder".

3.47 Clearly the likelihood or foreseeability of the type of injury is likely to reflect changes in the knowledge of (a) which types of individual, and (b) which types of employment are more susceptible to psychological or stress-related disorders. According to the report by the Health and Safety Executive, "Stress Research and Stress Management: putting theory to work",[62] both physical and psychosocial factors can have an effect on the incidence of occupational stress. When the knowledge that the presence of hazards and the lack of control over work content and speed of work have been found to induce stress while certain pathologies are associated with stress (heart disease, bronchitis, obesity and peptic ulcers) is placed in the context of risk assessment and health surveillance as required by the Management of Health and Safety at Work Regulations 1999, the test of foreseeability may be more easily overcome, and the connection between work rate and work load, and health and safety must now be regarded as beyond doubt in light of the Working Time Regulations 1998.[63] The Regulations proceed on the basis that in general, workers should not be required to work more than 48 hours in a week, on average, should have adequate rest breaks and paid annual leave and should have their night work restricted; particularly where the pattern of work according to which an employer organises work is such as to put health and safety of the worker at risk, the employer must ensure the worker is given adequate rest breaks.[64] While it is not possible to cite firm statistical evidence, work-related stress occurs frequently. As Amanda Griffiths has reported,[65] while the estimated prevalence of work-related disorders had changed little from 1990 to 1995, the contribution of musculo-skeletal disorders, and anxiety and depression has increased in relation to other diseases.[66] Psychological injury can frequently be caused by the behaviour of superiors and colleagues, and there are reported instances of employers settling actions in which employees have claimed to have suffered harm through bullying. However, such complaints have generally been based on statutory provisions which render unlawful subjecting an employee to a detriment on sexual or racial

---

[62] ISBN 07176 0084 8.

[63] See paras 4.48 *et seq.*

[64] Working Time Regulations 1998, reg. 8. And see the Discussion Document published in 1999 by the Health and Safety Commission "Managing Stress at Work" in which a Code of Practice is suggested.

[65] "Work-related illness in Great Britain", *Work & Stress*, 1998, vol. 12, no. 1, p. 1.

[66] When self reported work-related illness is concerned the largest category was found to be musculo-skeletal conditions (57%), while 25% reported a work-related stress, anxiety and depression or a physical condition ascribed to stress at work.

grounds,[67] or being harassed by not taking appropriate action to discipline the alleged harasser or conduct a serious investigation into the allegations. In such cases it is sufficient if the complainant shows that he or she has been subjected to a detriment, and it is not necessary that the treatment results in a physical or psychological injury—the tribunal being able to compensate a successful complainant for injury to feelings. However, there would seem to be no reason why an employer who fails to take action to prevent an employee suffering a psychological illness caused by bullying or harassment by colleagues or managers would not be in breach of his common law duty of care to the employee.[68] Indeed the matter has come before the Scottish courts as a preliminary matter in *Ward v. Scotrail Railways Ltd*[69] in which the pursuer claimed damages from her employer after she suffered an anxiety disorder and depression as a result of which she was absent from work and lost wages. The pursuer alleged that a fellow employee had written to her a letter which had a sexual connotation, stared at her, swapped shifts to be able to work alongside her, made efforts to show that he knew where she was working, and that after she had complained the employers took insufficient action to prevent her having to come into contact with the other employee. While the Lord Ordinary was unable to say that the alleged conduct could amount to "persecution" he was prepared to let the allegations of the employer's being in breach of their duty of care go to proof.

VICARIOUS RESPONSIBILITY

3.48 Vicarious responsibility is of importance to third parties injured as a result of the negligence of employees and to employees themselves whose employer has instituted and operates a safe system of work but which, because of the negligence of another employee, is not followed. Although the employer is not personally liable for any injury, in that he has fulfilled his duty by

---

[67] See for example *Porcelli v. Strathclyde Regional Council* [1986] I.C.R. 564 (I.H.); *Dobbin v. Denholm Ship Management (U.K.) Ltd* (E.T., S/5310/94, unreported).

[68] See, for example, the settlement—without liability being admitted—of the action brought by a residential social worker employed by Strathclyde Regional Council who took early retirement on health grounds when she became depressed; the summons alleged the employers failed in their duty of care by not providing a safe working environment, providing competent and co-operative colleagues and by not taking steps to reduce the risk of the pursuer's health suffering by steps to resolve the dispute between the pursuer and her superior or by removing one of them to a different place of work; *Ballantyne v. South Lanarkshire Council*, I.R.S. H.S.B, July 1996.

[69] 1999 S.C. 255, O.H.

instituting and operating a safe system of work, he will be vicariously liable for the injuries caused to an employee by virtue of the casual negligence of a fellow employee. This form of liability is based on the legal policy[70] enshrined in the maxims *qui facit per alium facit per se* (he who does something by another does it himself) and *repondeat superior* (let the master (or employer) be responsible) and may be seen as cutting across the general proposition that *culpa tenet suos auctores* (blame attaches to its originators). However, the last-mentioned maxim is observed in that although the employer may be vicariously liable for his employee's failure to take reasonable care, the employee himself is not released from liability[71] and, at least in the context of the employment contract, may be required to indemnify the employer for any loss the latter sustains as a result of his (the employee's) lack of care.[72]

3.49 The effect is that an employer is vicariously liable for the injuries sustained by one of his employees through the negligence of another employee provided the negligent employee was at the relevant time acting in the course of or in the scope of his employment.[73] Whether an employee is acting in the course of his employment is probably a mixed question of fact and law, although there are some useful general propositions. In *Kirby v. NCB*[74] Lord President Clyde indicated that there were four situations:

1. where the employer authorises the particular act;

2. where the employee performs an authorised act in an unauthorised way;

3. where the employee exceeds his authority by doing work he is not employed to do;

4. where the employee uses his employer's time or tools for his own purposes.

In the first two situations the employee will be acting within the scope of his employment, while in the last two situations he will

---

[70] For a detailed discussion of the legal policy see Atiyah, *Vicarious Liability* (1967) and Williams, "Vicarious Liability and the Master's Indemnity" (1957) 20 M.L.R. 220.

[71] Of course in most cases the action will be against the employer who, in the case of injury to an employee is required to maintain a policy of insurance; see *post*, para. 7.46.

[72] This is based on the employee's implied obligation to carry out his contractual duties with reasonable care; see Craig V. and Miller K., *Employment Law in Scotland* (2nd ed.), Chap. 3.

[73] It has been stated that there is no difference between "scope" of and "course" of employment: *McCready v. Securicor Ltd*, I.R.L.I.B. 460, 12, N.I.C.A.

[74] 1958 S.C. 514.

not. Accordingly, when Kirby and several other miners sustained injuries caused by one of them lighting a cigarette during a break, their employer was not vicariously liable as the offending employee was acting in breach of statutory provisions which prohibited possessing matches or cigarettes underground and was in an area where he was not supposed to be; he was in effect pursuing a purpose of his own. However, a deviation from an authorised method or route will not take the employee outside the scope of his employment. Accordingly, where a driver deviated from the authorised route he was acting in the course of his employment because he was still carrying out the predominant purpose of the authorised journey, namely, the transport of passengers.[75] Similarly a milkman was acting in the course of his employment when by driving negligently he injured a 13-year-old boy whom he had, contrary to his employer's instructions, engaged to assist him in making deliveries because he was merely performing his work in an unauthorised or prohibited way.[76] On the other hand, where the employee does something he is not employed to do (as distinct from merely adopting an unauthorised method) such as where a bus conductor drove a bus[77] or a miner did the work of a shot-firer,[78] he will not be acting in the course of his employment.[79]

3.50 Travelling to and from a place of work can present problems, although the modern trend is to view travel and refreshment breaks as in the course of employment.[80] Indeed in *Nancollas v. Insurance Officer*[81] the Court of Appeal has recognised that early cases which concentrate on whether an employee was carrying out his employer's instruction have been overtaken by developments in society and the relationship of employment which is no longer based on orders but on contractual rights and mutual cooperation. Thus where an employee, (who had to cover a wide area of the

---

[75] *Williams v. A. W. Hemphill Ltd*, 1966 S.C. (H.L.) 31. *Cf. Century Insurance Co. v. Northern Ireland RTB* [1942] A.C. 509 (tanker driver lighting match when awaiting transfer of petrol from tanker).

[76] *Rose v. Plenty and Co-operative Retail Service* [1976] I.R.L.R. 60, CA. *Cf. Portsea Island Mutual Co-operative Society v. Leyland* [1978] I.R.L.R. 556 (criminal vicarious liability).

[77] *Iqbal v. London Passenger Transport Executive, The Times*, June 6, 1973.

[78] *Alford v. N.C.B.*, 1951 S.C. 248.

[79] An employee's authority may be extended by implication: see *Neville v. C & A Modes*, 1945 S.C. 175, in which a shop assistant's authority was held to extend to protection of the employer's property so that a defamatory allegation that a customer had stolen a dress was in the course of the assistant's employment. *Cf. Heasmans v. Clarity Cleaning Co. Ltd, The Times*, January 23, 1987, CA (employee authorised to clean and disinfect telephones not authorised to use them).

[80] *Harvey v. R. G. O'Dell Ltd* [1958] 1 All E.R. 657. *Cf. Crook v. Derbyshire Stone*, 1956 1 W.L.R. 432.

[81] [1985] 1 All E.R. 833, CA.

country) travelled from his usual office in Worthing to the
Guildford office where it was decided that he should travel the next
day to Aldershot, it was held he was acting in the course of his
employment that (next) day when he left his home and went
directly to Aldershot[82] and in *Smith v. Stages and Darlington
Insulation Co. Ltd*[83] Lord Lowry set out the following propositions:

1. Except where the employee is obliged to use transport
   provided by his employer and employee travelling to his
   regular place of work from his ordinary residence is not
   acting in the course of his employment;

2. Travelling in the employer's time between workplaces or
   in the course of a peripatetic occupation is in the course
   of employment;

3. Receipt of wages but not travelling allowance indicates
   the employee is travelling in the employer's time even
   where he has discretion as to the mode and time of travel;

4. Travelling in the employer's time from his ordinary residence to a workplace other than his regular workplace, or
   in the course of a peripatetic occupation or to the scene of
   an emergency is in the course of employment[84];

5. A deviation from or interruption of a journey undertaken
   in the course of employment (unless merely incidental
   thereto) will for the time being (including overnight
   interruption) take the employee out of the course of his
   employment;

6. Return journeys are to be treated on the same footing as
   outward journeys.[85]

Thus where an employee (Stages) who normally worked at
Drakelow Power Station was, with a colleague instructed to work
for a week at Pembroke Power Station, he was acting in the course
of his employment when driving home, in his own car, immediately
after a long spell (from 8.30 a.m. Sunday to 8.30 a.m. on Monday)
of work, so that when his colleague was injured when (his) Stages'
fatigue caused an accident the employer was liable. Since the
employer could have prohibited the employee from travelling
immediately after the spell of work and had not done so the

---

[82] And see *Ball v. Insurance Officer* (C.A., case 85/88, unreported).

[83] [1988] I.R.L.R. 107 (HL).

[84] This would probably embrace any employee who is called out to respond to
perform a task unexpectedly and outside normal hours.

[85] However, averments must be sufficiently precise at least to infer a situation of
vicarious liability: *McGowan v. Mein*, 1975 S.L.T. (Sh.Ct) 10.

homeward journey was an authorised journey in the course of Stages' employment.[86]

3.51 Difficulty may also arise where the employee is engaged on a "frolic of his own"—a phrase which may describe an act of personal vengeance, or a prank or workplace horseplay. Thus a bus conductress whose private act of malice or spite caused her to signal the driver to move off when a passenger was in the process of alighting would not be acting in the course of her employment,[87] and the correct test is whether at the relevant time the employee was doing something he was authorised to do although doing it in an unauthorised way, and not whether the reasonable man would say the act was part and parcel of the employee's employment in the sense of being incidental to it.[88] Thus an apprentice who inserted a high pressure hose into the rectum of another apprentice, causing internal injuries, was not acting in the course of his employment[89]; nor was an employee who, as a prank, attempted to shut a colleague into a walk-in safe, even although the employee was authorised to open and close the safe at night or in an emergency because he was not acting for the employer but for his own purpose entirely,[90] and an employee who is taking industrial action is likely to be regarded as doing something insufficiently related to the authorised acts as not to be in the course of his employment.[91]

3.52 Generally where a person engages an independent contractor through the medium of a contract *locatio operis* that person is not liable for the negligence of the independent contractor,[92] although it has been argued that the increase in the number of atypical workers requires a reassessment of that proposition,[93] and recent cases may suggest that the Scottish courts are aware of the

---

[86] And see *Thomson v. The British Steel Corporation*, 1977 S.L.T. 26.

[87] *Power v. Central SMT*, 1949 S.C. 367. And see *Keppel Bus Co. Ltd v. Sa'ad Bin Ahmad* [1974] 1 W.L.R. 1082 (conductor assaulting passenger who had intervened on behalf of another passenger).

[88] *Aldred v. Nacanco* [1987] I.R.L.R. 292, CA (employee injured in washroom while another employee was trying to startle her), disapproving *Harrison v. Michelin Tyre Company Ltd* (1985) 1 All E.R. 919.

[89] *Smith v. Crossley Brothers* (1951) 95 S.J. 655.

[90] *McCready v. Securicor Ltd*, 1992 I.R.L.I.B. 460 at 12 (NICA).

[91] *General Engineering Services Ltd v. Kingston and St Andrew Corporation* [1989] I.C.R. 88 (PC) (firemen on a "go-slow").

[92] *Stephen v. Thurso Police Commissioners* (1876) 3 R. 535, *per* Lord Justice-Clerk Inglis at p. 540. And see *MacLean v. Russell* (1850) 12 D. 887; *Esso Petroleum Company Ltd v. Hall Russell & Co. Ltd, The Times*, October 7, 1988, HL. *Cf. Moir v. Wide Arc Services Ltd*, 1988 H.S.I.B. 146, regarding employment *pro hac vice*.

[93] See E. McKendrick, "Vicarious Liability and Independent Contractors—a Re-examination", 1990 53 M.L.R. 770.

results of applying too rigid a policy where atypical workers are involved.[94] However, it has to be emphasised that this general proposition assumes that the contractor is truly independent and not subject to control by the person who instructs him. Thus where a contractor/electrician who was called in by an employer to rectify an electrical fault negligently caused injury to an employee, it was held the employer who had called him in was vicariously liable for the injuries to the employee, and this was so even although the electrician was a person with special expertise because he was under the supervision and control of the employer.[95] In such a case the principal though not exclusive issue is "personal control or power over the acting or mode of acting of the subordinate" in the sense of "control or direction of the person in opposition to the mere right to object to the quality of the work done".[96] Additionally the instructor of an independent contractor may be personally liable for the actings of the contractor where the instructor has himself been negligent by, for example, careless selection of an incompetent contractor[97] instructing the contractor to carry out dangerous work,[98] or where work is to be done on a public road.[99] Finally an employer cannot escape liability by delegating the performance of a personal duty to others including a truly independent contractor, and this is of particular importance because such duties would include absolute duties imposed to protect employees,[1] duties laid on employers, and contractors carrying out certain types of work.[2] Many employment and health and safety statutes create vicarious liability for acts done by employees in the course of their employment, but the approach of courts and tribunals to the scope of the concept of "course of employment" in a statutory context has been coloured more by the layperson's understanding of course of employment and the policy issues of the statutes themselves,[3] and decisions regarding the meaning of course of employment in relation to statutory matters must be treated with care and are "not particularly helpful when

---

[94] See *Rennie v. Dorans*, 1991 S.L.T. 443; *Marshall v. William Sharp & Sons Ltd*, 1991 S.L.T. 114; *United Wholesale Grocers v. Sher* (1992) 12 C.L.Y 988.

[95] *Marshall v. William Sharp & Sons Ltd*, 1991 S.L.T. 114 (I.H.).

[96] *Stephen v. Thurso Police Commissioners* (1876) 3 R. 535, *per* Lord Gifford at 542, and adopted by Lord Justice-Clerk Ross in *Marshall v. William Sharp & Sons Ltd*, 1991 S.L.T. 114.

[97] See for example *Pinn v. Rew* (1916) 32 T.L.R. 451.

[98] See, for example, *Boyle v. Glasgow Corporation*, 1949 S.C. 254 and *Honeywill and Stein Ltd v. Larkin Brothers* [1934] 1 K.B. 191.

[99] See *Stephen v. Thurso Police Commissioners* (1876) 3 R. 535; *Tarry v. Ashton* (1876) 1 Q.B. 314; *Holliday v. National Telephone Company* [1899] 2 Q.B. 392.

[1] Factories Act 1961, ss. 12, 13 and 14.

[2] See for example *Donaghey v. O'Brien* [1966] 1 W.L.R. 1170. And see *Riverstone Meat Co. Pty Ltd v. Lancashire Shipping Co. Ltd* [1961] A.C. 807.

[3] See for example *Jones v. Tower Boot Company* [1997] I.C.R. 254, CA.

one is concerned with the meaning of course of employment in a common law context."[4]

Volenti non fit injuria

3.53 *Volenti non fit injuria*, literally "to one who is willing no legal wrong is done", may operate as a complete defence against an action based on a failure to take reasonable care. Thus in *Morris v. Murray*[5] the plaintiff, having spent the afternoon drinking with a friend, went for a flight in the friend's light aircraft. The aircraft, which was piloted by the plaintiff's friend, crashed injuring the plaintiff who sued his friend's representatives who pleaded *volenti*. The defence was sustained because the plaintiff had willingly boarded the plane knowing that the pilot was so drunk that he could not perform his duty to take reasonable care for the plaintiff's safety, while he, although drunk he was not incapable of appreciating the nature and extent of the risk involved. It may also be successfully pleaded in sporting situations, although it is unlikely that a spectator will be held to have accepted the risk of injury.[6] However, the scope for the defence to operate in the field of employment is limited in several ways.[7] First because there must be evidence[8] to the effect that the pursuer freely and voluntarily undertook the risk of the particular harm that in fact he suffered[9]: the very fact of an employment relationship may itself indicate that the employee did not freely accept that risk.[10] Secondly, as the

---

[4] *per* Lord Reed in *Ward v. Scotrail Railways Ltd*, 1999 S.C. 255.

[5] [1991] 2 W.L.R. 195, CA.

[6] *Murray v. Haringey Arena* [1951] 2 K.B. 146; *Wooldridge v. Sumner* [1962] 2 All E.R. 978. And see *Stair Memorial Encyclopaedia*, Vol. 19 (Recreation and Sports), para. 1242.

[7] In *Bowater v. Rowley Regis Corporation* [1944] 1 All E.R. 465, CA, Goddard L.J. urged that in the case of employer and employee *volenti* must be applied with extreme caution and "it can hardly ever be applicable where the act to which the servant is said to be 'volens' arises out of his ordinary duty unless the work is one in which danger is necessarily involved" and Scott L.J. opined that a man cannot "be truly willing unless he is in a position to choose freely and freedom of choice predicates not only full knowledge of the circumstances . . . so that he may be able to choose wisely"; there must be "absent from his mind any feeling of constraint so that nothing shall interfere with the freedom of his will".

[8] Whether the pursuer had freely and voluntarily accepted the risk is a question of fact: *Smith v. Baker* [1891] A.C. 326 (HL).

[9] Alternatively it may expressed as agreement by the pursuer; the defender would be discharged from his duty to take reasonable care for his (the pursuer's) safety or a waiver of that duty. For an interesting analysis of the maxim see A. J. E. Jaffey, "*Volenti non fit injuria*", Camb.L.J. 1985, p. 87.

[10] See *Cvetkovic v. Princes Holdings* (1989) 51 S.A.S.R. 365, in which an amusement arcade doorman who was injured while attempting to eject undesirable customers could not be met with the plea of *volenti* when acting on his superior's instructions where the employer had failed to take reasonable care for his safety by refusing to call the police as he (the doorman) had suggested.

employee must be *volens* (willing) and not merely *sciens* (knowing) it is not enough that the employee continued in the employment with full knowledge and understanding of the dangers involved.[11] Thirdly, the maxim only operates as a complete defence where the employer's liability is vicarious and not personal.[12] And too ready an application of *volenti* could result in the reintroduction of the doctrine of common employment which Parliament has deliberately abolished.[13]

3.54 A realistic appreciation of the employee's position is seen in *Smith v. Baker*[14] in which the House of Lords approved the Scottish decision of *Sword v. Cameron.*[15] Smith had, for a period of several months, been employed to drill holes in a rock face near a crane operated by fellow employees. The crane swung stones over Smith's head without warning and he admitted that he knew of the danger. He sued his employers when he was injured by a stone falling from the crane; their plea of *volenti* was rejected because although he undertook and continued in the employment with full knowledge and understanding of the danger arising from the systematic neglect to give warning, that did not justify the finding that he voluntarily undertook the risk of injury. However, although in more recent cases[16] the plea has been upheld it has to be noted that these are not cases in which the employer has been at fault. Thus in *Shatwell*[17] one of two men in a team of shot-firers was injured when the men combined to disobey their employer's order deliberately and act in contravention of a statutory prohibition even although they knew the risk involved; the plea of *volenti* was sustainable both in respect of an action by the injured man against the other and against the employer on the grounds of vicarious liability.

3.55 Consideration has also to be given to express contractual terms which may seek to limit or exclude liability—as in cases where the employee agrees to undertake the work in exchange for an additional premium. Can they operate as substitutes for *volenti*? As the basis for *volenti* is agreement it follows that an express term in an employment contract which excludes liability is capable of having the same effect. However, while it has to be noted that the

---

[11] *Smith v. Baker* [1981] A.C. 325 (HL); *ICI v. Shatwell* [1965] A.C. 656 (HL).

[12] *Wheeler v. New Merton Board Mills* [1933] K.B. 669; *ICI v. Shatwell* [1965] A.C. 656 (HL); *Hugh v. The National Coal Board*, 1972 S.C. 252.

[13] See para. 3.3 above.

[14] [1891] A.C. 326 (HL)

[15] 1839 1 D. 493.

[16] *ICI v. Shatwell* [1965] A.C. 656 (HL); *Hugh v. The National Coal Board*, 1972 S.C. 252.

[17] *ibid.*

Unfair Contract Terms Act 1977 applies to contracts of employment and apprenticeship,[18] a contractual term (or a non contractual notice) which purports to exclude or restrict liability for breach of duty arising in the course of any business in respect of death or personal injury shall be void.[19]

[18] Unfair Contract Terms Act 1977, s. 15(2)(b).
[19] Unfair Contract Terms Act 1977, s. 16, as amended by the Law Reform (Miscellaneous Provisions) (Scotland) Act 1990, s. 68

CHAPTER 4

THE STATUTORY REGIME

INTRODUCTION

4.1 This chapter concerns the importance of legislation as a mechanism for setting standards and enforcing health and safety law. For many years the legal position was regulated by older statutes like the Mines and Quarries Act 1954, the Offices, Shops and Railway Premises Act 1963 and particularly the Factories Act 1961 whose roots can be traced back to the Victorian era. One of the purposes of the Health and Safety at Work Act 1974 was to ensure the repeal of these earlier statutes and their replacement by regulations and voluntary codes of practice. By 1992 many of the older provisions had been repealed and replaced, and responsibility for enforcement of the legislation had passed to the Health and Safety Executive. The process of repeal has been hastened by regulations[1] made under section 15 of the Health and Safety at Work Act 1974 which are intended to comply with European Directives on this subject. These regulations repeal many of the remaining important provisions of the earlier legislation and they took effect on January 1, 1993. However, in some cases the repeal was not immediately effective[2] so that there was a transitional period when both the "European" Regulations and the older legislation were operative. At present, although the higher courts

---

[1] For the initial batch of Regulations see the Management of Health and Safety at Work Regulations 1999 (S.I. 1999 No. 3242); the Workplace (Health, Safety and Welfare) Regulations 1992 (S.I. 1992 No. 3004); the Provision and Use of Work Equipment Regulations 1998 (S.I. 1998 No. 2306); the Personal Protective Equipment at Work Regulations 1992 (S.I. 1992 No. 2966); the Manual Handling Operations Regulations 1992 (S.I. 1992 No. 2793) and the Health and Safety (Display Screen Equipment) Regulations 1992 (S.I. 1992 No. 2792).

[2] See, for example, the Workplace Regulations which make it clear that the regulations would not apply to existing workplaces until January 1, 1996 (although they do apply immediately to any new workplaces which came into existence after December 31, 1992). Equally, the fencing provisions of the Work Equipment Regulations did not apply to existing machinery provided before January 1, 1993, until January 1, 1997. This issue is discussed in *English v. North Lanarkshire Council*, 1999 S.C.L.R. 310.

may still be dealing with cases under the old law, the new legal regime based upon the regulatory framework created by European Directives and implemented in Great Britain by means of statutory instruments holds sway. As regards the initial "six pack" of Regulations made in 1992 and which came into force on January 1, 1993, all apart from the Management of Health and Safety at Work Regulations 1992[3] give rise to civil liability. Generally, the "European" Regulations apply to a much wider category of premises than simply factories or shops.

ROLE OF THE LAW

4.2 In Chapter 3 we saw how the common law regulated health and safety through the implied duties owed by employers to employees under the contract of employment and by the application of the general principles of negligence to compensate victims of accidents at work. The most significant role for the common law is to impose a civil liability on employers to take reasonable care for their employees' health and safety. It would be rare for the common law to impinge upon employers in another sense through the application of common law crimes. To be sure, there have been occasions when both employees[4] and employers[5] have been prosecuted or threatened with prosecution for culpable homicide for accidents which cause death. However, in the modern era it would be necessary to show that the accused was guilty of

---

[3] S.I. 1999 No. 3242, reg. 22 declares specifically that a breach of duty imposed by the Management Regulations does not confer a right of action in any civil proceedings (except for the risks to new or expectant mothers and the protection of young persons).

[4] See, for example, *William Paton and Richard McNab* (1845) 2 Broun 525. In March 1990, a plumber, Ross Fontana, was convicted of culpable homicide for causing the deaths of two people through the improper installation of a gas fire. See *Glasgow Herald*, March 30, 1990.

[5] See, for example, *William Baillie and James McCurrach* (1870) 1 Couper 442. In the modern era the critical issue has been whether it is possible for corporate employers to be prosecuted for culpable homicide. The prosecution of P. & O. European Ferries for manslaughter following the disaster aboard the *Herald of Free Enterprise* in 1987 failed largely because the trial judge was not satisfied that the company's directors and senior managers ought to have known that there was an obvious and serious risk when the ship sailed with its bow doors open. See D. Bergman, "Recklessness in the Boardroom" (1990) 140 N.L.J. 1496. The failure of this prosecution undoubtedly influenced the decision of the Lord Advocate not to prosecute Occidental Petroleum for corporate culpable homicide after the *Piper Alpha* disaster. The difficulties of prosecuting companies for crimes are discussed by J. Ross in "Corporate Liability for Crime", 1990 S.L.T. (News) 265. For a consideration of the more recent case law and analysis of corporate responsibility under different statutes, see J. Ross, "Corporate Criminal Responsibility: One Form or Many Forms", 1999 J.R. 49.

gross or wicked negligence.[6] Generally, however, the fact that other crimes which involve injury to a victim are crimes of intention minimises their scope in the context of accidents at work.

4.3 Nonetheless, when we turn to examine the statutory law on health and safety it is clear that both the civil law and the criminal law have a role to play. This is because breach of many of the important statutes can give rise to both a civil damages action and a criminal penalty.[7] As far as the civil law is concerned statute law not only creates another basis for legal action by an employee but also enables a more flexible approach as regards the standard of care to which employers must adhere. As we have seen, the common law operates in a way which generally obliges employers to take reasonable care.[8] In the civil area, the provisions of a statute can be drafted in such a way that the duty owed by employers does not have to be based upon the common law standard of negligence. Statute can adopt a more positive role by laying down obligations which employers must fulfil irrespective of the practical difficulties. In such circumstances the liability owed by employers can be strict with minimal scope for defences.[9] Moreover, statute can also deal specifically with particularly dangerous operations or processes of manufacture. It has been one of the features of British health and safety laws in the past that there has been much delegated legislation where laws have been made which are directed at specific industries or types of activity. Indeed, until the Health and Safety at Work Act 1974 the major health and safety statutes[10] were themselves aimed at premises where particular forms of work were being carried out.

4.4 It is also true that in the criminal area statutory provisions can move away from the application of *mens rea* principles towards

---

[6] The development of the law in this area is discussed by G. H. Gordon, *The Criminal Law of Scotland*, (2nd ed., 1978) at paras 26–01 to 26–16. He points out that prosecutions for culpable homicide of this type are now largely confined to road traffic cases and argues that prosecutions for accidents at work have dried up because of "the complex nature of modern factories and mines which makes it very difficult to single out the negligent party" (para. 26.09). Instead, prosecutions under the Health and Safety at Work Act 1974 are much more likely. See, for example, the successful prosecutions of Arco British Ltd and Odeco Ltd for breaches arising out of the death of a wireless operator aboard the drilling rig, *Ocean Odyssey*, in the North Sea. See *The Scotsman*, August 11, 1993.

[7] There can be no civil liability for breach of the general duties created by ss. 2–8 of the Health and Safety at Work Act; see 1974 Act, s. 47(1). However, s. 47(2) declares that any regulations made under s. 15 of the 1974 Act do give rise to civil liability for breach of statutory duty unless the regulations provide otherwise.

[8] Although, as we saw in Chap. 3, the extent of this duty will vary depending upon the circumstances and the proclivities of the employee. See, for example, *Porteous v. NCB*, 1967 S.L.T. 117.

[9] See, for example, *Millar v. Galashiels Gas Co.*, 1949 S.C. (H.L.) 31.

[10] Mines and Quarries Act 1954; Factories Act 1961 and Offices, Shops and Railway Premises Act 1963.

other standards of criminality which reduce the importance of the mental element or avoid it entirely. This enables statutory criminal law to exercise a regulatory role and to fashion offences consistent with the risks. Thus one of the principal reasons for enacting statutory provisions on health and safety has been to create offences which need not necessarily be based on the requirement of intention or *mens rea*. Indeed, the earliest statutes were largely enforced by means of penalties in the criminal courts.[11] In modern times, the Health and Safety at Work Act 1974, section 47, excludes civil liability for breach of any of the duties specified in sections 2 to 7 or any contravention of section 8. Thus as far as the general duties created by the 1974 Act are concerned, the only appropriate means of enforcement through the courts is by criminal prosecution. As regards the earlier health and safety statutes (Mines and Quarries Act 1954, Factories Act 1961 and Offices, Shops and Railway Premises Act 1963), they were capable of enforcement both through criminal prosecution and by civil damages actions. Moreover, as has already been noted, as far as the "European" Regulations are concerned, with the exception of the Management of Health and Safety at Work Regulations 1999,[12] the other five sets of regulations which took effect on January 1, 1993 also permit the possibility of dual enforcement.

Statutory Criminal Law

4.5 It is important, therefore, to consider the nature, role and significance of statutory offences under health and safety legislation before considering those statutory provisions which permit civil actions for breach of statutory duty. It is worth remembering, of course, that under the Health and Safety at Work Act 1974 the only means of enforcing the general duties is by criminal penalty and, therefore, we shall discuss these separately.[13] Some statutory provisions like the Management Regulations or the Construction (Design and Management) Regulations 1994[14] are enforced primarily by criminal sanction but do permit civil action in certain limited circumstances.[15] In other areas such as the other five original "European" Regulations it is quite possible for a particular breach to give rise to both criminal penalty and civil liability. For

---

[11] J. Munkman, *Employer's Liability*, (11th ed., 1990) at p. 17.
[12] S.I. 1999 No. 3242.
[13] See Chap. 5.
[14] S.I. 1994 No. 3140.
[15] In the case of the Management Regulations, this operates in relation to the risks applying to new and expectant mothers; reg. 15. In the case of the Construction (Design and Management) Regulations, they permit civil liability in only two circumstances relating to the construction phase starting without a health and safety plan and co-operation between contractors; reg. 21.

present purposes we shall consider those statutes where civil action is also competent and examine the interaction between the civil and criminal law under such provisions.

4.6 Most of the older statutes also contained provisions for the creation of offences.[16] This had implications for the way that the provisions of such statutes were interpreted.[17] However, it is also important generally to establish the fundamental requirements for the commission of an offence. One important issue has been to decide whether or not the offence requires *mens rea*. If *mens rea* is not required then there would be no need to establish a mental element; for the commission of the offence it would be enough for conviction that the accused committed the unlawful act regardless of his knowledge or intention.

4.7 In law there is a presumption in favour of the application of *mens rea* in criminal statutes—though this presumption can be rebutted. As Sheriff Gordon points out this is a matter which is likely to depend upon the terms of the statutory provision. However, there are criteria which the courts have developed for deciding whether or not *mens rea* is required for the commission of a statutory offence. The most important are the wording of the statutory provision creating the offence, the gravity of the offence, the nature of the penalty and the object of the statute.[18] Looking to this final element, the fact that health and safety statutes involve "the regulation for the public welfare of a particular activity"[19] means that offences under them generally do not require *mens rea* unless the particular provision requires it. Thus criminal responsibility is strict, although all the statutes provide for certain defences and, in many cases, permit the generic defence that the accused had done all that was reasonably practicable in the circumstances.

Breach of Statutory Duty

4.8 As we have seen, it is arguable that the primary means of enforcing the older legislation was by criminal prosecution. The question which is now to be discussed is how health and safety legislation can also give a right of civil action to those who are injured or killed in accidents caused by a contravention of the

---

[16] See, for example, the Factories Act 1961, s.155(1), which made the occupier guilty of offences for contraventions of the Act.

[17] See below.

[18] See generally, G. H. Gordon, *The Criminal Law of Scotland* (2nd ed., 1978), Chap. 8.

[19] *Lim Chin Aik v. The Queen* [1963] A.C. 160, at 174.

statutory provisions. In the case of regulations made under the Health and Safety at Work Act 1974, section 15, it is declared specifically that a breach of a duty created by them does give rise to civil liability where damage is caused unless the regulations provide otherwise.[20] In any event, nowadays, a civil action for breach of statutory duty is well-established. The basic requirement for such an action is that where a statute places obligations on an individual in such a way that a particular category of persons is intended to benefit from such a duty, a person who falls within this category and who is injured as a result of a contravention has a right to sue. As Lord Kinnear put it in the context of coal mines legislation in *Black v. Fife Coal Co. Ltd*[21]:

> "There is no reasonable ground for maintaining that a pro-
> ceeding by way of penalty is the only remedy allowed by the
> statute . . . . We are to consider the scope and purpose of the
> statute and in particular for whose benefit it is intended. Now
> the object of the present statute is plain. It was intended to
> compel mineowners to make due provision for the safety of
> the men working in their mines, and the persons for whom all
> those rules are to be enforced are the persons exposed to
> danger. But when a duty of this kind is imposed for particular
> persons, there arises at common law a correlative right in
> those persons who may be injured by its contravention."

4.9 Before an action based on breach of statutory duty will be competent the following basic elements[22] must be established:

(1) that the statutory provision, properly construed, imposes upon the defender a duty which is intended to protect a class of persons of which the pursuer was one;

(2) that the defender has failed to perform this duty;

(3) that this breach of duty has caused injury to the pursuer of a kind contemplated by the statute.

It is intended to say a few words about each of these elements in the context of health and safety legislation.

4.10 As regards the first element, it is clear that the relevant statutory provision must be examined to ensure that it places a direct obligation on the defender. As we shall see, there may be

---

[20] 1974 Act, s. 47(2).
[21] 1912 S.C. (H.L.) 33.
[22] For a more detailed and exhaustive analysis see D. M. Walker, *The Law of Delict in Scotland*, (2nd ed., 1981), Chap. 9.

circumstances where the language of the statute is not sufficiently mandatory to be capable of creating an enforceable duty.[23] If the statute does create a duty it is necessary for that duty to be placed on the defender. In *Gallagher v. Wimpey & Co. Ltd*,[24] for example, the court had to decide whether an obligation to fence machinery which the statute had placed on persons who work or use it gave the pursuer a cause of action against his employer. Finally, under the first element it must be shown that the pursuer is one of the class of persons who is intended to benefit from the provision. In *Hartley v. Mayoh & Co.*,[25] for example, it was held that a fireman who was electrocuted when fighting a fire in a factory could not sue for breach of statutory duty because the relevant statutory provision was only for the benefit of persons employed. In the context of health and safety legislation it has generally been assumed that the class of persons who are intended to benefit are employees. However, much will turn on the construction of the relevant statutory provision and there may be occasions where the intention is to benefit a broader category of person.[26]

4.11 As far as the second element is concerned it is for the pursuer to show two things. First, the standard of the duty imposed upon the defender, and second, the fact that the duty was breached by the required standard not having been satisfied. Under factories legislation the standard placed upon defenders could be strict. In *John Summers & Sons Ltd v. Frost*,[27] for example, a factory owner was held to have breached the fencing provisions of the Factories Act which required that dangerous machinery had to be securely fenced even although to have fenced the dangerous part in this case would have made it impossible to use the machine. In other cases the statutory duty is hedged by requirements that the obligation is to act so far as is reasonably practicable[28] or that it is

---

[23] See the speech of Lord Kinnear in *Black v. Fife Coal Co. Ltd*, 1912 S.C. (H.L.) 33; and *Harrison v. NCB* [1951] A.C. 639.

[24] 1951 S.C. 515.

[25] [1954] 1 Q.B. 383.

[26] *Wigley v. British Vinegars Ltd* [1964] A.C. 307 (under the Factories Act 1961, s. 29, "any person" was construed as to benefit all those who entered the factory in order to work there so that a window cleaner who was employed by the factory owner as an independent contractor was covered).

[27] [1955] A.C. 740.

[28] See, for example, Factories Act 1961, s. 29(1), as regards the provision of safe means of access, and the Workplace Regulations 1992, reg. 12, which requires every floor and the surface of every traffic route be kept free from obstructions. Both provisions impose a standard of reasonable practicability. "Practicable" is that which is capable of being carried out in action or feasible: *Lee v. Nursery Furnishings Ltd* [1945] 1 All E.R. 387. The addition of "reasonably" creates a qualification which involves balancing the quantum of risk on the one hand and the measures necessary to avert the risk on the other. See *Sharp v. Coltness Iron Co. Ltd*, 1937 S.C. (H.L.) 68; and *Edwards v. NCB* [1949] 1 K.B. 704, approved by the House of Lords in *Marshall v. Gotham Co. Ltd* [1954] A.C. 360.

impracticable[29] to avoid or prevent the contravention. It will be for the court to establish whether or not the defender has breached the relevant standard based upon its interpretation of the statutory provision and the facts of the case. In *Latimer v. AEC Ltd*,[30] for example, it was held that there had been no breach of the statutory duty to ensure that floors were properly maintained where it was clear that the lack of safety arose from some transient or exceptional condition.

4.12 Under the third requirement it is necessary to show that the harm that the pursuer suffered was of a type which the statute was intended to protect. A simple example of this arises from the old case of *Gorris v. Scott*[31] where sheep were swept overboard from a ship because of an absence of pens. However, the subsequent damages action failed because the relevant statute required that the pens be provided in order to prevent disease and not to prevent accidents. Clearly everything depends upon the court's interpretation of the purpose of the statute. In *Grant v. NCB*,[32] the fact that the House of Lords interpreted the mines and quarries legislation as intending to safeguard miners against accidents generally and not just against the collapse of the roof meant that the pursuer had a cause of action when he was injured by the derailment of a bogie. In the context of the fencing of machines under factories legislation, one critical question has been to decide what is the purpose of such fencing. Generally the court's approach has been to require fencing in order to prevent the worker from coming into contact with the machine. This means that workers cannot sue when they are injured when either part of the material being worked, or part of the machine, flies out.[33]

4.13 Finally, under the third requirement it is necessary to establish a causal link between the breach of duty and the injury. The onus is upon the employee to prove on a balance of probabilities that the breach of duty caused or materially contributed to his injuries.[34] It is significant that the test applies the lesser

---

[29] See, for example, the Mines and Quarries Act 1954, s. 157, which provided a defence for a contravention of the Act if it was impracticable to avoid or prevent the contravention. This phrase has been interpreted strictly since it relieves a statutory obligation. Thus the fact that compliance with the statutory duty would involve unreasonable time and expense is irrelevant. See generally *Jayne v. NCB* [1963] 2 All E.R. 220.

[30] [1954] A.C. 643.

[31] (1874) L.R. 9 Ex. 125.

[32] 1956 S.C. (H.L.) 48.

[33] *Carroll v. Andrew Barclay & Sons Ltd*, 1948 S.C. (H.L.) 100; *Nicholls v. Austin (Leyton) Ltd* [1946] A.C. 493.

[34] *Wardlaw v. Bonnington Castings Ltd*, 1956 S.C. (H.L.) 26, *per* Lord Reid at 31.

standard of material contribution. This can be particularly important in industrial disease cases where it would be exceedingly difficult to prove that the breach was the sole or exclusive cause of the disease. Usually, prolonged exposure to the disease-creating conditions will suffice,[35] and an inference of liability may be created where, after a person has been exposed to conditions likely to cause the disease, it starts in a way typical of the way the disease would start in such conditions.[36] On the other hand, it is a potential defence in a case where injuries were alleged to have been caused by a failure to fulfil a statutory duty to provide safety equipment for the employer to show that the employee would not have used that equipment even if it had been provided.[37]

4.14 Unless the above requirements can be established it will not be competent for there to be a civil action for breach of statutory duty. Moreover, it does not follow that simply because some provisions of a statute do give rise to an action for breach of statutory duty that this is true for all the provisions of an Act. There was some doubt, for example, as to whether breaches of the welfare provisions of the Factories Act 1961 (namely sections 57 to 60) could give rise to actions for breach of statutory duty. It seemed that whilst breaches of section 58(1) (provisions of washing facilities) and section 59(1) (accommodation for clothing) gave rise to civil liability, the interpretation of the remaining provisions was uncertain.[38] These provisions have been repealed and replaced by regulations 21 to 25 of the Workplace (Health, Safety and Welfare) Provisions 1992,[39] and it will be interesting to see to what extent the courts construe these essentially welfare provisions as giving rise to civil liability for breach of statutory duty.

4.15 It is well established that an employer cannot argue as a defence in an action for breach of statutory duty that he delegated the duties to other persons such as employees or independent contractors. As Lord Atkin declared in *McMullan v. Lochgelly Iron & Coal Co. Ltd*[40]; "the duty is imposed upon the employer, and it is irrelevant whether his servants had disregarded his instructions or whether he knew or not of the breach". Generally, therefore, it is

---

[35] *Quinn v. Cameron & Roberton Ltd*, 1957 S.C. (H.L.) 22.

[36] *Gardiner v. Motherwell Machinery & Scrap Co. Ltd*, 1961 S.C. (H.L.) 1. *Cf. McGhee v. NCB*, 1973 S.L.T. 14.

[37] *Qualcast (Wolverhamton) Ltd v. Haynes* [1959] A.C. 743; *McWilliams v. Sir Wm Arrol & Co. Ltd*, 1962 S.C. (H.L.) 70.

[38] See the General Introduction to Redgrave, Fife and Machin, *Health and Safety* (1990). The matter is discussed by the First Division of the Court of Session in *Reid v. Westfield Paper Co. Ltd*, 1957 S.C. 218.

[39] S.I. 1992 No. 3004.

[40] 1933 S.C. (H.L.) 64.

no defence for the employer to argue that he delegated the duty to others. However, there is certainly one type of case where it is a defence for the employer to show that the pursuer was injured as a result of a breach of duty which had been delegated, so long as the delegation is to the injured employee himself. In *Smith v. A. Baveystock & Co. Ltd*,[41] for example, a skilled operator was held to have no remedy when he was injured by a circular saw when it was proved that he had not adjusted the guard properly before use as the regulations required. Essentially, in this type of case the issue is to decide—whose fault was it?[42]

4.16 An action for breach of statutory duty has been described as an action for negligence.[43] This is true in the sense that the pursuer must prove the defender's breach of duty and establish a causal connection between the breach and the harm suffered. However, in another sense the analogy can be somewhat misleading because the standard of care required of a defender under statute can differ from that required by the common law. An action for breach of statutory duty may entail fulfilling the common law standard of reasonable care. Yet, as we have seen, everything turns on the statutory language and it is clear that a statutory provision can impose a higher standard than the common so that liability can be strict or even absolute. In *Millar v. Galashiels Gas Co. Ltd*,[44] for example, the occupiers were held liable for the death of a workman who was killed by the failure of an automatic braking system in a lift, despite the fact that the failure was one which nobody could account for and which could not have been detected beforehand.

4.17 Given the different basis for the action, therefore, there is nothing to prevent a pursuer raising both a common law action for negligence and an action for breach of statutory duty. Moreover, the competent defences can vary as between the two types of action. For example, although the defence of *volenti non fit injuria* is relevant in common law actions, it is not generally available in cases of breach of statutory duty[45] unless employees have breached a statutory duty which is placed upon them for their own safety.[46]

4.18 The above discussion concerned cases where the statute is silent as regards the potential for civil damages actions, and the

---

[41] [1945] 1 All E.R. 531.
[42] See Pearson J. in *Ginty v. Belmont Building Supplies Ltd* [1959] 1 All E.R. 414.
[43] *McMullan v. Lochgelly Iron & Coal Co. Ltd*, 1933 S.C. (H.L.) 64.
[44] 1949 S.C. (H.L.) 31. See also the speech of Lord Normand in *Carroll v. Andrew Barclay & Sons Ltd*, 1948 S.C. (H.L.) 100, who argued that the duty to fence dangerous machinery under the Factories Act was absolute because the duty must be actually fulfilled.
[45] *Wheeler v. New Merton Board Mills Ltd* [1933] 2 K.B. 669, CA.
[46] *ICI Ltd v. Shatwell* [1965] A.C. 656.

courts have had to construe the statutory provisions in accordance with the above rules in order to discover whether a civil damages action for breach of statutory duty is competent. Obviously, there is nothing to prevent the statute declaring specifically that a breach of one of its provisions will give rise to civil liability. As already indicated, this is exactly the position as regards regulations which are made under section 15(1) of the Health and Safety at Work Act 1974. As section 47(2) of the 1974 Act makes clear, breach of a duty imposed by any such regulations is, so far as it causes damage,[47] actionable unless the regulations provide otherwise. As we know, apart from a breach of the Management Regulations, breaches of the other five original "European" Regulations do give rise to civil liability.

The Interpretation of Health and Safety Statutes

4.19 As we have seen, the original health and safety legislation in statutes like the Mines and Quarries Act 1954, the Factories Act 1961 and the Offices, Shops and Railway Premises Act 1963 create criminal offences so that they could have been considered as being primarily penal in nature. There is a rule of statutory interpretation in favour of the strict construction of such statutes so that where a provision is ambiguous the benefit of the doubt must be given to the person against whom the penalty is directed.[48] However, it is also the case that health and safety statutes are intended to protect workers so that they could just as easily be construed as being remedial. In this latter case the statute should be read in such a way as to effect its object in so far as the wording fairly and reasonably permits.[49] This entails adopting an interpretation which seeks to prevent accidents at work.[50] Generally it has been this latter approach which has been favoured as regards health and safety statutes.[51] If the Act is intended to protect workers it would be "an illegitimate method of interpretation" to interpret the statute in such a way as to reduce that protection.[52] However, courts must be careful when interpreting health and safety legislation that they do not place a strained meaning on the statutory language simply in order to achieve a social purpose.[53]

---

[47] "Damage" includes the death of, or injury to, any person (including any disease and any impairment of a person's physical or mental condition); s. 47(6).

[48] See *Stair Memorial Encyclopaedia*, Vol. 12, para. 1184.

[49] *Harrison v. NCB* [1951] A.C. 639.

[50] *Norris v. Syndic Manufacturing Co. Ltd* [1952] 2 Q.B. 135, CA.

[51] In *McCarthy v. Coldair Ltd* [1951] 2 T.L.R. 1226, Lord Denning argued that the rule in favour of a strict construction was a rule of last resort which should only be applied when other rules fail.

[52] See the speech of Viscount Simonds in *John Summers & Sons Ltd v. Frost* [1955] A.C. 740 at 751.

[53] See the speech of Lord Diplock in *Haigh v. Charles W. Ireland Ltd*, 1974 S.L.T. 34.

The Regulatory Framework

4.20 It is now time to consider some of the most important statutory provisions which regulate health and safety at work and which enable employees to sue their employers when they are injured at work because of a breach of the statutory provisions. Since the repeal of the fencing provisions in sections 12 to 16 of the Factories Act 1961 by the Provision and Use of Work Equipment Regulations 1992,[54] regulation 27 and Schedule 2, and the repeal of the workplace safety requirements in sections 28 and 29 of the Factories Act 1961 by the Workplace (Health, Safety and Welfare) Regulations 1992, regulation 27 and Schedule 2, it is only necessary to consider these Regulations on order to obtain an appreciation of the present state of the law.

A. PRESENT STATUTORY ARRANGEMENTS

The Provision and Use of Work Equipment Regulations 1998

4.21 These Regulations revoke and re-enact the original regulations which were made in 1992 and which were intended to implement E.C. Directive 89/655/EEC on the minimum safety and health requirements for the use of work equipment. The regulations are augmented by Guidance Notes published by the Health and Safety Executive, and the current regulations came into force on December 5, 1998. The new regulations ensure compliance with both E.C. Directive 89/655/EEC and E.C. Directive 95/63/EEC and incorporate provisions regarding the safety of power presses which were previously to be found in the Power Presses Regulations 1965.[55] They apply to employers in Great Britain and in the North Sea[56] in respect of work equipment provided for use or used by employees at work.[57] They also apply to self-employed persons as regards their own work equipment and to other persons who have control of work equipment, who use or supervise or manage the use of work equipment, or who control the way in which work equipment is used.[58] Generally, the regulations do not apply to a ship's work equipment—although there are special rules which amongst other things make the shore employer responsible for

---

[54] See now the Provision and Use of Work Equipment Regulations 1998 (S.I. 1998 No. 2306).

[55] S.I. 1965 No. 1441.

[56] reg. 3(1). See the Health and Safety at Work Act 1974 (Application Outside Great Britain) Order 1995 (S.I. 1995 No. 263).

[57] reg. 3(2).

[58] reg. 3(3) and (4).

ensuring that the work equipment complies with merchant shipping requirements.[59] It has been argued that since the regulations are intended to give effect to a European Directive, an approach based on the Factories Act 1961 is fundamentally misconceived.[59a]

4.22 "Work equipment" means any machinery, appliance, apparatus, tool or installation for use at work.[60] This phrase should be given its ordinary meaning so that, for example, "apparatus" is wide enough to cover bolts used to join two pieces of rail.[60a] "Use" is also broadly defined to mean any activity involving work equipment and includes starting, stopping, programming, setting, transporting, repairing, modifying, maintaining, servicing and cleaning.[61]

4.23 The regulations contain detailed provisions concerning the suitability of work equipment. Every employer must ensure that work equipment is so constructed or adapted as to be suitable[62] for the purpose for which it is used or provided.[63] In selecting work equipment, employers must have regard to the working conditions and to the risks to the health and safety of persons which exist in the premises or undertaking in which that equipment is to be used, and any additional risk posed by its use.[64] Employers must also ensure that work equipment is used only for operations for which, and under conditions for which, it is suitable.[65] These provisions are central and address the safety of work equipment in three ways. They are intended to ensure the initial integrity of work equipment, the place where it will be used, and the purpose for which it will be used.

4.24 Work equipment must be maintained in an efficient state, in efficient working order and in good repair, and where employers

---

[59] See generally reg. 3(6)–(10).

[59a] *Per* Lord Reed in *English v. North Lanarkshire Council*, 1999 S.C.L.R. 310, 319.

[60] reg. 2(1). The Guidance Notes make clear work equipment can include single machines such as power presses and photocopiers, tools such as portable drills and apparatus such as laboratory equipment like bunsen burners. The definition also includes arrangements for the assembly of components like a bottling plant. Work equipment does not include livestock, substances like acids, structural items, and private cars.

[60a] *Kelly v. First Engineering Ltd*, 1999 G.W.D. 21-1016.

[61] reg. 2(1).

[62] "Suitable" means suitable in any respect which it is reasonably foreseeable will affect the health and safety of any person; reg. 4(4).

[63] reg. 4(1). This provision has been interpreted broadly to cover equipment in use for its specific purpose but also whilst being cleaned: *English v. North Lanarkshire Council*, 1999 S.C.L.R. 310.

[64] reg. 4(2).

[65] reg. 4(3).

maintain a maintenance log, that log must be kept up to date.[66] The Guidance Notes make clear that "efficient" relates to how the condition of the equipment might affect health and safety; it is not concerned with productivity. There is no legal requirement that a maintenance log be kept, though the Guidance Notes certainly recommend this. Where the use of work equipment is likely to involve a specific risk to health and safety, regulation 7 requires employers to restrict its use, repair and maintenance to specific persons. It is the view of the Health and Safety Executive that this particular regulation does not require employers to take any additional measures other than those required by existing legislation. It is also important for employers to ensure that, where the safety of work equipment depends upon the installation conditions, inspection arrangements are in place when it is first installed and at regular intervals thereafter.[67]

4.25 There are also requirements as regards information and training. Employees who use work equipment and supervisors and managers of such equipment must have available to them adequate health and safety information and, where appropriate, written instructions about the use of that equipment.[68] In particular such information should include (a) the conditions and the methods for use of the equipment; (b) foreseeable abnormal situations and the action for such situations; and (c) any conclusions to be drawn from experience in using the equipment.[69] Any such information must be readily comprehensible to those concerned.[70] There are also requirements for users of work equipment, and supervisors and managers to receive adequate training for health and safety purposes, including training in the methods for use of the equipment, any risks which such use may entail and precautions to be taken.[71]

4.26 The regulations also contain specific rules about dangerous parts of machinery, protection against specified hazards, controls and control systems and maintenance requirements.

(a) Dangerous Parts

4.27 Regulation 11 replaces section 14 of the Factories Act 1961 and requires employers to ensure that effective measures are taken

---

[66] reg. 5(1) and (2). To establish liability, a pursuer must show a causal link between the alleged failure of the equipment and the accident: *Gordon v. British Airways plc* (O.H., July 1999, unreported).

[67] reg. 6.

[68] reg. 8(1) and (2).

[69] reg. 8(3).

[70] reg. 8(4).

[71] reg. 9(1) and (2). The adequacy of training is only available as a defence to the employer where it has been shown that the equipment was suitable: *English v. North Lanarkshire Council*, 1999 S.C.L.R. 310.

to prevent access to any dangerous part of machinery or to any rotating stock-bar,[72] or to stop the movement of any dangerous part or rotating stock-bar before any part of a person enters a danger zone.[73] It is clear that this provision follows the approach of section 14 by requiring that measures need only be taken to prevent the contact of employees with the machinery.[74]

4.28 On the other hand, unlike section 14 which placed an absolute obligation on employers to fence dangerous parts of machinery, the new regulations introduce a hierarchy of measures based upon the risks and hazards associated with the process and the practicability of the measures. Employers must consider each level of the hierarchy in turn and select measures from that level so far as they are practicable. As important, the selection process must also ensure that the measures which are taken are effective in overcoming the risks and satisfying the requirements of regulation 11(1).[75] The four levels of measure are (a) fixed enclosing guards,[76] (b) other guards[77] and protection devices,[78] (c) protection appliances[79] like jigs, holders and push-sticks, and (d) the provision of information, instruction, training and supervision.

4.29 All guards and protection devices must:

(a) be suitable for their purpose;

(b) be of good construction, sound material and adequate strength;

(c) be maintained in an efficient state, in efficient working order and in good repair;

---

[72] "Stock-bar" means any part of a stock-bar which projects beyond the head-stock of a lathe; reg. 11(5).

[73] reg. 11(1). "Danger zone" means any zone in or around machinery in which a person is exposed to a risk to health or safety from contact with a dangerous part of machinery or a rotating stock bar; reg. 11(5).

[74] For case law under the Factories Act 1961, see, for example, *Carroll v. Andrew Barclay & Sons Ltd*, 1948 S.C. (H.L.) 100 and *Close v. Steel Co. of Wales Ltd* [1962] A.C. 367 (HL). But note the cautionary words of Lord Reed in *English v. North Lanarkshire Council*, 1999 S.C.L.R. 310.

[75] The Guidance Notes suggest that the selection process will often result in a combination of measures being taken.

[76] The Guidance Notes define guards as physical barriers which prevent access to the danger zone and fixed guards should have no moving parts and be fastened in a constant position relative to the danger zone; app. 3, para. 1.

[77] "Other guards" include moveable guards, adjustable guards, automatic guards and fixed guards that are not fully enclosing; app. 3, para. 2.

[78] "Protection devices" are devices which do not prevent access to the danger zone but stop the movement of the dangerous part before contact (*e.g.* photoelectric devices); app. 3, para. 3.

[79] "Protection appliances" are used to hold or manipulate in a way which allows operators to control and feed a loose workpiece at a machine while keeping their body clear of the danger zone; app. 3, para. 4

(d) not give rise to any increased risk to health and safety;

(e) not be easily bypassed or disabled;

(f) be situated at sufficient distance from the danger zone;

(g) not unduly restrict the view of the operating cycle of the machinery, where such a view is necessary;

(h) be so constructed or adapted that they allow operations necessary to fit or replace parts and for maintenance work, restricting access so that it is allowed only in the area where the work is to be carried out and, if possible, without having to dismantle the guard or protection device.[80]

(b) Protection Against Specified Hazards

4.30 The Regulations place new responsibilities upon employers to take measures to ensure that the exposure of persons using work equipment to any risk to health or safety from specified hazards is either prevented or, where that is not reasonably practicable, adequately[81] controlled.[82] The measures envisaged by this provision are measures other than the provision of personal protective equipment or of information, instruction, training and supervision, so far as reasonably practicable, and include, where appropriate, measures to minimise the effects of the hazard as well as to reduce the likelihood of the hazard occurring.[83] The hazards specified by this provision are:

(a) the falling or ejection from work equipment of any article or substance[84];

(b) the rupture or disintegration of parts of work equipment[85];

(c) work equipment catching fire or overheating;

(d) the unintended or premature discharge of any article or of any gas, dust, liquid, vapour or other substance which is produced, used or stored in the work equipment;

---

[80] reg. 11(3). If protection appliances are provided, then, they must comply with paras (a) to (d) and para. (g).

[81] "Adequately" means adequately having regard only to the nature of the hazard and the nature and degree of exposure to the risk; reg. 12(4).

[82] reg. 12(1).

[83] reg. 12(2).

[84] In contradistinction to the Factories Act 1961 this provision creates protection against parts of the material flying out.

[85] Again, unlike the Factories Act this provision protects operators from parts of the machinery breaking off and flying out.

(e) the unintended or premature explosion of any work equipment or any article or substance produced, used or stored in it.[86]

4.31 These protections for specified hazards do not apply where certain other regulations require measures to be taken to prevent or control risks to health and safety. The types of hazard which are excluded from the scope of the Regulations because they are regulated by other provisions are operations involving lead, ionising, and asbestos as well as substances hazardous to health, noise and head protection in the construction industry.[87] The Regulations also require appropriate protection for work equipment and substances kept in work equipment which is at a high or very low temperature so as to prevent burns, scalds or sears.[88]

(c) Controls and Control Systems

4.32 The Regulations introduce new rules as regards the provision of controls and control systems in work equipment. This is a new departure, since in the past requirements for controls only applied in particular areas such as woodworking machines. There are requirements for appropriate controls for starting work equipment (including restarting after a stoppage) or for controlling any change of speed, pressure or other operating conditions of work equipment where the change leads to greater or different risks.[89] Employers are also required to ensure that, where appropriate, work equipment is provided with readily accessible controls to stop the machinery,[90] and there are provisions requiring the installation of readily accessible emergency stop controls which will operate in priority to any other stop control.[91]

4.33 Employers must ensure that all work equipment controls are clearly visible and identifiable and, except where necessary, no control is in a position where persons operating the control are exposed to a risk to their health and safety.[92] All control systems must, so far as reasonably practicable, be safe and a control system will not be safe unless (a) its operation does not create any increased risk to health and safety, (b) it ensures, so far as reasonably practicable, that any fault or damage to the system or

---

[86] reg. 12(3). Examples of the types of hazard which are covered by this regulation are provided in the Guidance Notes, para. 121.
[87] reg. 12(5).
[88] reg. 13.
[89] reg. 14(1).
[90] reg. 15.
[91] reg. 16.
[92] reg. 17(1) and (2).

any loss of energy supply will not result in additional or increased risk to health and safety, and (c) it does not impede the operation of stop controls or emergency stop controls.[93]

(d) Maintenance and Other Requirements

4.34 The Regulations also introduce rules about the isolation of work equipment from all its sources of energy,[94] the stabilisation of work equipment,[95] the provision of suitable and sufficient lighting,[96] markings,[97] and warnings and warning devices.[98] Regulation 22 requires employers to take appropriate measures to ensure that work equipment is so constructed or adapted that, so far as reasonably practicable, maintenance operations which involve a risk to health and safety can be carried out while the work equipment is shut down unless maintenance operations can be carried out without a risk to health or safety, or appropriate measures can be taken to protect persons carrying out maintenance operations which involve a risk to health and safety. This provision resolves some of the difficulties associated with the construction and maintenance requirements of section 16 of the Factories Act 1961, particularly as regards whether or not the machinery is in motion or use.[99] Moreover, the Guidance Notes provide examples of the sorts of measures which can be taken in order to minimise risks to health and safety when machinery is running or working during maintenance operations.[1]

(e) Mobile Work Equipment and Power Presses

4.35 Employers must ensure that their employees are not carried by mobile work equipment unless it is suitable and incorporates features to reduce risks (including risks from wheels or tracks) to as low as is reasonably practicable.[2] There are also obligations on employers to minimise risks to their employees from mobile equipment rolling over or fork-lift trucks overturning,[3] and there are special provisions preventing the use by unauthorised persons

---

[93] reg. 18.

[94] reg. 19.

[95] reg. 20.

[96] reg. 21.

[97] reg. 23.

[98] reg. 24.

[99] See, for example, *Richard Thomas & Baldwins Ltd v. Cummings* [1955] A.C. 321 (H.L.).

[1] See para. 213, which recommends that the design of work equipment should ensure that the power, speed or range of movement of dangerous parts be restricted during maintenance.

[2] reg. 25.

[3] regs 26 and 27.

of self-propelled work equipment.[4] The Regulations also contain detailed provisions relating to the examination and inspection of power presses, guards and protection devices and require the notification of defects to the employer after examination or inspection as well as record-keeping functions.[5]

The Workplace (Health, Safety and Welfare) Regulations 1992

4.36 The Factories Act 1961 also contained detailed provisions on the safety of floors, stairs and passages (section 28) and as regards safe means of access to places of work (section 29). These provisions were repealed by the Workplace (Health, Safety and Welfare) Regulations 1992 as from January 1, 1993—although there were transitional provisions for existing workplaces so that in their case the regulations took effect on January 1, 1996. The present regulations provide a more modern and realistic framework for the protection of employees at their place of work.

4.37 These Regulations are intended to implement the E.C. Directive on Minimum Health and Safety Requirements at the Workplace.[6] There is also an Approved Code of Practice to accompany the Regulations. A workplace is defined as any premises or part of premises which are not domestic premises and are made available to any person as a place of work.[7] The definition includes any place within the premises to which a person has access while at work and any room, lobby, corridor, staircase, road or other place used as a means of access to or egress from that place of work or where facilities are provided for use in connection with that place of work other than a public road.[8] The following workplaces are excluded from the definition:

(a) a workplace which is in or on a ship;

(b) a workplace where the only activities being undertaken are building operations or engineering construction works;

(c) a workplace where the only activities being undertaken are the exploration for or extraction of mineral resources;

(d) a workplace which is situated in the immediate vicinity of another workplace where the only activities being undertaken are the exploration for or extraction of mineral resources.[9]

---

[4] reg. 28.
[5] regs 32–35.
[6] 89/654/EEC.
[7] reg. 2(1).
[8] reg. 2(1)(a) and (b).
[9] reg. 3(1).

There are also special rules as regards the application of the regulations to temporary worksites where only the provisions in regulations 20 to 25 on sanitary conveniences, washing facilities, drinking water, clothing accommodation, changing facilities, and facilities for rest and eating meals apply.[10]

4.38 Employers have a statutory duty to ensure that every workplace which is under their control and where any of their employees works complies with any of the requirements of the Regulations.[11] The Regulations are also specifically applied to the occupiers of factories[12] and to persons who have control of any workplace in connection with trade, business or other undertaking (whether for profit or not).[13] Thus as well as applying the Regulations to persons who already had obligations under the Factories Act 1961, the Regulations also apply to workplaces in institutions such as hospitals, schools and universities which were not previously the subjects of specific statutory regulation.

4.39 The workplace and the equipment, devices and systems (*i.e.* mechanical ventilation systems) must be maintained (including cleaned as appropriate) in an efficient state, in efficient working order and in good repair.[14] It is clear from the Code of Practice that "efficient" in this context means efficient from the view of health, safety and welfare. Such equipment, devices and systems must be subject, where appropriate, to a suitable system of maintenance.[15] The Code of Practice recommends that a suitable system of maintenance should include regular maintenance, remedying potentially dangerous defects, proper remedial work and the keeping of a suitable record to ensure that the maintenance system has been properly implemented.

4.40 There must be effective and suitable provision to ensure that every enclosed workplace is ventilated by a sufficient quantity of fresh and purified air and any plant used for this purpose must include an effective device to give visible and audible warning of

---

[10] reg. 3(2). Workplaces which are or are in or on aircraft, locomotives or rolling stock, trailers or semi-trailers when stationary in a workplace (but not when on a public road) are generally exempt from the regulations save for reg. 13 (falls or falling objects) (reg. 3(3)). Also excluded are agricultural or forestry workplaces which are outdoors and away from the undertaking's main buildings save for the requirements on sanitary conveniences, washing facilities and drinking water in regs 20–22 (reg. 3(4)).
[11] reg. 4(1).
[12] reg. 4(5).
[13] reg. 4(3).
[14] reg. 5(1).
[15] reg. 5(2).

any failure of the plant for reasons of health and safety.[16] There are also provisions requiring the temperature in all workplaces during working hours to be reasonable and for the provision of thermometers.[17] The aim here is to provide reasonable comfort without the need for special clothing.[18] However, where, despite the provision of local heating or cooling, workers are exposed to temperatures which do not give reasonable comfort, then suitable protective clothing and rest facilities should be provided. Every workplace must also have suitable and sufficient lighting and, so far as is reasonably practicable, this should be by natural light.[19] Workplaces together with any furniture, furnishings and fittings must be kept sufficiently clean as must the surfaces of floors, walls and ceilings, and there are also provisions aimed at preventing the accumulation of waste materials except in suitable receptacles.[20]

4.41 In any room where a person works there must be sufficient floor area, height and unoccupied space for purposes of health, safety and welfare.[21] The Regulations do not provide guidance on the amount of space required. However, the Code of Practice does make recommendations about the minimum amount of space which should be provided. Regulation 11(1) requires that every workstation[22] must be so arranged as to be suitable both for the person required to work there and for the work that is likely to be done there. Suitable seats must also be provided where the work or a substantial part of it must be done sitting.[23] In the case of workstations outdoors there is a requirement that they be so arranged that (a), so far as reasonably practicable, they provide protection from adverse weather; (b) they enable people working there to leave it swiftly; and (c) persons there are not likely to slip or fall.[24] It is interesting that a test of reasonable practicability is introduced for workstations outdoors, whereas the test for other workstations is based solely upon suitability.

---

[16] reg. 6(1) and (2).
[17] reg. 7(1) and (3).
[18] The Code of Practice recommends that the temperature in workplaces should normally be at least 16° Celsius unless much of the work involves severe physical effort, where it should be at least 13° Celsius.
[19] reg. 8(1) and (2).
[20] reg. 9(1)–(3).
[21] reg. 10(1).
[22] Workstations where visual display screens, etc., are used are also subject to the Health and Safety (Display Screen Equipment) Regulations 1992.
[23] reg. 11(3). This can also entail the provision of suitable footrests (reg. 11(4)(b)).
[24] reg. 11(2).

4.42 Regulation 12(1) requires that every floor in a workplace and the surface of every traffic route[25] in a workplace must be of such construction that the floor or surface is suitable for the purpose for which it is used. To some extent this provision echoes some of the language of section 28(1) of the Factories Act 1961. However, regulation 12 also lays down particular requirements that the floor, or surface of the traffic route should have no hole or slope, or be uneven or slippery so as to expose any person to a risk to health or safety, and that every floor has effective means of drainage.[26] There are also provisions which seek to avoid obstructions and prevent persons from slipping. Regulation 12(3) requires that, so far as reasonably practicable, every floor in a workplace and every surface of a traffic route are kept free from obstructions and from any article or substance which may cause a person to slip, trip or fall. This provision also echoes section 28(1) of the Factories Act 1961 and it is anticipated that the courts will adopt the same approach to the issue of reasonable practicability in regulation 12(3) as was applied under the older legislation. Finally, there are provisions about the provision of suitable and sufficient handrails for staircases except where a handrail could not be provided without obstructing a traffic route.[27]

4.43 Regulation 13 requires that, so far as reasonably practicable, suitable and effective measures are taken to prevent any person falling a distance likely to cause personal injury[28] or being struck by a falling object likely to cause personal injury. So far as reasonably practicable, the required measures should entail measures other than the provision of personal protective equipment, information, instruction, training or supervision. It is clear, therefore, that the primary obligation is to provide fencing or covers.[29] There is a higher obligation where there is a tank, pit or structure and there is a risk of persons falling into a dangerous substance[30] in the tank, etc. In such a case the duty is to securely cover or fence, so far as is practicable.[31]

---

[25] "Traffic route" means a route for pedestrian traffic, vehicles or both and includes any stairs, staircase, fixed ladder, doorway, gateway, loading bay or ramp (reg. 2(1)).

[26] reg. 12(2).

[27] reg. 12(5). The Code of Practice recommends that a handrail should be provided on one side of a staircase, except where there is a particular risk of falling, where handrails should be provided on both sides.

[28] Unlike the Factories Act 1961, s. 29(2), reg. 13(1) and (3) does not specify any minimum distance. However, the Code of Practice does recommend the provision of secure fencing at any place where a person might fall two metres or more and fencing in other cases where there is an increased likelihood of falling.

[29] See generally Code of Practice, paras 108–118.

[30] For the definition of dangerous substance, see reg. 13(7).

[31] reg. 12(5).

4.44 Windows, and transparent and translucent doors, gates and walls must, where necessary for reasons of health and safety, be of safety material or be protected against breakage and be appropriately marked.[32] There are also provisions concerning the safe opening of windows, skylights and ventilators,[33] and the safe cleaning of windows and skylights.[34]

4.45 Regulation 17 introduces important provisions as regards the organisation of traffic routes. Every workplace must be organised in such a way that pedestrians and vehicles can circulate in a safe manner, and traffic routes must be suitable for the persons or vehicles using them; sufficient in number, in suitable positions and of sufficient size.[35] Traffic routes do not satisfy the last requirement unless suitable measures have been taken to ensure that (a) pedestrians or vehicles can use them without causing danger to the health and safety of persons at work near it; (b) there is sufficient separation of any traffic route for vehicles from doors or gates or from pedestrian traffic routes which lead into it; and (c) where vehicles and pedestrians use the same traffic route, there is sufficient separation between them.[36]

4.46 Doors and gates must be suitably constructed (including being fitted with any necessary safety devices).[37] In particular, sliding doors must have a device to prevent them coming off their tracks during use, upward opening doors must have a device to prevent them falling back, powered doors or gates must have suitable and effective features to prevent them causing injury by trapping any person and must be capable of being opened manually, and doors and gates which open either way must be constructed in such a way as to provide a clear view of the space close to both sides.[38]

4.47 Escalators and moving walkways must function safely, be equipped with any necessary safety devices and be fitted with one or more emergency stop controls which are easily identifiable and readily accessible.[39] Finally, there are detailed provisions on the

---

[32] reg. 14(1).
[33] reg. 15.
[34] reg. 16.
[35] reg. 17(1) and (2). It should be noted that reg. 17(2) and (3) are, so far as is reasonably practicable, to be applied to existing workplaces. See reg. 17(5).
[36] reg. 17(3). Further detailed guidance is provided in the Code of Practice, paras 159–182. It should be noted that some of the guidance provided in this section applies to existing workplaces.
[37] reg. 18(1).
[38] reg. 18(2).
[39] reg. 19.

provision of suitable and sufficient sanitary provisions, suitable and sufficient washing facilities, an adequate supply of wholesome drinking water, suitable and sufficient accommodation for clothing, suitable and sufficient facilities for changing clothing, and suitable and sufficient rest facilities.[40] It should be noted that regulation 25(3) creates a specific obligation to ensure that in the provision of rest facilities suitable arrangements are made to protect non-smokers from tobacco smoke. Suitable facilities must also be provided for pregnant women or nursing mothers to rest.[41]

The Working Time Regulations 1998

4.48 Until the introduction of these Regulations[42] and subject to the employer's duty to take reasonable care for the health and safety of the employee, employers and employees were generally free to make such contractual provisions regarding hours of work as they wished. That position was changed considerably by the Working Time Regulations 1998, which give effect to the Working Time Directive[43] and the Young Workers Directive,[44] and became effective on October 1, 1998. The Regulations however frequently do nothing more than "copy out" the text of the Directives, leaving it up to courts and tribunals to apply the rather opaque statutory wording.[45] On the other hand in some cases the Regulations considerably enhance the wording of the Directive.[46]

4.49 The DTI has published guidance on the Regulations but while it may be helpful, it does not have the status of the guidance published under the Disability Discrimination Act 1996 or of a Code of Practice, so that courts and tribunals are not required to take account of the guidance. Before dealing with the substantive provisions of the Regulations it is necessary to discuss their scope and extent.

---

[40] regs 20–25.

[41] reg. 25(4).

[42] S.I. 1998 No. 1833.

[43] Council Directive 93/104.

[44] Council Directive 94/33. A young worker is someone who is between school-leaving age (in Scotland see the Education Scotland Act 1980, s. 31) and under 18 years of age (reg. 2(1)), and certain articles of the Young Workers Directive have already been introduced by the Health and Safety (Young Persons) Regulations 1997 and the Children (Protection at Work) Regulations 1998 (S.I. 1998 No. 276) which deal with the employment of schoolchildren, effective on August 4, 1998.

[45] See for example reg. 8 (pattern of work), reg. 20 (unmeasured work time) and reg. 21 (exclusions for special cases).

[46] See the definition of the civil protection services in reg. 2 to *include* the "police, the fire brigades, ambulance services, customs and immigration officers, the prison service, the coastguard service, lifeboat crew and other voluntary rescue services".

Scope of the Regulations

4.50 Although much modern employment law confers rights only on employees,[47] the Regulations apply to "workers" who are defined to include those with contracts of employment and those with any other contract by which an individual agrees to perform personally any work for another party to the contract, whose status is not that of a client or customer of any profession or business undertaking carried on by the individual.[48] This definition would not necessarily include agency workers and, in keeping with the government's policy of extending employment rights[49] to prevent such workers falling outside the Regulations, it is specially provided[50] that they are to be treated as if they had a contract with the agency or the principal with the employer being whichever has the responsibility for paying the worker or whichever does in practice pay the worker.[51]

Working time

4.51 Perhaps the most important definition in the Regulations is that for "working time". Although this largely copies out the definition in Article 2.1 of the Directive, to the effect that it means "any period during which the worker is working, at the employer's disposal and carrying out his activity or duty", significantly it adds to that definition "any period during which the worker is receiving relevant training" and "any additional period which is to be treated as working time . . . under a relevant agreement".[52] The Regulations themselves[53] give no guidance regarding whether "on-call" hours are part of working time or not, but clearly it is the intention that such hours will be regulated by a relevant agreement. In a slightly different context the House of Lords has, in relation to "on-call" hours, distinguished a duty to be available for work from actual work itself, and such a distinction would seem to be applicable in the context of working time so that "on-call" hours would generally not be taken into account.[54] However, the effect of

---

[47] Namely those who have contracts of employment.
[48] reg. 2(1).
[49] See *Fairness at Work*, Cm. 3968 (1998) and the Employment Relations Act 1999, s. 23.
[50] reg. 36.
[51] reg. 2(1). And note provision is made for non-employed trainees who are to be regarded as workers employed by the organisation or the person who provides the training; reg. 42.
[52] reg. 2(1).
[53] *cf.* the Guidance issued by the Department of Trade and Industry (para. 2.1.2).
[54] *Suffolk County Council v. Secretary of State for Environment and Alcock* [1984] I.C.R. 882 (HL).

the expanded definition in the Regulations is that if an employer and employee are in doubt about whether a period is to be treated as working time they are able to enter into an agreement by which that uncertainty is removed. Such an agreement might provide that all contractual working hours or all times during which the worker is on the premises of the employer are to be regarded as working time. However, the agreement cannot provide that a period when a worker is working, at the employer's disposal, and is carrying out his duties or activities, or is receiving training, is not to be regarded as working time because that is the definition contained in the Directive which the Regulations are not free to reduce.

THE SUBSTANTIVE ENTITLEMENTS AND PROTECTIONS

Maximum working week

4.52 A worker's average working time—including overtime—shall not exceed 48 hours for each seven-day period.[54a] There are special rules for calculating the average working week of a worker and, while the normal reference period for calculating the average is 17 weeks, that period may be extended to 52 weeks by collective or workforce agreement and, if certain conditions are met, to 26 weeks for other workers. For example a worker engaged in household refuse collection or the postal services may have his average working week worked out by reference to a period of 26 weeks.[55]

4.53 An employer and a worker are free to agree in writing—but not irrevocably—indefinitely or for a particular period that the 48-hour limit shall not apply to that worker.[56] The employer need now only keep up-to-date records of all workers who have agreed to work in excess of the 48-hour limit.[56a] Even where there is no agreement that the 48-hour limit should not apply, the employer must keep records to show whether that limit is being complied with and retain them for two years.[57]

4.54 The only exceptions permitted from the 48-hour limit are in respect of (1) domestic servants and (2) workers whose working

---

[54a] reg. 4(1). This provision creates free-standing legal rights and obligations under the contract of employment which can be enforced by legal action in the courts: *Barber v. RJB Mining (U.K.) Ltd* [1999] I.R.L.R. 308.

[55] regs 4(5) and 23(b).

[56] regs 4 and 5.

[56a] reg. 4(2), as inserted by the Working Time Regulations 1999 (S.I. 1999 No. 3372). These Regulations also repeal the more extensive record keeping requirements to be found in the original version of the Regulations.

[57] reg. 9.

time "is not measured or predetermined or can be determined by the worker himself" on account of the specific characteristics of the activity in which the worker is engaged such as managing executives or others with autonomous decision-making powers, family workers, or workers officiating at religious ceremonies—a wonderfully opaque piece of Brussels jargon to which the United Kingdom courts will have to give meaningful content.[58]

4.55 An obvious defect in the Regulations (and the Directive) was the failure to make provision for workers who work for more than one employer. Clearly if long working hours contribute to poor health and safety it makes no difference whether the hours are worked for only one employer or several employers, and it might have been expected that the Directive and the Regulations would make special provision to deal with this. The Regulations themselves are silent on this matter beyond providing that an employer shall take all reasonable steps to ensure that the 48-hour working week limit or the night work limits are complied with in the case of each worker employed by him. However, the guidance published by the DTI suggests that where a worker has more than one job, taking reasonable steps would include inquiring whether the worker was working elsewhere and, if he was working elsewhere, to adjust his hours of work accordingly. Clearly this can be done by the employer entering into an agreement with the worker which allows the 48-hour limit to be exceeded, but the night work limits cannot be avoided by individual agreement and it might have been expected that the Regulations would include an obligation on the worker to inform his employer of the existence of a second job. What may become of importance is section 7 of the Health and Safety at Work Act 1974, which imposes an obligation on employees (but not workers) to take reasonable care for their own safety and the safety of others, and this could include informing their employer of the existence of other jobs whose hours, when aggregated, result in the limits set out in the Regulations being breached. Section 7 also requires an employee to co-operate with his employer so far as is necessary to enable him to perform any duty imposed on him under any health and safety regulations.

Night work

4.56 Night-time means a period of seven hours, including the hours between midnight and 5 a.m., as determined by a relevant

---

[58] reg. 20; and see the addition of reg. 20(2) by the Working Time Regulations 1999 which applies to cases where a worker's working time is partly measured, predetermined or determined by the worker, and partly not. In such cases, the provisions on working time will only apply in relation to that part of the worker's work that is measured, predetermined or cannot be determined by the worker himself.

agreement or, in default of such an agreement, the period between 11 p.m. and 6 a.m., and a night worker is (1) one who on the majority of days works three of his working hours at night time or (2) one who during night time works such proportion of his annual working hours as is set out in a collective agreement or workforce agreement.[59]

4.57 Except where there are special hazards or heavy physical or mental strain is involved[60] in which case the night worker must not work for more than eight hours in any 24-hour period during which the night worker performs night work,[61] a night worker's normal hours of work shall not exceed an average of eight hours in a 24-hour period,[62] and no worker may be assigned to night work unless the employer has ensured the worker has the opportunity of a free health assessment and, where a night worker suffers from health problems related to night work, he is to be transferred to other suitable (non-night) work whenever possible.[63] However, the employer's duty is dependent on a registered medical practitioner advising him that the worker is suffering from health problems which the practitioner considers are connected with night work. An employer of night workers is required to keep records going back two years to show that the limits on working hours of night workers are being adhered to and that health assessments are being carried out. The exceptions to the 48-hour week relating to domestic service[64] and unmeasured time workers[65] also apply to night work but—unlike the 48-hour rule which may be avoided only by individual agreement—the limits on night work may be excluded in many other special cases when certain conditions apply, ranging from where the worker's activities are such that his place of work and his place of residence are distant from one another, to where his activities are affected by an accident or an imminent risk of accident and may be excluded or modified by collective or workforce agreement.[66]

---

[59] reg. 2(1).

[60] Work is to be regarded as involving such hazards or strains if it is identified as such in a collective or workforce agreement or a risk assessment; reg. 4(8).

[61] The result is that during days (24-hour periods) when the worker is not performing night work, his working hours are not limited other than by the need to ensure that the 48-hour limit is not exceeded.

[62] reg. 6(1) and (7).

[63] reg. 7. There is a minor exception for workers who have already had a health assessment which the employer believes is still valid (reg. 7(1)(a)(ii)) and the result of an assessment shall not be disclosed except to the worker unless the worker has given his consent or the assessment is confined to whether the worker is fit to take up or continue night work (reg. 7(6).

[64] reg. 19.

[65] reg. 20.

[66] regs 21 and 23.

Rest periods

4.58 A worker is entitled to a daily rest beak of 11 consecutive hours in each 24 hour period[67] and a weekly rest period of not less than 24 hours in each seven-day period he works for the employer, but an employer is entitled to substitute for this two uninterrupted periods of 24 hours each in a 14-day period, or one uninterrupted period of 48 hours in a 14-day period. The weekly rest period is to be in addition to the daily rest period unless objective technical or work organisation conditions justify it, although where the worker is a shift worker[68] he is not entitled to the 11-hour daily rest period or the 24-hour weekly (or 48-hour fortnightly) rest period where he changes from one shift to another. Where a worker's working day is more than six hours he is entitled to a rest break (away from his work station[69]) of not less than 20 minutes uninterrupted, unless provision is made for a rest break by a collective or workforce agreement.

Annual leave

4.59 A worker—whether full or part time—who has 13 weeks' continuous employment[70] is entitled to four weeks' paid leave per year.[71] However, the rules regarding continuity of employment in the Employment Rights Act 1996 are avoided by the Regulations providing that a worker is to be regarded as continuously employed for 13 weeks if his relations with his employer have been governed by a contract during the whole or part of each of those weeks, so that any week in which there is no contract means the accumulation process must start again. There is no provision for the basic entitlement to paid annual leave to be modified or excluded by collective or workforce agreement, and except where the employment is terminated there can be no payments in lieu. However, where termination occurs during the leave year, special provision is made to ensure that the worker receives a payment in respect of leave not yet taken.[72] Where the worker has at the point of

---

[67] But note the exceptions created for by unmeasured time workers (reg. 20), special cases (reg. 20) and by collective and workforce agreements (reg. 23).

[68] Shift work is defined in reg. 22(2), and means any method of organising work in shifts whereby workers succeed each other at the same work stations according to a certain pattern, including a rotating pattern, and which may be continuous or discontinuous, entailing the need for workers to work at different workstations over a given period.

[69] This effectively means that an employer may have to provide an area at which the break can be taken.

[70] It is the case that the 13 weeks must fall after the date on which the Regulations become effective to avoid making them retrospective.

[71] reg. 13. It is a breach of the Regulations to include an element for holiday pay in basic pay: *Acherman v. Stratton*, August 27, 1999, E.T., unreported.

[72] reg. 14.

termination taken more leave than he is (having regard to the period of the leave year that has elapsed) pro rata entitled to, the employer's right to recover any excess payment depends on there being a binding agreement to that effect between the employer and the worker, a workforce agreement or a collective agreement. Particularly where the employer proposes to rely on a workforce agreement to recover holiday pay excess, he will have to ensure that there is an agreement in writing by the worker (or that the worker has been given written notice of his oral agreement) in order to comply with the provisions of Part II of the Employment Rights Act 1996. There are complicated provisions regarding when leave may be taken and when an employer may prevent a worker taking leave,[73] but these provisions may be varied by a binding agreement between the worker and the employer or by a collective or workforce agreement, and this flexibility would seem to be attractive for many employers and may allow them merely to adhere to current practice.

Group or sector exclusions

4.60 Certain groups of workers are excluded either in part (domestic servants[74]) or in respect of all entitlements and protections (particular sectors of activity; namely air, road, rail and sea transport, activities of doctors in training, activities of the armed forces and the civil protection services, which inevitably conflict with the Regulations[75]). By excluding the "sector of activity" as distinct from the type of work, the surprising result is that the booking clerk employed by a railway company is excluded. According to the Guidance, employers will need to consider whether particular workers fall within a sector or not and the location of the work, for example a port, railway station, or airport will not necessarily mean that those doing it are excluded. Furthermore, neither will workers involved in the movement of goods or people to or from a mode of transport (for example, in docks, or loading or unloading onto or from road vehicles) necessarily be excluded. Where workers are directly involved in the operation of the sector, such as baggage handlers, and signal and maintenance staff, they are more likely to be excluded from the Regulations, but where they are not (*e.g.* construction workers at an airport) the exclusion

---

[73] See reg. 165.

[74] reg. 19 excludes them from reg. 4 (maximum working week), reg. 6 (length of night work) reg. 7 (health assessment for night workers) and reg. 8 (monotonous work or work at pre-determined rates).

[75] reg. 18 excludes them from regs 4, 6, 7, 8, 10, 11, 12, 13 and 16. According to the Guidance it will be for such services to identify the activities which conflict with the regulations.

is not likely to apply. Also "own account" transport operations (for example, a retail chain operating a fleet of vehicles to deliver goods to its own stores) are excluded from the Regulations on the basis that they fall within the road transport sector. Such operations will often be almost identical to those undertaken by businesses operating for hire, which are clearly excluded. Nor do the Regulations apply to the activities of doctors in training—namely pre-registration house officer, house officer, senior house officer, registrar, senior registrar and specialist registrar.

4.61 However, workers in these excluded sectors or areas of activity must be distinguished from workers to whom the Regulations do not apply if certain conditions are met.[76] Regulation 21 contains many special circumstances in which the regulations do not apply to a worker because of the work the worker does. These circumstances may be classified as below, with the Guidance in italics.

(a) A worker's "activities are such that his place of work and place of residence are distant from one another or his different places of work are distant from one another". *This may apply to workers where, because of the distance from home, it is desirable for them to work longer hours for a short period to complete the task more quickly, or where continual changes in the location of the work make it impractical to set a pattern of work.*

(b) A worker who is "engaged in security and surveillance activities". *This may apply to security and surveillance work where there is a need for a round-the-clock presence to protect property or a person.*

(c) A worker's activities involve the need for continuity of service or production. *This applies where there is a need for round-the-clock activity. The Regulations cite a list of examples, as set out in the Working Time Directive. These include hospitals, residential institutions, prisons, docks or airports, press, radio, television, film production, postal and telecommunications services, civil protection services, gas, water and electricity production, transmission and distribution, household refuse collection and incineration, industries in which work cannot be interrupted on technical grounds (as may be the case where there is a need to keep machinery running), research and development activities; and agriculture.*

---

[76] The onus of proving the existence of the conditions would be on the employer.

(d) There is a foreseeable surge of activity. *The examples suggested in the Working Time Directive are agriculture, tourism and postal services.*

(e) A worker's "activities are affected by an occurrence due to unusual and unforeseeable circumstances . . . or exceptional events, the consequences of which could not have been avoided . . . or an accident or the imminent risk of an accident". *The very nature of unforeseeable circumstances makes it difficult to identify examples in advance. However, this provision relates essentially to emergency situations or those that arise outside the normal course of events. The flexibility it provides is not, of course, something that could be used on a routine basis.*

However, in the event that the employer may rely on such special circumstances, he is required to give compensatory time off, or if that is not possible afford the worker "appropriate protection".[77] According to the Guidance an equivalent period of rest should be considered to be a period of rest as long as that the worker was entitled to but not able to take and should be provided within a reasonable time from when the entitlement to rest was modified. Probably occasions where it is not possible to take compensatory rest due to "exceptional circumstances" will be rare, but will also be self-evident and quite properly the Guidance states that the flexibility provided for here is not, of course, something that could be used on a routine basis.

Modification or exclusion by agreement

4.62 In several respects the scope of the Regulations may be extended or defined by agreement between the employer and the workforce or their representatives.[78] Although the general rule is that an agreement may not exclude or limit the operation of the Regulations except where they expressly provide,[79] many of the Regulations are subject to variation by a "relevant agreement"; namely an agreement between (1) the employer and the worker (an individual agreement),[80] (2) the employer and the workforce or

---

[77] reg. 24.
[78] Thus the definition of night time will normally be the period between 11 p.m. and 6 a.m., unless determined otherwise by agreement between the workforce and the employer, or indeed the worker and the employer so that by agreement night time may be 10 p.m. to 5 a.m. (reg. 2); and night worker will normally be one who works at least three hours of his daily working time during the night time or someone who works a proportion of his annual hours as specified in a collective or workforce agreement but not an agreement between the employer and the worker.
[79] reg. 35(1)(a).
[80] Such an agreement must be in writing and be legally enforceable (reg. 2(1)).

their representatives (a workforce agreement), or (3) the employer and the trade unions (a collective agreement).

4.63 Collective agreements are well understood and are defined in legislation,[81] but it has to be emphasised that a collective agreement may only be used to modify or exclude the provisions of the Regulations where the trade union which is party to the agreement is an independent trade union,[82] so that an employer will not be able to conclude a collective agreement with an informal grouping of union members (as an alternative to a workforce agreement) because such an informal grouping would be unlikely to be an independent trade union, and where an employer proposes to conclude a collective agreement he will have to ensure that he is dealing with properly authorised representatives of the independent trade union.

4.64 Workforce agreements are an innovation, however, and are defined in Schedule 1 to the Regulations. They will be of particular significance to employers who do not recognise trade unions but nevertheless wish to exploit the opportunities the Regulations give for flexibility. Thus by workforce agreement (or collective agreement) the reference period for the maximum working week may be increased from 17 to 52 weeks,[83] or the provisions relating to night work, daily and weekly rest periods and rest breaks excluded or modified in respect of particular workers or groups of workers.[84] The significance of this cannot be overestimated because, unlike other provisions which allow for modification or exclusion (for example Regulation 21), it is not dependent on any conditions being met except the grant of an equivalent period of compensatory rest or other "appropriate protection".[85]

4.65 A workforce agreement need not apply to *all* members of the workforce whose conditions are not provided for in a collective agreement. The Regulations expressly allow for a workforce agreement to apply to all *or particular groups* (which may be defined by function, place of work, or by belonging to a department or unit within the employer's business) of workers.[86] It is important to note that unless the workforce is fewer than 21 (on the date the agreement is made available for signature), the employer will require to have the agreement signed by elected representatives of

---

[81] Trade Union and Labour Relations (Consolidation) Act 1992, s. 178.
[82] reg. 2(1).
[83] reg. 23(b).
[84] reg. 23(a).
[85] reg. 24.
[86] Sched. 1, para. 1(c)(ii).

the workforce or of the group. The option of putting the agreement to the group or the workforce as a whole is not available so that the employer is required to arrange for the election of representatives.

Contracting-out

4.66 In keeping with modern employment law statutes, the Regulations do not permit contracting out or exclusion of their rights and duties or to preclude the bringing of proceedings in an employment tribunal, but this does not prevent concluding an agreement to settle a complaint and refrain from bringing tribunal proceedings where a conciliation officer has taken action or by a compromise agreement.[87] However, where a worker has a contractual entitlement to a rest period or annual leave and an entitlement under the provisions of the Regulations, although he may not exercise the two rights separately he may take advantage of whichever right is most beneficial to him.[88]

Enforcement and remedies

4.67 There are three ways in which the Regulations can be enforced:

(1) An employer who fails to comply with Regulations regarding the 48-hour working week,[89] the length of night workers' work and their entitlement to health assessment and transfer to non-night work, the provision of rest breaks for monotonous or fixed rate work and keeping records in respect of the working week, night work and health assessments, commits an offence.[90] The offences are dealt with under the Health and Safety at Work Act 1974 and will be enforced by the Health and Safety Executive (HSE) or local authority Environmental Health Departments. Generally the HSE is responsible for enforcing the working time limits where they apply in factories, building sites, mines, farms, fairgrounds, quarries, chemical plants, nuclear installations, schools and hospitals. Local Authority Officers are responsible for retailing, offices, hotels and catering, sports, leisure and consumer services.

---

[87] reg. 35.
[88] reg. 17.
[89] The High Court has held that the Working Time Regulations have created a contractual right that a worker may not be required to work more than 48 hours a week on average (*Barber v. RJB Mining* [1999] I.R.L.R. 308).
[90] reg. 29.

(2) It is also possible for a worker who suffers injury or loss by virtue of the employer's failure to comply with these Regulations to sue in the ordinary courts for breach of statutory duty.[91]

(3) Other provisions (the worker's *entitlements*[92]) are enforced through complaints to the employment tribunal. These entitlements are: daily rest, weekly rest, rest breaks, annual leave (including failure to pay wages during leave) and compensatory rest.[93] However, the EAT has held[94] that, as it was the duty of the national court to apply national law in such a way as to ensure the fulfilment of the obligation arising from a Directive to achieve the result envisaged by the Directive; and as a result a swimming instructor employed by a local authority (which was regarded as an emanation of the state), who was paid an hourly rate and was not paid during school holidays, was entitled to four weeks' paid annual leave under Article 7 of the Working Time Directive. The Directive was concerned with the further harmonisation of health and safety conditions within the community and granting minimum annual periods of rest in order to ensure safety of workers, and Article 7 was clear and precise and admitted of no ambiguity or conditionality.

Where a complaint is well founded the tribunal shall make a declaration to that effect and may make an award of compensation which shall be such amount as the tribunal considers just and equitable, having regard to the employer's default and any loss sustained by the worker or, where the complaint concerns non-payment during annual leave, the amount the employer is due the worker.[95] Complaint may also be made to the employment tribunal that the employer has dismissed the worker or subjected him to a detriment for (a) not complying with a requirement imposed in contravention of the employer's duties under the regulations, (b) refusing to forego a right under the Regulations, (c) failing to sign a workforce agreement, (d) being a representative of the workforce

---

[91] Also where the claim was based on the employer's common law duty of reasonable care the standards set by the Regulations could be refereed to determine reasonableness.

[92] Because they are entitlements there is nothing to prevent a worker "waiving" his entitlement and it is not unlawful for an employer to allow him to waive an entitlement.

[93] reg. 30.

[94] *Gibson v. East Riding Of Yorkshire District Council, The Times,* February 12, 1999, EAT.

[95] reg. 30(4) and (5).

or a candidate in an election for representatives, and (e) bringing proceedings against the employer or alleging that an employer infringed a right conferred on the worker. Where the worker is dismissed for one of the above reasons he is regarded as unfairly dismissed.[96]

B. OTHER GENERAL STATUTORY ARRANGEMENTS

Fire Precautions (Workplace) Regulations 1997

4.68 These Regulations[97] are intended to give effect to provisions in both the Framework Directive[98] and the Workplace Directive[99] which relate to fire precautions. The basic obligation on employers is to ensure that all the workplaces (excluding domestic premises) which are under their control meet the requirements of the Regulations.[1] This necessitates the employer in ensuring where there are fire hazards that, in order to safeguard the safety of employees, the workplace is equipped with appropriate fire-fighting equipment (with fire-detectors and alarms) and that any non-automatic fire-fighting equipment is easily accessible, simple to use and indicated by signs.[2] There must be routes to emergency exits and those exits must be kept clear at all times.[3] The workplace and any fire safety equipment and devices must be subject to a suitable system of maintenance and be maintained in an efficient state, in efficient working order and in good repair.[4]

4.69 It is the duty of every fire authority to enforce the legislation in workplaces within their area.[5] The authority has the power to serve an enforcement notice on any person where it is of the opinion that there has been a failure to comply with the Regulations and the failure places employees at serious risk in the case of fire.[6] The notice will give reasons for the opinion, specify the steps necessary to remedy the failure within a specified period of time being not less than 21 days from the service of the notice and

---

[96] regs 31 and 32 which insert new ss. 45A and 101A into the Employment Rights Act 1996.

[97] S.I. 1997 No. 1840.

[98] E.C. Directive 89/391.

[99] E.C. Directive 89/654.

[1] reg. 3(1). Certain workplaces are exempted because more specific fire safety requirements apply to them or because they are not covered by the Directives.

[2] reg. 4(1).

[3] reg. 5.

[4] reg. 6.

[5] reg. 10(1).

[6] reg. 13(1). It is a criminal offence to fail to comply with such a notice; reg. 15.

explain the rights to and effect of an appeal.[7] There is a right of appeal against the service of an enforcement notice to the sheriff court.[8] In less serious cases the fire authority is likely to apply to the sheriff court for an enforcement order where it appears that a person has failed to comply with the Regulations.[9] The court will order compliance where it is satisfied that the person has failed to take action that he is obliged to take under the Regulations.[10] It is an offence to fail to comply with the Regulations where that failure places employees at serious risk in case of fire and that failure is due to intentional or reckless conduct.[11] Otherwise enforcement is by administrative remedy.

Lifting Operations and Lifting Equipment Regulations 1998

4.70 These Regulations[12] are intended to comply with the lifting equipment requirements of the Work Equipment Directive[13] and apply to employers in Great Britain and in other places where the Health and Safety at Work Act 1974 (Application Outside Great Britain) Order 1995 operates.[14] They have minimal application to ships.[15] It is the duty of every employer to ensure that lifting equipment is of adequate strength and stability for each load, having regard in particular to the stress induced at its mounting or fixing point, and that every part of the load and anything attached to it and used in the lifting is of adequate strength.[16] Lifting equipment for lifting persons must be such as to prevent a person using it being crushed, trapped, struck or falling from the carrier.[17] The employer must also ensure that lifting equipment is positioned or installed in such a way as to reduce to as low as reasonably practicable the risk of the equipment or load striking a person, or the load drifting, falling free or being released unintentionally and is otherwise safe.[18] Lifting equipment should be marked to indicate its safe working load[19] and the lifting operation should be planned by a competent person, appropriately supervised and carried out in a safe manner.[20] All lifting equipment must be examined or

---

[7] reg. 13(1)(i)–(iv).
[8] reg. 14(1) and (5).
[9] reg. 16(1)(a).
[10] reg. 16(1)(b).
[11] reg. 11 (1). "Serious risk" means being subject to a risk of death or serious injury which is likely to materialise.
[12] S.I. 1998 No. 2307.
[13] E.C. Directive 89/655, as amended by E.C. Directive 96/53.
[14] S.I. 1995 No. 263.
[15] reg. 3(6)–(11).
[16] reg. 4.
[17] reg. 5(1).
[18] reg. 6(1).
[19] reg. 7.
[20] reg. 8.

inspected before being used for the first time or after installation, and there are detailed rules for the subsequent examination and inspection of such equipment.[21] Employers must keep records of inspection, and if the equipment has an E.C. declaration of conformity, such declaration must be kept for as long as the lifting equipment is operated.[22]

---

[21] See generally reg. 9. There are also reporting duties on the person carrying out the examination; reg. 10.

[22] reg. 11.

CHAPTER 5

HEALTH AND SAFETY AT WORK ACT 1974

INTRODUCTION

5.1 It was noted in chapter four that the pre-1974 statutory regime was workplace-specific, in that the various statutes tended to regulate health and safety at particular places of work or to control specific industrial activities or substances. Each statute possessed its own body of inspectors to enforce its provisions and, as has already been noted, although these statutes made provision for criminal sanction the most likely legal action was a civil damages claim for breach of statutory duty. This regime was the subject of close scrutiny by a Committee of Inquiry chaired by Lord Robens which was appointed in 1970 by the then Secretary of State for Employment, and its report was published on June 9, 1972.[1] It identified a number of weaknesses in the health and safety statutes of that time. It criticised the existing approach to health and safety as being out-dated, over-complex and inadequate, and advocated a new approach which gave a far greater emphasis to the idea of self-regulation.

5.2 The Robens Committee believed that the most important single reason for accidents at work was apathy. This was largely because the individual experience of people at work was not conducive to safety awareness. Serious accidents at work were fortunately rare, but even rarer was any personal awareness of the hazards and diseases associated with an unhealthy working environment. For Robens it was vital to foster safety awareness through a variety of ways "through education and training, through the provision of better information and advice, through practical, co-operative organisation and action, through legal sanctions where necessary, through research, publicity and so on".[2] One particular reason for the lack of awareness about health and safety

---

[1] Cmnd. 5034.
[2] Robens, para. 13.

was the amount and complexity of the law.[3] Not only was there too much law but the existing provisions were intrinsically unsatisfactory. The legislation was badly drafted, over-elaborate and too detailed and largely unintelligible to those who were most affected by it. In addition, the application of the law was largely negative since it tended to operate only after accidents had happened either through the prosecution of the employer or, more likely, by means of a civil damages action.

5.3 The fact that the legislation was largely dependent upon the type of workplace created another series of problems. First, it meant that many workers fell through the safety net. Robens accepted that something like five million workpeople were employed at premises not subject to any statutory provisions on occupational health and safety. Secondly, each statute possessed its own separate enforcement agency so that enforcement of health and safety statutes was fragmented and the pattern of control bewilderingly complex.[4] Thirdly, the varying definitions of premises and activities in the different statutes affected the standing and operation of the inspectorates who were required to enforce the statutory provisions. Finally, the fragmentation of administrative responsibility for health and safety had implications for policy formulation and law making at national level. It was impossible for any government department with health and safety responsibilities to develop initiatives without close and extensive consultation with several other departments. The Robens Committee believed that such a state of affairs contributed to the obsolescence and inadequacies of many of the existing statutory provisions.

5.4 The Robens Committee believed that there were "severe practical limits on the extent to which progressively better standards of health and safety at work can be brought about through negative regulation by external agencies".[5] Thus the Committee's most significant recommendation was to argue for a much more effective self-regulating system. In Robens' view the primary responsibility for doing something about the risks of accident or disease must lie with those who create the risks and those who work with them.[6] Moreover, Robens recommended that the existing statutory provisions should be replaced by a comprehensive and

---

[3] Robens pointed out that there were nine main groups of safety statutes supported by nearly 500 statutory instruments which were being added to every year. See para. 28.

[4] Robens calculated that there were nine separate groups of safety statutes with enforcement bodies administered in England alone by five government departments, together with local authorities. See para. 32.

[5] See para. 41.

[6] See para. 28.

orderly set of revised procedures under an enabling Act. The new Act should contain a clear statement of the basic principles of safety responsibility, and should be supported by regulations and by non-statutory codes of practice. The basic principles would be enunciated by restating the common law duties of employers and employees in broad terms. However, it was also necessary to revise, harmonise and up-date the existing statutory provisions in order to simplify their style and to reduce their number. Any new law should be extended to cover all employers and employees, and the self-employed should also be covered where their conduct could affect other workers or the general public.

5.5 Robens also recommended that the existing separate inspectorates should be amalgamated to form a unified service under a new authority and this new authority should also have responsibility for the administration of the new Act. It is clear that the Robens Committee preferred administrative enforcement of the law over criminal sanctions, though they did accept that criminal penalties were appropriate where punishment would be generally expected and supported by the public. As far as administrative sanctions were concerned the most significant recommendation was Robens' proposal that inspectors should have the power to issue improvement notices (requiring remedial action to specific faults) and prohibition notices (preventing the use of equipment until faults are remedied) with a right of appeal to employment tribunals.

THE FRAMEWORK OF THE 1974 ACT

5.6 The framework of the 1974 Act reflects closely the philosophy of the Robens Committee, and the provisions of the Act implement the vast majority of their recommendations. First and foremost it creates a series of general duties applicable to employers, the self-employed, persons in control of premises, manufacturers, suppliers, importers and the like, and employees. The general duties are not workplace-based and apply to persons rather than the occupiers of premises.[7] They are based largely on the implied duties of the common law. The general duties do not give rise to civil liability and the only court-based remedy is by criminal sanction.[8] The 1974 Act, section 33(1), makes it clear that

---

[7] It has been estimated that something between seven and eight million were brought within the ambit of protective legislation by the 1974 Act. See Selwyn, *Law of Health and Safety at Work* (1982), at para. 3.2.

[8] 1974 Act, ss. 33(1) and 47(1).

it is an offence to fail to discharge a duty under sections 2 to 7 or to contravene sections 8 and 9. Additionally, section 15 empowers the Secretary of State to make regulations consistent with the general purposes of the Act and for a whole range of purposes which are listed in Schedule 3. Such regulations are intended to play a vital role in the repeal of the older provisions and their progressive replacement by a system of regulations and codes of practice aimed at improving and maintaining health, safety and welfare standards. A breach of duty created by any regulation made under section 15 does give rise to civil liability, except in so far as that regulation provides otherwise.[9]

5.7 Consistent with the notion of self-regulation, the 1974 Act also grants powers to the Health and Safety Commission to approve and issue Codes of Practice with the consent of the Secretary of State and after consulting any government department and such other bodies as appear to the Commission to be appropriate.[10] Although a failure to observe any provision of an approved Code of Practice does not create any civil or criminal liability, a breach of any provision of a code can be used in evidence in criminal proceedings.[11]

5.8 The Act also ensures the integration of health and safety law and creates the Health and Safety Commission (HSC) which has overall responsibility for the general operation of the unified health and safety regime.[12] In addition, there is also a Health and Safety Executive (HSE), which has operational responsibility for enforcing the relevant statutory provisions[13] on health and safety and also has the power to appoint inspectors.[14] Inspectors have important powers of entry, examination and investigation[15] and can issue both improvement notices[16] and prohibition notices.[17]

THE APPLICATION AND GENERAL PURPOSES OF THE ACT

5.9 As already noted, the 1974 Act applies generally to persons rather than to premises. However, there is an exclusion for persons

---

[9] 1974 Act, s. 47(1).
[10] 1974 Act, s. 16(1) and (2).
[11] 1974 Act, s. 17.
[12] 1974 Act, s. 11.
[13] This is defined as meaning the health, safety and welfare provisions of the 1974 Act, the health and safety regulations provided for by s. 15, and the existing statutory provisions like the Factories Act 1961 and the Offices, Shops and Railway Premises Act 1963.
[14] 1974 Act, ss. 18 and 19.
[15] 1974 Act, s. 20.
[16] 1974 Act, s. 21.
[17] 1974 Act, s. 22.

who employ another, or are themselves employed, as domestic servants in a private household.[18] The Act and any regulations made under it apply to the Crown[19] subject to a number of important qualifications. Thus the provisions on improvement notices and prohibition notices do not apply to the Crown,[20] nor do the provisions as to offences.[21] Despite the fact that the offences provisions do not apply to the Crown, they do apply to persons in the public service of the Crown as they do apply to other persons.[22] Crown immunity no longer extends to a health authority or a health board[23]; nor does it apply to NHS Trusts.[24] The Act grants powers to Her Majesty by Order in Council to extend the operation of the health, safety and welfare provisions of the Act outside Great Britain.[25] This power has been exercised to extend the 1974 Act within United Kingdom territorial waters adjacent to Great Britain or a designated area[26] in order to cover workers employed on the offshore installations for the oil and gas industry and in mining, wells and pipelines and also divers.[27]

5.10 The health, safety and welfare provisions of the 1974 Act have effect with a view to:

(a) securing the health, safety and welfare of persons at work[28];

(b) protecting persons other than persons at work against risks to health or safety arising out of or in connection with persons at work;

(c) controlling the keeping and use of explosive or highly flammable or otherwise dangerous substances, and generally preventing the unlawful acquisition. possession and use of such substances; and

---

[18] 1974 Act, s. 51.

[19] 1974 Act, s. 48(1).

[20] 1974 Act, ss. 21–25.

[21] 1974 Act, ss. 33–42.

[22] 1974 Act, s. 48(2). It should be noted that the Crown employees are not prosecuted in lieu of the Crown. For a discussion of prosecution policy on this matter see "Employment", *Stair Memorial Encyclopaedia*, Vol. 9, para. 409.

[23] See National Health Service (Amendment) Act 1986, s. 2, repealed and replaced by the National Health Service and Community Care Act 1990. See in particular s. 60.

[24] 1990 Act, Pt II.

[25] 1974 Act, s. 84(3).

[26] An area so designated by an order made under the Continental Shelf Act 1964.

[27] See the Health and Safety at Work etc. Act 1974 (Application Outside Great Britain) Order 1995 (S.I. 1995 No. 263).

[28] "Work" means work as an employee or as a self-employed person. 1974 Act, s. 52(1)(a).

(d) controlling the emission into the atmosphere of noxious or offensive substances from prescribed premises.[29]

This provision sets the parameters for the operation of the Act. However, it also influences the powers of HSC to make regulations under section 15, and it also sets the framework for the exercise of the general duty by HSC to do such things and make such arrangements as it considers appropriate.[30] It is declared that risks arising out of or in connection with the activities of persons at work are to be treated as including risks attributable to the manner of conducting an undertaking, the plant or substances used for the purposes of an undertaking, and the condition of premises so used or any part of them.[31]

The general duty

5.11 The 1974 Act, section 2(1), lays down the basic general duty placed upon every employer which is to ensure, so far as reasonably practicable, the health, safety and welfare at work of all his employees. The notion of "employer" has been interpreted broadly when applied to companies so that there is no need to show that the offence was committed by a senior manager who can be identified with the company itself. The basis of the employer's responsibility for the acts and omissions of employees is vicarious liability so that the employer can be liable under section 2(1) for the conduct of less senior employees who allowed the risk to develop.[32] Like many of the other duties created by the 1974 Act, the general duty under section 2(1) is not absolute but depends upon the notion of reasonable practicability. In considering the meaning of this phrase the courts have approved expressly the interpretation placed upon the same phrase in the earlier factories legislation.[33] It is clear that the mere fact that a precaution is physically possible does not mean that it is reasonably practicable.[34] Equally, the existence of a universal practice is not conclusive

---

[29] 1974 Act, s. 1(1). Para. (d) is repealed by the Environmental Protection Act 1990, s. 162, Sched. 16, Pt I. However, at time of writing there has been no appointed day.

[30] 1974 Act, s. 11(1).

[31] 1974 Act, s. 1(3).

[32] *R. v. Gateway Foodmarkets Ltd* [1997] I.C.R. 382, CA.

[33] See, for example, the decision of McNeill J. in *West Bromwich Building Society v. Townsend* [1983] I.C.R. 257 applying the reasoning of the Court of Appeal in *Edwards v. NCB* [1949] 1 K.B. 704 and the House of Lords in *Marshall v. Gotham Co. Ltd* [1954] A.C. 360. See also the decision of the High Court of Justiciary in *Lockhart v. Kevin Oliphant Ltd*, 1993 S.L.T. 179 which also applies *Edwards* and *Marshall*.

[34] Dictum of Asquith L.J. in *Edwards* at 712 applied in both *Townsend* and *Lockhart*.

evidence that it is not reasonably practicable to use some other safer method; though it should be given as much weight as is appropriate depending on the surrounding circumstances of the case.[35] The correct approach is to make a computation in which the *quantum* of risk is balanced against the sacrifice in terms of cost, time or trouble involved in the measures necessary for averting that risk. Employers will only satisfy this test when they can show that there is a gross disproportion in the computation so that the risk is insignificant in relation to the sacrifice.[36] It should be noted that it is not the precautions in themselves which have to be reasonably practicable. It is the observance of the precautions that is required so far as may be reasonably practicable.[37] The 1974 Act, section 40 makes it clear that in any criminal proceedings involving a failure to comply with a duty or requirement to do something so far as practicable or so far as reasonably practicable, the onus of proof is placed on the accused.

The particular duties

5.12 There are also a series of specific duties in section 2(2) which are without prejudice to the generality of an employer's duty under section 2(1). In *Bolton Metropolitan Borough Council v. Malrod Insulations Ltd*[38] Tudor Evans J. argued that the opening words of section 2(2) ensure that the general duty in section 2(1) is imported into section 2(2) and in *R. v. Swan Hunter Shipbuilders Ltd*[39] the Court of Appeal made it clear that the specific duties in section 2(2) were merely aspects of the wider general duty created by section 2(1). Nevertheless, where the prosecutor does rely on one of the specific duties in section 2(2) and the circumstances of the case do not establish this, it is not competent to fall back on the general duty in section 2(1) in order to obtain a conviction since this does not give the accused fair notice of the charge against him.[40] It has also been argued in *West Bromwich Building Society v. Townsend*[41] that for a competent charge under section 2(1) to be laid particulars of the breach have to be given which indicate a breach independent of the specific duties listed in section 2(2). It was the view of McNeill J. in this case that section 2(1) was a safety net designed to catch any breaches which could not be libelled under section 2(2). This latter view appears to underplay the

---

[35] *Martin v. Boulton and Paul (Steel Construction) Ltd* [1982] I.C.R. 367, DC.
[36] *per* Asquith L.J. in *Edwards* at 712.
[37] *per* Lord Keith of Avonholm in *Marshall* at 377.
[38] [1993] I.C.R. 358.
[39] [1981] I.C.R. 831.
[40] *Cardle v. David Carlaw Engineering (Glasgow) Ltd*, 1991 S.C.C.R. 807.
[41] [1983] I.C.R. 257.

importance of section 2(1) and does not necessarily accord with prosecution practice.[42]

5.13 Section 2(2) places specific duties on employers and fleshes out the broad general duty created by section 2(1). Thus the matters to which the general duty extends include in particular:

(a) the provision and maintenance of plant[43] and systems of work that are, so far as reasonably practicable, safe and without risks to health;

(b) arrangements for ensuring, so far as reasonably practicable, safety and absence of risks to health in connection with the use, handling, storage and transport of articles and substances[44];

(c) the provision of such information, instruction, training and supervision as is necessary to ensure, so far as reasonably practicable, the health and safety at work of employees;

(d) so far as reasonably practicable as regards any place of work under the employer's control, the maintenance of it in a condition that is safe and without risks to health and the provision and maintenance of means of access to and egress from it that are safe and without such risks;

(e) the provision and maintenance of a working environment for employees that is, so far as reasonably practicable, safe, without risks to health, and adequate as regards facilities and arrangements for their welfare at work.

These duties provide a statutory articulation of the common law obligations of employers towards their employees.[45]

5.14 The duty on employers under paragraph (a) to provide and maintain safe and risk free plant and systems of work for their employees applies to all employees "at work",[46] and is not confined

---

[42] The matter is discussed in more detail in "Employment", *Stair Memorial Encyclopaedia*, Vol. 9, para. 427.

[43] "Plant" includes any machinery, equipment or appliance. See 1974 Act, s. 53(1).

[44] "Substance" means any natural or artificial substance (including micro-organisms), whether in solid or liquid form or in the form of a gas or vapour. See 1974 Act, s. 53(1).

[45] This matter is discussed by McNeill J. in *West Bromwich Building Society v. Townsend* [1983] I.C.R. 257 at 261.

[46] Employees are at work throughout the time when they are in the course of their employment but not otherwise. See 1974 Act, s. 52(1)(b).

to those engaged in the specific process for which the plant in question was made available.[47] The word "provide" has been given the same meaning as under factories legislation; namely "to supply or to make available".[48] This means that where there is a duty to provide safe plant, for example, and an employer makes available plant which is not safe there will be a breach of duty even though the unsafe plant in question has not been used or is not being used.[49]

5.15 The extent of the duty under paragraph (c) may be wider than first appears. In *R. v. Swan Hunter Shipbuilders Ltd*[50] where the employers were not only charged with failing to provide a safe system of work under paragraph (a), but also with a failure to provide sufficient information and instruction under paragraph (c), the Court of Appeal held that this latter duty might entail providing information and instruction as to potential dangers to non-employees who are working in connection with an employer's business. In the present case, it was held that Swan Hunter did owe a duty under paragraph (c) to inform the employees of contractors of potential dangers since the dangers arose in circumstances which affected the health and safety of the employers' own employees. It has been held that information as to how an accident happened is sufficient notice to employees and others of the existence and nature of a risk of injury to them.[51] The duty to inform is further extended by Regulations which require information relating to the health, safety and welfare of employees to be provided to them by means of posters or leaflets in the form approved by the Health and Safety Executive.[52]

5.16 The duty under paragraph (d) to provide a safe and risk-free place of work applies to any place which is under the employer's control. The fact that the duty is not linked to ownership but to the employer's ability to control means that this duty could apply even where employees are working at the premises of another, so long

---

[47] *Bolton Metropolitan Borough Council v. Malrod Insulations Ltd* [1993] I.C.R. 358.

[48] See, for example, *Norris v. Syndic Manufacturing Co. Ltd* [1952] 2 Q.B. 135. Equally, there is no definition of the word "maintain" in the 1974 Act. If the courts' approach to the meaning of "provide" is followed it is likely that they would apply the meaning of "maintained" to be found in the Factories Act 1961, s. 176(1), where it means maintained in an efficient state, in efficient working order, and in good repair.

[49] *Bolton Metropolitan Borough Council v. Malrod Insulations Ltd* [1983] I.C.R. 358.

[50] [1981] I.C.R. 831.

[51] *Maersk Co. Ltd v. Vannet*, 1997 S.L.T. 1097.

[52] See the Health and Safety Information for Employees Regulations 1989 (S.I. 1989 No. 682).

as the employer has control of those premises. HSC has suggested that "place of work" should have a broad meaning to include such things as open-air sites and temporary structures, and that the duty itself is wide-ranging.[53] Under paragraph (e) a safe working environment is likely to cover such things as heating, lighting, ventilation and noise, and facilities for welfare at work should include the provision of washing facilities.[54]

Health and safety policy

5.17 The 1974 Act, section 2(3), requires employers to prepare, and as often as may be appropriate revise, a written statement of their general policy with respect to the health and safety at work of their employees, and the organisation and arrangements for the time being in force for carrying out that policy and to bring the statement and any revisions to the notice of all their employees. There is an exemption from this requirement for an employer who carries on an undertaking to which, for the time being, less than five employees are employed.[55] The basic duty placed upon the employer under section 2(3) is to prepare and thereafter revise a safety policy, and to bring this policy and any revisions to the notice of all employees. This is the extent of the duty and there is no further statutory guidance on the structure or content of such policies, nor any advice on how they should be brought to the attention of employees: though HSC has published Guidance Notes for such policies.[56] This provision has been criticised on the basis that it merely requires employers to prepare safety policies. It does not require them to be adequate.[57]

Employee involvement in health and safety

5.18 The 1974 Act, section 2(4), empowers the Secretary of State to provide for the appointment by recognised trade unions of safety representatives from amongst the employees.[58] Such representatives must represent the employees in consultations with the

---

[53] See *A Guide to the Health and Safety at Work, etc. Act 1974*.

[54] See HSC Guide.

[55] See the Employers' Health and Safety Policy Statements (Exception) Regulations 1975 (S.I. 1975 No. 1584) discussed in *Osborne v. Bill Taylor of Huyton Ltd* [1982] I.C.R. 168, where it was held that the phrase "for the time being" should be construed as meaning "at any one time".

[56] *Guidance Notes on Employers' Health and Safety Policy Statements for Health and Safety at Work* (1980).

[57] See P. James, "Reforming British Health and Safety Law: A Framework for Discussion" (1992) 21 I.L.J. 83 at p. 87.

[58] Under the 1974 Act, s. 2(5), it was possible for safety representatives to be appointed by workforce election. However, this provision was repealed by the Employment Protection Act 1975, ss. 116 and 125(3), Sched. 15, para. 2 and Sched. 18.

employer. Moreover, employers have a duty to consult these representatives with a view to the making and maintenance of arrangements which will enable them and their employees to co-operate effectively in promoting and developing measures to ensure the employees' health and safety at work, and in checking the effectiveness of such measures.[59] There is a further duty on employers, if requested to do so by the safety representatives, to establish a safety committee which has the primary function of keeping under review the measures taken to ensure the health and safety at work of employees.[60]

5.19 The details of employee involvement in health and safety are provided by the Safety Representatives and Safety Committees Regulations 1977[61] and there is also an HSC Approved Code of Practice. Safety representatives can only be appointed by a recognised trade union[62] from amongst the employees, where one or more employees are employed by an employer by whom it is recognised.[63] Employees appointed as safety representatives should so far as reasonably practicable have been employed by the employer throughout the preceding two years or have had at least two years experience in similar employment.[64] Employees cease to be safety representatives when the trade union which appointed them notifies the employer in writing that their appointment has been terminated, or they cease to be employed at the workplace[65] or they resign.[66]

5.20 As well as having the general function under the 1974 Act, section 2(4), to represent employees in consultation with the employer, safety representatives have the following functions:

---

[59] 1974 Act, s. 2(6).

[60] 1974 Act, s. 2(7).

[61] S.I. 1977 No. 500, as amended by the Management of Health and Safety at Work Regulations 1992 (S.I. 1992 No. 2051).

[62] "Recognised trade union" means an independent trade union as defined by the Trade Union and Labour Relations (Consolidation) Act 1992, s. 5, which the employer concerned recognises for the purpose of negotiations relating to or connected with one or more of the matters specified in s. 178 of that Act. See reg. 2(1).

[63] reg. 3(1). There is an exception for employees employed in a mine within the meaning of the Mines and Quarries Act 1954, s. 180. There are also special rules for members of the British Actors' Equity Association and the Musician's Union. See reg. 8.

[64] reg. 3(4).

[65] However, where safety representatives are appointed to represent employees at more than one workplace they need not cease to be safety representatives so long as they continue to be employed at any one of them. See reg. 3(3)(b).

[66] reg. 3(3)(a)–(c).

(a) to investigate potential hazards and dangerous occurrences at the workplace[67] (whether or not they are drawn to their attention by the employees they represent) and to examine the causes of accidents at the workplace;

(b) to investigate complaints by any employee they represent relating to that employee's health, safety or welfare at work;

(c) to make representations to the employer on matters arising from the above two paragraphs;

(d) to make representations to the employer on general matters affecting the health, safety or welfare at work of employees at the workplace;

(e) to carry out certain inspections;

(f) to represent the employees they were appointed to represent in consultation at the workplace with inspectors of HSE and of any other enforcing authority;

(g) to receive certain information from inspectors;

(h) to attend meetings of safety committees where they attend in their capacity as safety representatives in connection with any of the above functions.[68]

5.21 Further guidance on the functions of safety representatives is provided by paragraph 5 of the Code of Practice. It recommends that safety representatives should:

(a) take all reasonably practical steps to keep themselves informed of:

   (i) the legal requirements relating to the health and safety of persons at work, particularly those they represent;

   (ii) the particular hazards of the workplace and the measures deemed necessary to eliminate or minimise the risk deriving from these hazards;

   (iii) the employer's health and safety policy and the organisation and arrangements for fulfilling that policy;

(b) encourage cooperation between their employer and the employees in promoting and developing essential measures to ensure the health and safety of employees and in checking the effectiveness of these measures;

---

[67] "Workplace" means any place or places where the group or groups of employees a safety representative is appointed to represent are likely to work or are likely to frequent in the course of their employment or incidentally to it. See reg. 2(1).

[68] reg. 4(1)(a)–(h).

(c) bring to the employer's notice normally in writing[69] any unsafe or unhealthy conditions or working practices or unsatisfactory arrangements for welfare at work which come to their attention whether on an inspection or day-to-day observation. The report does not imply that all other conditions and working practices are safe and healthy or that the welfare arrangements are satisfactory in all other respects.

5.22 There are now additional duties of consultation placed upon employers by the Regulations.[70] Employers must consult safety representatives in good time with regard to:

(a) the introduction of any measure at the workplace which may substantially affect the health and safety of the employees the safety representatives concerned represent;

(b) arrangements for nominating or appointing competent persons to assist them in undertaking the measures necessary to comply with the requirements and prohibitions imposed by the relevant statutory provisions[71];

(c) any health and safety information they are required to provide to the employees by any relevant statutory provision;

(d) the planning and organisation of any health and safety training they are required to provide to the employees by any relevant statutory provision;

(e) the health and safety consequences for the employees of the introduction and planning of new technologies into the workplace.[72]

Employers must also provide such facilities and assistance as safety representatives may reasonably require in order to carry out their functions.[73]

---

[69] The Code also recommends that making a written report does not preclude a direct oral approach in the first instance, particularly in situations where speedy remedial action is necessary. Oral discussion is also most appropriate for minor matters.

[70] See reg. 4A, inserted by the Management of Health and Safety at Work Regulations 1992 (S.I. 1992 No. 2051), reg. 17, Sched.

[71] Under the Management of Health and Safety at Work Regulations 1999 (S.I. 1999 No. 3242), reg. 7 employers must appoint competent persons to assist in health and safety matters, and under reg. 8(1)(b) they must nominate a sufficient number of competent persons to implement evacuation procedures from premises in the event of serious or imminent danger.

[72] reg. 4A(1)(a)–(e).

[73] reg. 4A(2).

5.23 Safety representatives have the power to carry out inspections in three circumstances. First, they are entitled to inspect the workplace or a part of it if they have given the employer or his representative reasonable notice in writing of their intention to do so and they have not carried out an inspection in the previous three months.[74] However, further inspections can be carried out within the three-month period where there has been a substantial change in the conditions of work (whether because of the introduction of new machinery or otherwise), or new information has been published by HSC or HSE relevant to the hazards of the workplace since the last inspection and the employer has been consulted before the intended inspection.[75] The employer is required to provide such facilities and assistance as the safety representatives may reasonably require (including facilities for independent investigation by them and private discussion with the employees) for the purposes of an inspection, but nothing in this provision precludes the employer or his representative from being present in the workplace during an inspection.[76]

5.24 Safety representatives also have specific inspection functions where there has been a notifiable accident or dangerous occurrence in a workplace or a notifiable disease[77] has been contracted there. In such circumstances they may inspect the part of the workplace concerned and, so far as is necessary for determining the cause, they may inspect any other part of the workplace and where it is reasonably practicable to do so they must notify the employer or his representative of their intention to carry out the inspection. Such an inspection will only be appropriate when it is safe for an inspection to be carried out and the interests of employees in the group which safety representatives are appointed to represent might be involved.[78] As with the general inspection power, employers are required to provide such facilities and assistance as the safety representatives may reasonably require; though the employer can be present on the premises during the inspection.[79]

5.25 The third inspection power which safety representatives possess is to inspect relevant documents. If safety representatives

---

[74] re.g 5(1). More frequent inspections can be carried out by agreement with the employer.

[75] reg. 5(2).

[76] reg. 5(3).

[77] "Notifiable accident or dangerous occurrence" and "notifiable disease" mean any accident, dangerous occurrence or disease, as the case may be, notice of which is required to be given by virtue of any of the relevant statutory provisions. See reg. 6(3).

[78] See generally, reg. 6(1).

[79] reg. 6(2).

have given the employer reasonable notice, they are entitled to inspect and to take copies of any document relevant to the workplace or to the employees they represent which the employer is required to keep under any relevant statutory provision; except the health records of identifiable individuals.[80] Employers must also make available to safety representatives the information, within their knowledge, necessary for safety representatives to fulfil their functions except:

(a) any information the disclosure of which would be against the interests of national security; or

(b) any information which they could not disclose without contravening a statutory prohibition; or

(c) any information relating specifically to individuals, unless they have consented to its disclosure;

(d) any information the disclosure of which would, for reasons other than its effect on health, safety and welfare at work, cause substantial injury to the employer's undertaking or, where the information was supplied by some other person, to the undertaking of that other person; or

(e) any information obtained by the employer for the purpose of bringing, prosecuting or defending any legal proceedings.

5.26 The Code of Practice recommends that the sorts of information which should be provided by employers should include:

(a) information about the plans and performance of their undertaking and any changes proposed in so far as they affect the health, safety and welfare at work of their employees;

(b) information of a technical nature about hazards to health and safety and precautions deemed necessary to eliminate or minimise them, in respect of machinery, plant, equipment, processes, systems of work and substances in use at work, including any relevant information provided by consultants or designers or by the manufacturer, importer or supplier of any article or substance used, or proposed to be used, at work by their employees;

(c) information which the employer keeps relating to the occurrence of any accident, dangerous occurrence or notifiable industrial disease and any statistical records relating to such matters;

---

[80] reg. 7(1).

(d) any other information specifically related to matters affecting the health and safety of employees, including the results of any measurements taken in the course of checking the effectiveness of health and safety arrangements;

(e) information on articles or substances which an employer issues to homeworkers.

Health and Safety (Consultation with Employees) Regulations 1996

5.27 As already indicated, the original duty to consult with employees on health and safety was only triggered when a recognised independent trade union appoints safety representatives from amongst the employees. The original provisions of the Health and Safety at Work, etc. Act 1974 did permit the election by employees of safety representatives; but this was repealed in 1975 by the Employment Protection Act. This approach was adopted because the Labour Government of the time believed that without the involvement of recognised trade unions safety representatives would be unable to ensure that their rights were enforced and their role respected by management.

5.28 However, the legal and industrial relations scene has altered considerably since 1975. From a legal perspective, ever since the adoption of the Framework Directive on European Health and Safety in 1989,[81] there have been doubts as to the legality of the British system for employee involvement in health and safety matters. As already indicated, the 1974 Act and the Safety Representatives and Safety Committees Regulations 1977 apply the medium of the recognised independent trade union as the exclusive legal mechanism for the appointment of safety representatives. As already noted, the Management of Health and Safety at Work Regulations 1992 extended the obligations of consultation placed upon employers as required by the Framework Directive, but did nothing to extend rights away from recognised trade unions. Such an approach was of doubtful validity given that the Framework Directive required consultation with workers and/or their representatives. In two cases brought under redundancy and transfer of undertakings laws the United Kingdom Government was held to have breached the relevant Directives by not providing for the compulsory designation of worker representatives and, instead, relying on representatives of recognised independent trade unions.[82] Such an approach breached the Directives because it did

---

[81] E.C. Directive 89/391/EEC.
[82] *E.C. Commission v. U.K.* (C–382/92 and C–383/92) [1994] I.C.R. 664 (ECJ).

not ensure that there was a system where the existence of worker representatives could be guaranteed.

5.29 It is no surprise, therefore, that the duty to consult on health and safety matters has been extended to employers who do not recognise trade unions. The 1996 Regulations[83] are intended to ensure fuller compliance with the consultation requirements of the Framework Directive. They can be regarded as top-up regulations because they build upon the existing framework for employee representation in health and safety created by the 1977 Regulations. It should be noted that the current arrangements which provide for representation through the medium of the recognised independent trade union remain unaffected by the changes introduced by the 1996 Regulations. However, where there is no recognised trade union, consultation is required with either the employees directly or with "representatives of employee safety".[84] This latter group is made up of employees who have been elected for the purposes of health and safety consultation. There is no guidance in the Regulations as to how such elections as representatives of employee safety are to be conducted. However, employers who use the Regulations must be aware of such issues as constituencies, frequency of elections, number of representatives, conduct of elections. Where an employer chooses to consult with representatives of employee safety he must inform the employees of the names of those representatives and the group of employees who are covered by such representation.[85]

5.30 Where consultation is with employees or representatives of employee safety such information must be made available to them as will enable them to participate fully and effectively in those consultations.[86] There are similar exemptions as those in the 1977 Regulations as regards the non-disclosure of information which is against the interests of national security, would contravene statute, relates to an individual, would cause substantial injury to the employer's undertaking or was obtained in connection with legal proceedings.[87]

5.31 Consultation must be in good time on matters relating to the employee's health and safety at work. In particular, employers must consult over the introduction of health and safety measures, arrangements for appointing competent persons under the Management Regulations or the Fire Precautions (Workplace) Regulations 1997, any relevant health and safety information, the

---

[83] S.I. 1996 No. 1513.
[84] reg. 4(1)(a), (b).
[85] reg. 4(2).
[86] reg. 5(1).
[87] reg. 5(3).

planning and organisation of health and safety training, and the health and safety consequences of the introduction of new technology.[88] These requirements are the same as those inserted into the 1977 Regulations by the Management Regulations so as to comply with the consultation requirements of the Framework Directive. "In good time" would suggest that before making a decision an employer should allow time to provide information about what is proposed, give the employees or their representatives an opportunity to express their views and to take account of such responses.

5.32 Representatives of employee safety have the following functions:

(a) to make representations to the employer on potential hazards and dangerous occurrences at the workplace which affect the group of employees he/she represents. This right can be compared with the 1977 Regulations, reg. 4 which allows safety representatives to investigate and to examine causes of accidents;

(b) to make representations on general matters affecting the health and safety at work of the employees he/she represents and, in particular, in the areas where the representatives have specific consultation rights;

(c) to represent the employees in consultations at the workplace with health and safety inspectors.[89]

It is noteworthy that the 1996 Regulations go no further than to ensure compliance with the consultation requirements of the Framework Directive and are therefore less extensive than the 1977 Regulations. For example, safety representatives have additional functions under the 1977 Regulations such as investigation and inspection powers which have not been provided to representatives of employee safety.

Safety committees

5.33 A safety committee must be established by an employer where at least two safety representatives request the employer in writing to establish one.[90] Where such a request is made employers must comply with the following procedure:

(a) they must consult with the safety representatives who made the request and with the representatives of recognised trade unions whose members work in any workplace

---

[88] reg. 3.
[89] reg. 6.
[90] reg. 9(1).

where it is proposed that the safety committee will function;

(b) they must post a notice stating the composition of the committee and the workplace(s) to be covered by it in a place where it may easily be read by the employees;

(c) the committee must be established not later than three months after the request for it.

As already noted, the general function of a safety committee is to keep under review the measures taken to ensure the health and safety at work of the employees. It is obvious that the functions of safety representatives and those of safety committees are different. The functions of safety representatives are much more pro-active, whereas the basic function of safety committees is to consider and appraise management's health and safety policies. It is vital, therefore, that there is effective co-ordination between the two groups.

The right to time off

5.34 An employer must permit a safety representative to take such time off with pay during the employee's working hours as is necessary for the purposes of his functions[91] and to undergo training in aspects of those functions as may be reasonable in all the circumstances, having regard to any relevant provisions of an HSC approved code of practice relating to time off for training.[92] The Code of Practice recommends that as soon as possible after their appointment, safety representatives should be permitted time off with pay to attend basic training facilities approved by the TUC or by the union which appointed them. Further training, similarly approved, should be undertaken where the safety representative has special responsibilities or where such training is necessary to meet changes in circumstances or relevant legislation. Equally, representatives of employee safety have the right to such training as is reasonable in the circumstances to enable them to perform their functions, and the employer must meet the reasonable costs associated with such training, including travel and subsistence costs.[93] They are also entitled to such time off with pay as is necessary to enable them to perform their functions or to enable them to undergo the type of training noted above.[94]

---

[91] Namely the general functions in the 1974 Act, s. 2(4), and the specific functions listed in reg. 4(1)(a)–(h).

[92] reg. 4(2). See the Code of Practice: Time Off for the Training of Safety Representatives (1978).

[93] 1996 Regs, reg. 7(1)(a).

[94] 1996 Regs, reg.7(1)(b).

5.35 The length of training for safety representatives cannot be rigidly prescribed. However, the Code recommends that basic training should take into account the functions of safety representatives, of safety committees and of trade union policies and practices in relation to:

(a) the legal requirements relating to health and safety at work, particularly the group of persons they directly represent;

(b) the nature and extent of workplace hazards, and the measures necessary to eliminate or minimise them;

(c) the health and safety policy of employers, and organisation and arrangements for fulfilling those practices.

5.36 The Code also suggests that safety representatives will have to acquire new skills in order to carry out their functions, including safety inspections, and in using basic sources of legal and official information and information provided by the employer on health and safety matters.

5.37 The Code also explains the obligations of trade unions as far as the training of safety representatives is concerned. When a trade union wishes a safety representative to receive relevant training it should inform management of the course that it has approved and supply a copy of the syllabus, indicating its contents, if the employer asks for it. Unions should give at least a few weeks' notice of the safety representatives who have been nominated for a particular course and the numbers attending should be that which is reasonable in the circumstances, bearing in mind such factors as the frequency of such courses and the operational requirements of the employer. As the Code makes clear many of these issues are best resolved by agreement between management and unions. In considering whether time off for training is necessary it has been held that the Code carries great weight but it is not decisive of the issue.[95] Further, although the Code recommends that training courses should be approved by the TUC or a union this is not a mandatory legal requirement.[96] Thus although union approval for courses is a factor to be taken into account, it is not illegal for employers to organise their own courses. In such a case it will be a question for the industrial tribunal to decide as to whether an

---

[95] *White v. Pressed Steel Fisher* [1980] I.R.L.R. 176 (EAT).

[96] *cf.* the provisions on time off for union duties in the Trade Union and Labour Relations (Consolidation) Act 1992, s. 168. It is provided by s. 168(2) that any training courses in aspects of industrial relations must be approved by the TUC or an independent trade union.

employer-provided course is adequate particularly as regards the representational responsibilities of safety representatives.[97]

5.38 Where the employer has either failed to permit a safety representative or a representative of employee safety to take time off or has failed to pay him for any time off, there is a right of complaint to an employment tribunal.[98] A safety representative must submit such a complaint within three months of the date when the failure occurred or within such further period as the tribunal considers reasonable where it is satisfied that it was not reasonably practicable for the complaint to be presented within the three months.[99] Where the tribunal finds the complaint to be well-founded it will make a declaration to that effect and can award compensation of such amount as it considers just and equitable in all the circumstances having regard to the employer's default and the employee's loss.[1] Where the tribunal finds that the employer has failed to pay the employee the whole or part of the required amount, the tribunal must order the employer to pay to the employee the amount which it finds due.[2]

Protection of safety representatives and safety committee members

5.39 There is now legislation which protects safety representatives and members of safety committees from being subjected to any detriment,[3] and which makes it unfair[4] to dismiss them where they have performed, or propose to perform, any functions as a safety representative or a member of a safety committee. There are also protections for employees who have been designated by the employer to carry out activities in connection with preventing or reducing health and safety risks, and for employees who bring to the employer's attention harmful circumstances where there is either no safety representative nor any safety committee, or it was not reasonably practicable for the employee to raise the matter through them.[5] Employees who leave or propose to leave or refuse to return to their place of work in circumstances of danger which

---

[97] *White v. Pressed Steel Fisher* [1980] I.R.L.R. 176 (EAT).

[98] The Safety Representatives and Safety Committees Regulations 1977, reg. 11(1); Health and Safety (Consultation with Employees) Regulations 1996, reg. 7(3) and Sched. 2.

[99] reg. 11(2).

[1] reg. 11(3).

[2] reg. 11(4).

[3] See the Employment Rights Act 1996, s. 44.

[4] Employment Rights Act 1996, s. 100(1)(b). There is no qualifying period or upper age limit applicable to such health and safety dismissals. See ERA 1996, ss. 108, 109.

[5] ERA 1996, s. 44(1)(a) and (c) (detriment); s. 100(1)(a) and (c) (dismissal).

they reasonably believe to be serious and imminent, or who take or propose to take appropriate steps to protect themselves or other persons from danger in similar circumstances, are also protected.[6] Representatives of employee safety, candidates for such posts and employees who have been consulted directly have the same protections as regards being subjected to a detriment or being dismissed as is enjoyed by safety representatives.[7]

Duties of Employers and the Self-Employed to Persons other than Employees

5.40 Employers must conduct their undertakings in such a way as to ensure, so far as reasonably practicable, that persons not in their employment who may be affected thereby are not exposed to risks to their health and safety.[8] A similar duty also applies to the self-employed to conduct their undertakings in such a way as to ensure that they and other persons (not being their employees) are not exposed to health and safety risks.[9] The Secretary of State also has the power, by regulations, to prescribe the circumstances and the manner in which employers and the self-employed must give prescribed information to persons other than employees who may be affected by the way that the undertaking is conducted as might affect their health and safety.[10]

5.41 The section 3(1) duty raises three obvious points. First the duty is owed by employers to persons other than their own employees; secondly, the standard is one of reasonable practicability; and thirdly the duty arises out of the conduct of the undertaking. It is intended to complement section 2(1) which places a duty on employers to ensure, so far as is reasonably practicable, the health, safety and welfare at work of all their employees. It is noteworthy that the operation of this latter duty does not involve the conduct of the undertaking. Despite this, in *H.M. Inspector of Factories v. Austin Rover Group Ltd*,[11] Lord Jauncey argued that sections 2 and 3 imposed duties in relation to safety on a single person, whether an individual or a corporation,

---

[6] ERA 1996, s. 44(1)(d) and (e) (detriment); s. 100(1)(d) and (e) (dismissal).

[7] ERA 1996, s.44(1)(ba) (detriment); s.100(1)(ba) (dismissal).

[8] 1974 Act, s. 3(1).

[9] 1974 Act, s. 3(2). The scope of this duty has been amended by the Genetically Modified Organisms (Contained Use) Regulations 1992 (S.I. 1992 No. 3217) and the Health and Safety (Dangerous Pathogens) Regulations 1981 (S.I. 1981 No. 1011) so as to apply to any activity involving genetic modification or dangerous pathogens.

[10] 1974 Act, s. 3(3). At time of writing no regulations have been made under this provision.

[11] [1989] I.R.L.R. 404 (HL).

who is in a position to exercise complete control over the matters to which the duties extend. It has been the element of control which until recently has been the major issue for prosecution under section 3(1). In *R. v. Swan Hunter Ltd*,[12] for example, the Court of Appeal held that the section required employers to provide information to visiting workers to avoid them exposing themselves to risk. However, the court was less clear on whether there was also an obligation on the employer to take control of the situation if the visiting workers had been supplied with the information and then failed to follow the safe system specified there.

5.42 In *R. v. Mara*[13] there was an accident in a store on a Saturday caused by a faulty cleaning machine which had been left out by cleaning contractors who had a weekday contract. This was at a time when the cleaning contractors were not at work. Nevertheless, the court made it clear that making equipment available to others was sufficient for the application of section 3(1). Indeed, in that case Parker L.J. specifically considered the case where a factory is closed down for cleaning by a contractor and concluded that there would be a breach of section 3(1) if the contractor's employees were exposed to risks. However, a much more restrictive approach was adopted by the Divisional Court in *RMC Roadstone Products Ltd v. Jester*[14] where it was held that there had been no breach of section 3(1) because of an absence of control on the part of the employers. It was argued that, before an activity could be within the conduct of an employer's undertaking, the employer had to exercise some *actual* control over it or be *under a duty* to do so. This case was therefore responsible for the startling proposition that an employer could escape liability under section 3(1) if he left the contractor to do the work in the way the contractor thinks fit.

5.43 The law has now been resolved authoritatively by the House of Lords in *R. v. Associated Octel Co. Ltd*,[15] where it was made clear that section 3(1) was not a provision dealing with vicarious liability which is essentially a matter governed by the nature of the contractual relationship between the parties. So section 3(1) is not a provision which places a liability on the employer for the vicarious acts of the contractor. Essentially, section 3(1) imposes a duty upon the employer *per se*. Such a duty is defined by reference to a certain kind of activity namely the conduct by the employer of his undertaking whether or not there is a contractual relationship. As far as the meaning of the conduct of the undertaking is

---

[12] [1981] I.C.R. 831, CA.
[13] [1987] I.C.R. 165.
[14] [1994] I.C.R. 456.
[15] [1996] I.C.R. 973.

concerned this is essentially a question of fact. However, the vital question is simply whether the particular activity can be described as part of the employer's undertaking and is not dependent upon the presence or absence of control. Thus the basic requirement under section 3 is for the employer to ensure, subject to reasonable practicability, that he does not create risks to a person's health and safety in the way the undertaking is run. The reference to control by Lord Jauncey in *Austin Rover* should simply be viewed as a "self-evident proposition" that a person conducting his own undertaking is free to decide how he will do so.

5.44 The House of Lords also considered the nature of the reasonable practicability defence which is available to the employer once it is proved that the activity is part of his undertaking.[15a] An employer must take reasonably practicable steps to avoid risks to the contractor's employees which arise not merely from the physical state of the premises, but also from the inadequacy of the arrangements which he makes with the contractor as to how the work will be done. This means that the employer must assess the risks and develop procedures to limit the risk of injury to contractors and their employees. It may require the employer to ensure that the self-same precautions are taken for the health and safety of employees of contractors as are taken for his own employees.[16]

5.45 It is clear that the general duty provided for by section 3(1) can impose a duty to inform persons who are not the employer's own employees. In *R. v. Swan Hunter Shipbuilders Ltd*[17] the Court of Appeal held that the duty under section 3(1) to conduct the undertaking in such a way as to avoid risks to the health and safety of persons other than employees was wide enough to include an obligation to provide information and instruction to the employees of others. The fact that section 3(3) specifically requires an employer to give information to persons not in his employment does not limit any obligation under section 3(1), since the former provision refers only to limited information in limited circumstances to be prescribed by regulations which have not yet been made. This approach has been followed in Scotland, where it has been confirmed that there is no mutual inconsistency between sections 3(1) and 3(3), since section 3(3) is limited in application and relates only to prescribed cases, prescribed circumstances, and prescribed information in a prescribed manner.[18] On the other

---

[15a] See also *R. v. Nelson Group Services (Maintenance) Ltd* [1999] I.R.L.R. 646, CA (issue essentially one of facts).

[16] *R v. Rhone Poulenc Rorer Ltd* [1997] I.C.R. 1054, CA.

[17] [1981] I.C.R. 831. See also *Maersk Co. Ltd v. Vannet*, 1997 S.L.T. 1097.

[18] See *Carmichael v. Rosehall Engineering Works Ltd*, 1984 S.L.T. 40; [1983] I.R.L.R. 480.

hand, section 3(1) requires information and instruction on how to avoid risks to health and safety subject only to the requirement of reasonable practicability.

5.46 A prosecution under section 3(1) is competent so long as there is a risk of exposure to danger; it is not necessary to prove that the risk has actually materialised. Thus, in a case involving the risk of legionella infection from an air conditioning cooling tower, it was sufficient for conviction merely to prove that legionella bacteria might emerge so as to expose members of the public to the possibility of danger: it was not necessary also to show that the bacteria did get into the atmosphere and was available to be inhaled.[19]

Duties of Persons concerned with Premises to Persons other than Employees

5.47 The 1974 Act also imposes general duties on owners, occupiers and others, such as maintenance contractors, as regards their control of non-domestic premises. A duty is owed by persons to those who are not their employees but who use non-domestic premises[20] made available to them as a place of work or as a place where they may use plant or substances provided for their use there, and the duty applies to such premises and other non-domestic premises used in connection with them.[21] The duty applies to persons having control of any premises or matter in connection with the carrying on by them of a trade, business or other undertaking (whether for profit or not).[22] The application of this duty is wide enough to cover the common parts of a block of flats (the hall, landing, and staircases and lifts) since the common parts are not domestic premises and, therefore, in accordance with section 53(1) if they are premises at all they must be non-domestic premises.[23] Such common parts will be made available as a place of work or as a place where plant and substances might be used as required by section 4(1) when lift engineers or electricians attend at the block to maintain or repair the lifts or electrical installations or when the common parts are redecorated by contractors.[24]

---

[19] *R. v. Board of Trustees of the Science Museum* [1993] I.C.R. 876.

[20] There is no specific definition of non-domestic premises in the 1974 Act. However, s. 53(1) defines "domestic premises" as meaning premises occupied as a private dwelling (including any garden, yard, garage, outhouse or other appurtenance which is not used in common by the occupants of more than one such dwelling), and directs that "non-domestic premises" should be construed accordingly.

[21] 1974 Act, s. 4(1).

[22] 1974 Act, s. 4(4).

[23] *Westminster City Council v. Select Management Ltd* [1985] I.C.R. 353.

[24] *ibid.* See, in particular, the judgment of Parker L.J. at 357.

5.48   Any person who has, to any extent, control of premises[25] or of the means of access to or egress from them or of any plant or substance in such premises has a duty to take such measures as it is reasonable for a person in his position to take to ensure, so far as is reasonably practicable, that the premises, all means of access or egress, and any plant or substance, are safe and without risks to health.[26] This provision requires a prosecutor to establish three things. The prosecutor must prove, first, that the premises are unsafe and constitute a risk to health; secondly, what persons have at that time any degree of control of those premises; and thirdly, that it is reasonable for one or more of the persons having a degree of control to take measures which would ensure safety. Once a prosecutor has fulfilled these requirements the onus shifts to the accused to prove that it was not reasonably practicable to take the measures in question.[27] The reasonableness of the measures is to be judged in the light of the person's knowledge of the anticipated use for which the premises have been made available, and of the extent of his control and knowledge, if any, of the actual use thereafter. But the person need not to take further measures against unknown and unexpected events.[28] A person is to be treated as a person who has control of premises when he has, by virtue of any contract or tenancy, an obligation of any extent in relation to the maintenance or repair of any non-domestic premises or of any means of access to or egress from them or as regards the safety or health risks arising from plant or substances in those premises.[29]

Management of Health and Safety at Work Regulations

5.49   The above provisions constitute the core duties created by the Act since they apply to employers as regards their own employees (section 2), employers and the self-employed as regards persons who are not their employees (section 3) and the controllers of premises (section 4). Persons who may owe duties under any of these provisions should also take into account the provisions of the Management of Health and Safety at Work Regulations 1999.[30] These regulations provide more specific direction as to how to

---

[25] The fact that the control can be to any extent means that this provision has been widely construed. In *T. Kilroe & Sons Ltd v. Gower* [1983] Crim. L.R. 548, contractors who were hired to demolish a factory were held to have sufficient control of the premises even though most of the work had been delegated to sub-contractors.

[26] 1974 Act, s. 4(2).

[27] *HM Inspector of Factories v. Austin Rover Group Ltd* [1989] I.R.L.R. 404 (HL).

[28] *ibid.* See the speech of Lord Jauncey at 410–411.

[29] 1974 Act, s. 4(3).

[30] S.I. 1999 No. 3242. These regulations are also discussed in Chap. 8.

carry out the general duties of sections 2 to 4 and, most importantly, introduce the principle of risk assessment. Regulation 3(1) requires every employer to make a suitable and sufficient assessment of the risks to the health and safety of his employees to which they are exposed whilst they are at work,[31] and the risks to the health and safety of others who are not in his employment arising out of the conduct of his undertaking. Where the persons working in the undertaking include women of child-bearing age and the work is of a kind which could involve risk to the health and safety of a new or expectant mother[32] or to that of her baby, the risk assessment must include an assessment of risk as regards any processes or working conditions, or physical, biological or chemical agents which might affect the health and safety of that mother or baby.[33] Where the risk cannot be avoided by taking action which is required to be taken under the relevant statutory provisions the employer must, if it is reasonable to do so, and would avoid such risks, alter the new or expectant mother's working conditions or hours of work.[34] If it is not reasonable to alter the working conditions or hours of work, or it would not avoid such risk, the employer must suspend the employee from work for so long as it is necessary to avoid the risk.[35] The duties to alter working conditions or hours of work and the duty to suspend from work do not apply unless the new or expectant mother has notified the employer in writing that she is pregnant, has given birth within the previous six months or is breastfeeding.[36] It should be noted that, unlike the rest of the Management Regulations, the risk assessment duties owed by an employer to new or expectant mothers and young persons do give rise to civil liability.[37] Generally, the assessment is to be done for the purpose of identifying the measures the employer needs to take to comply with the requirements and

---

[31] There are special obligations owed to young persons (*i.e.* those under 18) who cannot be employed by the employer unless there has been a review of the risk assessment which takes account of their lack of experience, lack of awareness of risks, and immaturity; reg. 13(4), (5).

[32] "New or expectant mother" means an employee who is pregnant who has given birth during the previous six months, or who is breastfeeding. See reg. 1(2).

[33] reg. 16(1). References to risk, in relation to infectious or contagious disease, are references to a level of risk at work which is in addition to the level to which a new or expectant mother may be expected to be exposed outside the workplace; reg. 16(4).

[34] reg. 16(2).

[35] reg. 16(3).

[36] reg. 18. The employer is also entitled to request the employee to produce a certificate from a registered medical practitioner or a registered midwife showing that she is pregnant; reg. 17.

[37] It is unlawful under European Law for the employer either to impose a blanket ban against women working at night or to refuse to employ them on health and safety grounds: *Commission of the European Communities v. Italian Republic*, Case C–207/46, ECJ, and *Land Mecklenburg v. Vorpommern*, Case C–207/98, ECJ.

prohibitions imposed by the relevant statutory provisions and the Fire Precautions (Workplace) Regulations 1997, Part II. A similar assessment should be conducted by self-employed persons as regards risks to their own health and safety, and the health and safety of persons not in their employment arising out of the conduct of their undertaking.[38] Employers and the self-employed are also required to keep their risk assessments under review and to make any necessary changes.[39] Employers who employ five or more employees must record the significant findings of the assessment and any group of employees who are especially at risk.[40] A failure to carry out a suitable and sufficient risk assessment is a criminal offence and in any prosecution the accused is entitled to be told in what respect the risk assessment was insufficient.[41] Regulation 4 now requires employers to implement any preventive and protective measures required by the risk assessments in accordance with principles specified in the regulations. These indicate a range of measures which employers must consider when implementing health and safety precautions.

5.50 The purpose of risk assessment is best described by the Approved Code of Practice which has been produced by the HSC. It declares:

"The purpose of the risk assessment is to help the employer or self-employed person to determine what measures should be taken to comply with the employer's or self-employed person's duties under the 'relevant statutory duties'. This phrase covers the general duties in the [1974 Act] and the more specific duties in the various Acts and Regulations (including these Regulations) associated with [it]. Regulation 3 does not itself stipulate the measures to be taken as a result of the risk assessment. The measures in each workplace will derive from compliance with other health and safety duties . . . taking carefully into account the risk assessment. In essence, the risk assessment guides the judgment of the employer or the self-employed person, as to the measures they ought to take to fulfil their statutory obligations".[42]

5.51 The Regulations also place a number of additional duties on employers which complement and enhance the basic requirement of risk assessment. Employers must make and give effect to

---

[38] reg. 3(2).
[39] reg. 3(3).
[40] reg. 3(6).
[41] *Carmichael v. Marks & Spencer plc*, 1996 S.L.T. 1167.
[42] See paras 7 and 8.

appropriate health and safety arrangements, having regard to the nature of the activities and size of undertaking, for the effective planning, organisation, control, monitoring, and review of preventive and protective measures[43] and provide such health surveillance as is appropriate to the health and safety risks identified by the assessment.[44] Competent persons can be appointed by employers to assist them in undertaking the measures necessary to comply with the requirements and prohibitions of the relevant statutory provisions.[45] Employers must also establish procedures to be followed in the event of serious and imminent danger to persons at work in the undertaking.[46] They must nominate a sufficient number of people to implement these procedures as far as evacuation from the premises is concerned, and no employee should have access to a restricted area unless he has reviewed adequate health and safety instructions.[47] The Regulations also ensure that employees become aware of these arrangements by requiring the employer to provide them with comprehensible and relevant information on:

(a) the risks to their health and safety identified by the assessment;

(b) the preventive and protective measures;

(c) procedures for serious and imminent danger and measures for fighting fires;

(d) the identity of persons nominated to implement evacuation and fire-fighting procedures;

(e) the risks associated with any shared workplace.[48]

There are also special information obligations placed on employers before employing a child to inform the child's parent about the health and safety risks, the preventive and protective measures, and the risks in shared workplaces.[49]

5.52 Further, the Regulations also contain provisions which are relevant to the duties owed by controllers of premises under the

---

[43] reg. 5(1). Employers with five or more employees must record their arrangements; reg. 5(2). "Preventive and protective measures" are the measures which have been identified in the assessment as the measures required to be taken so as to comply with the requirements and prohibitions imposed by the relevant statutory provisions; reg. 1(2).

[44] reg. 6.

[45] reg. 7(1).

[46] reg. 8(1)(a).

[47] reg. 8(1)(b) and (c).

[48] reg. 10(1).

[49] reg. 10(2). A child is a person not over school age under the Education (Scotland) Act 1980, s. 31; reg. 1(2).

1974 Act, section 4. Employers who share a workplace must co-operate with one another so as to ensure compliance with the requirements and prohibitions of the relevant statutory provisions, take all reasonable steps to co-ordinate those measures, and inform the other employers concerned of the health and safety risks to their employees.[50] Employers and self-employed persons must ensure that the employer of any employees from an outside undertaking who are working in their undertaking are provided with comprehensible information on the risks to those employees' health and safety and the measures which have been taken to comply with the requirements and prohibitions of the relevant statutory provisions.[51]

Duties of persons in control of premises

5.53 The 1974 Act, section 5, placed duties on persons having control of a prescribed class[52] of premises to use the best practicable means for preventing the emission into the atmosphere from the premises of noxious or offensive substances, and for rendering harmless and inoffensive such substances as may be emitted. The provision has been the subject of considerable amendment by the Environmental Protection Act 1990, section 162(1), Schedule 15, paragraph 14, and was prospectively repealed by section 162(2) and Schedule 16, Part I of that Act.

Duties of manufacturers as to articles for use at work

5.54 The 1974 Act, section 6,[53] imposes a series of duties in respect of articles and substances for use at work. This provision has been the subject of considerable amendment; most importantly by the Consumer Protection Act 1987. The basic thrust of the provision is to place duties on any person who designs, manufactures, imports or supplies[54] any article for use at work,[55] or any article of fairground equipment. The duties only operate in relation

---

[50] reg. 11(1). These duties also extend to the self-employed; reg. 11(2).

[51] reg. 12(1).

[52] See the Health and Safety (Emissions into the Atmosphere) Regulations 1983 (S.I. 1983 No. 943) which prescribes the class of premises covered by this provision and the substances which are to be treated as noxious or offensive.

[53] The provisions of s. 5 preventing harmful emissions into the atmosphere were repealed by the Environmental Protection Act 1990, s. 162(2), Sched. 16, Pt I.

[54] "Supply" means supplying articles by way of sale, lease, hire, or hire-purchase, whether as principal or agent for another; 1974 Act, s. 53(1).

[55] It is necessary that the article be designed, etc., for use at work. This requirement is critical and it will mean, for example, that there is unlikely to be any protection under s. 6(1) when the article is being tested to discover whether it is suitable for use at work. See *Mckay v. Unwin Pyrotechnics Ltd* [1991] Crim. L.R. 547.

to things done in the course of a trade, business or other undertaking and to matters within their control.[56] The key duties are:

(a) to ensure, so far as reasonably practicable, that the article is so designed and constructed that it will be safe and without risks to health at all times when it is being set, used, cleaned or maintained by a person at work;

(b) to carry out or arrange for the carrying out of such testing and examination as may be necessary for performing the above duty;

(c) to take such steps as are necessary to secure that persons supplied with an article are provided with adequate information about the use for which the article has been designed or has been tested and about any conditions necessary to ensure that it is safe and without risks to health;

(d) to take such steps as are necessary to secure, so far as is reasonably practicable, that revisions of the information are provided as are necessary by reason of its becoming known that anything gives rise to a serious risk to health and safety.[57]

5.55 The 1974 Act, section 6(2), requires designers and manufacturers of articles for use at work to carry out any necessary research with a view to the discovery, and so far as is reasonably practicable, the elimination or minimisation of health and safety risks. There are also duties placed upon those responsible for the erection or installation of any article for use at work to ensure, so far as is reasonably practicable, that nothing about the way in which the article is erected or installed makes it unsafe or a risk to health.[58] Manufacturers, importers and suppliers of any substance must:

(a) ensure, so far as is reasonably practicable, that the substance will be safe and without risk to health at all times when it is being used, handled, processed, stored or transported by a person at work or in non-domestic premises;

(b) carry out or arrange for the carrying-out of any necessary testing and examination;

(c) take such steps as are necessary to secure that persons supplied with the substance are provided with adequate information about any risks to health and safety to which

---

[56] 1974 Act, s. 6(7).
[57] 1974 Act s. 6(1)(a)–(d).
[58] 1974 Act, s. 6(3).

the inherent properties of the substance may give rise, about the results of any relevant tests and about any necessary conditions as regards the use, etc., or disposal of the substance;

(d) take such steps as are necessary to secure, so far as is reasonably practicable, that all necessary revisions of information are provided.[59]

Duties of Employees at Work

5.56 It is the duty of employees to take reasonable care for the health and safety of themselves and of other persons who may be affected by their acts or omissions at work.[60] Employees also owe a duty of co-operation as regards any duty or requirement imposed on the employer or any other person by any of the relevant statutory provisions so far as is necessary to enable that duty or requirement to be performed or complied with.[61] Both the duty of care and the duty of co-operation only apply while the employee is at work. Employees are at work throughout the time that they are in the course of their employment, but not otherwise.[62] This issue was discussed in *Coult v. Szuba*,[63] where the court observed that, although there were masses of authority on the meaning of course of employment in a civil law context, this was the first time that the phrase had had to be interpreted in the context of penal legislation. In the context of the civil cases it is necessary for the phrase to be liberally construed. But that approach should not be applied when interpreting criminal legislation. In the end of the day the issue is primarily one of fact. However, the mere fact that an employee has clocked-in for work does not necessarily mean that he is automatically within the course of his employment.

5.57 The duties of employees have been extended by the Management of Health and Safety at Work Regulations 1999. Under regulation 14(1) employees have duties to use any machinery, equipment, dangerous substance, transport equipment, means of production or safety device provided by the employer in accordance with any training and instruction in the use of that equipment which is provided by the employer in compliance with the requirements and prohibitions of any relevant statutory provision. Moreover, employees must also inform their employer, or any other employee with specific responsibility for health and safety, of any

---

[59] 1974 Act, s. 6(4)(a)–(d).
[60] 1974 Act, s. 7(a).
[61] 1974 Act, s. 7(b).
[62] 1974 Act, s. 52(1)(b).
[63] [1982] I.C.R. 380.

work situation which could reasonably be considered a serious and immediate danger to health and safety, and of any matter which could reasonably be considered to represent a shortcoming in the employer's protection arrangements for health and safety. These latter duties only arise where the situation or matter either affects the health and safety of the employee or arises out of or in connection with his own activities at work, and has not previously been reported to the employer or to any other employee.[64]

Other Duties

5.58 No person shall intentionally or recklessly interfere with or misuse anything provided in the interests of health, safety and welfare in pursuance of any of the relevant statutory provisions.[65] HSC has made it clear that the things which are covered by this provision include fire escapes and fire extinguishers, perimeter fencing, warning notices for particular hazards, protective clothing, guards for machinery, and special containers for dangerous substances.[66] It must be shown that the thing was provided in the interests of health, safety or welfare. Thus it is not a breach of this provision to interfere with or misuse a thing which has been provided for another purpose.[67]

5.59 No employer is to levy or permit to be levied on any employee any charge in respect of anything done or provided in pursuance of any specific requirement of the relevant statutory provisions.[68] This prohibition against charging only operates where there is a specific statutory requirement to do or provide a thing. It will not apply in relation to the general duties of sections 2 to 6 of the 1974 Act which, in any case, are usually hedged by requirements of reasonable practicability.[69]

Administration

5.60 The 1974 Act creates two bodies corporate, called the Health and Safety Commission (HSC) and the Health and Safety Executive (HSE).[70] HSC consists of a chairman appointed by the Secretary of State, and between six and nine other members who are also appointed by the Secretary of State.[71] Before appointing

---

[64] See generally, reg. 14(2).
[65] 1974 Act, s. 8.
[66] Discussed in *Stair Memorial Encyclopaedia*, Vol. 9, para. 467.
[67] *Tearle v. Cheverton & Laidler Ltd* (1969) 7 K.I.R. 364 (a case under the Factories Act 1961, s. 143(1) (repealed)).
[68] 1974 Act, s. 9.
[69] See, for example, *Associated Dairies Ltd v. Hartley* [1979] I.R.L.R. 171.
[70] 1974 Act, s. 10(1).
[71] 1974 Act, s. 10(2).

the members of the Commission, the Secretary of State is required to consult with organisations representing employers (for three members), organisations representing employees (for three other members) and as to any other members, organisations representing local authorities and such other organisations, including professional bodies, the activities of whose members are concerned with the general purposes of the Act.[72] HSE consists of three persons of whom one is appointed by the Commission with the approval of the Secretary of State to be director and the other two are appointed by the Commission with the approval of the Secretary of State and after consulting the director.[73] The functions of HSC and HSE, and of their officers and servants, are performed on behalf of the Crown.[74]

5.61 HSC has the general duty to do such things and make such arrangements as it considers appropriate for the general purposes of the Act.[75] This general function is subject to the duty (a) to submit to the Secretary of State, from time to time, particulars of what it proposes to do in order to perform its functions; (b) to ensure that its activities are in accordance with proposals approved by the Secretary of State; and (c) to give effect to any directions given by the Secretary of State.[76] HSC also has the following specific duties:

(a) to assist and encourage persons concerned with matters relevant to the general purposes to further those purposes;

(b) to make such arrangements as it considers appropriate for the carrying out of research, the publication of the results of research and the provision of training and information in connection with those purposes, and to encourage research and the provision of training and information;

(c) to make such arrangements as it considers appropriate for securing that government departments, employers, employees, organisations representing employers and employees respectively, and other persons concerned with matters relevant to any of those purposes are provided with an information and advisory service, and are kept informed of, and adequately advised on, such matters;

---

[72] 1974 Act, s. 10(3)(a)–(c).
[73] 1974 Act, s. 10(5).
[74] 1974 Act, s. 10(7).
[75] 1974 Act, s. 11(1).
[76] 1974 Act, s. 11(3).

(d) to submit from time to time to the authority having power to make regulations under any of the relevant statutory provisions such proposals as it considers appropriate for the making of regulations.[77]

5.62 HSC also possesses a number of other powers. It can enter into agency agreements with government departments or other persons to perform functions on behalf of either HSC or the Executive and can by agreement undertake functions of a Minister of the Crown, government department or other public authority[78] (with or without payment), being functions which in the opinion of the Secretary of State can appropriately be performed by the Commission in connection with any of its functions.[79] HSC also has the power to provide (with or without payment) services or facilities to government departments and public authorities,[80] to appoint persons or committees to advise it[81] and to carry out or arrange for or make payments for research, and to disseminate information derived from that research.[82]

5.63 HSC also has powers to direct investigations and inquiries.[83] This power can be exercised as regards any accident, occurrence or other matter whatsoever which HSC thinks it necessary or expedient to investigate for any of the general purposes of the Act or with a view to making regulations for those purposes.[84] In such circumstances it is immaterial whether or not HSE has responsibility for enforcing any of the relevant statutory provisions which relate to the matter in question.[85] Accordingly, HSC may at any time (a) direct HSE or authorise any other person to investigate and make a special report on any matter, or with the consent of the Secretary of State direct that an inquiry be held into any such matter.[86] HSC has the power to make public any special report which it has commissioned.[87] Where the inquiry is concerned with a matter

---

[77] 1974 Act, s. 11(2).
[78] No regulation-making power can be delegated under this power. See 1974 Act, s. 13(2).
[79] 1974 Act, s. 13(1)(a) and (b).
[80] 1974 Act, s. 13(1)(c).
[81] 1974 Act, s. 13(d). HSC can remunerate such persons and has the power to pay travelling and subsistence allowances; s. 13(1)(e).
[82] 1974 Act, s. 13(1)(f).
[83] See generally 1974 Act, s. 14.
[84] 1974 Act, s. 14(1).
[85] 1974 Act, s. 14(1).
[86] 1974 Act, s. 14(2). See also the Health and Safety (Inquiries) Procedure Regulations 1975 (S.I. 1975 No. 335), as amended by S.I. 1976 No. 1246. Inquiries should be held in public except where the regulations provide otherwise; 1974 Act, s. 14(3).
[87] 1974 Act, s. 14(5).

which has caused the death of any person, unless the Lord Advocate otherwise directs, no inquiry with regard to that death can be held under the Fatal Accidents and Sudden Deaths Inquiries (Scotland) Act 1976.[88]

5.64 HSE has the specific duties to exercise on behalf of HSC, such of its functions as HSC directs it to exercise, and to give effect to any directions given to it by HSC; although HSC cannot give directions as to the enforcement of the relevant statutory provisions in any particular case.[89] HSE must also, if so requested by a Minister of the Crown, provide him with information about HSE's activities in connection with any matter with which he is concerned and provide him with relevant expert advice from any of its officers or servants.[90] HSE also has the power to do anything (except borrow money) which is calculated to facilitate, or is conducive or incidental to, the performance of any of its functions.[91]

Enforcement

5.65 It is the duty of HSE to make adequate arrangements for the enforcement of the relevant statutory provisions, except to the extent that some other authority or class of authorities is made responsible for their enforcement.[92] The Secretary of State has the power by Regulations to make local authorities responsible for the enforcement of the relevant statutory provisions.[93] The Regulations may also make provision for the division of responsibilities between the Executive and local authorities and for securing that notice of any such division is brought to the notice of persons affected by it.[94] The Secretary of State has made Regulations which assign enforcement responsibilities to both HSE and local authorities.[95] The Regulations authorise local authorities in Scotland to enforce the relevant statutory provisions for certain types of activities in non-domestic premises.[96] A local authority will be the enforcing authority where the main activity relates to such matters as the sale of goods for retail or wholesale distribution, office activities, catering activities, consumer services or the arts, sports, games, entertainments or other cultural or recreational activities.[97]

---

[88] 1974 Act, s. 14(7).
[89] 1974 Act, s. 11(4).
[90] 1974 Act, s. 11(5).
[91] 1974 Act, s. 11(6).
[92] 1974 Act, s. 18(1).
[93] 1974 Act, s. 18(2)(a).
[94] 1974 Act, s. 18(2)(b).
[95] See the Health and Safety (Enforcing Authority) Regulations 1989 (S.I. 1989 No. 1903).
[96] reg. 2(1).
[97] reg. 3(1) and Sched. 1.

On the other hand, HSE has the power of enforcement in such areas as mines and quarries, fairgrounds, construction work and agricultural activities.[98] HSC has the power to resolve any uncertainties as regards the division of responsibilities.[99]

5.66   Where a local authority has designated the enforcing authority, it is the duty of that authority to make adequate arrangements for the enforcement within its area of the relevant statutory provisions and to perform the enforcement duty and any other functions conferred on it in accordance with any guidance given by HSC.[1] HSC has powers to investigate and report to the Secretary of State in the case of a local authority which is defaulting as regards its enforcement responsibilities.[2] The Secretary of State has the power to make a default order which may require the authority to perform specified enforcement functions within a specified time.[3] A failure to comply with the order may result in the authority's responsibilities being transferred to HSE.[4]

5.67   Day-to-day enforcement lies with the inspectors who are appointed by enforcing authorities.[5] Under section 19(1), every enforcing authority may appoint as inspectors such persons having suitable qualifications as it thinks necessary for carrying into effect the relevant statutory provisions within its field of responsibility, and may terminate such appointments. Every appointment of a person as an inspector must be made by an instrument in writing specifying which of the powers conferred on inspectors by the relevant statutory provisions are to be exercisable by the person so appointed, and an inspector can only exercise the powers as are so specified.[6] Inspectors, when seeking to exercise their powers, may be required to produce their instruments of appointment or duly authenticated copies.[7]

Powers of Inspectors

5.68   Inspectors can exercise the following powers so as to carry into effect any of the relevant statutory provisions within the field of responsibility of their enforcing authority:

---

[98] reg. 3(1) and Sched. 2.
[99] reg. 6(2).
[1] 1974 Act, s. 18(4).
[2] 1974 Act, s. 45(1).
[3] 1974 Act, s. 45(3) and (4).
[4] 1974 Act, s. 45(5).
[5] For further information on how HSE organises its six inspectorates see *Stair Memorial Encyclopaedia*, Vol. 9, paras 486 and 487.
[6] 1974 Act, s. 19(2).
[7] 1974 Act, s. 19(4).

(a) at any reasonable time (or in dangerous situations, at any time) to enter any premises;

(b) to take with them a constable if they have reasonable cause to apprehend any serious obstruction in the execution of their duty;

(c) on entering premises, to take with them any other person duly authorised by their enforcing authority and any necessary equipment or materials;

(d) to make such examination and investigation as may be necessary in the circumstances;

(e) to direct that premises where there is a power of entry must be left undisturbed (whether generally or in particular respects) for so long as is reasonably necessary to enable examination and inspection;

(f) to take such measurements and photographs and make such recordings as are necessary for any examination or investigation;

(g) to take samples of any articles or substances found in any premises where there is power of entry, and of the atmosphere in or in the vicinity of those premises;

(h) in the case of articles or substances likely to cause danger to health or safety, to cause them to be dismantled or subjected to any process or test[8];

(i) to take possession of such articles or substances for so long as is necessary in order to examine them, prevent any tampering with them, and to ensure that they are available in any proceedings for an offence[9];

---

[8] This power must be exercised in the presence of persons who have responsibilities in relation to those premises where that person so requests, unless the inspector considers that such an arrangement would be prejudicial to the safety of the State; 1974 Act, s. 20(4). The inspector also has duties to consult appropriate persons in order to ascertain the dangers of dismantling the article or substance or subjecting it to any process or test; 1974 Act, s. 20(5).

[9] An inspector who exercises this power must leave a notice with a responsible person or fixed to a conspicuous position giving particulars of the article or substance and stating that he has taken possession of it. Where it is practicable a portion of any sample that is taken away must be given to the responsible person; 1974 Act, s. 20(6). It is interesting that, although an inspector exercising powers under para. (i) must fulfil notice requirements, no such requirement operates under para. (g) which grants the inspector a specific power to take samples. See *Laws v. Keane* [1982] I.R.L.R. 500 (HJC), doubting *Skinner v. John G. McGregor (Contractors) Ltd*, 1977 S.L.T. (Sh.Ct) 83.

(j) to require any person whom there is reasonable cause for believing may have information relevant to any examination or inspection to answer questions and sign a declaration of the truth of the answers[10];

(k) to require the production of, inspect, and take copies of any books or documents required by the relevant statutory provisions and any other books or documents which must be seen for the purpose of any examination or investigation;

(l) to require any person to afford such facilities and assistance as are necessary to enable inspectors to exercise their powers;

(m) to exercise any other power which is necessary for carrying into effect the relevant statutory provisions within the field of responsibility of the enforcing authority.

The powers of an inspector do not extend to compelling the production by any person of any document which could be withheld on grounds of legal professional privilege from production in an action in the Court of Session on an order for the production of documents.[11]

Improvement Notices and Prohibition Notices

5.69 As was noted at the beginning of this chapter, the Robens Committee preferred administrative enforcement over criminal sanctions which they thought should only be applied where punishment would be generally expected and supported by the public. The most important recommendation as regards administrative sanctions was the grant of powers to inspectors to serve inspection notices and prohibition notices with a right of appeal to industrial tribunals. The 1974 Act, sections 21 to 24, fulfils these recommendations and creates the framework for the operation of these specific administrative powers and the arrangements for appeals.

5.70 If an inspector is of the opinion that a person is contravening one or more of the relevant statutory provisions or has contravened one or more of those provisions in circumstances that make it likely that the contravention will continue or be repeated, he can serve an improvement notice. The notice will:

---

[10] Such questioning should take place in camera except for any persons nominated by the individual and persons who are allowed to be present by the inspector; s. 20(2)(j).
[11] 1974 Act, s. 20(8).

(a) state that he is of the opinion that a relevant statutory provision is being contravened;

(b) specify the provision which is being contravened;

(c) give particulars of the reasons for the inspector's opinion; and

(d) require the person to remedy the contravention within such period as may be specified in the notice.[12]

It is insufficient for the inspector to assert in an improvement notice that he is of the opinion that the employer is contravening the general duties of section 2(1) without stating which of the particular provisions are being contravened. Such a defect will not be cured by the inspector giving reasons for his opinion. A proper notice should either identify the contravention by reference to the specific duties or, if some contravention not so identifiable is alleged, give particulars of it.[13]

5.71 The more draconian administrative remedy, a prohibition notice, applies to any activities which are being or are likely to be carried on, by or under the control of any person, being activities to which the relevant statutory provisions apply.[14] A prohibition notice can be served by an inspector where he is of the opinion that the above activities involve a risk of serious personal injury and will be served on the person who is carrying on or is likely to carry on those activities or who has control of them.[15] The prohibition notice must:

(a) state that the inspector has the required opinion;

(b) specify the matters which in his opinion give rise to the risk;

(c) where in his opinion any of those matters involves a contravention of any of the relevant statutory provisions, he must state that he is of that opinion, specify the provision(s) as to which he is of that opinion, and give particulars as to why he is of that opinion; and

---

[12] 1974 Act, s. 21. The notice may (but need not) include directions as to the measures to be taken to remedy the contravention specified in the notice, and any such directions may be framed by reference to approved codes of practice and so as to afford the employer the choice of different ways of remedying the contravention; s. 23(2).

[13] *per* McNeill J. in *West Bromwich Building Society Ltd v. Townsend* [1983] I.C.R. 257 at 269.

[14] 1974 Act, s. 22(1).

[15] 1974 Act, s. 22(2).

(d) direct that the activities to which the notice relates shall not be carried on by or under the control of the person on whom the notice is served, unless the matters specified in the notice as giving rise to the risk and any associated contraventions of specified provisions have been remedied.[16]

Such a direction can take effect either at the end of the period specified in the notice or, if the notice so declares, immediately.[17]

5.72 There is a right of appeal to an employment tribunal against the service of either of the above notices.[18] Such an appeal is instigated by sending a notice of appeal to the Secretary of State within 21 days from the date of service of the notice.[19] The tribunal has the power either to cancel or affirm the notice and, if it affirms it, can do so either in its original form or with such modifications as the tribunal may in the circumstances think fit.[20] In the case of an appeal against an improvement notice, the bringing of that appeal has the effect of suspending the operation of the notice until the final disposal of the appeal.[21] The bringing of an appeal against a prohibition notice has the same effect if, but only if, on the application of the appellant the tribunal so directs (and then only from the giving of the direction).[22]

Grounds for Appeal

5.73 It would seem that the employer's financial position is not a relevant ground on which to base an appeal against a notice. In *Harrison (Newcastle-under Lyme) Ltd v. Ramsey*,[23] where the company argued that it could not comply with the notice because it was in financial difficulties, the tribunal rejected such a defence because otherwise the company would be able to make economic gains and undercut competitors at the expense of the safety of its employees. However, there may be circumstances where the tribunal will be

---

[16] 1974 Act, s. 22(3). See also s. 23(2) as regards references to approved codes of practice in directions and affording employees the choice between different ways of remedying the contravention.

[17] 1974 Act, s. 22(4).

[18] 1974 Act, s. 24. For the procedure applicable to such appeals see generally the Employment Tribunals (Constitution and Rules of Procedure) (Scotland) Regulations 1993 (S.I. 1993 No. 2688), Sched. 4.

[19] Sched. 4, reg. 2(1). Although this period can be extended where the tribunal is satisfied that it was not reasonably practicable for the appeal to be brought within the time; reg. 2(2).

[20] 1974 Act, s. 24(2).

[21] 1974 Act, s. 24(3)(a).

[22] 1974 Act, s. 24(3)(b).

[23] [1976] I.R.L.R. 135.

prepared to extend the time for compliance with the notice for financial reasons.[24]

5.74 Much may turn on the relevant statutory provisions which form the basis of the notice and the standard of care which those provisions create. If the provisions create absolute requirements then there will be no scope for assessing the risk as against the cost of the necessary remedial action.[25] On the other hand, in many cases tribunals may have to conduct such an assessment because the relevant statutory provisions require employers to do all that is reasonably practicable. In *Associated Dairies Ltd v. Hartley*,[26] where the company appealed against a notice requiring suitable safety footwear to be provided free of charge, the tribunal considered that there was no statutory requirement that such footwear should be provided and that the general duty under the 1974 Act, section 2, for securing safety at work was based on the standard of reasonable practicability. In such circumstances, the tribunal concluded that, since the cost of providing the necessary footwear free of charge was disproportionate to the risk of employees being injured, it was not reasonably practicable for such footwear to be supplied without charge. Nonetheless, in other cases tribunals have been prepared to accept the terms of the notice unmodified because the sacrifice in terms of cost is not disproportionate to the risks involved.[27] Equally, it is no defence to argue that the breach is a trivial one which is also being committed by many other employers who have not been served with notices.[28] On the other hand, the mere fact that an activity is dangerous *per se* is not a ground for serving a prohibition notice, since the critical issue is for the employer to ensure that the employees are safe in the way that the work is carried out.[29]

5.75 As we have already seen, the 1974 Act, section 24(2), empowers tribunals to modify notices. This power enables tribunals not only to reduce the scope of the notice but also to add to or increase its requirements.[30] However, this power does not permit a

---

[24] *Otterburn Mill v. Bullman* [1975] I.R.L.R. 223 (time limit extended because of the impact on the business of fencing all the machines at once). Extensions of time may also be given for other reasons. See, for example, *D. J. M. Campion and A. J. Campion v. Hughes* [1975] I.R.L.R. 291 (extension of time to enable consent for work from the local authority).

[25] See, for example, *Sutton & Co. Ltd v. Davies* (1978) IDS Brief 149 (although no accident in 27 years notice affirmed because duty to fence was absolute).

[26] [1979] I.R.L.R. 17.

[27] See, for example, *Belhaven Brewery Co. Ltd v. McLean* [1975] I.R.L.R. 370 (risk justified expensive requirement of improvement notice).

[28] *South Surbiton Co-operative Society v. Wilcox* [1975] I.R.L.R. 292.

[29] *Canterbury City Council v. Hewletts & Port Lympne Estates Ltd* [1997] I.C.R. 925.

[30] *Tesco Stores Ltd v. Edwards* [1977] I.R.L.R. 120.

tribunal to amend a notice so as to include allegations that the employer was breaching other provisions of the Act which are not specified in the notice.[31] But tribunals may have the power to amend a notice in order to correct technical matters where there is evidence of a plain and continuing breach of the Act.[32] Moreover, where it is alleged that the notice is invalid as being imprecise or vague, a tribunal should not deal with that matter as a preliminary point. Instead, the tribunal should hear the whole case and, if it concludes that the notice is imprecise or vague, it should modify the notice so as to remedy this defect.[33]

Other Powers

5.76 Inspectors also have powers to deal with causes of imminent danger. Where an inspector finds an article or substance in premises which he has power to enter and which he believes is a cause of imminent danger of serious personal injury, he may seize it and cause it to be rendered harmless (whether by destruction or otherwise).[34] Before it is rendered harmless the inspector must take a sample of the article or substance, if it is one of a batch, and if practicable give it to a responsible person at the premises where it was found.[35] There are also requirements obliging the inspector, after the article or substance has been rendered harmless, to give a written report of his action to the responsible person, and the owner of the article or substance where the owner is not the responsible person.[36] There are also provisions in the 1974 Act concerning the power of customs officers to detain articles and substances,[37] indemnification of inspectors,[38] the power of HSC, HSE and the enforcing authorities to obtain information which HSC needs for the discharge of its functions[39] and as regards restrictions on the disclosure of any such information.[40]

Offences

5.77 It is an offence under the 1974 Act for a person:

---

[31] *British Airways Board v. Henderson* [1979] I.C.R. 77. But note also *West Bromwich Building Society v. Townsend* [1983] I.C.R. 257 discussed at para. 5.57 above.

[32] *Harrison (Newcastle-under-Lyme) v. Ramsey* [1976] I.R.L.R. 135.

[33] *Chrysler (U.K.) Ltd v. McCarthy* [1978] I.C.R. 939 (DC).

[34] 1974 Act, s. 25(1).

[35] 1974 Act, s. 25(2).

[36] 1974 Act, s. 25(3).

[37] 1974 Act, s. 25A.

[38] 1974 Act, s. 26.

[39] 1974 Act, s. 27.

[40] 1974 Act, s. 28.

(a) to fail to discharge a duty created by sections 2 to 7;

(b) to contravene sections 8 or 9;

(c) to contravene any health or safety regulations or any requirements or prohibition imposed under any of these regulations (including any requirement or prohibition to which he is subject by virtue of the terms of or any condition or restriction attached to any licence, approval, exemption, or other authority issued, given or granted under the regulations);

(d) to contravene any requirement imposed by or under any regulations made under section 14 for the purpose of directing investigations and inquiries, or intentionally obstructing any person exercising powers in connection with investigations or inquiries;

(e) to contravene any requirement imposed by an inspector under section 20 (general powers) or section 25 (power to deal with cause of imminent danger);

(f) to prevent or attempt to prevent any other person from appearing before an inspector or from answering any questions that the person is required to answer under section 20(2);

(g) to contravene any requirement or prohibition imposed by an improvement notice or a prohibition notice[41];

(h) intentionally to obstruct an inspector or to obstruct a customs officer in the exercise or performance of their powers or duties;

(i) to contravene any requirement imposed by a notice requiring the disclosure of information under section 27(1);

(j) to use or disclose any information for another purpose in contravention of section 27(4) or section 28;

(k) to make a statement which he knows to be false or recklessly to make a statement which is false where the statement is made in purported compliance with a statutory requirement to furnish any information, or for the purpose of obtaining the issue of a document to himself or another person;

---

[41] It is no defence to such a charge that the accused has complied with the notice so far as reasonably practicable since this is irrelevant to an offence under s. 33(1)(g). See *Deary v. Mansion Hide Upholstery Ltd* [1983] I.C.R. 610.

(l) intentionally to make a false entry in any register, book, notice or other document required by the relevant statutory provisions to be kept, served or given or, with intent to deceive, to make use of any such entry which he knows to be false;

(m) with intent to deceive, to use a document issued, or authorised to be issued, under any of the relevant statutory provisions or required for any purpose, or to make or have in his possession a document so closely resembling any such document as to be calculated to deceive;

(n) falsely to pretend to be an inspector;

(o) to fail to comply with an order made by a court under section 42.[42]

5.78 The Act also creates a series of penalties applicable to the above offences. A person guilty of an offence which consists of a failure to discharge a duty imposed by sections 2 to 6 is liable on summary conviction to a fine not exceeding £20,000,[43] and on conviction on indictment to an unlimited fine.[44] A person guilty of an offence under paragraph (d), (f), (h) or (n), or an offence under paragraph (e) where it consists of a requirement imposed by an inspector under section 20, is liable on summary conviction to a fine not exceeding level 5 on the standard scale.[45] A person guilty of an offence under paragraph (g) or (o) is liable on summary conviction to imprisonment for a term not exceeding six months, or a fine not exceeding £20,000, or both, and on conviction on indictment to imprisonment for a term not exceeding two years, or an unlimited fine, or both.[46] A person guilty of any other offence created by section 33(1) or of an offence under any of the existing statutory provisions, being an offence for which no other penalty is specified, is liable on summary conviction to a fine not exceeding £5,000, and on conviction on indictment, if the offence is covered by section 33(4), to imprisonment for a term not exceeding two years, or an unlimited fine, or both, and in any other case to a fine.[47] The offences covered by section 33(4) where a higher penalty can be imposed on indictment are:

---

[42] 1974 Act, s. 33(1)(a)–(o).

[43] It is clear that there is no yardstick by which one can test whether a fine of £20,000 is excessive, except by considering whether all the relevant circumstances have been taken into account. See *Kvaerner Govan Ltd v. HMA*, 1992 S.C.C.R. 10. One relevant circumstance will be the serious consequences of the risk for employees. See *R. v. Sanyo Electrical Manufacturing (U.K.) Ltd* (1992) 156 J.P. 863, CA.

[44] 1974 Act, s. 33(1A), as inserted by the Offshore Safety Act 1992, s.4(2) and (6).

[45] 1974 Act, s. 33(2).

[46] 1974 Act, s. 33(2A) as inserted by the Offshore Safety Act 1992, s. 4(3) and (6).

[47] 1974 Act, s. 33(3).

(a) an offence consisting of a contravention of any of the relevant statutory provisions by doing otherwise than under the authority of a licence issued by HSE where such a licence is necessary under the relevant statutory provisions;

(b) an offence consisting of a contravention of a term, condition or restriction attached to any such licence;

(c) an offence consisting of acquiring or attempting to acquire, possessing or using, an explosive article or substance in contravention of the relevant statutory provisions;

(d) an offence under paragraph (j).

There are special provisions in section 34 concerning time limits for bringing criminal proceedings under section 33.[48]

Special Provisions on Offences

5.79 Where the commission by any person of an offence under any of the relevant statutory provisions is due to the act or default of some other person, that other person is guilty of an offence, and the person may be charged with and convicted of the offence, whether or not proceedings are taken against the first-mentioned person.[49] "Act or default" requires the wrongful act or default of the other person.[50] Accordingly, no prosecution will be competent when the act or default of the other person only became unlawful as a result of legislation enacted subsequently.[51] There is no need to prove *mens rea* or negligence under this provision if the original offence is constituted without the need for *mens rea* or negligence.[52] It is competent to prosecute persons for wrongful acts or defaults where the original offence would have been committed by the Crown, but for the fact that section 33 does not bind the Crown.[53] It should also be noted that the above provisions are subject to what may be specified in health and safety regulations.[54]

5.80 It is trite law that, when a statute declares that the act or default of any person is an offence, such an offence applies equally to bodies corporate.[55] However, the 1974 Act creates additional

---

[48] For a discussion on s. 34 see *Stair Memorial Encyclopaedia*, Vol. 9, para. 513.

[49] 1974 Act, s. 36(1).

[50] *Noss Farm Products Ltd v. Lilico* [1945] 2 All E.R. 609 (DC).

[51] *ibid.*

[52] *Lamb v. Sunderland and District Creamery Ltd* [1951] 1 All E.R. 923 (DC).

[53] 1974 Act, s. 36(2).

[54] 1974 Act, s. 36(3).

[55] Interpretation Act 1978, s. 5 and Sched. 1.

rules which ensure that not only the body corporate but also its directors, managers, secretary and other similar officers can be prosecuted. It is provided by section 37(1) that where an offence under any of the relevant statutory provisions committed by a body corporate is proved to have been committed with the consent or connivance of, or to have been attributable to any neglect on the part of, any director, manager, secretary or other similar officer of the body corporate, or a person who was purporting to act in such a capacity, he as well as the body corporate is guilty of an offence and can be proceeded against and punished accordingly.[56]

5.81 There appears to be no direct authority on the meaning of the word "connivance", although it has been submitted that the state of mind is one of "wilful blindness", *i.e.* an intentional shutting of the eyes to something of which the percipient would, in his own interests, prefer to remain unaware.[57] "Neglect" presupposes the existence of some obligation or duty on the part of the person charged with neglect[58] and applies to any neglect in duty to which the contravention of the safety provisions was attributable.[59] The need for the offence to be attributable to the neglect is also broadly construed. In *Wotherspoon v. HMA*[60] the court considered that:

> "any degree of attributability will suffice and in that sense it is evident that the commission of a relevant offence by a body corporate may well be found to be attributable to failure on the part of each of a number of directors, managers or officers to take certain steps which he could and should have taken in the discharge of the particular functions of his particular office."

The director of roads of a regional council has been held to fall within the class of person who can be prosecuted under this provision.[61] However, it would seem that only managers who have the power and responsibility for deciding corporate policy and strategy are capable of being prosecuted.[62]

---

[56] Where the affairs of a body corporate are managed by its members, the provision applies in relation to the acts and defaults of a member in connection with his functions of management as if he were a director of the body corporate; 1974 Act, s. 37(2).

[57] See J. Hendy and M. Ford, *Health and Safety* (2nd ed., 1993), Introductory Note 6.

[58] *Wotherspoon v. HMA* 1978 J.C. 74.

[59] *Armour v. Skeen*, 1977 J.C. 15.

[60] 1978 J.C. 74.

[61] *Armour v. Skeen*, 1977 J.C. 15.

[62] *R. v. Boal* [1992] Q.B. 591.

The Use of Regulations and Approved Codes of Practice

5.82 It is clear that one of the principal objectives of the 1974 Act is for the older laws on health and safety to be progressively replaced by a system of regulations and approved Codes of Practice operating with other provisions of the 1974 Act, so as to improve standards of health safety and welfare.[63] The 1974 Act, sections 15 and 16, play a crucial role in achieving this objective by granting powers to make Regulations and by authorising HSC to approve and issue codes of practice.

5.83 The Secretary of State for Employment, the Minister of Agriculture, Fisheries and Food, or the Secretary of State and the Minister acting jointly have the power to make regulations for any of the general purposes of the Act.[64] Regulations can also be made for any of the purposes specified in Schedule 3 to the Act.[65] Health and safety regulations:

(a) may repeal or modify any of the existing statutory provisions;

(b) may exclude or modify for specified classes of case any of the general duties in sections 2 to 9 or any of the existing statutory provisions;

(c) may make a specified authority or class of authorities responsible, to such extent as may be specified, for the enforcement of any of the relevant statutory provisions;

(d) may impose requirements by reference to the approval of HSC or any other specified body or person;

(e) may provide for references in the Regulations to any specified document to operate as references to that document as revised or reissued from time to time;

(f) may provide (either conditionally or subject to conditions, and with or without limit of time) for exemptions from any requirement or prohibition imposed by or under any of the relevant statutory provisions;

---

[63] 1974 Act, s. 1(2).
[64] 1974 Act, s. 15(1).
[65] These include the manufacture, supply, design, construction, guarding, repair, maintenance, marking, testing, import and transport of articles and substances; the licensing of activities; the regulation of persons allowed to perform certain functions; health; conditions of work; welfare; protective clothing; fire risks; emission of substances; training; notification and recording of accidents; animals; dangers to premises or persons; powers of search in connection with fire risks; action after accidents; power to employers and others to make rules and give directions; and powers to local and public authorities to make bye-laws.

(g) may enable exemptions from any requirement or prohibition imposed by or under any of the relevant statutory provisions to be granted (either conditionally or subject to conditions, and with or without limit of time) by any specified person or by any person authorised in that behalf by a specified authority;

(h) may specify the persons or classes of person who, in the event of a contravention of a requirement or prohibition imposed by or under the Regulations, are to be guilty of an offence, whether in addition to or to the exclusion of other persons or classes of persons;

(i) may provide for any specified defence to be available in proceedings for any offence under the relevant statutory provisions either generally or in specified circumstances;

(j) may exclude proceedings on indictment in relation to offences consisting of a contravention of a requirement or prohibition imposed by or under any of the existing statutory provisions, the general duties of sections 2 to 9 or health and safety regulations;

(k) may restrict the punishments which can be imposed in respect of any of the offences mentioned in paragraph (j) other than the maximum fine on conviction on indictment;

(l) in the case of Regulations made for any purpose mentioned in the Offshore Safety Act 1992, section 1(1), may provide that any offence consisting of a contravention of the Regulations, or of any requirement or condition imposed by or under them, shall be punishable on conviction on indictment by imprisonment for a term not exceeding two years, or a fine, or both.[66]

It is legitimate for health and safety regulations to take the form of Regulations applying to particular circumstances only or to a particular case only (for example, Regulations applying to particular premises only).[67]

5.84 HSC has the power for the purposes of providing practical guidance with respect to the general duties of sections 2 to 7 or of health and safety regulations, or of any of the existing statutory provisions to approve and issue such codes of practice (whether prepared by it or not) as in its opinion are suitable for that purpose.[68] HSC may also approve such codes of practice issued or

---

[66] 1974 Act, ss. 15(2)–(6).
[67] 1974 Act, s. 15(8).
[68] 1974 Act, s. 16(1)(a).

proposed to be issued by other bodies.[69] HSC cannot approve a Code of Practice without the consent of the Secretary of State, and must, before seeking his consent, consult any government department or other body that appears to HSC to be appropriate, and may have to consult such government departments and other bodies by virtue of the directions of the Secretary of State.[70] HSC also has the power from time to time to revise the whole or any part of a Code of Practice or withdraw its approval from any code subject to the consent of the Secretary of State and after appropriate consultation.[71] There are also notification requirements as regards the approval, revision, or withdrawal of approval for any code.[72]

5.85 A failure to observe a provision of a Code of Practice does not of itself render a person liable to any civil or criminal proceedings; but there are special provisions where in any criminal proceedings a party is alleged to have committed an offence by reason of a contravention of any health and safety provision for which there is an approved Code of Practice.[73] In such a case any provision of the code which appears to the court to be relevant to the requirement or prohibition alleged to have been contravened is admissible in evidence in the proceedings. If it is proved that there was at any material time a failure to observe any provision of the code, that matter must be taken as proved, unless the court is satisfied that the requirement or prohibition could be complied with other than by way of observance of the code.[74]

---

[69] 1974 Act, s. 16(1)(b).
[70] 1974 Act, s. 16(2).
[71] 1974 Act, s. 16(4) and (5).
[72] 1974 Act, s. 16(3) and (6). In the case of the approval of a code, HSC is required to issue a notice in writing identifying the code, stating the date on which it takes effect and specifying the provisions for which it is approved.
[73] 1974 Act, s. 17(1).
[74] 1974 Act, s. 17(2).

CHAPTER 6

SELECTED AREAS OF STATUTORY REGULATION

INTRODUCTION

6.1 It is the purpose of this chapter to consider some of the delegated legislation made under the Health and Safety at Work Act 1974, section 15, in more detail. First, we shall consider some basic statutory regulations of general effect such as the Health and Safety (First-Aid) Regulations 1981.[1] Thereafter we will discuss certain specific and specialised statutory provisions which regulate health and safety in particular industries or in relation to particular types of activity. In this part of the chapter we shall consider certain regulations such as the Control of Lead at Work Regulations 1998[2] and the Control of Substances Hazardous to Health Regulations 1999,[3] which comply largely with earlier European Directives. Next we shall examine the remaining regulations made in 1992, which were intended to comply with the more recent European Directives made under Article 118a of the Treaty of Rome and which have not yet been discussed in this book.[4] Finally, the chapter will conclude with a brief examination of the regulatory regime applicable in offshore installations. This regime has been revolutionised as a result of the recommendations of the Cullen Report,[5] which led to the enactment of the Offshore Safety Act 1992 and the making of the Offshore Installations (Safety Case) Regulations 1992.[6]

---

[1] S.I. 1981 No. 917.

[2] S.I. 1998 No. 543. See also the Lead and Ionic Compounds Directive 82/605.

[3] S.I. 1999 No. 437. These Regulations are intended to give effect to a range of European Directives, such as the Chemical, Physical and Biological Agents at Work Directive 80/1107 and the Carcinogens Directive 90/394.

[4] The Personal Protective Equipment at Work Regulations 1992 (S.I. 1992 No. 2966); the Manual Handling Operations Regulations 1992 (S.I. 1992 No. 2793) and the Health and Safety (Display Screen Equipment) Regulations 1992 (S.I. 1992 No. 2792). We shall also consider some aspects of the Management of Health and Safety at Work Regulations 1999 (S.I. 1999 No. 3242).

[5] Cm. 1310 (1990).

[6] S.I. 1992 No. 2885.

SELECTED GENERAL REGULATIONS

(a) Health and Safety (First-Aid) Regulations 1981

6.2   These Regulations[7] require employers[8] to provide equipment
and facilities and such number of suitable persons as is adequate
and appropriate in the circumstances so that first-aid[9] can be
rendered to employees who are injured or become ill at work.[10]
Persons will not be suitable to provide first-aid unless they have
undergone such training and have such qualifications as HSE may
approve for the time being and have such additional training, if
any, as may be appropriate in the circumstances of the case.[11]
Where a suitable person is absent in temporary and exceptional
circumstances it is sufficient compliance if the employer appoints a
person to take charge of the situation throughout the period of the
absence, both in relation to an injured or ill employee who will
need help from a medical practitioner or nurse, and the adequate
and appropriate equipment and facilities which must be provided.[12]
Employers would usually be expected to provide suitable persons
qualified in first-aid.[13] However, it is possible for them to appoint a
person to take charge instead of providing a person qualified in
first-aid where, having regard to the nature of the undertaking, the
number of employees at work and the location of the establishment, it would be adequate and appropriate to do so.[14] Employers
also have an obligation to inform their employees about arrangements for first-aid, including the location of equipment, facilities
and personnel,[15] and self-employed persons are required to take
care of their own health and safety by the provision of adequate
and appropriate first-aid equipment.[16]

---

[7] S.I. 1981 No. 917. There is also an Approved Code of Practice and a Guidance
Note published by HSE.

[8] For exemptions from the Regulations, see reg. 7. For the special position of
mines see regs 7(e) and 8, and for the application of the Regulations offshore, see
reg. 9.

[9] "First-aid" means (a) in cases where a person will need help from a medical
practitioner or nurse, treatment for the purposes of preserving life and minimising
the consequences of injury and illness until such help is obtained; and (b) treatment
of minor injuries which would otherwise receive no treatment or which do not need
treatment by a medical practitioner or nurse. See reg. 2(1).

[10] reg. 3(1) and (2).

[11] reg. 3(2)(a) and (b).

[12] reg. 3(3).

[13] See Code of Practice, para. 32.

[14] reg. 3(4).

[15] reg. 4.

[16] reg. 5.

(b) Health and Safety Information for Employees Regulations 1989

6.3 These Regulations[17] require employers to furnish information relating to health, safety and welfare to their employees, either by means of a poster in a form approved and published by HSE or by means of a similarly approved leaflet which is given to each employee.[18] It is the duty of the employer to ensure that any approved poster is kept displayed in a readable condition and at a reasonably accessible place, and in such a position in that place so that it can be easily seen and read.[19] The Regulations also require that the name and address of the enforcing authority and the address of the employment medical advisory service be written clearly and indelibly on the poster in the appropriate space.[20] Where employers distribute the leaflet to their employees, the same information should be provided in a written notice which accompanies it.[21]

(c) Control of Major Accident Hazards Regulations 1999

6.4 The purpose of these Regulations[22] is to comply with the Directive on the control of major accidents[23] involving dangerous substances. The Regulations apply to any operation in an installation[24] which involves one or more dangerous substances,[25] unless that operation is incapable of producing a major accident hazard, or except in relation to transport.[26]

6.5 An operator[27] who has control of the operation at an installation must take all measures necessary to prevent major accidents and limit their consequences, and prepare and keep a major

---

[17] S.I. 1989 No. 682, as modified by S.I. 1995 No. 2923.

[18] regs 3 and 4. The HSE now has the power to approve posters or leaflets which are specific to particular classes of employment; reg. 3(4) added by S.I. 1995 No. 2923, reg. 2(b).

[19] reg. 4(1)(a). HSE has the power to approve revisions to the posters and leaflets, and employers must incorporate such changes into their literature. See regs 3(2) and 4(3).

[20] reg. 5(1).

[21] reg. 5(3).

[22] S.I. 1999 No. 743. The regulations are intended to implement Council Directive 82/501 on the major accident hazards of certain industrial activities.

[23] Directive 96/82. The Regulations have wide effect. However, they do not apply to nuclear installations, defence installations, mines or quarries, or waste land fill sites. See reg. 3.

[24] See reg. 2(1).

[25] For the definition of "dangerous substance", see reg. 2(1) and Sched. 1.

[26] See reg. 3(2).

[27] "Operator" means a person having control of an industrial activity. See reg. 2(1).

accident prevention policy document.[28] The operator must also notify the HSE as the competent authority of specified matters at specified times, and provide a safety report to HSE and revise that report periodically, and not start the construction or operation of the installation until he has received the conclusions of the HSE on the report.[29] He must also prepare an on-site emergency plan for certain purposes which must contain specified information.[30-37]

6.6 The local authority[38] in whose area the activity is being carried on has a corresponding obligation to prepare and keep up-to-date an adequate off-site emergency plan.[39] The operator also has a responsibility to prepare and supply information to persons likely to be in the area of the activity and to make that information publicly available.[40] HSE is also required to disseminate relevant information to other establishments.[41]

(d) The Reporting of Injuries Diseases and Dangerous Occurrences Regulations 1995

6.7 These Regulations[42] (RIDDOR) are intended to simplify and rationalise the law relating to the reporting of dangerous occurrences. The 1995 Regulations apply to all work activities covered by the Health and Safety at Work, etc. Act 1974. This means, for example, that the separate reporting arrangements for the railways and for offshore activities have been abolished, so that the one set of reporting rules now apply to all of industry, including offshore oil and gas exploration and extraction (though there are separate regulations for Northern Ireland).

General requirements

6.8 Regulation 3(1) now makes it necessary to report the following:

---

[28] regs 4 and 5. "Major accident" means an occurrence (including, in particular, a major emission, fire or explosion) resulting from uncontrolled developments in the course of an industrial activity, leading to a serious danger to persons, whether immediate or delayed, inside or outside the installation, or to the environment, and involving one or more dangerous substances. See reg. 2(1).

[29] regs 6 and 7 and Scheds 3 and 4.

[30-37] reg. 9 and Sched. 5.

[38] The appropriate local authority is the council for the local government area. See reg. 2(1).

[39] reg. 10. This plan should be prepared subject to exemptions from HSE.

[40] reg. 14(1). The manufacturer can consult the local authority and appropriate persons, but remains responsible for the accuracy, completeness and form of the information. See reg. 12(2).

[41] reg. 15.

[42] S.I. 1995 No. 3163.

(a) the death of any person as a result of an accident arising out of or in connection with work;

(b) a major injury to any person at work as a result of an accident arising out of or in connection with work;

(c) where any person not at work suffers any injury as a result of an accident arising out of or in connection with work there will be a duty to report when that person is taken from the site of the accident to a hospital for treatment for the injury;

(d) there is a dangerous occurrence.[43]

In addition, regulation 3(2) requires the responsible person to report as soon as practicable and, in any event, within 10 days of the accident, any injury where the injured employee is incapacitated for work for more than three consecutive days. This calculation does not involve counting the day of the accident but does include days which would not have been working days. Further, the responsible person must, as soon he knows, inform the enforcing authority in writing of the death of an employee as a result of an accident at work which is the cause of his death within one year of the accident, whether or not the accident has already been reported.[44]

6.9 If any of the above incidents takes place it is the duty of the responsible person to forthwith notify the enforcing authority of the accident by the quickest practicable means,[45] and within 10 days of the accident happening send a report to the authority on an approved form (see Form F2508) or by some other means approved by HSE.[46] In the case of accidents to employees the responsible person required to report will usually be the employer, since the regulations place the obligation to report on the persons having control of the premises—though there are special rules for mines, offshore installations, pipelines, wells and diving projects.[47] "Accident" includes an act of non-consensual physical violence done to a person at work, and an act of suicide which occurs on a relevant transport system like a railway or tramway.[48] This means that for the first time reporting is required for acts of violence committed against staff at work whether by members of the public

---

[43] There are exemptions for accidents arising out of medical operations or treatment; reg. 10.
[44] reg. 4.
[45] This appears to permit reporting by means of the telephone.
[46] reg. 3(1)(i) and (ii).
[47] reg. 2(1)(a)(i)–(viii).
[48] reg. 2(1)(a) and (b).

or other employees. "Major injury" includes fractures, amputations, dislocations, loss of sight, chemical or hot metal burns to the
eye, electric shocks or chemical burns, loss of consciousness caused
by asphyxia and acute illness caused by exposure to a biological
agent.[49] It is also necessary to report "dangerous occurrences".[50]
However, if an injury occurs and is reportable under one of the
other heads then the dangerous occurrence does not have to be
reported separately. If, however, the injury would not otherwise be
reportable then the dangerous occurrence must be reported.

(ii) Reporting of diseases

6.10 There are also reporting requirements where a person at
work suffers from any of the occupational diseases listed in
Schedule 3 and his work involves one of the corresponding
activities also listed. Under regulation 5 it is the duty of the
responsible person to forthwith send a report of this fact to the
relevant enforcing authority on an approved form (see Form
F2508A) or by some other means approved by HSE. Such a duty
only applies where the responsible person has received a written
statement prepared by a registered medical practitioner diagnosing
the disease as one specified in Schedule 3.[51] Basically the employer
must report when he has received a written diagnosis from a
registered medical practitioner indicating that an employee suffers
from a prescribed occupational disease *and* the ill employee's work
involves the corresponding work activity listed in Schedule 3.[52]

(iii) Record-keeping and defences

6.11 Employers are required to keep records of all the events
which were required to report under reg. 3 and all diseases
reported under reg. 5.[53] It is a defence in any criminal proceedings
brought under RIDDOR for the accused to prove that he was not
aware of the event requiring notification and/or reporting to the
relevant enforcing authority and that he had taken all reasonable
steps to have all such events brought to his notice.[54]

---

[49] reg. 2(1) and Sched. 1.
[50] See reg. 2(1) and Sched. 2, where an extensive definition dealing with general
situations and then specific activities is provided.
[51] reg. 5(2).
[52] There is an additional and more extensive list applied to offshore workplaces;
Sched. 3. Pt II.
[53] reg. 7.
[54] reg. 11.

SPECIAL REGULATIONS

(a) Control of Lead at Work Regulations 1998

6.12 These Regulations[55] place duties on employers to protect their employees and other persons who are exposed to lead at work.[56] They are accompanied by an Approved Code of Practice, which provides detailed guidance for each regulation. The exposure to lead must come through the use of lead in such a form that it is likely to be inhaled, ingested or otherwise absorbed by persons: the regulations do not apply to lead given off from the exhaust systems of motor vehicles on public roads.[57] It would seem that any such exposure should be significant and that there will be no breach of duty when the work involves merely intermittent exposures of short duration.[58] The basic duty is for employers and the self-employed, where any work may expose persons to lead, to carry out a suitable and sufficient risk assessment to determine the nature and degree of that exposure.[59] Employers should ensure that the exposure of their employees to lead is either prevented or, where this is not reasonably practicable, adequately controlled by means of appropriate control measures.[60] Employers also have obligations to ensure that adequate[61] information, instruction and training is given to their employees who are liable to be exposed to lead so that they are aware of the risks from lead and the precautions which should be observed.[62]

6.13 There are also a series of regulations which are intended to control the exposure to and spread of contamination by lead at the work place. Thus every employer must, so far as is reasonably practicable, provide such control measures for materials, plant and processes as will adequately control the exposure of employees to lead otherwise than through the use of respiratory protective equipment or protective clothing.[63] However, there are also special provisions requiring the provision of appropriate respiratory equipment to employees who are liable to be exposed to airborne lead.[64]

---

[55] S.I. 1998 No. 543. These Regulations comply substantially with the Lead and Ionic Compounds Directive 82/605.

[56] reg. 3.

[57] See generally the definition of lead in reg. 2(1).

[58] *Hewett v. Alf Brown's Transport Ltd* [1992] I.C.R. 530, CA.

[59] reg. 5. There are also prohibitions against the use of any other glaze except a leadless glaze in pottery, and against the employment of a young person or a woman of reproductive capacity; reg. 4.

[60] reg. 6.

[61] "Adequate" means adequate having regard only to the nature and degree of exposure to lead.

[62] reg. 11.

[63] reg. 6.

[64] reg. 6(4).

The Regulations also place obligations on employers to ensure that suitable arrangements are made for employees to eat, drink and smoke in a place which is not liable to be contaminated with lead,[65] and to secure the cleanliness and efficiency of control measures required to prevent or minimise employees exposure to lead.[66] Most importantly, employers are required to have adequate air monitoring procedures,[67] and there are detailed rules about the medical surveillance of employees who are employed on work which involves exposure to lead.[68]

(b) Control of Asbestos at Work Regulations 1987

6.14 A similar safety regime to that applicable for lead was created for asbestos by the 1987 Regulations.[69] The Regulations impose duties on employers for the protection of employees who may be exposed to asbestos at work and of other persons who are liable to be affected by such work.[70] Employers are not permitted to carry out any work involving exposure to asbestos unless they have identified the type of asbestos involved in the work and have treated it accordingly.[71] Moreover, there must be an adequate assessment of the nature and degree of exposure to asbestos and an indication of the steps to be taken to prevent or reduce to the lowest level reasonably practicable that exposure.[72] Employers must also notify the enforcing authority when work with asbestos is to be undertaken[73] and must ensure that adequate information, instruction and training is given to employees about the risks from asbestos and the precautions to be observed.[74] The basic obligation placed upon employers is to prevent the exposure of their employees to asbestos, but, where this is not reasonably practicable, to reduce exposure to asbestos to the lowest level reasonably practicable by measures other than by the use of respiratory protective equipment.[75] Thereafter, the Regulations impose control mechanisms, maintenance requirements and medical surveillance along similar lines to those already discussed for the Control of Lead at Work Regulations.[76]

---

[65] reg. 10.
[66] reg. 8.
[67] reg. 9.
[68] See generally, reg. 10.
[69] S.I. 1987 No. 2115 (as amended by S.I. 1988 No. 712, S.I. 1992 No. 2966 and S.I. 1992 No. 3068). They fulfil the requirements of the Asbestos Directive 83/477 (as amended by E.C. Directive 91/382).
[70] reg. 3.
[71] reg. 4.
[72] reg. 5(1) and (2).
[73] reg. 6.
[74] reg. 7.
[75] reg. 8.
[76] See regs 9–17.

(c) Control of Substances Hazardous to Health Regulations 1999

6.15 These Regulations[77] constitute some of the most important and far-reaching provisions on health and safety promulgated since the 1974 Act. They are intended to provide a comprehensive and systematic approach to the control of exposure to most substances hazardous to health in all types of work and workplace. The original regulations which implement some of the earlier Directives of the European Union[78] were the subjects of considerable amendment in 1992 in order to comply with the Carcinogens at Work Directive, and the present regulations are also intended to ensure compliance with the Biological Agents Directive.[79] The effect of the consolidation of the regulations in 1994 has been to create an extensive but flexible code of conduct as regards the health risks associated with virtually all work activities[80] where substances which are hazardous to health are used or produced. The regulations are also accompanied by a general Approved Code of Practice and by a number of other Codes of Practice which focus attention on the health risks associated with specific substances and specific activities.

6.16 The principal purpose of the Control of Substances Hazardous to Health Regulations 1994 (COSHH Regulations) is to protect persons against risks to their health, whether immediate or delayed, arising from exposure to substances hazardous to health. The cornerstone of these Regulations is regulation 3, which places a duty on all employers[81] as regards the health risks of their employees and other persons, whether at work or not, who may be affected by the work carried on by employers as regards substances hazardous to health. A substance means any natural or artificial substance, whether in solid or liquid form, or in the form of a gas or vapour (including micro-organisms).[82] Such a substance becomes hazardous to health if it satisfies any of the following:

    (a) it is a substance which is listed as being dangerous for supply within the meaning of the Chemicals (Hazard Information and Packaging) Regulations 1994,[83] and for

---

[77] S.I. 1999 No. 437.

[78] See, for example, the Chemical, Physical and Biological Agents at Work Directive 80/1107.

[79] 90/394 and 90/679.

[80] There are some limited exceptions where the COSHH Regulations do not apply. See reg. 5. For our purposes the most important exclusions are where the activities are already covered by the Control of Lead at Work Regulations 1998 or the Control of Asbestos at Work Regulations 1987.

[81] For the purposes of these Regulations a self-employed person is to be treated as both an employer and employee except for monitoring and health surveillance purpose. See reg. 3(2).

[82] reg. 2(1).

[83] S.I. 1994 No. 3247.

which an indication of danger specified for that substance by the 1994 Regulations is very toxic, harmful, corrosive or irritant;

(b) it is a substance for which the COSHH Regulations specify a maximum exposure limit[84] or for which HSC has approved an occupational standard;

(c) it is a micro-organism which creates a hazard to the health of any person;

(d) it involves dust of any kind, when present at a substantial concentration in air;

(e) it is a substance which is not already covered but which creates comparable hazards to the health of any person.[85]

6.17 Key to the application of the Regulations is regulation 6, which places obligations on employers not to carry on any work which is liable to expose any employees to any substances hazardous to health unless they have made a suitable and sufficient assessment of the health risks created by that work and of the steps that need to be taken in order to comply with the Regulations. Any such assessment must be reviewed regularly and forthwith if there is reason to suspect that the assessment is no longer valid or there has been a significant change in the work to which it relates.[86] It is clear that the focus for the health risk assessment is the employer's own work activities, and that the preventive and precautionary measures which an employer will be required to introduce as a result of that assessment will be consistent with the risks which it has identified. Nevertheless, the Regulations provide guidance as to the sorts of precautions which employers should introduce.

6.18 These are as follows:

(1) preventing exposure to substances hazardous to health or, where this is not reasonably practicable, securing adequate control of exposure[87];

(2) taking all reasonable steps to ensure that any control measure, personal protective equipment, or other thing or facility so provided is properly used and applied[88];

---

[84] See Sched. 1.
[85] reg. 2(1).
[86] reg. 6(2).
[87] reg. 7(1). So far as reasonably practicable, such prevention is to be secured by measures other than the provision of personal protective equipment; reg. 7(2). It should be noted, however, that there are special rules for carcinogens. See reg. 7(3).
[88] reg. 8(1).

(3) ensuring that any control measure is maintained in an efficient state, in efficient working order and in good repair[89];

(4) monitoring the exposure of employees to substances hazardous to health in accordance with a suitable procedure[90];

(5) ensuring that employees who are, or are liable to be, exposed to a substance hazardous to health are subject to suitable health surveillance arrangements[91];

(6) providing employees who may be exposed to substances hazardous to health with such information, instruction and training as is suitable and sufficient for them to know the risks to health created by such exposure and the precautions which should be taken.[92]

(d) Electricity at Work Regulations 1989

6.19 These Regulations[93] are intended to provide a comprehensive framework of control as regards the use of electricity at work, and they place duties of compliance on employers, the self-employed, managers of mines or quarries, and employees.[94] Regulation 3(1) lays down a general requirement that all electrical systems[95] must at all times be of such construction as to prevent danger. There are also similar requirements as regards the maintenance of electrical systems.[96] In addition, every work activity, including operation, use, and maintenance of a system and work near a system must be carried out in such a manner as not to give rise to danger.[97] All of these duties are based upon the standard of reasonable practicability, indicating that a balance should be struck between the steps necessary to prevent the dangers and the dangers themselves. However, as the HSE's Guidance Notes make clear, given that the most obvious danger associated with electricity is electrocution, the Regulations may in practice impose a fairly high standard of care.

---

[89] reg. 9(1).

[90] reg. 10(1).

[91] reg. 11(1).

[92] reg. 12(1).

[93] S.I. 1989 No. 635.

[94] See generally, reg. 3. The Regulations do not apply to the master or crew of a sea-going vessel or their employer, nor do they apply to any person in relation to an aircraft or hovereraft moving under its own power; reg. 32.

[95] "System" means an electrical system in whch all the electrical equipment is, or may be, electrically connected to a common source of electrical energy, and includes such source and such equipment; reg. 2(1).

[96] reg. 4(2).

[97] reg. 4(3).

6.20 There are also other duties created by the Regulations where the standard is one of reasonable practicability. Thus, under regulation 6, electrical equipment[98] which may reasonably foreseeably be exposed to mechanical damage; the effects of the weather, natural hazards, temperature or pressure; the effect of wet, dirty, dusty or corrosive conditions; or any flammable or explosive substance, must be of such construction or as necessary protected so as to prevent, so far as reasonably practicable, danger arising from such exposure. Equally, under regulation 7 there are duties, so far as reasonably practicable, to ensure that all conductors in a system which may give rise to danger are either suitably covered with insulating material or have such precautions taken in respect of them as will prevent danger. It has been held under the equivalent provision of earlier regulations that the purpose of this regulation is to protect employees against the consequences of doing things by reason of inadvertence or inattention which they would not normally do.[99]

6.21 Other duties impose a standard which is strict, so that they do not involve issues of reasonable practicability. Any protective equipment provided to persons working on or near electrical equipment must be suitable for the use for which it is provided, be maintained in a condition suitable for that use, and be properly used.[1] No electrical equipment should be put into use where its strength and capability may be exceeded in such a way as may give rise to danger.[2] The Regulations also impose requirements through earthing, or by other suitable means, to prevent dangers arising from conductors becoming charged[3] and as regards the need for suitable precautions to prevent dangers from breaks in the electrical continuity when a circuit conductor is connected to earth.[4] Every joint and connection in a system must be mechanically and electrically suitable for use,[5] and efficient means, suitably located, must be provided for protecting every part of the system from excess of current.[6]

---

[98] "Electrical equipment" includes anything used, intended to be used or installed for use, to generate, provide, transmit, transform, rectify, convert, conduct, distribute, control, store, measure or use electrical energy.

[99] See *R. v. Sanyo Electrical Manufacturing (U.K.) Ltd* (1992) 156 J.P. Reps 863, CA (decided under the Electricity (Factories Act) Special Regulations 1944 (S.R. & O. 1944 No. 739)).

[1] reg. 4(4).

[2] reg. 5.

[3] reg. 8.

[4] reg. 9.

[5] reg. 10.

[6] reg. 11.

6.22 There must be suitable means for cutting off the supply of electricity to any electrical equipment and for isolating that equipment,[7] and adequate precautions must be taken to prevent electrical equipment which has been made dead becoming electrically charged when work is being carried out on or near it.[8] There are regulations about the need for adequate precautions for electrical equipment made dead,[9] as regards work on or near live conductors,[10] and in relation to the provision of adequate space, access and lighting for work on or near all electrical equipment.[11] Finally, it is unlawful for a person to work on any activity where technical knowledge or experience is necessary to prevent danger or injury, unless he possesses such knowledge or experience, or is properly supervised.[12]

6.23 As already noted, the Regulations place obligations of compliance as far as matters which are within their control on employers, the self-employed, and managers of mines and quarries.[13] As far as employees are concerned they have duties while at work to co-operate with their employer so far as is necessary to enable any duty placed upon that employer to be complied with, and to comply with the regulations in relation to matters which are within their control.[14] This ensures that both the employer and employee can be guilty of an offence under the regulations, and that actions for breach of statutory duty are also competent against both. This state of affairs may cause problems for employees suing on the basis of the employer's alleged breach of duty where it is claimed that they were also in default under the regulations.[15]

(e) Construction (Design and Management) Regulations 1994

6.24 These Regulations[16] are intended to implement the design and management aspects of the Temporary or Mobile Construction Sites Directive.[17] The underlying principles of the Construction (Design and Management) Regulations 1994 (CDM Regulations) are to consider the health and safety aspects of construction projects from the outset; involve all those who are

---

[7] reg. 12(1).
[8] reg. 13.
[9] reg. 13.
[10] reg. 14.
[11] reg. 15.
[12] reg. 16.
[13] reg. 3(1). For the special provisions for mines and quarries, sec Pt III.
[14] reg. 3(2).
[15] See, for example, *Ginty v. Belmont Building Supplies Ltd* [1959] 1 All E.R. 414.
[16] S.I. 1994 No. 3140.
[17] E.C. Directive 92/47.

engaged in construction projects through proper planning and co-ordination, ensure that health and safety will be adequately resourced by proper persons; share and communicate information and record information for the future so as to promote the safety of subsequent parts of the project.

6.25 The Regulations apply to construction work, which means the carrying out of any building, civil engineering or engineering construction work, and includes demolition, fitting out, repair, redecoration, maintenance (including cleaning) and temporary sites.[18] There is an exclusion for construction work (but not demolition or dismantling work) where the client has reasonable grounds for believing that the project is not notifiable (broadly projects of less than 30 days duration) and the number of workers required to carry out the work at any one time is less than five.[19] There are also exemptions for work carried out for a domestic client (except domestic client work involving a developer). The Regulations place duties on clients, designers and contractors, and create the roles of planning supervisor and principal contractor who have particular functions.

(i) The Client

6.26 "Client" means any person for whom a project is carried out, whether it is carried out by another person or is carried out in house.[20] Thus clients would encompass such people as the owner of the building or a developer. Clients have the following responsibilities:

(a) to appoint the planning supervisor and principal contractor[21];

(b) to be reasonably satisfied as to the competence of the planning supervisor, designer and contractor, and that adequate resources have been allocated so as to enable the planning supervisor, designer or contractor to perform their functions[22];

(c) to ensure that the planning supervisor is provided with all relevant information about the state or condition of any premises where the construction work is to be carried out (such information should be provided as soon as reasonably practicable, but in any event before the commencement of the work)[23];

---

[18] reg. 2(1).
[19] reg. 3(2).
[20] reg. 2(1).
[21] reg. 6(1).
[22] reg. 8.
[23] reg. 11.

(d) to ensure that so far as reasonably practicable the construction phase of the project does not start unless a health and safety plan has been prepared for that project[24];

(e) to take reasonable steps to ensure that the information in any health and safety file is available for inspection by any person who may need the information so as to comply with the relevant statutory provisions.[25]

These duties cannot be delegated, although the Regulations do permit the appointment of an agent or another client to act as the only client for a project.[26] A client cannot appoint any person as an agent unless the client is reasonably satisfied that the person has the competence to perform the duties placed upon the client by the CDM Regulations.[27]

(ii) Designers

6.27 "Designer" means any person who carries on a trade, business or other undertaking which involves preparing a design or arranging for any person under his control (including employees) to prepare a design.[28] "Design" includes drawing, design details, specification, and bill of quantities (including specification of articles or substances).[29] Designers have the following duties:

(a) except in the case of in-house work, no designer shall prepare a design unless reasonable steps have been taken to ensure that the client is aware of the duties placed upon him by the Regulations and any practical guidance issued by HSC[30];

(b) to ensure, so far as reasonably practicable, that any design includes among the design considerations adequate regard to the need (i) to avoid foreseeable risks to the health and safety of any person, (ii) to combat at source risks to the health and safety of any person at work, and (iii) to give priority to measures which will protect all persons at work[31];

---

[24] reg. 10. It should be noted that this is one of only two provisions in the Regulations which give rise to civil liability; reg. 21.
[25] regs 11 and 12.
[26] reg. 4(1).
[27] reg. 4(2).
[28] reg. 2(1).
[29] reg. 2(1).
[30] reg. 13(1).
[31] reg. 13(2)(a).

(c) to ensure, so far as reasonably practicable, that the design includes adequate information about any aspect of the project which might affect the health or safety of any person at work[32];

(d) to co-operate with the planning supervisor and any other designer involved in the project to enable each of them to comply with their duties under the relevant statutory provisions.[33]

(iii) Planning Supervisor

6.28 This is the person appointed by the client at the outset of the project. He is there to act as co-ordinator for health and safety. A planning supervisor has the following duties:

(a) to ensure, so far as reasonably practicable, that the design of any structure includes among the design considerations adequate regard to the health and safety needs of persons who will work there, and adequate information about any aspect of the project which might affect health and safety[34];

(b) to take reasonable steps to ensure co-operation between designers so as to enable them to comply with their duties under the Regulations[35];

(c) to be in a position to give adequate advice to (i) any client and any contractor as regards the competence of and resources available to any designer, and (ii) any client as regards the competence of and resources available to any contractor, as well as the preparation of the health and safety plan and the need to ensure that the construction phase does not start until the plan is prepared[36];

(d) to ensure that a health and safety file is prepared for each structure in the project containing the health and safety information which must be included with the design, and any other information which it is reasonably foreseeable will be necessary for health and safety purposes[37];

(e) to review, amend or add to the health and safety file as necessary to ensure that it contains the required health and safety information when it is delivered to the client[38];

---

[32] reg. 13(2)(b).
[33] reg. 13(2)(c).
[34] reg. 14(a).
[35] reg. 14(b).
[36] reg. 14(c).
[37] reg. 14(d).
[38] reg. 14(e).

(f) to ensure that, on the completion of the construction work on each structure in the project, the health and safety file is delivered to the client.[39]

In addition, it is the duty of the planning supervisor to ensure that a health and safety plan for the project has been prepared in good time, and that it contains general information and more specific details about the project.[40] It is also the responsibility of the planning supervisor to ensure that notice of the project is given to HSE before it starts and to ensure that the relevant particulars are contained in the notice.[41]

(iv) Contractors and Principal Contractor

6.29 "Contractor" means any person who carries on a trade, business or other undertaking (whether for profit or not) who undertakes to, or does, carry out or manage construction work, or arranges for any person at work under his/her control (including employees) to carry out or manage construction work.[42] The principal contractor is the contractor so appointed by the client at the outset of the project. The principal contractor has the following duties:

(a) to take reasonable steps to ensure co-operation between all contractors (whether or not there is a shared worksite under the Management of Health and Safety at Work Regulations 1999) so far as is necessary to enable each of the contractors to comply with the requirements and prohibitions of the relevant statutory provisions[43];

(b) to ensure, so far as reasonably practicable, that every contractor and every employee working on the project complies with the rules of the health and safety plan[44];

(c) take reasonable steps to ensure that only authorised persons are allowed on to the construction site[45];

(d) to ensure that the particulars contained in the notice given to HSE are displaycd in a readable condition in a position where they can be read by any person at work[46];

---

[39] reg. 14(f).
[40] reg. 15(1)–(3).
[41] reg. 7(1).
[42] reg. 2(1).
[43] reg. 16(1)(a). This is the only other provision in the Regulations which gives rise to civil liability.
[44] reg. 16(1)(b).
[45] reg. 16(1)(c).
[46] reg. 16(1)(d).

(e) promptly provide the planning supervisor with any information which is in the possession of the principal contractor or which could be ascertained by making reasonable inquiries of contractors, which it is reasonable to believe that the planning supervisor would include in the health and safety file and which is not in the planning supervisor's possession.[47]

The principal contractor also has the power to give reasonable directions to any contractor so as to enable the principal contractor to comply with the above duties and to include, in the health and safety plan, rules for the management of the construction work which are reasonably required for health and safety reasons.[48] There are also requirements placed upon the principal contractor to ensure, so far as reasonably practicable, that every contractor is provided with comprehensible information on health and safety risks, and that contractors provide their employees with relevant information and the right to time off for training.[49] In addition, the principal contractor must ensure that employees and self-employed persons working on the site are able to discuss and offer advice on health and safety matters, and that these views and those of employees' representatives are co-ordinated.[50]

6.30 In order to ensure that the principal contractor can comply with the above duties contractors have the following responsibilities:

(a) to co-operate with the principal contractor over health and safety[51];

(b) so far as reasonably practicable, to promptly provide the principal contractor with any information which might affect the health or safety of any person at work or might justify a review of the health and safety plan[52];

(c) comply with the reasonable directions of the principal contractor[53];

(d) comply with the applicable rules of the health and safety plan[54];

---

[47] reg. 16(1)(e).
[48] reg. 16(2).
[49] reg. 17.
[50] reg. 18.
[51] reg. 19(1)(a).
[52] reg. 19(1)(b).
[53] reg. 19(1)(c).
[54] reg. 19(1)(d).

(e) promptly provide the principal contractor with information about any death, injury, condition or dangerous occurrence[55];

(f) promptly provide the principal contractor with any information which is in the possession of the contractor, which should be supplied to the planning supervisor by the principal contractor, but which the principal contractor does not possess.[56]

Contractors must also supply certain health and safety information to their employees and the self-employed.

Enforcement

6.31 The sole enforcing authority for these Regulations is HSE.[57] The Executive has at its disposal the full range of administrative remedies which are provided by the 1974 Act (including improvement notices and prohibition notices). Apart from the two provisions already identified the Regulations can only be enforced by criminal penalty.

(f) Construction (Health, Safety and Welfare) Regulations 1996

6.32 These Regulations[58] complement the CDM Regulations and are intended to comply with Annex 4 of the Temporary and Mobile Constructions Sites Directive. The 1996 Regulations are not dissimilar to the Workplace (Health, Safety and Welfare) Regulations 1992, although they also tackle issues which are of particular importance to the construction industry. The opportunity has been taken to replace and update in consolidated form the earlier construction legislation to be found in the Construction (General Provisions) Regulations 1961, the Construction (Working Places) Regulations 1966, the Construction (Health and Welfare) Regulations 1966 and the Construction (Health and Welfare) (Amendment) Regulations 1974. The 1996 Regulations apply the same definition of "construction work" as is contained in the CDM Regulations. They apply generally to employers, the self-employed and employees wherever construction work is being conducted. They now cover such matters as falls, traffic routes, doors and gates, inspection, fire detection, fire-fighting and enforcement in respect of fire, emergency routes and exits, temperature and weather, good order of construction sites, and welfare facilities.

---

[55] reg. 19(1)(e).
[56] reg. 19(1)(f).
[57] reg. 22.
[58] S.I. 1996 No. 1592, as amended by S.I. 1999 No. 3242, reg. 27.

OTHER "EUROPEAN" REGULATIONS

6.33 The acceptance of the Single European Act by the Member States of the European Community in 1987 has had a major impact on the development and implementation of health and safety laws throughout the European Union. The amendments to the Treaty of Rome which SEA brought about not only ensured that for the first time there was a specific article namely Article 118a dealing with health and safety issues, but they also enabled approval for such measures to be given by means of a system of qualified majority voting in the Council of Ministers. There can be no doubt that the directives of the European Union which have been made since the Framework Directive[59] was approved in 1989 constitute a major source of law on health and safety matters. As has already been noted, the United Kingdom Government has accepted these European initiatives and has enacted the necessary compliance measures by means of regulations made under section 15 of the Health and Safety at Work Act 1974. Some of these regulations have already been discussed in earlier chapters. For example, the Workplace (Health, Safety and Welfare) Regulations 1992[60] and the Provision and Use of Work Equipment Regulations 1998[61] were discussed in Chapter four, and the risk assessment require-ments of the Management of Health and Safety at Work Regu-lations 1999[62] were discussed in Chapter five. It is now time to consider some of these Regulations in a different context and to examine other "European" regulations which have not yet been discussed in this book.

(a) Management of Health and Safety at Work Regulations 1999

6.34 As well as implementing the Framework Directive,[63] these Regulations are also intended to comply with the Temporary Workers Directive.[64] As already noted, their most significant contribution to United Kingdom health and safety laws has been the introduction of detailed requirements for risk assessment. The 1999 Regulations now require employers, in regulation 4, to comply with principles of prevention which are listed in Schedule

---

[59] See the E.C. Council Directive on the introduction of measures to encourage improvements in the safety and health of workers at work; 89/391.

[60] S.I. 1992 No. 3004.

[61] S.I. 1998 No. 2306.

[62] S.I. 1999 No. 3242.

[63] E.C. Directive on the introduction of measures to encoumge improvements in the safety and health of workers at work; 89/391.

[64] 91/383. HSC has published an Approved Code of Practice to accompany the Regulations.

1.[65] Employers now have an obligation to conduct a risk assessment exercise both for their employees and for others, so as to identify the measures that should be taken in order to comply with health and safety laws.[66] There are similar obligations placed on the self-employed as regards risks to their own health and safety and those of others.[67] However, there can be no doubt that the Management of Health and Safety at Work Regulations 1999 (Management Regulations) also strengthen the United Kingdom health and safety regime by creating a number of additional obligations on both employers and employees. Much of what follows arises as a logical extension of the risk assessment exercise and the conclusions which it reaches. It is central to such an exercise that information about the risks and the preventive and protective measures is distributed widely. Accordingly, the Management Regulations also contain provisions intended to ensure that employees and other persons are aware of the hazards and their own responsibilities in relation to them.

6.35 Key aspects of the rest of the regulations are as follows:

(1) Health and Safety Arrangements and Health Surveillance

Employers must make and give effect to appropriate arrangements having regard to the nature of their activities and the size of their undertakings for the effective planning organisation, control, monitoring and review of any preventive and protective measures.[68] Employers must also provide such health surveillance as is appropriate to the risks identified by the assessment.[69]

(2) Health and Safety Assistance

Employers are required to appoint one or more competent persons to assist them in undertaking the necessary measures to comply with the requirements and prohibitions imposed by any of the relevant statutory provisions and the Fire Precautions (Workplace) Regulations 1997, Part II.[70] A person can be regarded as competent where he has sufficient training and experience or knowledge,

---

[65] See paras 5.49–5.52.

[66] reg. 3(1).

[67] reg. 3(2).

[68] reg. 5(1). Employers employing five or more employees must record their arrangements; reg. 5(2).

[69] reg. 6.

[70] reg. 7(1). The number of persons appointed, the time available to fulfil their functions and the means at their disposal must be adequate having regard to the size of the undertaking, the risks and the distribution of those risks through the undertaking; reg. 7(3).

and other qualities to enable him properly to assist in undertaking the necessary measures.[71] Such a person need not necessarily be an employee (although the 1999 Regulations now state explicitly that employees are to be referred), and special information responsibilities are placed upon the employer when the competent person is not in his employment.[72] Employers may also have to inform the competent person(s) about persons working in the undertaking who are on fixed-term contracts or are employed in an employment business.[73]

(3) Procedures for Serious and Imminent Danger

Every employer must establish and give effect to appropriate procedures which should be followed in the event of serious and imminent danger to workers in the undertaking. Competent persons must be nominated to implement these procedures as far as evacuation from premises is concerned, and the employer must ensure that no employee should have access to an area which is restricted on health and safety grounds, unless adequate health and safety instruction has been provided to the employee concerned.[74] In particular, the appropriate procedures must, so far as is practicable, ensure that persons at work who are exposed to serious and imminent danger are informed of the nature of the hazard and the steps which have been taken to protect them from it, enable those persons to stop work and immediately proceed to a place of safety when they are exposed to serious, imminent and unavoidable danger, and prevent those persons from resuming work where there is still a serious and imminent danger.[75] There are also new rules about arranging contacts with external services as regards first aid, emergency medical care and rescue work.[75a]

(4) Information to Employees

Employers are required to provide their employees with comprehensible[76] and relevant information on the risks to their health and safety identified by the assessment, the preventive and protective measures, the procedures for serious and imminent danger, the persons responsible for evacuation procedures, and the risks associated with shared workplaces.[77]

---

[71] reg. 7(5).
[72] See reg. 7(4)(a) and (8).
[73] reg. 7(4)(b).
[74] reg. 8(1).
[75] reg. 8(2).
[75a] reg. 9.
[76] The Code of Practice advises that for information to be comprehensible it must be capable of being understood by the employees to whom it is addressed.
[77] reg. 10.

(5) Shared Workplaces and Visiting Workers

Employers who share a workplace must co-operate with one another in order to comply with the requirements and prohibitions of the relevant statutory provisions and take all reasonable steps to co-ordinate their preventive and protective measures, and inform the other employers of the risks to their employees' health and safety from the conduct of their undertakings.[78] Every employer and self-employed person must provide comprehensible information to the employer of employees from an outside undertaking who are working in his undertaking as regards the health and safety risks associated with that undertaking, and the requirements and prohibitions of any of the relevant statutory provisions.[79]

(6) Capabilities and Training

Employers must take into account an employee's health and safety capabilities when entrusting tasks, and must provide adequate health and safety training to new employees and those exposed to new or increased risks either because of a transfer or change of responsibilities or through the introduction of new work equipment, new technology or a new or changed system of work.[80] Training must be repeated periodically where appropriate, be adapted to take account of any new or changed health and safety risks, and take place during working hours.[81]

(7) Duties of Employees

Employees have duties to use any machinery, equipment, dangerous substance, transport equipment, means of production or safety device in accordance with the training that they have received, and the instructions regarding use which have been provided to them in compliance with the requirements and prohibitions of any relevant statutory provisions.[82] Employees must also inform their employer or any other employee with specific health and safety responsibilities as regards any work situation which represents a serious and immediate danger to health and safety and any shortcoming in the employer's protection arrangements for health and safety.[83]

(8) Temporary Workers

Regulation 15 is intended to comply with the Temporary Workers Directive by placing information responsibilities on employers and

---

[78] reg. 11(1).
[79] reg. 12(1).
[80] reg. 13(1) and (2).
[81] reg. 13(3).
[82] reg. 14(1).
[83] reg. 14(2). These duties are discussed in more detail at para. 5.57.

the self-employed for employees on fixed term contracts, those employed to perform a specific task, and those provided by employment agencies. Such people must be provided with information about any special occupational qualifications or skills to be held by such employees if they are to carry out their work safely, and health surveillance requirements. This information should be provided before the employees commence their duties.

(9) Worker Participation

As already noted,[84] the original 1992 Regulations amended the Safety Representatives and Safety Committees Regulations 1977[85] by placing additional responsibilities on employers to consult, in good time, safety representatives as regards (a) the introduction of protective and preventive measures; (b) the arrangements for the appointment of safety assistants and those responsible for implementing evacuation arrangements; (c) the health and safety information provided to employees; (d) the planning and organisation of health and safety training; and (e) the health and safety consequences of new technology.[86]

(10) Duties to New or Expectant Mothers and Young Workers

As already noted, a risk assessment must take account of the health and safety risks to new and expectant mothers.[87] Moreover, employers must suspend from work a new and expectant mother[88] who works at night where a certificate from a registered medical practitioner or a registered midwife shows that it is necessary for her health and safety that she should not be at work for any period specified in the certificate.[89] Employers must also ensure that young persons employed by them are protected at work from any risks to their health and safety which are a consequence of their lack of experience, or absence of awareness of existing or potential risks or the fact that young persons have not yet fully matured.[89a] The Regulations also list a range of circumstances where young persons should not be employed.[89b]

---

[84] See para. 5.22.

[85] S.I. 1977 No. 500; and see also the Health and Safety (Consultation with Employees) Regulations 1996 (S.I. 1996 No. 1513).

[86] reg. 17 and Sched.

[87] See para. 5.49. It would seem that this duty is triggered when an employer employs a worker of child-bearing age; *Day v. T. Pickles Farms Ltd* [1999] I.R.L.R. 217 (EAT).

[88] "New or expectant mother" means an employee who is pregnant: who has given birth within the previous six months; or who is breastfeeding; reg. 1(2).

[89] reg. 17.

[89a] reg. 19(1). A "young person" means any person not yet 18: reg. 1(2).

[89b] reg. 19(2).

Finally, it should be noted that a breach of any duty imposed by the Regulations does not confer a right of action in any civil proceedings, except in relation to new or expectant mothers or young workers.[90]

(b) Workplace (Health, Safety and Welfare) Regulations 1992

6.36 These Regulations[91] are intended to implement the Workplace Directive[92] of the European Union, and are accompanied by an HSC Approved Code of Practice. They took effect for new workplaces on January 1, 1993, and apply to workplaces in existence before that date since January 1, 1996. They are discussed in detail in Chapter four.[93] As already noted, the Regulations provide very detailed rules about the health and safety requirements for the working environment and provide for both criminal and civil liability. They exclude from their compass workplaces which are in the nature of ships; building operations and engineering construction works; involving the extraction of mineral resources; or workplaces which are situated in the immediate vicinity of another workplace involving the extraction of mineral resources. The Regulations also repeal a whole host of earlier regulations[94] and some key provisions of the Factories Act 1961[95] and the Offices, Shops and Railway Premises Act 1963.[96]

(c) Provision and Use of Work Equipment Regulations 1998

6.37 These Regulations[97] are intended to implement the Work Equipment Directive,[98] and are accompanied by HSE Guidance Notes. As was noted in Chapter four,[99] one of the key aspects of these Regulations is the repeal of the fencing provisions of the Factories Act 1961.[1] Instead, the Regulations provide new provisions requiring measures to be taken to prevent access to

---

[90] reg. 22.

[91] S.I. 1992 No. 3004.

[92] See Directive 89/654, on minimum safety and health requirements for the workplace.

[93] See paras 4.36–4.47.

[94] See Sched. 2, Pt II.

[95] In particular, Factories Act 1961, ss. 1–7, 18, 28, 29, 57–60 and 69. See Sched. 2, Pt I.

[96] Offices, Shops and Railway Premises Act 1963, ss. 4–16. See Sched. 2, Pt I.

[97] S.I. 1998 No. 2306.

[98] Directive 89/655, on minimum safety and health requirements for the use of work equipment by workers at work.

[99] See paras 4.21–4.35.

[1] Factories Act 1961, ss. 12–16. The regulations also repeal ss. 17 and 19 and the offices, Shops and Railway Premises Act 1963, s. 17. See Sched. 2. Pt I. They also repeal a number of older regulations. See Sched. 2, Pt II.

dangerous parts of machinery or to any rotating stock bar, or to stop the movement of any dangerous part of machinery or rotating stock bar when any person enters a danger zone. The Regulations apply to new machinery from January 1, 1993 and, in the case of existing machinery, the obligations under these Regulations became effective from January 1, 1997. They can be enforced through both criminal penalty and civil liability.

(d) Personal Protective Equipment at Work Regulations 1992

6.38 These Regulations[2] are intended to implement the Personal Protective Equipment Directive[3] and are accompanied by HSE Guidance Notes. The basic obligation placed upon employers[4] is to ensure that suitable personal protective equipment is provided to their employees[5] who may be exposed to a risk to their health or safety while at work, unless it can be shown that the risk has been adequately controlled by other means which are equally or more effective.[6] "Personal protective equipment" means all equipment (including clothing affording protection against the weather) which is intended to be worn or held by a person at work, and which protects him against one or more risks to his health and safety, and any addition or accessory designed to meet that objective.[7] However, there are exclusions for personal protective equipment which involves any of the following:

(a) ordinary working clothes and uniforms which do not specifically protect the health and safety of the wearer;

(b) offensive weapons used as self-defence or as deterrent equipment;

(c) portable devices for detecting and signalling risks and nuisances;

---

[2] S.I. 1992 No. 2966.

[3] Directive 89/656, on minimum safety and health requirements for the use by workers of personal protective equipment at the workplace.

[4] There are exemptions for sea-going ships. See reg. 3(1).

[5] The Health and Safety at Work Act 1974, s. 9, ensures that an employer cannot charge the employee for the provision of such equipment.

[6] reg. 4(1). Self-employed persons must ensure that they are provided with suitable personal protective equipment for their own health and safety; reg. 4(2). Regulation 4 does not apply where other Regulations require personal protective equipment to be provided in respect of health and safety risks. For our purposes the most important of these other Regulations are the Control of Lead at Work Regulations 1998, the Control of Asbestos at Work Regulations 1987, and the COSHH Regulations 1994.

[7] reg. 2(1). For examples of relevant protective equipment, see para. 7 of the Guidance Notes. The Guidance Notes make clear that some types of personal protective equipment, such as ear protectors and most types of respiratory protective equipment, are unlikely to be covered by the PPE Regulations since they are covered by other regulations such as the COSHH Regulations.

(d) personal protective equipment used for protection while travelling on roads;

(e) equipment used during the playing of competitive sports.[8]

6.39 As noted above, the key requirement is for the personal protective equipment to be suitable. Equipment will not be suitable unless.:

(a) it is appropriate for the risks involved and the conditions at the place where the exposure to the risks may occur;

(b) it takes account of ergonomic requirements and the state of health of the wearer;

(c) it is capable of fitting the wearer correctly, if necessary. after adjustments;

(d) so far as practicable, it is effective to prevent or adequately control the risks involved without increasing overall risk;

(e) it complies with any British enactment implementing any relevant Community Directive[9] on design and manufacture of personal protective equipment.[10]

6.40 Although the need to provide suitable personal protective equipment is the key provision, the Regulations also place obligations on employers as regards the selection and compatibility, and use and maintenance of personal protective equipment. Thus, before choosing any personal protective equipment, employers must ensure that an assessment is made to determine whether that equipment is suitable.[11] This assessment must include (a) an assessment of the health and safety risks which have not been avoided by other means, (b) the definition of the characteristics the equipment must have to be effective against those risks, and (c) a comparison of those characteristics against the characteristics which the proposed equipment possesses.[12] Such an assessment must be reviewed if there is any reason to suspect that it is no longer valid or there has been a significant change in the matters to which it relates.[13] In addition, employers must ensure that where

---

[8] reg. 3(2).
[9] The relevant directives are Directive 89/686 and Directive 93/95 implemented in the U.K. by the Personal Protective Equipment (E.C. Directive) Regulations 1992 (S.I. 1992 No. 3139) (as amended by S.I. 1993 No. 3074).
[10] reg. 4(3).
[11] reg. 6(1).
[12] reg. 6(2).
[13] reg. 6(3).

employees are required to wear two or more items of personal protective equipment each item is compatible and continues to be effective against the risks in question.[14]

6.41 The Regulations also require employers to take all reasonable steps to ensure that any personal protective equipment provided to employees is properly used.[15] Central to this requirement are the provisions of regulation 9(1), which place obligations on employers to ensure that employees are provided with the necessary information, instruction and training. Any such information, etc., should be adequate and appropriate,[16] to enable employees to know (a) the risks which the personal protective equipment will avoid or limit, (b) the purpose for which and the manner in which that equipment is to be used, and (c) any action the employee needs to take to ensure that the equipment remains in an efficient state, in efficient working order and in good repair. There are corresponding obligations on employees to use personal protective equipment in accordance with any training and instructions as to its use,[17] and to report to their employer any loss of or obvious defect in that equipment.[18]

6.42 As regards the upkeep of such equipment, regulation 7(1) requires every employer to ensure that any personal protective equipment provided to employees is maintained (including replaced or cleaned as appropriate) in an efficient state, in efficient working order and in good repair. The Guidance Notes make it clear that it is essential for employers to introduce an examination and maintenance schedule for all personal protective equipment and to provide a sufficient stock of spare parts.[19] Employers are also required to provide appropriate accommodation for personal protective equipment when it is not being used[20] and employees must take all reasonable steps to ensure that it is returned to that accommodation after use.[21] The regulations can be enforced by the application of both the criminal and civil law and it is clear that both employers and employees can be responsible for breaches of statutory duty.

---

[14] reg. 5(1).
[15] reg. 10(1).
[16] Information and instruction will not be adequate and appropriate unless it is comprehensible to the employees concerned; reg. 9(2).
[17] reg. 10(2).
[18] reg. 11.
[19] See paras 45–47.
[20] reg. 8.
[21] reg. 10(4).

(e) Manual Handling Operations Regulations 1992

6.43   These Regulations[22] are intended to implement the Manual Handling Directive,[23] and are accompanied by HSE Guidance Notes. They repeal earlier provisions in both the Factories Act 1961, section 72, and the Offices, Shops and Railway Premises Act 1963, section 23, which concentrated solely on the weight of the load to be lifted. Instead the new regulations take a wider and more ergonomic approach to the problem of employees moving loads. The basic aim of the Manual Handling Operations Regulations 1992 (Manual Handling Regulations) is to prevent employees having to undertake any lifting operations which involve a risk of back injury: though the Regulations apply to the risk of any type of injury. Thus, the primary obligation placed upon employers[24] is, so far as is reasonably practicable, to avoid the need for employees to undertake any manual handling operations at work which involve the risk of their being injured.[25] "Manual handling operations" means any transporting or supporting of a load (including the lifting, putting down, pushing, pulling, carrying or moving of it) by hand or by bodily force.[26] A load is defined to include any person and any animal,[27] so that the Regulations apply equally to nurses lifting patients and to farm workers lifting animals.

6.44   Although the principal and first obligation on employers is to avoid employees lifting loads, the Regulations recognise that there may be situations where this cannot be achieved. Thus, where it is not reasonably practicable to avoid the need for employees to undertake any manual handling operations at work which involve the risk of injury, employers must:

---

[22] S.I. 1992 No. 2793.

[23] Directive 90/269, on the minimum safety and health requirements for the manual handling of loads where there is a risk particularly of back injury to workers.

[24] Similar duties are placed upon self-employed persons as regards themselves; reg. 2(2). There are also exemptions for sea-going ships; reg. 3.

[25] reg. 4(1)(a). A prima facie case will be made out under reg. 4(1) if the pursuer shows that he was involved in a manual handling operation and that it involved a risk of injury. Thereafter, his employers come under a duty to avoid the need for him to undertake that operation, unless they assume and discharge the onus of proving that it was not reasonably practicable to do so: *Hall v. City of Edinburgh Council*, 1999 S.L.T. 744, O.H. "Injury" does not involve injury caused by any toxic or corrosive substance which (a) has leaked or spilled from a load, (b) is present on the surface of a load but has not leaked or spilled from it, or (c) is a constituent part of the load, and "injured" is to be construed accordingly; reg. 2(1).

[26] reg. 2(1). It does not cover merely unscrewing a nut with a spanner: *King v. Carron Phoenix Ltd*, 1999 G.W.D. 9-437.

[27] reg. 2(1).

(a) make a suitable and sufficient assessment of all such operations[28];

(b) take appropriate steps to reduce the risk of injury to those employees involved in manual handling operations to the lowest level reasonably practicable; and

(c) take appropriate steps to provide such employees with general indications and, where it is reasonably practicable to do so, precise information on the weight of each load and the heaviest side of any load whose centre of gravity is not positioned centrally.[29]

The assessment must be reviewed by the employer if there is reason to suspect that it is no longer valid, or there has been a significant change in the operations to which it relates.[30] It would seem that the need to conduct such an assessment is not simply restricted to cases where the risk of injury arises from the imposition of a load. It is enough under the Regulations that the operation involved a risk of an employee being injured whether or not it was due to the imposition of a load.[31] Employees have a duty to make full and proper use of any system of work which the employer has instituted, so as to bring the risk of injury to the lowest level reasonably practicable.[32] The Regulations permit both criminal prosecutions and civil actions for breach of statutory duty.

(f) Health and Safety (Display Screen Equipment) Regulations 1992

6.45 These Regulations[33] are intended to implement the Display Screen Equipment Directive,[34] and are accompanied by HSE Guidance Notes. The effect of the Regulations is to ensure that for

---

[28] In this context employers must have regard to a list of factors and consider the corresponding questions, all of which are specified in Sched. 1. The factors include the tasks, the loads, the working environment and individual capacity. The questions include the posture of employee's bodies, the unwieldiness of loads, the conditions of the working environment, and whether the operations require unusual strength or height or could endanger pregnant women.

[29] reg. 4(1)(b). There is a very useful flow chart on p. 5 of the Guidance Notes, which indicates the hierarchy of responsibilities placed upon employers by reg. 4(1). See also *Logan v. Strathclyde Fire Board*, January 12, 1999, unreported: liability is based on a failure to fulfil the substantive duty of taking proper precautions rather than the procedural requirement of a risk assessment.

[30] reg. 4(2).

[31] *Cullen v. North Lanarkshire Council*, 1998 S.L.T. 847 (I.H.).

[32] reg. 5.

[33] S.I. 1992 No 2792.

[34] Directive 90/270, on minimum safety and health requirements for work with display screen equipment.

the first time in Britain there is a legal framework regulating the health and safety of persons using visual display units. The Regulations only apply where there is display screen equipment, and the duties that they create only apply when there are users and operators. "Display screen equipment" means any alphanumeric or graphic display screen, regardless of the display process involved.[35] However, exempted from the Regulations are the following:

(a) drivers' cabs or control cabs for vehicles or machinery;

(b) display screen equipment on board a means of transport;

(c) display screen equipment mainly intended for public operation;

(d) portable systems not in prolonged use;

(e) calculators, cash registers or any equipment having a small data or measurement display required for direct use of the equipment;

(f) window typewriters.[36]

6.46 "User" means an employee who habitually uses display screen equipment as a significant part of his normal work.[37] The critical question here is whether employees use a display screen as a *significant* part of their normal work, and the Guidance Notes are particularly helpful in indicating examples of users and non-users, and the criteria that should be adopted when resolving this issue.[38] "Operators" are self-employed persons who also habitually use display screen equipment as a significant part of their normal work.[39] The obligations under the Regulations fall largely on employers. As far as users are concerned, employers owe duties to their employees regardless of who it is that provided the work-station[40]; whereas in the case of operators, employers only owe duties to the self-employed when it is the employer who has provided the workstation and the operator uses that workstation for the employer's purposes.[41]

---

[35] reg. 1(2).

[36] reg. 1(4).

[37] reg. 1(2)(d).

[38] See the Guidance Notes at pp. 6–10. Some examples given or definite users are secretaries, journalists, air traffic controllers and graphic designers. Some examples of possible users are scientists and airline check-in clerks: whereas the Guidance Notes make clear that senior managers are definitely not users. These are merely examples and a better guide are the criteria listed in para. 12, and the chart provided on p. 10.

[39] reg. 1(2)(b).

[40] Thus employees working at home or at another employer's workstation are nonetheless covered.

[41] See generally, reg. 3.

6.47 It is clear that critical to the application of the regulations is the concept of the "workstation". A workstation is an assembly comprising:

  (a) display screen equipment (whether provided with software determining the interface between the equipment and the user, a keyboard, or any other input device);

  (b) any optional accessories to the equipment;

  (c) any disk drive, telephone, modem, printer, document holder, work chair, work desk, work surface or other item peripheral to the equipment; and

  (d) the immediate work environment around the equipment.[42]

Workstations first put into service on or after January 1, 1993 must comply with certain standards listed in the Schedule to the Regulations; whereas existing workstations (those in service on or before December 31, 1992) had to comply with these standards by December 31, 1996.[43]

6.48 Consistent with many of the other "European" Regulations, the Health and Safety (Display Screen Equipment) Regulations 1992 (Display Screen Regulations) require employers to carry out an assessment of the risks associated with display screen equipment. Thus regulation 2(1) requires employers to perform a suitable and sufficient analysis of workstations so as to assess the health and safety risks to which users and operators are exposed. Once this has been completed, employers must then reduce the risks identified by the assessment to the lowest extent reasonably practicable.[44] Any such assessment must be reviewed if there is reason to suspect that it is no longer valid or there has been a significant change in the matters to which it relates.[45] Employers must also plan the activities of users so that their daily work on display screen equipment is periodically interrupted by such breaks or changes of activity as reduce their workload at that equipment.[46]

6.49 A central provision of the Regulations concerns eye and eyesight tests for employees. Employers owe obligations both to

---

[42] reg. 1(2(e).

[43] See reg. 3 and Sched. The Schedule contains detailed rules on the equipment, environment and interface between computer and user/operator required for workstations.

[44] reg. 2(3).

[45] reg. 2(2).

[46] reg. 4. For general guidance on this issue see the Guidance Notes at paras 44 and 45.

users and to employees who are to become users to ensure that they are provided with an appropriate eye and eyesight test,[47] which must be carried out by a competent person.[48] Such tests should be carried out whenever an employee who is a user at the date of coming into force of the regulations, or who is an employee who is to become a user so requests it, at regular intervals thereafter, and on request where a user experiences visual difficulties which may reasonably be considered to be caused by work on display screen equipment.[49] No employee can be required to undergo an eye and eyesight test against their will.[50] Employers may also be required to provide users with special corrective appliances appropriate for their work where normal corrective appliances cannot be used and the result of any eye and eyesight test shows such provision to be necessary.[51]

6.50 Finally, the Regulations also place training and information responsibilities on employers. As regards training, users and employees who are to become users must be provided with adequate health and safety training in the use of any workstation upon which they may be required to work, and that training must be updated when a workstation is substantially modified.[52] As regards information, users and operators must be provided with adequate information about all aspects of health and safety relating to their workstations, and the measures taken in accordance with the risk assessment and the requirements for workstations specified in the Schedule to the Regulations.[53] Employers must also provide users with adequate information concerning their daily work routine and any substantial modification in their workstations, and also as regards eye and eyesight tests and training requirements.[54] The Regulations give rise to both criminal and civil liability.

THE OFFSHORE HEALTH AND SAFETY REGIME

6.51 Until recently, the major statute dealing with health and safety on offshore installations was the Mineral Workings (Offshore Installations) Act 1971. This Act enabled regulations to be

---

[47] This will be a "sight test", as defined by the Opticians Act 1989, s. 36(2). See Guidance Notes, para. 50.

[48] reg. 5(1).

[49] regs 5(1), 5(3) and (4). An original test should, in the case of users, be carried out as soon as practicable after the request and, in the case of employees who will become users, be carried out before that employee becomes a user; reg. 5(2).

[50] reg. 5(6).

[51] reg. 5(5). Under the Health and Safety at Work Act 1974, s. 9, an employer cannot charge the employee for such appliances.

[52] reg. 6.

[53] reg. 7(1).

[54] reg. 7(2) and (3).

made for the safety of offshore installations and for the safety, health and welfare of persons aboard such installations. It placed obligations on the concession owner and owner of the installation, and required the appointment of an installation manager who was given general responsibility for safety, health and welfare on the installation and who was also required to maintain order and discipline on the rig. Many of its provisions have now been repealed; though much remains, particularly as far as the responsibilities of the oil installation manager are concerned. Moreover, under the original provisions of the 1971 Act, responsibility for the enforcement of the Act was placed upon the Department of Energy—this responsibility has now been transferred to HSE.[55]

6.52 The legal catalyst for much of this change was the Offshore Safety Act 1992, which was enacted so as to implement the recommendations of the Cullen Report[56] into the *Piper Alpha* disaster which had claimed the lives of 165 men. This report was highly critical of the safety regime applicable on offshore installations, and made a number of significant and important recommendations. For our purpose, three of Lord Cullen's 106 recommendations are worthy of particular comment. The first was his recommendation that there should be regulations requiring the operator of every offshore installation to submit a "safety case" for acceptance by HSE. The safety case would have to demonstrate that the risks of a major accident had been assessed adequately, and that suitable measures had been applied to control risks and ensure the safety of everybody on board. The second major recommendation was that existing offshore health and safety legislation should be progressively repealed by new regulations. These new regulations were to be "goal-setting" rather than specific as to the measures which had to be taken. Thirdly, responsibility for offshore health and safety should be transferred to HSE.

6.53 The Offshore Safety Act 1992 fulfils three major purposes. First, it extends the general purposes of the Health and Safety at Work Act 1974, section 1(1)(a)–(d). The 1992 Act makes it clear that the general purposes will apply to:

(a) the safety, health and welfare of persons on offshore installations or engaged on pipeline works;

(b) the safety of such installations and the prevention of accidents on or near them;

---

[55] See generally, the Offshore Safety (Repeals and Modifications) Regulations 1993 (S.I. 1993 No. 1823).
[56] See the *Report of the Public Inquiry into the Piper Alpha Disaster*, Cm. 1310 (1990).

(c) the proper construction and safe operation of pipelines and the prevention of damage to them; and

(d) the safe dismantling, removal and disposal of offshore installations and pipelines.[57]

Secondly, it declares that current offshore safety legislation should be added to the list of relevant statutory provisions which are specified in the 1974 Act, Schedule 1.[58] As relevant statutory provisions, offshore safety legislation is now subject to the 1974 Act, section 1(2), and can be progressively replaced by a system of regulations and approved Codes of Practice. Moreover, it also ensures that offshore safety legislation can be enforced by HSE. Thirdly, section 1 ensures that the existing statutory provisions can be repealed or modified by health and safety regulations made under the 1974 Act, section 15, and allows for such regulations to be made about any of the matters which are specified in the general purposes of the 1974 Act, as modified for offshore installations by the 1992 Act.[59] The 1992 Act clearly enables earlier offshore safety legislation to be repealed and replaced by the goal-setting regulations which Lord Cullen has recommended. Just as important, it has enabled the Secretary of State to introduce regulations for safety cases.

(a) Offshore Installations (Safety Case) Regulations 1992

6.54 These Regulations[60] were made under powers granted to the Secretary of State by the 1974 Act, section 15, and the 1992 Act, section 1(2), and fulfil the recommendations of Lord Cullen on this issue. They are entirely consistent with the thrust of the "European" Regulations, since they require a full assessment of installations so as to identify the risks and introduce the necessary protective and preventive measures. There are also requirements for the carrying out of safety audits by independent persons. The key requirement is for operators to prepare a safety case for their installation and to send it to HSE.[61] No offshore installation can be operated until such a case has been prepared and sent to HSE and it has been accepted by the Executive.[62]

6.55 The Regulations specify the requirements for a safety case[63] and make it clear that any such case must include sufficient particulars to demonstrate:

---

[57] 1992 Act, s. 1(1).
[58] 1992 Act, s. 1(1) and (3).
[59] 1992 Act, s. 1(2).
[60] S.I. 1992 No. 2885 (as amended by S.I. 1995 No. 738 and S.I 1996 No. 913).
[61] reg. 4(1).
[62] reg. 4(2).
[63] See Sched. 1 for the safety case requirements for the design of a fixed installation, and Sched. 2 for the operation of a fixed installation. Schedule 3 lists the requirements for a mobile installation.

(a) the management system[64] is adequate to ensure that the relevant statutory provisions will be complied with in relation to the installation and any activity on or connected with it;

(b) adequate arrangements have been established for audits[65] and reports;

(c) all hazards with the potential to cause a major accident have been identified; and

(d) risks have been evaluated and measures taken to reduce the risks to persons affected by those hazards to the lowest level that is reasonably practicable.[66]

A safety case should be revised by the operator as often as is appropriate.[67] and there are obligations on the operator to ensure that the procedures and arrangements laid out in the safety case are followed.[68]

(b) Offshore Installations (Safety Representatives and Safety Committees) Regulations 1989

6.56 The importance of the oil installation manager in offshore health and safety matters has already been noted. Such persons have particular responsibility under the Offshore Installations (Safety Representatives and Safety Committees) Regulations 1989 (1989 Regulations)[69] as regards safety representatives and safety committees on offshore installations. These Regulations were made by the Secretary of State for Energy, under powers granted to him by the Mineral Workings (Offshore Installations) Act 1971, and are different from the Safety Representatives and Safety Committees Regulations 1977.[70] The major difference is that the 1989 Regulations do not depend upon the existence of an independent trade union recognised for collective bargaining purposes. Instead, the 1989 Regulations permit a workforce to nominate and elect safety representatives on the basis of constituencies established and maintained by the installation manager.

---

[64] "Management system" means the organisation and arrangements established by the operator for managing the undertaking; reg. 8(4)(b).

[65] "Audit" is a systematic assessment of the adequacy of the management system carried out by persons who are sufficiently independent of the system to ensure that the assessment is objective.

[66] reg. 8(1).

[67] reg. 9.

[68] reg. 10(1).

[69] S.I. 1989 No. 971.

[70] S.I. 1977 No. 500, discussed in Chap. 5, at paras 5.18–5.26.

6.57 There must be at least two constituencies on each installation with a maximum of 40 members, and every member of the workforce must be assigned to a constituency.[71] It is the duty of the installation manager to establish these constituencies and he can take into account such factors as the areas of the installation, its activities, the employers of members of the workforce and such other objective criteria as may be applied.[72] There must be a safety representative for each constituency, and any member of the constituency can stand for election so long as he is nominated and seconded by two other members of the constituency.[73] If there is more than one candidate nominated for election as a safety representative in a constituency, it is the duty of the installation manager to conduct a secret ballot where every member has the right to vote for one candidate.[74] Once elected, a safety representative has the right to conduct investigations and to make representations to the installation manager on behalf of the constituency members.[75] Safety representatives also have the right to paid time off, in order to exercise their functions and to undertake training.[76]

6.58 The owner of an offshore installation where one or more safety representatives have been elected also has a duty to establish a safety committee. This committee is chaired by the installation manager and is made up of all the safety representatives, together with one other person appointed by the manager and other persons co-opted unanimously by the committee.[77] The committee exercises important functions such as the power to keep under review the measures taken to ensure the occupational health and safety of the workforce and the arrangements for training of safety representatives, and the right to consider the causes of accidents, dangerous occurrences and causes of occupational ill health, and to make representations to the installation manager about them.[78]

---

[71] reg. 5(2).
[72] reg. 5(1).
[73] reg. 9(1).
[74] reg. 11(1).
[75] See generally, reg. 16.
[76] reg. 26.
[77] reg. 20.
[78] See generally, reg. 22(1).

CHAPTER 7

REMEDIES AND INSURANCE

INTRODUCTION

7.1 As has been made clear in earlier chapters, enforcement of performance of duties in the field of health and safety at work is the province of both criminal and civil procedure. Broadly[1] it can be asserted that those duties which are common law in their origin are the subject of civil procedures and remedies, while duties which are statutory are either enforced only through criminal sanctions or through both criminal sanctions and a civil law action for breach of statutory duty at the instance of a party suffering loss. This chapter seeks to outline those civil law remedies and insurance, both private and State.

The range of remedies

7.2 By far the most common civil law remedy for death or personal injury sustained at work is an action for damages for breach of the employer's duty of care. However, an action for damages may also lie for breach of statutory duty[2] and for breach of contract[3]; similarly, because of the ambit of the implied contractual term, a breach of duty may also justify use of self-help remedies like retention and lien as well as the rescission of the contract and ground a claim of constructive dismissal[4] and, although unlikely, there is no reason why persistently breaching the

---

[1] Of course there are many situations in which the common law triggers a criminal procedure as a result of a crime committed in the course of employment (*e.g.* assault on a fellow employee or employer or committing the crime of malicious mischief by deliberately damaging the property of the employer) but these sanctions would be the normal result of the criminal conduct and are not specific to work situations.

[2] See Chap. 4, paras 4.8 *et seq.*

[3] See Chap. 3, paras 3.4 *et seq.*

[4] *ibid.* And see *Day v. T. Pickles Farms Ltd* [1999] I.R.L.R. 217, in which the E.A.T. in England seems to accept that breach of statutory duty can found constructive dismissal.

duty of care owed to an employee could not lead to an employer being the subject of an interdict.[5] Far more likely the matter would be drawn to the attention of a Health and Safety Inspector (or other enforcing authority) who is empowered to issue an Improvement or Prohibition Notice.[6] The range of remedies open to an employee would also include (1) the special rights against action short of dismissal and dismissal itself, and (2) the maternity suspension provisions on health and safety grounds both introduced by the Trade Union Reform and Employment Rights Act 1993.[7]

Damages—contract or delict?

7.3 The purpose of an award of damages is "so far as possible, to effect *restitutio in integrum* and to restore the pursuer to the position he would have been in if the contract had been performed, or the legal duty to him duly implemented".[8] However, if the initial injury is made worse by the conduct of the pursuer, he cannot recover damages for loss attributable to his own lack of care.[9] Although the employer's duty to his employee may be expressed as contractual or delictual, it is important to note that the basis of the claim can produce different results and while one claim may be viable the other may not.[10] Thus it may be that an action in contract cannot proceed because of an exemption clause[11] or because the contract may have been retrospectively reduced. Also, and probably more importantly, the heads of loss recoverable in delict are different from those recoverable in contract. Thus the rules of remoteness of damage are not the same in contract and delict. In the former, liability extends only for the consequences of the breach which should have been contemplated at the time the contract was entered, so that loss not reasonably foreseeable by the defender at the time of contracting, having regard to his state of knowledge—imputed and actual—is too remote to be recoverable.[12] On the other hand, in a delictual action there is liability for

---

[5] See S. Robinson, *The Law of Interdict*, pp. 126 *et seq.*

[6] See Chap. 5, paras 5.69 *et seq.*

[7] Trade Union Reform and Employment Rights Act 1993, ss. 25 and 28; see *post*, para. 7.33. The provisions are now contained in the Employment Rights Act 1996, ss. 66–68, as amended by the Maternity and Parental Leave Regulations 1999.

[8] Walker, *Principles of Scottish Private Law*, Book IV, p. 292.

[9] *McKew v. Holland & Hannen for Cubitts*, 1970 S.L.T. 68 (HL); and see Chap. 3, para. 3.25.

[10] In this respect see the interesting article by Prof. J.M. Thompson "Delictual Liability between Parties to a Contract", 1994 S.L.T. 29.

[11] *Golden Sea Produce Ltd v. Scottish Nuclear plc*, 1992 S.L.T. 942. Note, however, that s. 16(1) of the Unfair Contract Terms Act 1977 prevents the exclusion of liability in respect of death or personal injury.

[12] Bell, *Comm.* I, 478–9; *Prin.* s. 33; *Hadley v. Baxendale* (1854) 9 Ex. 341; *Victoria Laundry v. Newman* [1949] 2 K.B. 528; and see the more recent review of the position in *Haberstich v. McCormick & Nicholson* 1975 S.C. 1.

the harm which immediately results from the breach of duty and for all the other direct consequences thereof provided these were reasonably foreseeable and, as has been pointed out,[13] although Lord Kinloch's statement that "[t]he grand rule on the subject of damages is, that none can be claimed except such as naturally and directly arise out of the wrong done and such as may reasonably be supposed to have been in the view of the wrongdoer"[14] was made *obiter* and may be said to contain two issues or criteria (namely direct consequences and reasonable forsight),[15] it is an accurate statement of Scots law governing liability for both the immediate and subsequent consequences of negligence when properly construed. Although there may be different views as to the correct test to be applied for determining questions relating to the remoteness of damage,[16] it is not disputed that the law of delict is generally more favourable to the pursuer in a personal injuries claim than the law of contract. While damages for breach of contract have included a sum in respect of *solatium*,[17] the dichotomy between contractual and delictual claims is amply illustrated by *Black v. Gibson*,[18] in which both breach of a building contract and negligence were pleaded. The Lord Ordinary allowed a proof before answer of the averments relating to damages for anxiety, worry and the onset or exacerbation of illness since the claim alleged fault as well as breach of contract.[19] Similarly, until recently as a result of the decision of the House of Lords in *Addis v. Gramophone Co. Ltd*[20] in an action for wrongful dismissal a pursuer was generally not entitled to a sum in respect of loss of reputation and injury to feelings. However that position has been changed following their Lordships' decision in *Malik v. BCCI*,[21] to the effect that *Addis* does not preclude the recovery of damages where there was breach of the implied term of trust and confidence, and that resulted in financial loss to the employee in the form of loss of reputation. However, damages will not be awarded for loss flowing from the manner of dismissal.[21a]

[13] Gloag and Henderson, *Introduction to the Law of Scotland* (9th ed. 1987), para. 34.14.

[14] *Allan v. Barclay* (1864) 2 M. 873 at 874.

[15] For a brief but interesting discussion see W.J. Stewart, *Delict* (3rd ed.), paras 4.40 *et seq*.

[16] For an interesting discussion of the test for remoteness of damage see W.A. Wilson, *Introductory Essays on Scots Law* (2nd ed., 1984), pp. 126 *et seq*.

[17] See the cases referred to by W.W. McBryde, *The Law of Contract in Scotland* (1987), p. 481.

[18] 1992 S.L.T. 1076.

[19] See also *Palmer v. Beck*, 1993 S.L.T. 485, in which an award of damages for *solatium* was refused in an action for breach of warrandice.

[20] 1909 A.C. 488; *per* V.-C. Browne-Wilkinson in *O'Laoire v. Jackel International Ltd (No. 2)* [1991] I.R.L.R. 170, CA. And see *In re BCCI* [1994] I.R.L.R. 282, in which the English High Court reviewed the law in *Addis*, and *O'Laoire*.

[21] [1997] I.R.L.R. 462 (HL).

[21a] *Johnson v. Unisys Ltd* [1999] I.R.L.R. 90, CA.

7.4 On the other hand, in a personal injuries claim based on delict or breach of statutory duty the pursuer is entitled to sums in respect of (a) *solatium*[22] for the pain and suffering caused by the injuries and for loss of faculties, mental or physical, including loss of or impairment of senses and, if the injured person's expectation of life has been reduced by the injuries and the injured person was or is likely to become aware of that, the court in assessing the amount of damages due by way of *solatium* will have regard to the extent the injured person will suffer in consequence of being aware of the reduction in the expectation of life[23]; (b) patrimonial loss including loss of earnings past and prospective[24] and, where the injuries cause diminished expectation of life, it is to be assumed that the pursuer will survive until the date when he would have been expected to die if he had not sustained the injuries, with account being taken of living expenses the pursuer would have reasonably incurred until the notional date of death[25]; and (c) expenses necessarily and reasonably incurred on, for example, medical treatment.

Calculating the award of damages

7.5 Detailed examination of the calculation of an award of damages is beyond the scope of this work,[26] but this section attempts to set out some general rules which may be of particular relevance to personal injuries claims and to offer some examples from case law of the rules in operation.

Provisional and interim damages

7.6 Until the enactment of the Administration of Justice Act 1982,[27] damages for personal injuries were assessed once and for all at the end of the proof.[28] However, that Act introduced a major innovation; namely, an award of provisional damages by providing that where (a) in an action for damages for personal injuries it is proved or admitted to be a risk that at some definite or indefinite

---

[22] *Solatium* may include an element for loss of congenial employment; *Stark v. Lothian and Borders Fire Board*, 1993 S.L.T. 652.

[23] Damages (Scotland) Act 1976, s. 9A, inserted by Damages (Scotland) Act 1993, s. 5. The effect of s. 9A is to supersede decisions like *Dalgleish v. Glasgow Corporation*, 1976 S.C. 32, which supported the award of *solatium* for reduced life expectancy even if the injured person was unaware of it.

[24] A multiplier is used depending on the number of years for which the loss may be expected to continue.

[25] Damages (Scotland) Act 1976, s. 9.

[26] For such a detailed coverage reference may be made to McEwan and Paton, *Damages in Scotland* (2nd ed. 1989).

[27] s. 12.

[28] Walker, *Delict* (2nd ed.), p. 462.

time in the future the injured person will, as a result of the act or omission which gave rise to the cause of action, develop or suffer some serious deterioration in his physical or mental condition; and (b) the responsible person was a public authority or public corporation or insured or otherwise indemnified in respect of the claim, the court may order damages be awarded to the injured person and that the injured person may apply for a further award of damages.[29] It is not enough merely to aver a possible future deterioration in condition; the pursuer has to aver and prove a causal link between that deterioration and the act or omission in question.[30] Provisional damages have been awarded where there was a serious risk of the injured person developing epilepsy[31] or mesothelioma but have been refused where the original injury was a damaged lumbar disc which gave rise to some risk of prolapse with ensuing complications.[32]

7.7 Provisional damages are to be distinguished from interim damages which are to mitigate the suffering of the injured person or to assist relatives pending the outcome of the action for damages. The procedure whereby an application for interim damages may be made was introduced in 1974,[33] and is competent at the instance of the pursuer after defences have been lodged. If the court is satisfied the defender has admitted liability or if the pursuer would succeed without a substantial finding of contributory negligence, it may order the defender to make a payment of interim damages.

Loss of earnings

7.8 Where personal injury has resulted in loss of earnings, the loss is calculated having regard to earnings after deduction of Income Tax,[34] National Insurance contributions[35] and pension contributions.[36] When the National Insurance scheme was introduced in 1948 it was provided[37] that in an action for damages for personal injuries (whether based on contract or delict) there shall,

---

[29] Administration of Justice Act 1982, s. 12; and see *Bonar v. Trafalgar House Offshore Fabrication*, 1996 S.L.T. 548 (O.H.).

[30] *Paterson v. Costain Mining Ltd*, 1988 S.L.T. 413.

[31] *Lappin v. Britannia Airways*, 1989 S.L.T. 181.

[32] *Meek v. Burton Gold Medal Biscuits Ltd*, 1989 S.L.T. 338; and see *McMenemy v. Argyll Stores Ltd*, 1992 S.L.T. 971.

[33] Rules of Court, r. 89A introduced by Act of Sederunt 14 May 1974; a similar procedure is available in the sheriff court.

[34] *British Transport Commission v. Gourlay* [1956] A.C. 185.

[35] *Gibney v. Eric Johnson Stubbs (Scotland) Ltd*, 1987 S.L.T. 132.

[36] *Dews v. NCB* [1987] 3 W.L.R. 38 (HL).

[37] Law Reform (Personal Injuries) Act 1948, s. 2.

in assessing those damages, be taken into account against any loss of earnings which has accrued or probably will accrue to the injured person from the injuries, one half of the value of any rights which have accrued or which will accrue in respect of certain state benefits. However, in order to permit the Government to recover monies paid out, there has now been introduced a new scheme which results in the deduction of the total amount of specified benefits.[38] Under the scheme, the Secretary of State is granted the right to recover from those making payments of damages for personal injuries a sum representing certain state benefits paid during the period of five years, or the period of until the making of the payment, if shorter. The defender must not make any payment under a decree or settlement until he has obtained from the Department of Social Security Compensation Recovery Unit a certificate of the total benefits paid to the pursuer, and must deduct that amount from the damages payable and account for it to the Department of Social Security. The benefits to which the scheme applies are (a) sickness benefit, (b) invalidity pension and allowance, (c) unemployment benefit, (d) attendance and mobility allowances, (e) retirement and severe disablement allowances, (f) family credit, and (g) income support.

7.9 However, certain payments are not to be taken into account to reduce the amount of damages.[39] Where a payment is not the subject of an express statutory provision its treatment must depend on its intrinsic nature and not its source,[40] and it has been held that a government retraining allowance should be deducted in full[41] but not Family Income Supplement, on the view that it is indistinguishable from wages.[42] Nor, in the absence of a contractual term to the effect, should there be deducted from an award of damages in

---

[38] Social Security Act 1989, s. 22, Sched. 4 now included in Pt IV of the Social Security Administration Act 1992.

[39] Administration of Justice Act 1982, s. 10, excludes from the scheme (a) contractual payments, (b) pensions payable out of public funds, (c) payments from public funds for period after date of award of damages designed to secure minimum subsistence level, (d) redundancy payments, (e) payments by an employer which employee is bound to repay, and (f) any payment of a benevolent nature, *e.g.* from British Coal under the NCB Pneumoconiosis Compensation Scheme. In *Lewicki v. Brown and Root Wimpey Highland Fabricators*, 1996 S.L.T. 1283, the Inner House held that payments made to an employee under his employer's long term disability plan were in the nature of a contractual pension or benefit rather than remuneration or earnings. *Cf. Hussain v. New Taplow Paper Mills Ltd* [1988] 2 W.L.R. 266 (HL), that payments to an incapacitated employee made under an employer's health insurance scheme have to be taken into account when assessing damages for loss.

[40] *per* Lord Reid in *Parry v. Cleaver* [1920] A.C. 1 at 15.

[41] *Ward v. Tarmac*, 1972 S.L.T. (Notes) 52.

[42] *Webb v. Macauley*, 1988 S.L.T. 138. *Cf. Gaskill v. Preston* [1981] 3 All E.R. 427.

respect of loss of earnings against an employer a sum representing
monies paid under an incapacity insurance to which the employer
and the employee have contributed.[43] In some recent cases an
award has been made for loss of employability to reflect the
modern economic conditions of inflation and unemployment,
which may result in a reluctance on the part of employers to
engage people with disabilities. The purpose of an award to reflect
loss of employability is to recognise the disadvantage of such
people in the employment market.[44] However, while the Scottish
courts have made awards specifically to reflect loss of employability,[45] in other situations the award is difficult to distinguish from
an award representing loss of future earnings.[46]

Other losses

7.10 Loss of future pension rights is recoverable,[47] as are the costs
of nursing care[48] and reasonable medical expenses.[49] Where necessary services like nursing care and attendance have been or are
likely to be rendered to the injured person by a relative, then in the
absence of an express agreement that no payment shall be made
for those services, the person who has incurred liability shall pay to
the injured person a sum which represents reasonable remuneration for those services and the injured person has a duty to account
to such a relative for any damages recovered,[50] and for that reason
the House of Lords has held in an English appeal that, where the
provider of the services was the tortfeasor, there could be no
ground for requiring him to pay to the injured plaintiff a sum
representing the value of the services which he had rendered, since
the plaintiff would then have to repay that sum to him (the
provider of the services).[51] Similarly, a person responsible for the

---

[43] *Wood v. British Coal Corporation* [1991] I.C.R. 449 (HL).

[44] This type of award seems to have originated in *Smith v. Manchester* [1974]
K.I.R. 1.

[45] *Kirkpatrick v. Scott Lithgow Ltd*, 1987 S.L.T. 654.

[46] See, *Douglas v. NCB*, 1977 S.L.T. 14; *Marshall v. Bertrams Ltd*, 1985 S.L.T. 80.

[47] *Barratt v. Strathclyde Fire Brigade*, 1984 S.L.T. 325.

[48] *MacIntosh v. NCB*, 1988 S.L.T. 348; *Tuttle v. Edinburgh University*, 1984 S.L.T.
172.

[49] As to whether these may include private medical treatment the Law Reform
(Personal Injuries) Act 1948, s. 2(4) provides that these shall be disregarded in
determining the reasonableness of such expenses, the possibility of avoiding or
reducing them by taking advantage of facilities available under the National Health
Service.

[50] Administration of Justice Act 1982, s. 8, as amended by Law Reform (Miscellaneous Provisions) (Scotland) Act 1990 s. 69. Note s. 8(4) provides a relative
shall have no right of action in delict against the person responsible for the personal
injuries. See for example *Prentice v. William Thyne Ltd*, 1989 S.L.T. 336 (£400
awarded for necessary services rendered by wife); *Kozikowska v. Kozikowska*, 1996
S.L.T. 386 (O.H.).

[51] *Hunt v. Severs* [1994] 2 A.C. 350.

personal injuries is made liable to pay to the injured person a reasonable sum in respect of the inability of the injured person to render certain personal services.[52] It is sufficient if the injured person or the deceased would personally have provided the services and they were provided for benefit of the person claiming.[53]

Multipliers

7.11 Resort is made to multipliers and multiplicands when assessing damages for future loss of, for example, wages, support and services, damages for nursing care,[54] and for damages for the expenses involved in a curatory.[55] The appropriate multiplier is to be determined by having regard to various factors including the age of the pursuer, his likely retirement age, the nature of his injuries and whether the incapacity is temporary or permanent, with discounts to reflect the investment opportunities arising on receipt of a large capital sum, the regularity of work record, supervening illness and the risk of redundancy. In England, the House of Lords had decided in *Wells v. Wells*[56] that as a starting point, reference should be made to the Ogden Tables; while the approach in Scotland stated by Lord President Hope in *O'Brien's Curator Bonis v. British Steel*[57] was that, where experience could be relied on (because there were sufficient comparable cases to which to refer), little more needed to be done to find a multiplier. In *McNulty v. Marshalls Food Group Ltd*[58] it was held that for the selection of a multiplier regard should be had to the Ogden Tables with the result that previous case law must no longer be regarded as an indicator of the appropriate mulitplier.[59]

7.12 Where a relative is injured, but not fatally, his family have no right to recover damages in respect of ruined family life,

---

[52] Administration of Justice Act 1982, s. 9. The services are such as (i) might have been expected of to have been rendered by the injured person, (ii) would ordinarily be obtainable on payment, and (iii) would have been given gratuitously to a relative. See *Worf v. Western SMT Co. Ltd*, 1987 S.L.T. 317 (injured father had tutored children before injuries), *Fox v. NCR (Nederland) B.V.*, 1987 S.L.T. 401 (son lost services (board and lodging and use of car) after parents' death).

[53] *Ingham v. John Russell (Transport) Ltd*, 1991 S.L.T. 739 (I.H.) (carrying out services in form of extensive DIY, maintenance and garden work held to fall within s. 9).

[54] *MacIntosh v. NCB*, 1988 S.L.T. 348.

[55] *Forsyth's Curator v. Govan Shipbuilders Ltd*, 1989 S.L.T. 91.

[56] [1998] 3 W.L.R. 329.

[57] 1991 S.C. 315 at 323.

[58] 1998 G.W.D. 36-1875 (O.H.), *per* Lord Macfadyen).

[59] In *Wells v. Wells* although the position in Scotland was not dealt with expressly the Scottish members of the Judicial Committee did not suggest that the position would be any different in Scotland.

solatium, expenses or loss of support,[60] and where a spouse has had to give up work to look after an injured spouse there is no right to damages for loss of earnings of the spouse who has had to give up work,[61] although the injured person himself may be able to claim for the loss of the spouse's earnings.[62] However, where the injuries are fatal, surviving relatives have a right to recover damages where there was an existing close relationship[63] between the relative and the deceased. According to the Damages (Scotland) Act 1976,[64] a loss of society award was to be made for the loss of such non-patrimonial benefit as the relative might have expected to derive from the deceased's society and guidance if he had not died, replacing the award of *solatium* for grief and suffering on the death of a relative.[65] However, more recently, following the recommendation of the Scottish Law Commission,[66] the basis of the award has been clarified to include compensation for all or any of the following—(a) distress and anxiety induced by the relative in contemplation of the suffering of the deceased person before his death, (b) grief and sorrow caused by the deceased's death, or (c) the loss of such non-patrimonial benefit as the relative might have been expected to derive from the deceased's society and guidance if he had not died,[67] and is no longer to be referred to as a loss of society award.[68] Also, relatives are entitled to the net loss of financial support since the date of death together with any reasonable expenses incurred in connection with the deceased's funeral.[69] To make a calculation of future loss of support a multiplier is used, and an award of provisional damages to an injured person does not, in the event of the injured person dying, bar a claim by relatives; but when quantifying loss of support, account must be taken of such part of the provisional award relating to future patrimonial loss as was intended to compensate the deceased for a period beyond the date on which he died.[70]

---

[60] *Robertson v. Turnbull*, 1980 S.C. 108; 1982 S.L.T. 96 (HL). Note the provisions of the Damages (Scotland) Act 1976, s. 1(5), which prevent account being taken of "any insurance money, benefit, pension or gratuity paid as a result of the deceased's death", applied in *Bews v. Scottish Hydro Electric plc*, 1992 S.L.T. 749 (O.H.).

[61] *Collins v. SSEB*, 1977 S.L.T. 93.

[62] *Jack v. Alexander McDougall & Co. (Engineers) Ltd*, 1973 S.C. 13, and see *Gordon v. Muir*, 1980 S.L.T. (Notes) 51.

[63] See Damages (Scotland) Act 1976, Sched.1.

[64] s. 1(4).

[65] *Dingwall v. Walter Alexander & Sons (Midland) Ltd*, 1981 S.L.T. 313.

[66] *Report on Effect of Death on Damages* (1992).

[67] Damages (Scotland) Act 1976, s. 1(4) as inserted by Damages (Scotland) Act 1993, s. 1(1).

[68] Damages (Scotland) Act 1993, s. 7(1).

[69] Damages (Scotland) Act 1976, s. 1(3). It is not necessary to establish a legal duty of support in order to prove dependency (*ibid.*, s. 1(6)).

[70] Damages (Scotland) Act 1976, s. 5A, inserted by Damages (Scotland) Act 1993, s. 1(3).

Provision is now made to transmit the rights of a deceased relative to his executor.[71] Thus for deaths on or after April 19, 1993 a claim for damages for both *solatium* and patrimonial loss is transmitted to the executor of a deceased person, but only in respect of the period prior to the death,[72] and any right to damages which is vested in the relative concerned immediately before his death is transmitted to the relative's executor, but only in so far as the period immediately before the relative's death.[73]

Interest

7.13 Under the Interest and Damages Act 1958 and the Damages (Scotland) Act 1971, a court, having made an award of damages, is required to consider the matter of interest on that award. Interest on patrimonial loss runs from the date of the injury or accident, although the court has a discretion to alter this[74] and the award has to be apportioned between past loss (up to the date of proof) and future loss. Interest may be awarded only on the former at one half of the average court rate from the date of the injury to the proof. Where the award includes a sum in respect of *solatium*, interest (at the average court rate for the period) is awarded on past *solatium* in respect of the period from the date of the injury to whenever the pain and suffering ended which may, of course, have been before the proof; in respect of *solatium* for the period after the proof, interest is awarded at one half of the average court rate until the time the court estimates the pain and suffering will reduce.[75] These rules regarding interest in personal injuries cases are in addition to the normal rules by which interest is awarded at the court rate from the date of decree until payment by the defender.

Prescription and limitation

7.14 Liability in respect of personal injuries or death prescribes after 20 years[76]; however a claim for reparation must be brought within three years.[77] In the case of a claim for personal injuries that period begins to run from (a) the date on which the injuries were sustained, or where the act or omission was a continuing one, the

---

[71] Damages (Scotland) Act 1976 ss. 1A and 3, as inserted by Damages (Scotland) Act 1993, ss. 2 and 3.

[72] *ibid.*

[73] Damages (Scotland) Act 1976, s. 1A, as inserted by Damages (Scotland) Act 1993, s. 2.

[74] *McRae v. Reid and Mallick Ltd*, 1961 S.L.T. 96.

[75] See *Keicher v. NCB*, 1988 S.L.T. 318; *Preston v. Grampian Health Board*, 1988 S.L.T. 435.

[76] Prescription and Limitation (Scotland) Act 1973, s. 7.

[77] *ibid.*, ss. 17 and 18.

date the act or omission ceased, whichever is the later; or (b) if later than the above date, the date on which the pursuer became aware (i) that the injuries were sufficiently serious to justify his bringing an action,[78] (ii) that the injuries were in part at least attributable to an act or omission, and (iii) that the defender was a person to whose act the injuries were attributable, or the employer of such a person.[79] A similar period of limitation operates where death has resulted from personal injuries.[80] However, in each case the court has a discretion to allow a later claim where it would be equitable to do so,[81] although a failure to give a truthful and accurate account of the history of the injury will result in the court's decision being set aside.[81a] Thus, where a member of the army claimed damages for alleged acts of violence and extortion suffered at the barracks where he was based until February 1992 did not raise his action until March 1995, his case was allowed to proceed where the pursuer had not been aware until 1994 that the bullying had caused physical and psychological injuries so that it was not until after February 1992 that he would be justified in bringing an action.[82]

Some examples of the principles in application

7.15 Detailed examination of the calculation of an award of damages for personal injury is beyond the scope of this work, but the following recent cases demonstrate by way of examples how the matter is approached by the courts.

Stark v. Lothian and Borders Fire Board[83]

7.16 S was a 26 year old firefighter who suffered burns to about 24 per cent of his body while fighting a fire. He developed post-traumatic stress disorder and had returned to employment which was less congenial. He sued his employers for damages to include a sum in respect of assistance (in the form of changing his bedding, dressing and undressing, cooking meals, changing bandages, applying medication and driving him about). The Lord Ordinary held

---

[78] *Ferla v. Secretary of State for Scotland*, 1995 S.L.T. 21 (O.H.); *Lowe v. Grampian Health Board*, 1998 S.L.T. 21 (O.H.).

[79] Periods of nonage and legal disability of the pursuer are disregarded (*ibid.*, s. 17(3)). And see *McLaren v. Harland & Wolff Ltd*, 1991 S.L.T. 85 (O.H.).

[80] Prescription and Limitation (Scotland) Act 1973, s. 18.

[81] *ibid.*, s. 19A; and see, for example, *Anderson v. John Cotton (Colne) Ltd*, 1991 S.L.T. 696 (O.H.); *Cunningham v. Western Automobile Co. Ltd*, 1998 G.W.D. 28-1446. And see *Heyes v. Pilkington* [1998] P.I.Q.R. 303, CA, or the equivalent English provision in the limitation Act 1980, ss. 11 and 14.

[81a] *Long v. Tolchard and Sons Ltd, The Times*, January 5, 2000.

[82] *Carnegie v. Lord Advocate*, 1998 S.L.T. 872 (O.H.).

[83] 1993 S.L.T. 652 (O.H.).

that he would never be fit enough to return to firefighting and that in his new work in the Board's community education department there were no promotion prospects and his employment was less secure. Had he remained a firefighter he would have had reasonable prospects of promotion to leading fireman by 1991. However, S would probably not have achieved any higher work.

Assistance and services. Counsel were agreed that £3,000 would be appropriate for services.

Future loss. A multiplier of 12 (years) was applied to £750; the difference between a leading fireman's salary and the salary in S's new job producing £9,000 and for future disadvantage in the labour market £3,000.

Solatium. An overall award of £26,000 for pain and suffering post-traumatic stress disorder and loss of job satisfaction.

McVey v. Central Regional Council[84]

7.17 M, a 33-year-old labourer, was injured when a pneumatic drill fell on his foot causing permanent ligament damage and rendering him unfit for any work involving prolonged walking or standing. He was probably fit for sedentary work but none was likely to be available. He sued his employers for damages.

Solatium. Agreed at £6,500.

Future loss. The difference between likely earnings and earnings had he not been disabled £12,638, to which a multiplier of five was applied producing £63,190.

Haining v. Babcock Energy Ltd[85]

7.18 H was a 59-year-old, right-handed, semi-skilled labourer whose left hand was trapped in a machine causing a crushing and degloving injury. Most of his index finger was affected by infection. He returned to work after six months but he suffered continuing pain and was unable to follow his pre-accident hobby of competitive rowing, and his injury interfered with his other hobby of breeding and keeping pigeons; also while he could still carry out home decorating after his accident he found this work was much more difficult and he could do it only very slowly, although he had not been required to employ professional decorators since the accident.

Solatium. Having heard evidence and submissions on solatium the Lord Ordinary stated:

> "Turning to the question of *solatium* counsel for the defenders submitted that the sum of £4,000 would be appropriate. In this

[84] 1994 S.L.T. 190.
[85] 1994 S.L.T. 107.

connection reference was made to *Boyes v. Carnation Foods Ltd*, 1986 S.L.T. 145 which involved the loss of the terminal phalanx of the right forefinger. The pursuer had been off work for 15 weeks and was awarded *solatium* of £2,250 which represented £3,352 in current monetary values. It was accepted that this case stood at the lower end of the scale. Reference was also made to *Jackson v. Tayside Health Board*, 1980 S.L.T. (Notes) 57 . . . in which solatium had been assessed at £2,000 . . . now £4,300. In *Lind v. Lord Advocate* 1982 S.L.T. 277 the pursuer had suffered injuries which resulted in partial amputation of the ring finger of the dominant right hand. The award of solatium was £2,250 . . . now £4,900. In *Anderson v. Thomas Case Ltd*, 1987 S.L.T. 564 there had been the loss by the pursuer of the top of the thumb of his dominant hand. This had resulted in an award of £4,000 . . . now £5,640. It was contended that that was a more serious injury than that of the pursuer. Finally reference was made to *Renwicks v. Bison Concrete Ltd*, 1988 S.L.T. 343 a case in which the pursuer's dominant right hand was crushed . . . leaving him with deformed fingers, a weakened grip and substantial reduction in manual dexterity. In that case solatium had been £4,250 . . . now £5,560. It was contended that this case was more serious than that of the pursuer.

It is quite apparent that the pursuer's ability to use his left hand has been materially reduced by them. He continues to find difficulty in performing certain tasks with that hand and continues to experience pain in it from time to time, especially in his employment . . . the injuries have brought about a very serious deterioration in the quality of the pursuer's non-working life. . . (for example) his ability to carry on his hobby of rowing, which plainly occupied a very large place in his life prior to the accident . . . and enjoy his hobby of breeding and racing pigeons. . . . While the injury involved in *Hodge v. British Coal Corporation (No. 2)*, 1992 S.L.T. 913[86] was plainly less severe than that of the pursuer the treatment carried out was by no means successful . . . in all the circumstances an award of £9,000 would be appropriate."

Home decorating costs. As the evidence demonstrated that the pursuer was still able to do home decorating, albeit with greater difficulty and more slowly, the Lord Ordinary opined "having regard to the pursuer's continued ability to do home decorating work. . . it would not be appropriate for me to make an award to represent that state of affairs.

---

[86] In *Hodge* the original injury was of a very minor nature, although following a complicated series of treatments including amputations the ultimate result was loss of the right middle finger and an award of £7,000 for *solatium* was made.

Williamson v. G B Papers plc[87]

7.19 W, a 59-year-old office cleaner injured herself in a fall on an oily substance on a factory floor. In her fall she twisted her ankle and also strained her neck. She was off work for about 12 weeks. She sued her employers for damages for, *inter alia*, out of pocket expenses and for services to be rendered by her husband and son. **Provision of services.** Lord Ordinary Cullen stated:

> "[f]inally the pursuer made a claim in respect of services which her husband and her son required to perform for her in dealing with activities such as working, ironing and shopping. The pursuer suggested under reference to the case of *Smith v. Chief Constable, Central Scotland Police*, 1991 S.L.T. 634 that a figure between £800 and £1,000 was justified with respect of the past, with £250–£300 in respect of the future. I do not consider that the evidence led was sufficiently detailed to enable figures of this magnitude to be awarded . . . it would be appropriate to assess the past services in the sum of £400 . . . and the future in the sum of £100."

McLaren v. Harland & Wolff Ltd[88]

7.20 M was employed as a plumber by H between 1953 and 1960, and thereafter worked as a driver. In 1983 he was diagnosed to be suffering from asbestosis, and while he claimed benefit from the Department of Health and Social Security, he made no claim against his former employers. After his death in 1988 his widow and children brought actions against H alleging that he died as a result of asbestosis while in employment with them.

On limitation Lord Migdale stated[89]:

> "I conclude that this is an action in which it seems to me to be equitable to allow this case to proceed in terms of section 19A of the 1973 Act. In coming to this conclusion I accept as relevant the various factors founded on by Counsel for the defenders [no reasonable excuse for M failing to appreciate the possibility raising an action against H, in 1985 M told a doctor who advised making claim to DHSS that the suggestion had already been made in 1983 when M was still working, by not following up the suggestion about a claim to the DHSS M indicated that he was merely inactive on the question of compensation from H] . . . in addition to the weighty point of

[87] 1994 S.L.T. 173.
[88] 1991 S.L.T. 85 (O.H.).
[89] *ibid.*, p. 89.

loss of benefit to the defenders by the termination of these proceedings. I do not however consider that any of these other factors are factors of great additional weight in the . . . present case. It is true that had M raised an action timeously H might have had him medically examined . . . prior to his death. There might possibly have been a *post mortem* examination. However it is clear that M's condition was thoroughly monitored by medical experts independent of any question of litigation during the period of seven years prior to his death. No material prejudice is expressly averred by H in relation to the question of medical causation and no medical evidence was led for H at the preliminary proof. . . . I regard it as at best for the defenders speculative whether they are prejudiced on the medical aspects and I am not satisfied that this factor has been shown to be weighty factor in favour of the defenders. So far as the loss of the evidence of M himself is concerned a partial but only partial answer to this point is that the loss of such evidence may well be more of a disadvantage in proving the case to M than to H rebutting it. . . . I regard it important that this action involves averments as to regular exposure of M to asbestos over a lengthy period and not for example to an allegation of a single transient event on which a witness no longer available could prospectively have provided evidence. There was evidence that in a case such as the present where employment in conditions involving exposure to asbestos dust is proved, where asbestosis is proved to be contracted many years later and where there is no other apparent significant exposure to asbestos dust, liability is not in practice a live issue.

On the other hand I consider that there are factors which as a matter of equity weigh heavily in favour of the pursuers. . . . I am satisfied that M was quite unaware at any time that he had a prospective right of action against H. Nor do I consider that any such unawareness was unreasonable. When he died M had been away from employment in the shipyards for 28 years. For the last 24 he was working as a driver. . . . As such he was a member of the TGWU and as a member of the transport section would not receive information about hazards and compensation regarding such matters as asbestosis. It appears that M did not happen to have contact . . . with anyone who might have suggested to him that he had a right to compensation from H namely a suggestion which would have caused M to go to a lawyer for advice . . . what is important for present purposes is that I am satisfied that it was no fault of the late M that no action was raised during his lifetime and there was no material delay in raising the action by the pursuers following his death. S. 19A provides aptly for the present action to proceed and I hold that it should be allowed to do so."

Statutory remedies

7.21 As previously indicated, some statutory provisions may ground an action at the instance of an employee injured at work.[90] However, in the context of an examination of health and safety at work it is also necessary to consider the relationship between general employment statutory provisions and health and safety. Thus the general principles of unfair dismissal and discrimination law impact on health and safety, particularly with regard to the introduction and enforcement of workplace rules which might cover a wide range of different matters, from a no-smoking policy to prevention of drug abuse or rules regarding hair length. It is beyond the scope of this work to consider the general principles of unfair dismissal or discrimination law but in view of the relationship between these, and other areas of law and health and safety at work, this section attempts to place the special issues of health and safety in the perspective of these more general issues.[91]

Health and safety aspects of unfair dismissal

7.22 In accordance with their statutory and common law duties to take reasonable care for the safety of employees, employers frequently introduce policies and/or rules designed to ensure the performance of those duties and the maintenance of a safe working environment. The introduction and application of such policies and rules may bring into consideration issues like (a) the fairness of a decision to dismiss an employee who fails to observe health and safety rules, (b) whether the state of health of an employee supports a fair dismissal having regard to the creation of risks for his safety and that of others, (c) whether an employer's failure to operate a reasonably safe system of work or provide adequate clothing or equipment is a basis for a constructive dismissal claim, and (f) ill-health dismissals *simpliciter*. As a result of the passage of the Disability Discrimination Act 1995 and the Public Interest Disclosure Act 1998 it is also necessary to consider the effect of these Acts on health and safety matters.

Breach of safety rules

7.23 It is clear that the dismissal of an employee for failure to observe a clearly stated safety rule will be for a reason related to

---

[90] See Chap. 4, paras 4.8 *et seq.*
[91] For coverage of the general principles of unfair dismissal and discrimination law, the reader is referred to V. Craig and K. Miller, *Employment Law in Scotland* (1996).

the conduct of the employee,[92] as will dismissal for conduct which poses a serious danger whether or not the precise conduct is covered by a particular safety rule. Thus in *Martin v. Galeshire Imperial Metals Ltd*[93] the reason for the dismissal of an employee who by-passed a safety device related to his conduct, even although the nearest company rule merely provided that employees could be dismissed "for disorderly conduct likely to endanger the well-being or safety of other employees".[94] While generally an employer is entitled to promulgate and apply rules for the safe operation of the workplace, it may be arguable that where the introduction of a new rule or policy breaches an existing contractual right[95] an employer may elect to obtain the employee's express consent by incorporating the rule into the contract of employment.[96] Such a procedure would seem to avoid difficulties which arise from the method adopted for the introduction of the rule. Thus the dismissal of an employee for smoking in breach of a no-smoking rule which was inconsistently applied was held to be unfair where there was no warning that the rule was now to be strictly applied.[97] Further, dismissal for breach of a rule prohibiting long hair which did not apply to women and was not specific was unfair,[98] while dismissal of a man for having hair which was 2½ feet long was fair where it followed several warnings and advice from the Factory Inspectorate.[99] Similarly, even a clearly stated and regularly applied rule does not allow the employer to fairly dismiss an employee who deliberately defies the rule without allowing the employee to state his case, although the fact that a disciplinary procedure would have made no difference would be reflected in the remedy to be awarded by the employment tribunal.[1]

Risks to employees and others

7.24 Where the health of an employee presents a risk to himself or others if he were to continue in employment, the reason for his

---

[92] Employment Rights Act 1996, s. 8(2); see *Ashworth v. John Needam & Sons*, 1978 H.S.I.B. 26.

[93] [1978] I.R.L.R. 440.

[94] And see *Frizzell v. Flanders*, 1979 H.S.I.B. 43 (fair dismissal for refusal to wear gas mask); *Singh v. J. Laing & Sons*, 1976 H.S.I.B. 10 (breach of rule regarding misusing toilet facility). *Cf. Mayhew v. Anderson (Stoke) Newington* [1978] I.R.L.R. 101 (unfair dismissal for refusal to wear cheap goggles which were uncomfortable).

[95] In *Dryden v. Greater Glasgow Health Board* [1992] I.R.L.R. 469 (EAT) it was argued, unsuccessfully, that the introduction of a no-smoking rule breached an implied term that the employee was entitled to have access to facilities for smoking during working hours.

[96] *Sutherland v. Sonat Offshore (UK) Inc.*, 1993 H.S.I.B 213 (EAT).

[97] *Bundall v. Paine and Betteridge* [1973] I.R.L.R. 44.

[98] *Talbot v. Hugh M. Fulton Ltd* [1975] I.R.L.R. 52 (EAT). *Cf. Smith v. Safeway Stores plc* [1995] I.R.L.R. 132 (EAT), as to whether rule was discriminatory.

[99] *Marsh v. Judge International Ltd*, 1977 H.S.I.B 15.

[1] *Wright v. Ladbrokes Ltd*, 1993 H.S.I.B. 211.

dismissal may be related to his capability.[2] However, the risk of illness cannot amount to grounds for a fair dismissal unless the nature of the employment is such that the risk is of such importance as to make it unsafe for the employee to continue in the job.[3] Thus the dismissal of an employee whose doctor could not give an assurance that there would be no recurrence of paranoid schizophrenia was held to be fair in light of the dangerous work taking place in a lead factory, and that the job required such a high degree of concentration that a relapse could have had devastating effects[4]. However, the risks must be real and not merely imagined.[5] Where the risks could be reduced or eliminated by attendance at a training course it has been held to be fair to dismiss an employee who refused to attend.[6] Where employee and employer disagree over the nature of the risks and the employee is dismissed for refusing to continue working, whether the employer's response to the refusal was reasonable is for the employment tribunal to determine, with only limited scope for its decision to be challenged.[6a] Thus in *Lindsay v. Dunlop Ltd*[7] the Employment Appeal Tribunal refused to disturb an employment tribunal's finding of a fair dismissal of an employee who refused to work in an atmosphere of hot rubber fumes in view of a report of the Health and Safety Executive on the carcinogenic properties of hot rubber fumes, even after the employer had agreed to deal with the fumes as quickly as possible and issue face masks as a temporary measure. Similarly, in *Piggott Brothers & Co. Ltd v. Jackson*[8] the Court of Appeal, highlighting the dangers inherent in the approach advocated by another division of the same court,[9] restored the employment tribunal's finding of unfair dismissal of employees who

---

[2] Employment Rights Act 1996, s. 98(3); and see *Harper v. NCB* [1980] I.R.L.R. 260 (EAT).

[3] *Converfoam (Darwen) Ltd v. Bell* [1981] I.R.L.R. 195 (EAT).

[4] *Singh-Deu v. Chloride Metals Ltd* [1976] I.R.L.R. 56. And see *Balogun v. Lucas Batteries Ltd*, 1979 H.S.I.B. 42 (continued employment with lead would have been harmful to employees with certain medical conditions); *Finch v. Betabake (Anglia) Ltd* [1977] I.R.L.R. 470 (motor mechanic with defective vision danger to himself and others).

[5] *Buck v. Letchworth Cinema* 1988 (unreported); dismissal of homosexual projectionist after objections from fellow employees who feared they might contract AIDS; and see R.A. Watt, "HIV dismissals" (1992) 21 I.L.J. 280.

[6] *Minter v. Willingborough Foundries Ltd*, 1981 I.D.S. Brief 202.

[6a] The direction of the EAT in *Haddon v. Van den Bergh (Foods) Ltd* [1999] I.R.L.R. 672 that an employment tribunal should judge the reasonableness of the employer's action having regard to the equity and merits of the case and their own experience, and not "the bands of reasonable responses" will further reduce the scope for challenge.

[7] [1980] I.R.L.R. 93 (EAT).

[8] [1991] I.R.L.R. 309.

[9] *Neale v. Hereford & Worcester County Council* [1986] I.R.L.R. 168, CA, in which the "my goodness that was certainly wrong" approach to the test of perversity was commended.

refused to work with materials which gave off unusual fumes after being certified unfit for work by their general practitioners. Neither the Health and Safety Executive nor the employers could identify the cause, but the employers had not obtained a chemical analysis or a toxicological report and it could not be said that the employment tribunal had misdirected itself in holding that the employers could reasonably have been expected to do more with a view to obtaining a definitive answer as to the cause of the employees' symptoms.

Constructive dismissal

7.25 Whether an employee is entitled to treat himself as constructively dismissed depends on whether the employer has repudiated the contract of employment[10] and it is in the context of such a test that the contractual nature of the employer's duty of safety is of significance, in that a failure to perform the duty in an important respect will allow the employee to leave and claim constructive dismissal. Thus a failure to provide safety equipment to the employee may justify rescission,[11] and it may be necessary not merely to make safety equipment available but to provide each individual employee with the relevant item.[12] The employer's duty is not performed by providing equipment or clothing which is inadequate,[13] and an employer will not act reasonably if he dismisses an employee to whom safety goggles costing 78p had been provided when she refused to wear them because they were uncomfortable and irritated her eyes without considering whether more expensive ones would have been acceptable to the employee.[14] A failure to provide security measures[15] and comfortable temperatures[16] have founded constructive dismissal claims, and the Scottish Employment Appeal Tribunal has recognised that there could be a constructive dismissal where an employee was required to work in intolerable conditions, for example where a serious danger to life was involved.[17] However, for a constructive

---

[10] *Western Excavating (ECC) Ltd v. Sharp* [1978] I.R.L.R. 27, CA, applied in *Greater Glasgow Health Board v. Pate*, 1983 S.L.T. 90. *Cf. Day v. T. Pickles Farms Ltd* [1999] I.R.L.R. 217 (EAT).

[11] *British Aircraft Corporation v. Austin* [1978] I.R.L.R. 332 (EAT) (prolonged failure to provide safety glasses).

[12] *Crouch v. BREL* [1988] I.R.L.R. 40, CA (employer's duty was to provide goggles for employee to keep in tool kit—not reasonable to require employee to walk considerable distance each time he required to use them).

[13] *Kirkcaldy District Council v. Baxter*, E.A.T. 540/78 (binmen were entitled to refuse to work when waterproofs provided by employer were not adequate).

[14] *Mayhew v. Anderson (Stoke Newington)* [1978] I.R.L.R. 101 (I.T.).

[15] *Keys v. Shoefayre Ltd* [1978] I.R.L.R. 476 (I.T.).

[16] *Mariner v. Domestic & Industrial Polythene Ltd*, 1978 H.S.I.B. 26; *Graham Oxley Tool Steels Ltd v. Firth* [1980] I.R.L.R. 135 (EAT).

[17] *Knight v. Barra Shipping Ltd*, 1992 H.S.I.B. 203, 187/92; and see *Popeye of Scotland Ltd v. McLay*, E.A.T. 309/76 (driver entitled to refuse to drive suspected unroadworthy vehicle).

dismissal case to succeed the employee has to show that it was the employer's breach of contract which led to him leaving,[18] and an employee who delays his decision to leave or give notice may be viewed as having accepted a variation of his contract.[19] Thus an employee who suffered a mental breakdown caused by allegations and complaints about her work failed to establish a constructive dismissal when she continued working for six months after her employer had taken remedial measures.[20] However, it has been held in Scotland that it is not open to an employee to affirm a contractual term which would undercut a minimum statutory wage,[21] and it would seem that the same reasoning would apply to an employee who continued working in the face of a contractual breach by the employer which was also the subject of a statutory provision like, for example, the Personal Protective Equipment at Work Regulations 1992 or the Provision and Use of Work Equipment Regulations 1998. In *Day v. Pickles*[22] the Employment Appeal Tribunal has indicated that constructive dismissal may consist in the failure to carry out a risk assessment as required by the Management of Health and Safety at Work Regulations 1999.

Dismissal for ill health

7.26 One of the potentially fair reasons for dismissal is the capability of the employee which is to be assessed by reference to, *inter alia*, "health or any other physical or mental quality".[23] Thus, provided the reason for the dismissal related to the capability of the employee for performing work of the kind he was employed to do and the employer acted fairly in other respects, an employee dismissed on grounds of ill health may have no claim against his employer. Unfair dismissal law in this respect seeks to hold a balance between the employer's need for the work to be done and the employee's need to be given time to recover from his illness.[24]

---

[18] *Walker v. Josiah Wedgwood & Sons Ltd* [1978] I.C.R. 744 (EAT).

[19] *Western Excavating (ECC) Ltd v. Sharp* [1978] I.C.R. 221, CA. *Cf. Marriott v. Oxford Co-operative Society (No. 2)* [1970] 1 Q.B. 186; *W.E. Cox Toner v. Crook* [1981] I.C.R. 823 (EAT). In *Day v. T. Pickles Farms Ltd* [1999] I.R.L.R. 217 the E.A.T. has expressed the view that a constructive dismissal claim failed because the employee had not given her employers an unequivocal communication that she was accepting the repudiation and wishing the contract at an end. However, in *Weathershield Ltd v. Sargent* [1999] I.R.L.R. 94, the Court of Appeal has rejected the proposition that there could be no acceptance of a repudiation by the employee unless he or she told the employer that he or she was leaving because of the employers' repudiation.

[20] *Wilton v. Cornwall & Isles of Scilly Health Authority*, 1993 H.S.I.B 482, CA.

[21] *Reid v. Comphill Engravers* [1990] I.C.R. 435 (EAT).

[22] [1999] I.R.L.R. 217 (EAT).

[23] Employment Rights Act 1996, s. 98(3).

[24] *Taylorplan Catering (Scotland) Ltd v. McInally* [1980] I.R.L.R. 53 (EAT); *East Lindsey District Council v. Daubney* [1977] I.R.L.R. 181 (EAT).

For unfair dismissal law to be activated, however, there has first to be a dismissal. It follows therefore that, in those cases where the ill health is so serious that the contract is brought to an end by impossibility of performance or frustration, there will be no dismissal. Where frustration truly operates, the contract of employment is terminated by operation of law and while an employer is always free to argue that termination has occurred by way of frustration it has to be noted (a) that the Employment Appeal Tribunal has cautioned employment tribunals against too easy an approach to the question of frustration of the contract of employment[25] and (b) in the event of the employer's argument being unsuccessful it is unlikely that his pre-termination procedures will come near to satisfying the standards of reasonableness imposed by Employment Rights Act 1996, section 98(4). In the leading cases of *Marshall v. Harland and Wolff Ltd*[26] and *The Egg Stores (Stamford Hill) Ltd v. Leibovici*,[27] the following factors were stated to be amongst those requiring to be considered to determine whether a contract of employment had been frustrated—(a) terms of contract including provisions regarding sick pay, (b) likely duration of employment if no illness, (c) nature of employment and whether employee is "key" personnel, (d) nature of illness and prospects of recovery, (e) period of past employment, (f) need for the sick employee's work to be done, (g) risk to employer of acquiring statutory employment obligations to replacement employees, (h) continuation of wages, (i) actions of employer including dismissal or failure to dismiss.[28] Two contrasting decisions can be found in *Hebden v. Forsey & Sons*[29] and *Scarr v. Goodyear*.[30] In the former the contract was not frustrated, principally because there was no reason why a surgical operation would not be successful, the employee had been kept on the employer's sick list and there had been no attempt to terminate his contract. In the latter the contract was frustrated because there was no prospect of the employee, whose work involved climbing ladders, being able to resume that work because of a heart condition.[31] However, whether a contract of employment is frustrated depends on the facts and circumstances of the case, and some earlier decisions which pre-date the caution advised by the Employment Appeal Tribunal in *Williams v.*

---

[25] *Williams v. Watson Luxury Coaches Ltd* [1990] I.R.L.R. 164 (EAT).
[26] [1972] 2 All E.R. 715 (NIRC).
[27] [1977] I.C.R. 260 (EAT).
[28] For a discussion of the issues involved see V. Craig, "Frustration or Dismissal" (1985) 53 S.L.G. at p. 85.
[29] [1973] I.C.R. 607 (NIRC).
[30] [1975] I.R.L.R. 166.
[31] Other examples include *Hart v. Marshall & Sons (Bulwell) Ltd* [1977] I.R.L.R. 51 (EAT) (one of two employees who contracted dermatitis); *Harman v. Flexible Lamps Ltd* [1980] I.R.L.R. 418 (absences caused by depression and hospitalisation).

Watson Luxury Coaches Ltd[32] should be treated with care, and although the Employment Appeal Tribunal in *Harman v. Flexible Lamps Ltd*[33] was wrong to say that the doctrine of frustration was not applicable to contracts of employment which could be brought to an end by notice, nevertheless the Court of Appeal in *Notcutt v. Universal Equipment Co. (London) Ltd*[34] did accept that it was correct to be cautious about applying the doctrine to such contracts. Of course contracting parties may expressly provide that a particular event will not frustrate the contract[35] and it would seem perfectly arguable that where a contract makes provision for sick pay that may be interpreted as an indication that in certain cases[16] the incapacity was anticipated by the contracting parties as one which would not frustrate the contract.[37]

7.27 Following the decision of the House of Lords in *Polkey v. A. E. Dayton Services*,[38] it is clear that whether or not a dismissal is fair depends, in the normal case, ultimately on whether the employer acted reasonably in treating the reason as one sufficient for dismissing the employee. Much attention is focussed on the pre-dismissal procedures adopted by employer, and the statement by Lord Bridge of Harwich in *Polkey*[39] that in the great majority of cases an employer will not be acting reasonably unless and until he has taken the steps which are necessary to justify his course of action, and "in the case of incapacity the employer will not normally act reasonably unless he gives the employee fair warning." In *A Links & Co. Ltd v. Rose*[40] after an employment tribunal had applied Lord Bridge's *dictum* literally and had concluded that the dismissal of an employee following two heart attacks was unfair because he had not been given any warning, the Inner House reasserted that, following *Polkey*, there was no inconsistency between that case and authorities like *Taylorplan Catering (Scotland) Ltd v. McInally*[41] which, while requiring consultation

---

[32] [1990] I.R.L.R. 164 (EAT).
[33] [1980] I.R.L.R. 418 (EAT).
[34] [1986] I.C.R. 414, CA.
[35] D.M. Walker, *The Law of Contracts and Voluntary Obligations in Scotland* (2nd ed.), para. 31.53.
[36] Immediate, total and lasting incapacity is the obvious exception.
[37] See too the similar arguments canvassed in *F.C. Shepherd & Co. Ltd v. Jerrom* [1986] I.C.R. 802, CA, regarding whether a contractual disciplinary procedure applying to misconduct might prevent frustration resulting from a sentence of imprisonment. And see *Jennison v. Airedale Health Authority* (I.T., 1987, unreported) in which it was accepted that sickness absences did not frustrate the contract in light of its provisions for sick pay.
[38] [1987] I.R.L.R. 503 (HL).
[39] *ibid.*
[40] [1991] I.R.L.R. 353 (I.H.).
[41] [1980] I.R.L.R. 53.

with a sick employee, indicated that warnings were inappropriate because, while warnings were not generally applicable to ill health of a more or less permanent character, there might be a case for warnings where the employee's ill health flowed directly from circumstances within his own control.[42] Following *Polkey* and in cases of intermittent absences, while a sympathetic approach has been recommended, eventually it may be appropriate to caution the employee that his absences have reached a stage where it is impossible to continue with his employment.[43] Regarding consultation, the employment tribunal must determine as a matter of fact and judgment (a) what consultation, if any, was necessary in the known circumstances of the case, (b) what consultation took place, and (c) whether it was adequate in all the circumstances.[44] Thus an employment tribunal was entitled in the exceptional circumstances of the case to conclude the dismissal of an employee—without any consultation—was fair because the director who took the decision not to engage in a face-to-face consultation did so to avoid the possibility of disclosing to an employee information about her health of which she was unaware.[45] While it is a management decision and not a medical one, it is a decision which has to be taken in the light of all the medical evidence.[46] Gathering the relevant information can be difficult, although the employee may agree to his own doctor preparing a report for transmission to the employer. However the Access to Medical Reports Act 1988 permits an employee to agree to a report being prepared by his own general practitioner (or other doctor who has had responsibility for the employee's clinical care) subject to his right to see the report in advance of it being made available to the employer and even to refuse its disclosure.[47] The Act provides that a person (*i.e.* an employer) shall not apply to a medical practitioner for a medical report about an individual (*i.e.* an employee) to be supplied to him for employment purposes[48] unless (a) that person has notified in writing the individual that he intends to make the application, and (b) the individual has notified in writing the applicant that he consents to the application[49] and, because of the

---

[42] Lord McCluskey instanced cases of obesity which could be cured with reasonable dieting and remedying a physical incapacity by simple operation which the employee, for no apparent reason, was neglecting to take (*A. Links & Co. Ltd v. Rose* [1991] I.R.L.R. 353 at 356).

[43] *Lynock v. Cereal Packaging Ltd* [1988] I.R.L.R. 510 (EAT).

[44] *ibid.*

[45] *Eclipse Blinds Ltd v. Wright* [1992] I.R.L.R. 133 (I.H.).

[46] *East Lindsey District Council v. Daubney* [1977] I.R.L.R. 181 (EAT).

[47] Access to Medical Reports Act 1988, ss. 3 and 4.

[48] "Employment purposes" are widely defined as the purposes in relation to any individual of any person by whom he is or has been, or is seeking to be, employed under a contract of service or otherwise (*ibid.*, s. 2(1)).

[49] *ibid.*, s. 3(1); the notice to the individual must set out his rights to withhold or restrict his consent.

difficulties the 1988 Act has produced, employers may wish to consider inserting a term into contracts of employment which require employees to submit to medical examination by a doctor nominated by the employer whose report would be disclosed directly to the employer. Of course, in the event that an employer proposed to dismiss an employee relying on such a report it would normally be necessary to make it available to the employee prior to taking the decision to dismiss,[50] but an inadequate medical report instructed by an employer may result in the employer not having conducted a proper investigation.[51] Even where an employee has become incapable of performing the work he is contracted to do, an employer will not act fairly if he does not at least consider alternative employment[52] although there is no duty to create a special job for a sick employee.[53]

Special health and safety rights

Dismissal and detrimental treatment

7.28   Until the enactment of special provisions in 1993, employees who were dismissed for performing health and safety functions or for raising health and safety issues with their employer could rely only on the general rules of unfair dismissal, with the effect that any employee with less than two years' continuous employment[54] could generally[55] be dismissed with impunity. Particularly as a result of certain parts of the Cullen Report into the *Piper Alpha* oil platform disaster,[56] it became clear that newly appointed employees felt uneasy about raising health and safety concerns because of their insecure employment, and to implement E.C. Directive 89/931, the Trade Union Reform and Employment Rights Act 1993[57] confers on all employees, irrespective of their length of

---

[50] *Louis v. Coventry Hood & Seating Co. Ltd* [1990] I.R.L.R. 324 (EAT); *cf. Eclipse Blinds Ltd v. Wright* [1992] I.R.L.R. 133 (I.H.).

[51] *Ford Motor Co. Ltd v. Nawaz* [1987] I.R.L.R. 163.

[52] *Dick v. Boots The Chemist* Ltd, E.A.T. 68/91 (unreported).

[53] *Merseyside and North Wales Electricity Board v. Taylor* [1975] I.R.L.R. 60 (EAT); *Carricks (Caterers) Ltd v. Nolan* [1980] I.R.L.R. 259 (EAT).

[54] By the Unfair Dismissal and Statement of Reasons for Dismissal (Variation of Qualifying period) Order 1999 the qualifying period for unfair dismissal was reduced to one year for dismissals taking effect on or after June 1, 1999.

[55] In some cases, of course, it was possible to argue that the real reason was trade union membership, and therefore automatically unfair (TULRCA, s. 152).

[56] Report of the Public Inquiry into the *Piper Alpha* Disaster (Cm. 1310); and see para 6.51.

[57] s. 28; Sched. 5.

continuous employment,[58] protection against dismissal[59] in particular health and safety cases.[60] Thus the dismissal[61] is unfair if it was because:

(a) the employee, having been designated by the employer to carry out activities in connection with preventing or reducing risks to health and safety, carried out or proposed to carry out such activities.[62] This has been held to apply where a manager who had suspended employees who had been drinking during lunch resigned after his decision was overturned by senior management; the constructive dismissal was because he had carried out health and safety duties having been designated to do so by the employers.[63]

(b) the employee, being a representative of workers on matters of health and safety at work or a member of a safety committee,[64] performed or proposed to perform any functions as a representative or a member of the committee.[65] This has been held to apply where a safety representative was dismissed after he visited premises of another employer (a supermarket) at which a colleague had been injured while making a delivery there; although the employment tribunal held that he was not dismissed for inspecting the workplace under the Safety Representatives and Safety Committee Regulations 1977 because the Regulations applied only to premises under the control of the employer, this was rejected by the Employment Appeal Tribunal.[66]

(c) the employee took part in consultation with the employer pursuant to the Health and Safety (Consultation with Employees) Regulations 1996 or in an election of employee representatives of health and safety.[67]

(d) the employee being employed at a place where (i) there was no representative or safety committee or (ii) where there was such a representative or committee but it was

---

[58] ERA, s. 108(3)(c).
[59] Similar protection is introduced against action short of dismissal (ERA, s. 44).
[60] ERA, s. 100.
[61] Selection for redundancy is also included (ERA, s. 105(2)).
[62] ERA, s. 100(1)(a).
[63] *Hunt v. A. W. Curtis and Sons Ltd* (Case No. 63969/95).
[64] For a fuller discussion of health and safety representatives and committees, see Chap. 5, paras 5.18 *et seq.*
[65] ERA, s. 100(1)(b).
[66] *Healey v. Excel Logistics Ltd*, I.D.S. Brief 622.
[67] ERA, s. 100(1)(ba).

not reasonably practicable for the matter to be raised via such representative or committee, brought to his employer's attention by reasonable means circumstances which the employee reasonably believed were potentially harmful to health or safety.[68] This has been held to apply to an employee who was constructively dismissed by her employer ignoring her reports of another member of staff mistreating a patient.[69]

(e) the employee, in circumstances of danger which he reasonably believed to be serious and imminent, and which he could not reasonably be expected to avert, left, or proposed to leave, or (while the danger persisted) refused to return to, his place of work or any dangerous part of his place of work,[70] and it is specifically provided that an employee who leaves his place of work and is dismissed therefor is not to be treated as taking industrial action thereby excluding the tribunal's jurisdiction from hearing the complaint.[71]

(f) the employee, in circumstances of danger which he reasonably believed to be serious and imminent, took or proposed to take, appropriate steps to protect himself or other persons from the danger.[72]

Some general observations need to be made about section 100. First the onus of proving that the reason for dismissal falls within section 100 is on the employee,[73] and although it has been held that in order to prove that there has been a constructive dismissal it is necessary for the employee to show that the breach of contract was a punishment for the employee's raising the health and safety matters,[74] it is respectfully suggested that such an approach imposes too heavy a burden on the employee, and a better approach is seen in *Griezans v. Ferguson t/a Tremayne Nursing Home*,[75] where a failure to take action against an employee whose practices, which created a risk to patients, had been drawn to the attention of the employer by the complainant was held sufficient to found constructive dismissal.

---

[68] ERA, s. 100(1)(c).

[69] *Griezans v. Ferguson* (Case No. 57605/95).

[70] ERA, s. 100(1)(d).

[71] See TULRCA, ss. 237(1A) and 238(2A). *Cf. Mariner v. Domestic and Industry Polythene Ltd*, 1978 H.S.I.B 26.

[72] ERA, s. 100(1)(e).

[73] *Parks v. The Landsdowne Club*, E.A.T. 310/93; *Tedeschi v. Hosiden Besson Ltd*, E.A.T. 959/95.

[74] *Baddeley v. Mehta t/a Supascoop* (Case No. 46041/94).

[75] Case No. 57605/95.

7.29   It is important to note that section 100(1)(c) only protects an employee who is dismissed for drawing matters directly to the attention of the employer where he does so by reasonable means and there is either no health and safety representative or committee at his place of work, or it is not reasonably practicable to raise the matter with a representative or committee and a failure to do so will result in the dismissal complaint being rejected.[76] Similarly, the employee must reasonably believe the circumstances were harmful or potentially harmful to health and safety. It was for this reason that the E.A.T. upheld the decision of the employment tribunal that an employee was not unfairly dismissed for refusing to take out a vehicle which by the end of the day could have become overloaded and unsafe, because there was a practice whereby the employee could telephone the depot to arrange for a second vehicle to assist—the employee's belief might have been genuine but it was not reasonable.[77] However the E.A.T. did remark that the fact that a second inquiry might allay an employee's fears would not necessarily mean that his belief was unreasonable. However, it would seem that an employee is protected only if his dismissal is for bringing the matter to the employer's attention; if he goes further and he is dismissed as a result of doing so, while he might be able to obtain the protection of ordinary unfair dismissal law he will not be able to bring his case into section 100(1)(c). Thus in *Brendon v. BNFL Chemicals Ltd*,[78] an employee/salesman was concerned that one of his employer's products (which was used in eye operations in some countries and was banned in the USA because it might cause blindness) might be exported illegally to the USA by one of his customers, and appears to have devoted much of his time to investigating the side effects of the product with the result that his sales figures fell and he was dismissed. According to the tribunal he was dismissed (fairly) because of his poor sales and not because of his having spent time investigating the side effects, because by doing so he would not be bringing the matter to his employer's attention by reasonable means. The inference is that he would be bringing the matter to the attention of the employer by unreasonable means, namely the fall in his sales achievements.

7.30   However, section 100(1)(c) is not confined to health and safety matters at the employee's place of work. Quite deliberately it would seem, it refers to "circumstances connected with his work which . . . are . . . potentially harmful to health and safety". Indeed in *Brendon* the E.A.T. recognised that section 100 would stretch beyond the workplace so that the employee would be protected if

---

[76] *Leake v. Commissioners of Inland Revenue*, Case No. 16889/94.
[77] *Kerr v. Nathan's Wastesavers Ltd*, E.A.T. 91/95.
[78] E.A.T. 766/95.

dismissed for raising concerns about the safety of others which would include the public, and this approach is reflected in other cases.[79] Accordingly, it would seem that if Brendon had been dismissed for bringing to the employer's attention his fear that the customer might illegally export the product to the USA, undoubtedly his case would have been successful, and the legitimacy of an employee's concern for the public is now endorsed by the E.A.T. in *Masiak v. City Restaurants (United Kingdom) Ltd*,[80] in which a chef who was concerned about cooking food which in his view would not be properly defrosted telephoned the Environmental Health Officer and reported his concerns to his manager. The response of the manager was to instruct the employee to cook the food or go home. The employee went home and claimed he had been unfairly dismissed relying on section 100(1)(e), which renders a dismissal unfair if the reason is that the employee took appropriate steps "to protect himself or other persons from danger". The employment tribunal dismissed the complaint on the ground that section 100(1)(e) concerned only fellow employees, but the E.A.T., noting that section 100(1)(e) was to implement Article 13 of the E.U. Directive 89/381—which makes a worker responsible for the health and safety of "other persons affected by his acts . . . at work"— held that it was wrong to limit section 100(1)(e) in that way. Although *Masiak* concerned section 100(1)(e), the same reasoning would apply to section 100(1)(c), so that the dismissal of an employee who brings to the attention of his employer by reasonable means circumstances connected with his work which are harmful or potentially harmful to the public would be automatically unfair. However, where a representative is dismissed, the manner in which a representative carries out his or her functions may take the complaint outside section 100.[81]

7.31 Because of the relationship between trade union membership and safety representatives and committees,[82] employees covered by section 100(1)(b) could previously have obtained protection had they been able to demonstrate that the reason for their dismissal was truly a reason covered by section.152 of the Trade Union and Labour Relations (Consolidation) Act 1992 (dismissal on grounds related to union membership or activities).

---

[79] *Lines v. Johnson* (E.T. 25000359/96) and *Barton v. Wandsworth Council* (E.T. 11268/94); the apprehension for the safety of passenger and patients respectively was sufficient to bring the complaint within s. 100(1)(c).

[80] [1999] I.R.L.R. 780 (EAT).

[81] Compare *Goodwin v. Cabletel UK Ltd* [1997] I.R.L.R. 665 (EAT) (confrontational approach by safety representative) with *Shillito v. Van Leer UK Ltd* [1997] I.R.L.R. 495 (EAT) (safety representative pursuing own personal agenda of embarrassing management).

[82] See Chap. 5, paras 5.18 *et seq.*

The addition of section 100(1)(a) and (c)–(f), although peppered with judgmental issues like "reasonable means", "reasonable belief", "serious and imminent" and "appropriate steps", undoubtedly enhances the position of all employees who are driven to take action in the interests of health or safety. For the purpose of section 100(1) the appropriateness of steps is to be judged having regard *inter alia* to the knowledge of the employee and the facilities and advice available to the employee at the time, and a dismissal shall not be regarded as unfair if the employer can show that it would have been so negligent for the employee to take the steps he did take that a reasonable employer might have dismissed him for taking them.[83] The connection between trade union membership and section 100(1)(a) and (b) above is confirmed by providing that dismissal for either of the reasons stated therein are to be "inadmissible" reasons giving access to the remedy of interim relief.[84] Where the reason for the dismissal falls into one of the section 100(1)(c)–(f), the employee is entitled to the usual unfair dismissal remedies.

Public Interest Disclosures

7.32 These provisions of the Employment Rights Act 1996 are to be seen in the context of the Public Interest Disclosure Act 1998 (PIDA) which supplements the 1996 Act[85] and which protects workers against dismissal or other detrimental treatment for making certain "qualifying disclosures." PIDA extends the provisions of sections 44(1)(c) and 100(1)(c) of the Employment Rights Act which protect an employee against detrimental treatment short of dismissal and dismissal,[86] but only where he was employed at a place where there was no health and safety representative or committee, or it was not practicable for the employee to raise the matter through those channels and he brought to his employers' attention by reasonable means circumstances connected with his work which he (the employee) reasonably believed were harmful to health and safety. First, PIDA protects workers as well as employees[87]; secondly in some circumstances it protects against disclosure or bringing the matter to the attention of someone other than the employer.[88] The Public Interest Disclosure (Prescribed

---

[83] ERA, s. 100(2) and (3).

[84] ERA, s. 129.

[85] The Public Interest Disclosure Act 1998 inserts a new Pt IVA into the Employment Rights Act 1996.

[86] See Public Interest Disclosure (Compensation) Regulations 1999 (S.I. 1999 No. 1548), which removes the limit on compensation for dismissal for making a protected disclosure.

[87] ERA, s. 43K as inserted by PIDA.

[88] ERA, ss. 43H and 43F allow for disclosure to "prescribed persons" who are listed in Public Interest Disclosure (Prescribed Persons) Order 1999 (S.I. 1999 No. 1549).

Persons) Order 1999 (PIDA) now contains a list of persons other than the employer to whom a worker can make a protected disclosure, and the matters in respect of which such a disclosure may be made. Thus, while a worker is protected for disclosing to the Health and Safety Executive "matters which may affect the health and safety of any individual at work and matters which may affect the health and safety of any member of the public arising out of or in connection with the activities of persons at work" he would not be protected if he disclosed these matters to the Rail Regulator unless they fell under the heading of "the provisions and supply of railway services".[89] Although it had been expected that certain trade union officers might have been prescribed persons, the Order emphasises the public interest element in the legislation by listing only public agencies like the Certification Officer, the Data Protection Registrar, the Civil Aviation Authority, etc.

The matters to which PIDA applies is information which the worker reasonably believes tends to show (a) a criminal offence has been or will be committed, (b) a person has failed to comply with a legal obligation, (c) a miscarriage of justice has occurred, (d) the health or safety of any individual has been or will be endangered, (e) the environment is being damaged, and (f) information tending to show one of the above has been committed is being destroyed or will be destroyed.[90] In most cases the disclosure has to be made in good faith but it is immaterial whether the failure occurs in the United Kingdom or elsewhere, although the worker must not commit an offence by making the disclosure.[91] The effect of the 1998 Act is to protect workers who "blow the whistle" on their employers in circumstances much wider than those which are covered by the Employment Rights Act 1996, sections 44 and 100.

Maternity and Pregnancy

Maternity leave

7.33   The E.U. Council Directive[92] on the introduction of measures to encourage improvements in the safety and health of (a) pregnant workers, (b) workers who have recently given birth or (c) who are breast feeding was adopted on October 19, 1992. In part implementation of the Directive, legislation was passed in 1993,[93]

---

[89] See the Schedule to Public Interest Disclosure (Prescribed Persons) Order 1999 (S.I. 1999 No. 1549).

[90] ERA, s. 43B, as inserted by PIDA.

[91] ERA, s. 43B(2) and (3).

[92] Directive 92/85.

[93] Trade Union Reform and Employment Rights Act 1993, ss. 23–25, Scheds 2 and 3.

and the current provisions are now in the Employment Rights Act 1996,[94] as amended by the Employment Relations Act 1999 and regulations made thereunder.[94a] These provisions insert a new Part VIII into the 1996 Act and will have the effect of extending the maternity leave period to 18 weeks and renaming it "ordinary maternity leave", (OML) altering the conditions for additional maternity leave (AML) and providing for a period of compulsory maternity leave (CML). The detailed provisions regarding maternity leave are beyond the scope of this text, but the law after the changes introduced by the Employment Relations Act 1999 and the regulations made thereunder which became effective on December 15, 1999 may be summarised as follows.

Compulsory maternity leave (CML)

7.34 This must not be less than two weeks, during which an employer may not permit an employee to work; it must fall within the period of ordinary maternity leave.[95] Any provision made under the Health and Safety at Work Act 1974 shall apply to that prohibition of work during the compulsory maternity leave period as if it were imposed by regulations under section 15 of the 1974 Act, and an employer who permits an employee to work during compulsory maternity leave shall be guilty of an offence and liable to a fine.[95a]

Ordinary maternity leave (OML)

7.35 This is given to all women irrespective of length of service, and is now increased to 18 weeks (from 14 weeks) or longer if necessary to include CML. The following conditions must be satisfied. 21 days before the commencement of OML she gives to her employer a notice of her pregnancy (not necessarily in writing), her expected week of childbirth (EWC) supported by a medical certificate if required, the date OML is to begin (in writing if employer requests) but this cannot be before beginning of eleventh week before EWC, and automatically it begins on first day after beginning of the sixth week before EWC if absent from work because of pregnancy. If a woman fails to give 21 days' notice it appears that she will lose her entitlement to OML. During OML, section 74(4) and (5) of the Employment Rights Act 1996 make clear that she is entitled to the benefit of her terms and conditions (except remuneration, defined to mean only "sums payable by way

[94] ss. 71–78.
[94a] Maternity and Parental Leave etc. Regulations 1999.
[95] ERA, s. 72, as inserted by Employment Relations Act 1999, Sched. 4.
[95a] ERA, s. 72 as inserted.

of wages or salary"[96]), provided the matters are connected with employment whether or not they arise under her contract, thereby allowing, for example, for the accrual of qualifying period for entitlement to paid annual leave under the Working Time Regulations 1998. During OML a woman is required to observe her contractual terms except those which are inconsistent with her being on OML.

7.36 There is no duty to inform her employer of her return to work after OML; it is assumed she will simply return at the end of OML. However if she wishes to return before the OML would normally expire she must give her employer 21 days' notice, and a woman who returns without proper notice is not entitled to be paid. She is entitled to return to the job she was employed in before the OML on terms which are not less favourable than those which would have operated it she had not been absent.

Additional maternity leave (AML)

7.37 The right to AML is now available to all women who have, by the beginning of the eleventh week before their EWC, one year's continuous employment. The result is that women who are pregnant and have one year's continuous employment on or after the December 15, 1999, will be entitled to AML.

7.38 The contract of employment (except the terms regarding remuneration) will continue throughout AML, but the regulations provide that (a) an employee on AML is entitled to the benefit of her employer's obligation of trust and confidence, and (b) is bound by her obligation of good faith and any express provisions prohibiting the disclosure of confidential information or competing with her employer.

7.39 AML will start on the last day of OML; now there is no requirement for the employee to notify her employer that she intends to commence AML on the expiry of OML unless she notifies her employer that she intends to return early. However, an employer is entitled to write to an employee no later than 21 days before the end of OML asking for (a) the date of childbirth and (b) whether she intends to return after AML, and the employee is required to reply within 21 days unless not reasonably practicable. Under the previous regime, if an employee did not reply to the employer's request she lost the right to return to work. Under the

---

[96] Thus any other terms and conditions to her benefit continue to apply; for example, the benefit of receiving her employer's contributions to an OPS, sports facilities provided by her employer, etc.

new regime, regulations 19 and 20, which protect an employee against dismissal or detrimental treatment if they occur as a result of taking AML, will not apply to an employee who does not reply to the employer's request, and a failure to reply might result in the employer taking disciplinary action. The result would appear to be that the employee who does not reply does not lose the right to return after the end of AML but may be disciplined therefor, and if the discipline included dismissal, the fairness of that would be judged according to the ordinary rules of unfair dismissal and not the special provisions contained in regulation 20.

7.40 Where an employee wishes to return to work before the end of AML she must give her employer 21 days' notice of her intention to return. If she does not do so the employer may delay her return so that he does receive the 21 days' notice, but that cannot go beyond the normal end of the AML.

7.41 Regulation 18 deals with the substance of the right to return by providing that, except where redundancy occurs during AML and OML, an employee who takes AML is entitled to return to the job in which she was employed before her absence, or if that is not reasonably practicable to return to another job which is suitable and appropriate for her in the circumstances. The right to return is on terms which are not less favourable than those which would have been applicable to her if not absent from work since the commencement of her OML which preceded the AML, with seniority and pension and similar rights as if her continuity of employment had not been broken.

Suspension from work on maternity grounds

7.42 An employee is to be suspended on maternity grounds where, in consequence of a requirement imposed by a relevant provision of any enactment or code of practice approved under the Health and Safety at Work Act 1974, she is suspended by her employer on the ground that she is pregnant, has recently given birth or is breast feeding.[97] A relevant provision is one which is specified as such by the Secretary of State, and regulation 16[98] of the Management of Health and Safety at Work Regulations 1999[99] has been so specified.[1] The Management of Health and Safety at

---

[97] ERA, ss. 66–68.
[98] Inserted by Management and Health and Safety at Work (Amendment) Regulations 1994 (S.I. 1994 No. 2865).
[99] S.I. 1999 No. 3242.
[1] Suspension from Work on Maternity Grounds Order 1994 (S.I. 1994 No. 2930), as amended by S.I. 1999 No. 3242.

Work Regulations extend the employer's general obligations to carry out a risk assessment, so that where the employees include women of child-bearing age and the work could involve a risk to the health and safety of a new or expectant mother (or her baby) from any substances, processes or working conditions (including, but not only, those specified in Annexes I and II of Directive 92/85), the risk assessment shall include an assessment of that particular risk.[1a] And it is expressly provided that if complying with a statutory provision would not avoid such a risk the employer shall, if it is reasonable to do so, (and it would avoid the risk) alter the woman's working hours or other conditions of work,[2] and if the risk cannot be avoided by such an alteration of conditions of employment the employee is required, subject to the statutory obligation to offer available suitable alternative work, to be suspended on maternity grounds.[3]

However nothing in the regulations requires an employer to take such steps in relation to an employee until she has notified him in writing that she is pregnant, has recently given birth, has miscarried or is breast feeding,[4] although it has to be noted that the more general duties of the Management Regulations and the Health and Safety at Work Act itself would require employers to take action to protect any worker they know to be pregnant, or breast feeding. Regulation 17 requires an employer—again subject to the obligation to offer alternative work—to suspend a new or expectant mother from night work (where she has a medical certificate that it is necessary that she should not work at night) for as long as is necessary for her health and safety. Neither the Directive nor the Management Regulations indicate what is meant by night work,[5] on the view that such a definition is unnecessary because what has to be avoided is the exposure to risk and in the meantime there is no evidence to show that the existence or the quality of a risk is determined by the time at which work is done.[6]

7.43 Although the Management of Health and Safety at Work Regulations generally do not confer a right of action in any civil proceedings, that limitation is expressly revoked in respect of any duty imposed by regulation 16,[7] so that an injury arising from a

---

[1a] Management of Health and Safety at Work Regulations 1999, reg. 16.

[2] *ibid.*

[3] ERA, ss. 67 and 68.

[4] Management of Health and Safety at Work Regulations 1999, reg. 16. And see reg. 18(2)(a) (relaxation of employer's duty where no certificate of pregnancy produced, etc).

[5] *cf.* the Working Time Regulations 1998.

[6] See *New and Expectant Mothers at Work—a guide for employers* (HSE Books, £6.95).

[7] Management of Health and Safety at Work Regulations 1999, reg. 22.

failure to carry out the assessment required by regulation 16(1) would give rise to liability for breach of statutory duty.

Dismissal

7.44 The above provisions are supplemented by the Employment Rights Act 1996, section 99, as amended by the Employment Relations Act 1999,[8] which extends the circumstances in which dismissal for pregnancy is unfair. Under these provisions no period of continuous employment is required, and a dismissal is unfair (a) if the reason for it is of a kind prescribed by regulations or (b) the dismissal takes place in prescribed circumstances. Regulation 20 of the Maternity and Parental Leave, etc. Regulations 1999[9] provides that an employee who is dismissed under section 99 of the Employment Rights Act 1996 shall be regarded as unfairly dismissed if the reason for the dismissal is (a) pregnancy or the fact that the employee has given birth to a child, (b) the application of a requirement or recommendation under section 66(2) of the 1996 Act (suspension on grounds of health and safety,[10] (c) the fact that she took time off or availed herself of the benefits of OML, and (d) the fact that she (i) took AML, parental leave or time off under section 57A of the 1996 Act (time off for dependants), (ii) refused to sign a workforce agreement, (iii) being a representative of the workforce or a candidate in a election for a workforce representatives, performed functions or activities of a candidate or representative. Dismissal is also unfair if the reason for it was that the employee was redundant and she was selected for redundancy for any of the reasons (a) to (d) above; and where during OML or AML it is not practicable by reason of redundancy for her employer to continue to employ her under her existing contract of employment, and the employer does not offer a suitable available vacancy, the employee is regarded as unfairly dismissed.

Medical suspension

7.45 It is also important to note the general provision by which an employee who is suspended from work on medical grounds is entitled to receive pay for up to 26 weeks.[11] An employee is suspended on medical grounds if he is suspended from work in consequence of (a) a requirement imposed under a provision of an enactment or an instrument made under an enactment,[12] or (b) a

---

[8] Sched. 4, Pt III.
[9] S.I. 1999 No. 3312.
[10] See para. 7.45.
[11] ERA, ss. 64 and 65.
[12] The provisions are reg. 16 of the Control of Lead at Work Regulations 1980, reg. 16 of the Ionising Radiations Regualtions 1985, and reg. 12 of the Control of Substances Harmful to Health Regulations 1988.

provision in a recommendation of a Code of Practice issued or approved under the Health and Safety at Work Act 1974, section 16.[13]

EMPLOYERS' LIABILITY INSURANCE

Introduction

7.46   As noted earlier,[14] the law imposes a wide variety of obligations designed to ensure the health and safety of people at work. Proper observance of these obligations is, in many cases, enforced by criminal sanction or the preventive Improvement or Prohibition Notices. Neither of these methods is principally[15] concerned with compensating a person injured at work, which is the province of the civil law. However, a sophisticated system of rules and obligations would be pointless if, having succeeded in establishing a case grounded either on the common law or a breach of statutory duty, a worker was confronted with a defender who was unable to pay the sum awarded in damages. To obviate such a result the Employers' Liability (Compulsory Insurance) Act 1969[16] requires every employer who conducts business in Great Britain[17] to maintain approved insurance with an authorised insurer for liability for bodily injury[18] or disease sustained by an employee arising out of and in the course of his employment[19] in Great Britain.[20] In light of the government's policy[21] of extending many

---

[13] ERA, s. 64(2).

[14] See Chap. 3.

[15] In some cases a Scottish court is empowered (subject to a statutory maximum) to require an offender to compensate a victim; such a power is intended to deal with simple cases in which the sum can be instantly calculated; Criminal Justice (Scotland) Act 1980, s. 58.

[16] The Act was conceived as a Private Members Bill and, although the government refused to sponsor the Bill it did assist the Bill's passage, prompted perhaps by the tragedy of the James Watt Street fire in which 22 employees died, in respect of whom there was no effective insurance although the General Accident Co. Ltd did offer *ex gratia* payments: see *The Scotsman*, September 6, 1969; H.L. Deb., Vol. 304., col. 1391.

[17] Great Britain comprises England, Scotland and Wales; Interpretation Act 1978, s. 22(1).

[18] In England the Court of Appeal has held in a criminal case that as a person's body included his nervous system, bodily injury might include injury to any of these parts of his body responsible for his mental and other faculties and that "actual bodily harm" could include psychiatric injury (*Regina v. Chan-Fook*, *The Times*, November 19, 1993, CA).

[19] As to the scope of "arising out of and the course of employment", see paras 3.48 *et seq.*

[20] Employers' Liability (Compulsory Insurance) Act 1969, s. 2(1). And see Offshore Installations and Pipelines Management (Administration) Regulations 1995, S.I. 1995 No. 738).

[21] See *Fairness at Work*, Cm. 3968 (1998).

employment right to workers[22] it seems remarkable that the Act does not extend to "workers", particularly in light of the fact that the Health and Safety at Work Act 1974 imposes a duty on employers to conduct his undertaking in such a way as to ensure that, so far as is reasonably practicable, persons not in his employment are not exposed to risks to their health or safety.[23] Also, except in so far as specifically provided by regulations,[24] the legislation does not extend to injury or diseases suffered or contracted outside Great Britain[25] and this, when combined with a judicial reluctance to extend the duty of care to employees working abroad,[26] dictates that employees who are dispatched abroad require to be satisfied in advance about the extent of their employer's liabilities and insurance therefor. Additionally it has to be emphasised that the 1969 Act merely requires the maintenance of approved insurance cover upon which the employer may call in the event of his liability for the employee's injury or disease being established in accordance with the rules discussed earlier.[27] The provisions regarding approved policies and certificates of insurance was revised in 1998 by the Employers' Liability (Compulsory Insurance) Regulations 1998,[28] which revoked and replaced earlier regulations.

Approved policies

7.47 The policy or policies must provide cover of £5 million[29] in respect of claims relating to any one or more of the employer's employees arising out of any one occurrence.[30] For a policy to be "approved" it must not contain any condition that there shall be no

---

[22] A worker is someone who works under a contract of employment or another contract whereby an individual undertakes to perform personally work or services for another party to the contract who is not a client or customer of any professional business undertaking carried on by the individual.

[23] s. 3(1).

[24] See the Offshore Installation (Application of Employers' Liability (Compulsory Insurance) Act 1969 Regulations 1975 (S.I. 1975 No. 1289).

[25] Employers' Liability (Compulsory Insurance) Act 1969, s. 1.

[26] See *Reid v. Rush & Tompkins Group plc* [1990] I.C.R. 61, CA; *Square D. Ltd v. Cook* [1992] I.R.L.R. 34, CA. *Cf. Crombie v. McDermott Scotland Ltd*, 1996 S.L.T. 1238.

[27] See in particular Chap. 3. For a detailed critical analysis of the 1969 Act see R. Hasson, "The Employers' Liability (Compulsory Insurance) Act 1969—A Broken Reed" (1974) 3 I.L.J. 79.

[28] S.I. 1998 No. 2573.

[29] Raised from £2 million by Employers' Liability (Compulsory Insurance) Regulations 1998.

[30] Employers' Liability (Compulsory Insurance) Regulations 1998, reg. 3 (S.I. 1998 No. 2573). Note that policies effected prior to January 1, 1991 may continue to be regulated by the previous Regulations (Employers' Liability (Compulsory Insurance) General Regulations 1971 (S.I. 1971 No. 1117)) until January 1, 2000.

liability (on the part of the insurer) (a) in the event of some specified thing being done or omitted to be done after the happening of the event which gave rise to the claim; (b) unless the policy holder takes reasonable care to protect his employees against risk of bodily injury or disease in the course of their employment; (c) unless the policy holder complies with any enactment for the protection of employees against such a risk in the course of their employment; and (d) unless the policy holder keeps specified records or provides the insurer with certain information. However, a term or condition which requires the policy holder to pay to the insurer sums the latter has, under the policy, paid out in respect of employees is permitted. Similarly, and rather oddly, there is nothing in the legislation to prevent an insurer inserting particular exclusions which may result in an injured employee's claim being excluded. Thus an approved policy may legitimately exclude cover for liability for silicosis, asbestosis and pneumoconiosis.[31] It has been suggested[32] that the effect of the legislation[33] is to permit an approved policy to contain terms which free the insurer of liability to indemnify the insured in the event of recklessness or gross negligence on the part of the insured, or in the event of the insured failing to advise the insurers of an increase in risk. An approved policy is not required to be maintained in respect of certain relatives who are employees[34] or employees who are not ordinarily resident in Great Britain.[35]

Certificates and enforcement

7.48 By agreement with the Department of Employment, the Health and Safety Commission has accepted responsibility for the enforcement of the 1969 Act.[36] Failure to effect and maintain insurance as required by the 1969 Act, is itself a criminal offence punishable by a fine for each day of the failure.[37] Accordingly, since the contract of insurance is a contract based on the utmost good faith, where an employer misrepresents or fails to disclose a material fact when effecting or renewing a policy risk, he does not

---

[31] *ibid.*, reg. 2.
[32] See R. Hasson, n. 27 above.
[33] reg. 2(1)(b) and (c).
[34] Employers' Liability (Compulsory Insurance) Act 1969, s. 2(2).
[35] However, such employees become covered by the 1969 Act if they are in Britain for a period of not less than 14 days; Employers' Liability (Compulsory Insurance) Regulations 1998, reg. 4.
[36] See Chap. 2, para. 2.6.
[37] Employers' Liability (Compulsory Insurance) Act 1969, s. 5A (added by S.I. 1995 No. 1738) and now in Criminal Procedure (Consequential Provisions) (Scotland) Act 1995.

just run the risk of the insurer reducing the contract but, if so, he will be liable to a fine for failing to maintain an approved policy.[38] An insurer who enters into an approved policy is required, within 30 days of commencement or renewal, to issue a Certificate of Insurance in statutory form,[39] and it is an offence for an employer, to whom such a Certificate(s) has been issued to fail to display or produce it.[40] Similarly it is an offence for an employer who has entered into a contract of insurance in accordance with the 1969 Act not to permit its inspection by an inspector authorised by the Secretary of State.[41]

STATE INSURANCE

Introduction

7.49 Full treatment of the state system of insurance benefits for industrial accident or disease (industrial injuries benefits) is outside the scope of this work, which is concerned primarily with the legal responsibilities of employers.[42] Nevertheless it is necessary to give here a general account of that system which, while hedged with many statutory conditions, is not dependent on the injured employee being able to establish legal liability (personal or vicarious) on the part of the employer. However, the converse is not the case in that in respect of an accident or injury suffered on or after January 1, 1989 (or where a prescribed disease is concerned a person first claimed benefit on or after that date) a person due to pay compensation to the victim of the accident, injury or disease (the compensator) may not make a payment[43] before obtaining a certificate of total benefit from the Secretary of State. The certificate requires the deduction from the compensation otherwise payable of the amount of the benefit paid or likely to be

---

[38] Ironically, the James Watt Street tragedy which acted as a catalyst for the 1969 Act would be dealt with no differently today; an insurer would still be able to reject claims on the grounds of misrepresentation or non-disclosure by the insured.

[39] The 1998 Regulations require more information regarding the cover provided to be stated in the Certificate.

[40] Certificates must be kept for 40 years and inspectors may require the production of current and previous certificates; employers of offshore employees are required to produce a copy of the certificate to an employee within 10 days of his/her request.

[41] Employers' Liability (Compulsory Insurance) Act 1969, s. 4; Employers' Liability (Compulsory Insurance) Regulations 1998, regs 5–8.

[42] For fuller treatment reference may be made to R. Lewis, *Compensation for Industrial Injury*, 1987, or *The Law of Social Security*, A. Ogus and E. Barendt (4th ed., 1995), Chap. 7.

[43] Certain compensation payments are exempt, *e.g.* under £2,500; Social Security Act 1989, s. 22(4).

paid during the period of five years from the date of the accident or injury (or in the case of a disease the date of first claim).[44]

Employed earner

7.50 A claim for industrial injuries benefits may only be made by an employed earner whose accident or disease was caused by employed earner's employment.[45] Broadly this embraces those who pay Class I National Insurance Contributions and those employees whose earnings are below the contribution threshold. Apprentices and other special groups are deemed to be in employed earner's employment[46] but certain close relatives are excluded.[47] Although the Industrial Injuries Advisory Council (IIAC) has recommended that the self-employed in construction and agriculture be brought within the scheme, the Government has not adopted it for reasons of principle and practice. Whether a person is an employed earner is a question reserved for decision by the Secretary of State,[48] who may also direct that where a contract of employment is void the employment is nevertheless to be treated as employed earner's employment for the purpose of industrial injuries benefits.[49]

Industrial accidents

7.51 The employed earner must have suffered "personal injury caused . . . by accident arising out of and in the course of his employment".[50] Personal injury is a "hurt to the body or mind"[51] it therefore includes psychological injury and nervous disorders[52] and may include damage to a prosthesis or artificial limb[53] but not to spectacles, a hearing-aid or crutch.[54] the claimant/victim must prove that the personal injury was "caused by accident", but it is not necessary that the accident is the single cause of the injury; a contributory cause is sufficient provided it is a *causa causans* and not merely a *causa sine qua non.*[55] "Accident" has been said to

---

[44] Further details of the procedure may be obtained from the Compensation Recovery Unit, Department of Social Security, Hebburn, Tyne and Wear NE31 1XB.

[45] Social Security (Contributions and Benefits) Act 1992, ss. 102 and 108.

[46] *e.g.* Ministers of religion, lecturers and off-shore workers (Employed Earners Employment and Industrial Injuries Regulations 1975).

[47] *ibid.*

[48] Social Security Contributions and Benefits Act 1992, s. 17.

[49] *ibid.,* s. 97.

[50] *ibid.,* s. 94(1).

[51] *Jones v. Secretary of State for Social Services* [1972] A.C. 944, *per* Lord Simon at 1020.

[52] R(I) 22/59.

[53] Compare R(I) 7/56 with R(I) 8/81.

[54] R(I) 1/82.

[55] R(I) 4/58 (burns employed earner suffered when his clothing, soaked in flammable liquid in accident at work, caught fire when it came into contact with cigarette he was lighting at home held to have been caused by lighting of cigarette (*causa causans*) and not the accidental soaking of clothing).

denote "an unlooked-for mishap or an untoward event which is not expected or designed",[56] but such a narrow understanding of "accident" has been superseded by decisions which recognise that injuries caused by (a) the deliberate and unlawful act of a third party,[57] or (b) performing a heavy or dangerous job where accidents are common,[58] are caused by accident. A more difficult issue arises in distinguishing an accident or "event" from a "process", only the former being covered by the scheme which is concerned with traumatic work injuries. The nature of the important distinction is best illustrated by observing that while the injury of an employed earner who suffered strain to his chest muscles by regular heavy lifting was the result of a process and not an event or accident,[59] the injury of an employed earner who experienced pains in his chest when lifting a heavy weight on a particular day was caused by an event or accident.[60] In *Fraser v. Secretary of State for Social Services*,[61] the Court of Session upheld the decision of a social security commissioner that refusing the claim of a civil servant who had developed an acute anxiety tension which was probably due to various strains and stress at work, namely, frustration over diminishing promotion prospects, anxiety over career prospects and transfers to departments for which he had no specialist skills. Commissioner Mitchell had stated that:

> "in the present case I am unable to hold that the [claimant's] condition was attributable to one or more events capable as being recognised as constituting injury by accident if . . . the claimant's incapacity was due . . . to the effect of strains arising over a period from his working conditions the relevant injury would . . . fall to be regarded as injury by 'process' rather than by accident . . . a change in the legislation would . . . be required before a nervous order due to a period of strain arising from uncongenial working conditions could be recognised as personal injury by accident."

More recently, it has been held that injury by "passive" smoking may be caused by accident,[62] but the facts there may be regarded as special in that the employed earner's evidence demonstrated she had inhaled considerable quantities of cigarette smoke on particularly identifiable occasions.

---

[56] *Fenton v. J. Thorley Ltd* [1903] A.C. 443, *per* Lord Macnaghten at 448.
[57] *Trim Joint District School v. Kelly* [1914] A.C. 667.
[58] CI 4/49.
[59] R(I) 42/51.
[60] R(I) 54/53; and compare R(I) 43/55 with R(I) 32/60.
[61] 1986 S.L.T. 386 (I.H.).
[62] R(I) 6/91.

7.52 It is necessary that the accident arises out of and in the course of employment. Whether an employee is acting *in the course of his employment* has already been discussed in the context of personal and vicarious responsibility.[63] However, for industrial injury it is also necessary that the accident arises *out of* the employed earner's employment. This additional requirement ensures that merely because an injury happens while a person is in the course of employed earner's employment is not sufficient to entitle a person to industrial injuries benefits. However, precisely how to formulate a test to separate accidents which do not arise out of employment from those which do has proved difficult.[64] In 1963 a Tribunal of Commissioners[65] stated that the critical issue is whether the claimant's own act creates a risk which is different from that created by the employment and in 1946 there was enacted a statutory presumption which now provides that an accident which arises in the course of an employed earner's employment shall be deemed in the absence of evidence to the contrary also to have arisen out of that employment.[66] However, this helpful provision has been narrowly construed by the Commissioners who have emphasised that the presumption is really only of much effect where there is no evidence to the contrary.[67] The result of the need for the accident to arise out of employment—even taking the presumption into account—is that an unexplained leg fracture while walking in the course of employment is not injury caused by accident arising out of employment[68] while slipping and fracturing the leg by falling to the ground is even if you are susceptible to injury because of brittle bones.[69] Thus that the employment merely sets the scene for the accident has to be distinguished from it materially contributing to the risk.[70] Violence or misconduct occasioned to employed earners in the course of their employment by third parties, it was decided in 1958,[71] was not an accident arising out of employment. The result was to deny industrial injuries benefits to a bus conductor who was attacked while on duty. Subsequent legislation now enacts[72] that such accidents shall arise out of the employed earner's employment if it is caused by another person's misconduct, skylarking or negligence

---

[63] See paras 3.12 and 3.48.
[64] Consider R(I) 26/59, R(I) 2/63, R(I) 27/60.
[65] R(I) 2/63.
[66] Social Security Contributions and Benefits Act 1992, s. 94.
[67] CI 3/49, CI 68/49. *Cf.* R(I) 1/64.
[68] R(I) 6/82.
[69] R(I) 12/52.
[70] R(I) 73/51.
[71] *R. v. National Insurance (Industrial Injuries) Commissioner, ex p. Richardson* [1958] 1 W.L.R. 851.
[72] Social Security Contributions and Benefits Act 1992, ss. 98–101.

or by the behaviour or presence of an criminal or consists in the employed earner being struck by any object or by lightning, provided the employed earner did not directly of indirectly induce or contribute to the happening of the accident by his conduct outside employment or by any act not incidental to the employment. Where an employed earner responds to an emergency, an accident happening to him in or about any premises at which he is for the time being employed for the purpose of his employer's business is deemed to arise out of and in the course of his employment.[73]

Industrial diseases

7.53 The British system has opted to compensate occupational disease by creating a list of prescribed diseases which are known to be typical of certain specified activities, and then requiring that a successful claimant demonstrate that he suffers from a prescribed disease as a result of working in an occupation prescribed for that disease. The disadvantage of this approach is that those who suffer from non-prescribed diseases are without a remedy, and advantages—encouragement of intensive study which leads to an improvement in prevention and rehabilitation—have little direct bearing on victims of occupational diseases. In 1981 the Industrial Injuries Advisory Council recommended that the system be amended to allow for individual victims to prove that although a disease was not prescribed nevertheless it was caused by their employment,[74] but even its modest proposals were not acceptable to the Government.[75] The British system remains one of inclusion or prescription. Thus current legislation[76] provides that to become prescribed by the Secretary of State, a disease ought to be treated in relation to particular employed earners as a risk of their occupations and not as a risk common to all persons, and is such that, in the absence of special circumstances, the attribution of particular cases to the nature of the employment can be established with reasonable certainty. Although the Secretary of State has power to prescribe a disease without reference to the Industrial Injuries Advisory Committee (IIAC)[77] this power has never been

---

[73] Social Security Contributions and Benefits Act 1992, s. 100. And see R(I) 6/63 (injury to milkman who helped at house on fire to which he delivered milk).
[74] Report on Industrial Diseases (Cm. 8393).
[75] Official Report, Written Answer, H.C., 52, col. 327. But note S.I. 1991 No. 1938 has enacted the recommendations of the IIAC in its reports on asthma (Cm. 1244) and zoonoses (Cm. 1243) by adding to the list of sensitising agents for asthma and introducing an open category thereby allowing for proof in an individual case.
[76] Social Security Contributions and Benefits Act 1992, s. 108(2).
[77] *ibid.*, ss. 171 and 172; Social Security (Consequential Provisions) Act 1992, ss. 173 and 176.

exercised and the IIAC has been criticised for the time taken to make recommendations and that it has recommended the inclusion of too few diseases.[78] Thus between 1906 when the scheme began and 1948 the list of diseases grew from six to 41, with about 12 being added until 1988. Since then, however, aviah and ovine chlamycliosis, Q fever and chronic bronchitis and emphysema in coal miners have been added to the list.

7.54 For a claim for industrial injuries benefits to be successful, an employed earner must therefore show that the disease from which he suffers is:

(a) a prescribed disease (listed in Schedule 1 (Part 1) to Prescribed Diseases Regulations 1985.[79] An initial decision is made by an Adjudication Officer or, on reference, an Adjudication Medical Authority from whom an appeal lies to a Medical Appeal Tribunal);

(b) that disease is prescribed in relation to his occupation (Schedule 1 lists the occupations or types of activity for which a disease is prescribed)[80]; and

(c) a causal link between the occupation and the disease. Normally[81] it is presumed that the disease was due to the nature of the occupation if the claimant was employed in it at any time within one month preceding the date the disease is treated as having developed.[82] The presumption is rebuttable by the Adjudication Officer adducing appropriate evidence; it is not necessary for the employment to be the sole cause of the disease but it must be the real and substantial cause.[83]

Industrial injuries benefits

7.55 Since October 1, 1986 all industrial injuries benefits are paid in the form of a pension, lump sum payments for disablement less than 20 per cent having been abolished by the Social Security Act

---

[78] Certain organisational changes have been made to ensure the IIAC operates more efficiently.

[79] S.I. 1985 No. 576.

[80] The text is one of actuality rather than legality; a successful claimant must show that he actually did the type of work and not merely that he was legally bound to do so (R(I) 3/78; R(I) 2/77).

[81] Special rules operate regarding certain respiratory diseases and occupational deafness (S.I. 1985 No. 967) and in some cases it does not apply at all (inflammation of nose, and non-infective dermatitis).

[82] S.I. 1985 No. 967.

[83] R(I) 10/53.

1986,[84] and are free of income tax.[85] The benefits are (a) disablement benefit, (b) reduced earnings allowance, (c) retirement allowance, and (d) industrial death benefit. However, as reduced earnings allowance and retirement allowance are being phased out[86] and industrial death benefit has been abolished for deaths before April 11, 1988[87] only disablement benefit is dealt with here.[88]

Disablement benefit

7.56 To become entitled to disablement benefit a claimant must show[89] that he suffers, as a result of an accident or prescribed disease, from loss of physical or mental faculty[90] which has been described as "impairment or proper functioning of part of the body or mind",[91] and has been held to include the malfunctioning of a kidney[92]; by express statutory provision disfigurement is to be considered an actual loss of physical faculty.[93] While a loss of faculty does not have to be permanent it must have been present for some time because disablement benefit is not available until after the expiry of 90 days beginning with the date of the accident or onset of the disease.[94] The extent to which the loss of faculty results in disablement is to be determined objectively without reference to the particular circumstances of the claimant except age, sex and physical and mental condition.[95] An important result of this is that the effect of a disablement on an individual's earning capacity is ignored.[96] For some conditions or injuries the degree of disablement is prescribed by regulation.[97] Thus, loss of a hand or foot is regarded as 100 per cent disability while, at the other extreme, loss of part of a small toe but with some loss of bone is

---

[84] The old rules still operate for assessments made on claims before October 1, 1986 (Social Security Act 1986, Sched. 3, para. 3(3).

[85] Income and Corporation Taxes Act 1988, s. 617, as amended.

[86] Social Security Act 1990, s. 3; no entitlement occurs where the onset of a prescribed disease or the accident occurs after September 30, 1990.

[87] Social Security Contributions and Benefits Act 1992, Scheds 7 and 8.

[88] For a detailed account of reduced earnings allowance and retirement allowance, see A. Ogus and E. Barendt, *The Law of Social Security* (4th ed., 1995).

[89] R(I) 1/62.

[90] Social Security Contributions and Benefits Act 1992, ss. 103, 108, 109, Scheds 4, 6 and 7.

[91] *Jones v. Secretary of State for Social Services* [1972] A.C. 944, *per* Lord Simon at 1020.

[92] R(I) 14/16.

[93] Social Security Contributions and Benefits Act 1992, Sched. 7.

[94] Social Security Act 1975, s. 57(4). Regarding the time for claiming, see Social Security (Claims and Payments) Regulations 1979, reg. 14.

[95] Social Security Contributions and Benefits Act 1992, s. 103, Scheds 4, 6 and 7.

[96] R(I) 3/84.

[97] General Benefit Regulations 1982, Sched. 2.

regarded as one per cent disability. However, these are prima facie assessments and are subject to increase or reduction as may be reasonable in the circumstances by the medical authorities.[98] Where a condition is not prescribed by regulation, assessment is dependent on the facts and circumstances of each case, and while the degree of disablement for prescribed conditions is relevant it is no more than a guide.[99] Since October 1, 1986, disablement benefit is paid only if the assessment of disablement is at least 14 per cent, except in cases of pneumoniosis, byssinosis or diffuse meso-thelioma, for which benefit is payable where the assessment is at least one per cent.[1] Rates of benefit are adjusted regularly but at the time of writing the weekly payment for a person over 18 who is assessed at 100 per cent disabled is £108.10, while a weekly payment for a person assessed between one per cent and 10 per cent disabled is £13.24.

OTHER STATE HELP

Criminal Injuries Compensation Board

7.57 Since 1964, where a person suffers personal injury directly attributable to a crime of violence or while attempting to stop someone committing a crime or while apprehending a suspected criminal, he is able to apply to the Criminal Injuries Compensation Board which may award a tax-free payment of compensation which is arrived at having regard to the principles applied by the civil courts.[2] There are some limitations to the scheme,[3] in that no award is made if the loss is caused by a road traffic accident unless it involved a deliberate running down. Also it is important that a claimant notifies and co-operates with the police and that neither his own conduct nor previous convictions justifies withholding or reducing an award. Nevertheless, as has been judicially noted,[4] an employee who could not substantiate a claim against his employer may successfully claim an award from the Board.

Pneumoconiosis

7.58 By the Pneumoconiosis, etc. (Workers' Compensation) Act 1979, special provision is made for workers who are disabled as a

---

[98] *ibid.*, reg. 11(b).
[99] *R. v. Industrial Injuries Commissioner, ex p. Cable* [1968] 1 Q.B. 729.
[1] Social Security Act 1975, s. 57(1); Industrial Injuries (Prescribed Diseases) Regulations 1985, reg. 20(1).
[2] Where a person is killed an award may be claimed by a dependant who may elect a flat-rate bereavement award.
[3] The Criminal Justice Act 1988 has placed the scheme on a statutory footing so that payments are no longer made *ex gratia*.
[4] *Charlton v. Forrest Printing Ink Co. Ltd* [1980] I.R.L.R. 331, CA, *per* Lord Denning.

result of pneumoconiosis, byssinosis or diffuse mesothelioma.[5] An applicant who satisfies the conditions is entitled to a lump-sum payment[6] from the Department of Employment.[7] At the time of writing,[8] the maximum payment to a disabled applicant is £55,118 and to dependants[9] is £25,050. The conditions of entitlement are (1) that disablement benefit is payable to the applicant in respect of the disease, (2) every relevant employer[10] has ceased to carry on business, and (3) he has not brought an action or settled any claim for damages in respect of the disablement.[11] Generally, applications must be made within 12 months of the date disablement benefit was awarded or, in the case of dependants, within 12 months of date of death.[12]

---

[5] The dependants of workers who have died while disabled by one of these diseases are also covered.

[6] The amount of the lump sum depends on the degree of disablement, assessed by a medical board, the period covered by the assessment and the applicant's age (S.I. 1985 No. 2035).

[7] Pneumoconiosis, etc. (Workers' Compensation) Act 1979, s. 1.

[8] The figures are revised annually.

[9] Pneumoconiosis, etc. (Workers' Compensation) Act 1979, s. 3; the Pneumoconiosis, etc. (Workers' Compensation) (Payment of Claims) Amendment Regulations 1998 (S.I. 1998 No. 1840).

[10] Any person by whom the applicant was employed during the time he was developing the disease against whom he might have had a claim for damages (*ibid.*, s. 2(3)).

[11] *ibid.*, 2(2); for dependants the conditions are slightly different.

[12] Pneumoconiosis, etc. (Workers' Compensation) (Determination of Claims) Regulations 1979.

APPENDIX

HEALTH AND SAFETY EXECUTIVE ORGANISATION

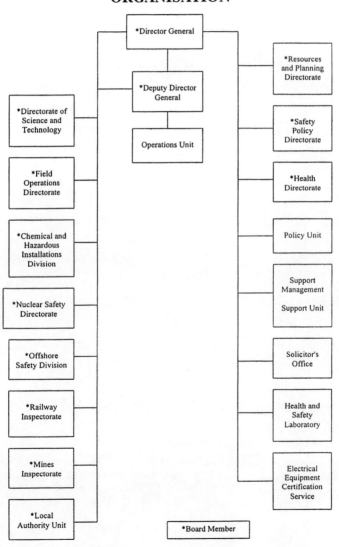

*Director General

*Resources and Planning Directorate

*Deputy Director General

*Directorate of Science and Technology

Operations Unit

*Safety Policy Directorate

*Field Operations Directorate

*Health Directorate

*Chemical and Hazardous Installations Division

Policy Unit

*Nuclear Safety Directorate

Support Management

Support Unit

*Offshore Safety Division

Solicitor's Office

*Railway Inspectorate

Health and Safety Laboratory

*Mines Inspectorate

Electrical Equipment Certification Service

*Local Authority Unit

*Board Member

INDEX